C000133370

Certified
Programming
with
Dependent
Types

Certified
Programming
with
Dependent
Types

A Pragmatic Introduction to the Coq Proof Assistant

Adam Chlipala

The MIT Press
Cambridge, Massachusetts
London, England

© 2013 Massachusetts Institute of Technology

All rights reserved. No part of this book may be reproduced in any form by any electronic or mechanical means (including photocopying, recording, or information storage and retrieval) without permission in writing from the publisher.

MIT Press books may be purchased at special quantity discounts for business or sales promotional use. For information, please email special_sales@mitpress.mit.edu or write to Special Sales Department, The MIT Press, 55 Hayward Street, Cambridge, MA 02142.

This book was set in 10/13 Lucida Bright by the author using LaTeX 2$_\varepsilon$. Printed and bound in the United States of America.

Library of Congress Cataloging-in-Publication Data

Chlipala, Adam, 1981–
      Certified programming with dependent types : a pragmatic introduction to the Coq proof assistant / Adam Chlipala.
            p.   cm
      Includes bibliographical references and index.
      ISBN 978-0-262-02665-9 (hardcover : alk. paper)
      1. Automatic theorem proving–Computer programs. 2. Computer programming. 3. Coq (Electronic resource) I. Title.
QA76.9.A96C45 2013
005.1—dc23

2013012837

10 9 8 7 6 5 4 3 2 1

Contents

III Proof Engineering   285

13 Proof Search by Logic Programming   287

14 Proof Search in Ltac   309

15 Proof by Reflection   339

IV The Big Picture   361

16 Proving in the Large   363

Acknowledgments

A version of this book has been available free of charge online since 2008, and I have been lucky to receive much useful feedback from many people. What follows is an incomplete list of contributors.

This book project began in the context of two classes I co-taught as a graduate student and postdoc: CS294-9 at the University of California, Berkeley, in fall 2006, with George C. Necula; and COMPSCI 252 at Harvard University in fall 2008, with Greg Morrisett. I thank those two advisers for giving me a chance to test preliminary materials with very capable students, and I thank those students for their feedback.

I used a later version of the book in teaching 6.892 at the Massachusetts Institute of Technology in fall 2011, and Benjamin C. Pierce used the book in CIS 670 at the University of Pennsylvania in fall 2012. The students in both classes generated voluminous feedback that I have used to improve the presentation.

Several readers of earlier versions have been kind enough to send me cover-to-cover detailed feedback, which has helped immensely in preparing this final version: Pierre Castéran, Nathan Collins, Peter Horst, Benjamin C. Pierce, Marko Schütz-Schmuck, and several anonymous referees.

I have also received many bug reports and more localized suggestions, including from Arthur Azevedo de Amorim, Andrew W. Appel, Thomas Braibant, Sébastien Briais, Gergely Buday, Ştefan Ciobâcă, Christophe Deleuze, Dan Friedman, Peter Gammie, Valentin Gatien-Baron, Jason Gross, Tom Harke, Catalin Hritcu, Brian Huffman, Dongseok Jang, Jens Katelaan, Jean-François Monin, Brandon M. Moore, César Muñoz, Duckki Oe, Erik Parmann, David Rajchenbach-Teller, Mark Raynsford, Valentin Robert, Andrew Sackville-West, Alan Schmitt, Peter Sestoft, Tobias Tebbi, Sam Tobin-Hochstadt, Andrew Tolmach, Luc Traonmilin, Daniel Wagner, Mitchell Wand, and Brent Yorgey.

I thank the MIT Press for agreeing to allow a version of this book to remain available online free of charge indefinitely. That medium is especially useful for experimenting with the source code in the book.

Finally, the most important acknowledgment: Many thanks to the Coq development team, which has done an amazing job going from theory to practice, constructing a fantastic practical tool that I hope readers will appreciate as much as I do.

1 Introduction

1.1 Whence This Book?

We would all like to have programs check that our programs are correct. Due in no small part to some bold but unfulfilled promises in the history of computer science, today most people who write software, practitioners and academics alike, assume that the costs of formal program verification outweigh the benefits. The purpose of this book is to convince you that the technology of program verification is mature enough today that it makes sense to use it in a support role in many kinds of research projects in computer science. Beyond the convincing, I also want to provide a handbook on practical engineering of certified programs with the Coq proof assistant. Almost every subject covered is also relevant to interactive computer theorem proving in general, such as for traditional mathematical theorems. In fact, I hope to demonstrate how verified programs are useful as building blocks in all sorts of formalizations.

Research into mechanized theorem proving began in the second half of the twentieth century, and some of the earliest practical work involved Nqthm [3], the Boyer-Moore theorem prover, which was used to prove such theorems as correctness of a complete hardware and software stack [25]. ACL2 [17], Nqthm's successor, has seen significant industry adoption, for instance, by Advanced Micro Devices, Inc. (AMD) to verify correctness of floating-point division units [26].

At the beginning of the twenty-first century, the pace of progress in practical applications of interactive theorem proving accelerated. Several well-known formal developments have been carried out in Coq, the system that this book deals with. In the realm of pure mathematics, Georges Gonthier built a machine-checked proof of the four-color theorem [13], a mathematical problem first posed more than one hundred years before, where the only previous proofs had required trusting ad hoc software to do brute force checking of key facts. In the realm of program verification, Xavier Leroy led the CompCert project to produce a verified C compiler back-end [19] robust enough to use with real embedded software.

Many other projects have attracted attention by proving important theorems using computer proof assistant software. For instance, the L4.verified project [18] led by Gerwin Klein has given a mechanized proof of correctness for a realistic microkernel, using the Isabelle/HOL proof assistant [29]. The amount of ongoing work in the area is so large that I cannot hope to list it all, so from this point I assume that readers are convinced that we ought to want machine-checked proofs and that such proofs are feasible to produce. (To readers not yet convinced, I suggest a Web search for "machine-checked proof.")

The idea of *certified program* features prominently in this book's title. Here "certified" does not refer to government rules for how the reliability of engineered systems may be demonstrated to sufficiently high standards. Rather, this concept of certification, a standard one in the programming languages and formal methods communities, has to do with the idea of a *certificate*, or formal mathematical artifact proving that a program meets its specification. Government certification procedures rarely provide strong mathematical guarantees, whereas certified programming provides guarantees about as strong as anything we could hope for. We trust the definition of a foundational mathematical logic, we trust an implementation of that logic, and we trust that we have encoded our informal intent properly in formal specifications, but few other opportunities remain to certify incorrect software. For compilers and other programs that run in batch mode, the notion of a *certifying program* is also common, where each run of the program outputs both an answer and a proof that the answer is correct. Any certifying program can be composed with a proof checker to produce a certified program, and this book focuses on the certified case while also introducing principles and techniques of general interest for stating and proving theorems in Coq.

A good number of tools are in wide use today for building machine-checked mathematical proofs and machine-certified programs. The following is a list of interactive proof assistants satisfying a few criteria. First, the authors of each tool must intend for it to be put to use for software-related applications. Second, there must have been enough engineering effort put into the tool that someone not doing research on the tool itself would feel time was well spent using it. A third criterion is an empirical validation of the second: the tool must have a significant user community outside its own development team.

ACL2	http://www.cs.utexas.edu/users/moore/acl2/
Coq	http://coq.inria.fr/
Isabelle/HOL	http://isabelle.in.tum.de/
PVS	http://pvs.csl.sri.com/
Twelf	http://www.twelf.org/

Isabelle/HOL, implemented with the proof assistant development framework Isabelle [32], is the most popular proof assistant for the HOL logic. The other implementations of HOL can be considered equivalent for purposes of the discussion here.

1.2 Why Coq?

This book is about certified programming using Coq, and I am convinced that it is the best tool for the job. Coq has a number of very attractive properties, which I summarize here, mentioning which of the other candidate tools lack which properties.

1.2.1 Based on a Higher-Order Functional Programming Language

There is no reason to give up the familiar comforts of functional programming when you start writing certified programs. All the tools I listed are based on functional programming languages and can be used without their proof-related features to write and run regular programs.

ACL2 is notable in this field for having only a *first-order language* at its foundation. That is, you cannot work with functions over functions and all those other treats of functional programming. By giving up this facility, ACL2 can make broader assumptions about how well its proof automation will work, but we can generally recover the same advantages in other proof assistants when we are programming in first-order fragments.

1.2.2 Dependent Types

A language with *dependent types* may include references to programs inside of types. For instance, the type of an array might include a program expression giving the size of the array, making it possible to verify absence of out-of-bounds accesses statically. Dependent types can go even further than this, effectively capturing any correctness property in a type. For instance, Section 2.2.3 introduces the technique of giving a compiler a type that guarantees that it maps well-typed source programs to well-typed target programs.

ACL2 and HOL lack dependent types outright. Each of PVS and Twelf supports a different strict subset of Coq's dependent type language. Twelf's type language is restricted to a bare-bones, monomorphic lambda calculus, which places serious restrictions on how complicated *computations inside types* can be. This restriction is important for the soundness argument behind Twelf's approach to representing and checking proofs.

In contrast, PVS's dependent types are much more general, but they are squeezed inside the single mechanism of *subset types*, where a normal type is refined by attaching a predicate over its elements. Each member of the subset type is an element of the base type that satisfies the predicate. Chapter 6 introduces that style of programming in Coq, and Chapters 7–12 deal with features of dependent typing in Coq that go beyond what PVS supports.

Dependent types are useful not only because they help express correctness properties in types. Dependent types also enable writing certified programs without writing anything that looks like a proof. Even with subset types, which in many contexts can be used to express any relevant property, the human driving the proof assistant usually has to build some proofs explicitly. Writing formal proofs is hard, so we want to avoid it as far as possible. Dependent types are invaluable for this purpose.

1.2.3 An Easy-to-Check Kernel Proof Language

Scores of automated decision procedures are useful in practical theorem proving, but it is unfortunate to have to trust in the correct implementation of each procedure. Proof assistants satisfy the de Bruijn criterion when they produce proof terms in small kernel languages, even when they use complicated and extensible procedures to seek out proofs in the first place. These core languages feature complexity on par with that in proposals for formal foundations for mathematics (e.g., ZF set theory). To believe a proof, we can ignore the possibility of bugs during *search* and just rely on a (relatively small) proof-checking kernel applied to the *result* of the search.

Coq meets the de Bruijn criterion, whereas ACL2 does not, because it employs fancy decision procedures that produce no evidence trails justifying their results. PVS supports *strategies* that implement fancier proof procedures in terms of a set of primitive proof steps, where the primitive steps are less primitive than in Coq. For instance, a propositional tautology solver is included as a primitive, so it is a question of taste whether such a system meets the de Bruijn criterion. The HOL implementations meet the de Bruijn criterion more manifestly; for Twelf, the situation is murkier.

1.2.4   Convenient Programmable Proof Automation

A commitment to a kernel proof language opens up wide possibilities for user extension of proof automation systems without allowing user mistakes to trick the overall system into accepting invalid proofs. Almost any interesting verification problem is undecidable, so it is important to help users build their own procedures for solving the restricted problems that they encounter in particular theorems.

Twelf features no proof automation marked as a bona fide part of the latest release; some automation code is included for testing purposes. The Twelf style is based on writing out all proofs in full detail. Because Twelf is specialized to the domain of syntactic metatheory proofs about programming languages and logics, it is feasible to use it to write those kinds of proofs manually. Outside that domain, the lack of automation can be a serious obstacle to productivity. Most kinds of program verification fall outside Twelf's scope.

Of the remaining tools, all can support user extension with new decision procedures by hacking directly in the tool's implementation language (such as OCaml for Coq). Since ACL2 and PVS do not satisfy the de Bruijn criterion (or at least do not satisfy it as strongly as Coq does), overall correctness is at the mercy of the authors of new procedures.

Isabelle/HOL and Coq both support coding new proof manipulations in ML in ways that cannot lead to the acceptance of invalid proofs. Additionally, Coq includes a domain-specific language for coding decision procedures in normal Coq source code, with no need to break out into ML. This language is called Ltac, and I think of it as the unsung hero of the proof assistant world. Not only does Ltac prevent the programmer from making fatal mistakes but it also includes a number of novel programming constructs that combine to make a "proof by decision procedure" style very pleasant.

1.2.5   Proof by Reflection

A surprising wealth of benefits follows from choosing a proof language that integrates a rich notion of computation. Coq includes programs and proof terms in the same syntactic class. This makes it easy to write programs that compute proofs. With rich enough dependent types, such programs are *certified decision procedures*. In such cases, these certified procedures can be put to good use without ever running them. Their types guarantee that if we did run them, we would receive proper ground proofs.

The critical ingredient for this technique, many of whose instances are referred to as *proof by reflection*, is a way of inducing nontrivial computation inside of logical propositions during proof checking. Further, most of these instances require dependent types in order to state the appropriate theorems. Of the proof assistants I listed, only Coq really provides support for the type-level computation style of reflection, though PVS supports very similar functionality via refinement types.

1.3   Why Not a Different Dependently Typed Language?

The logic and programming language behind Coq belongs to a type theory ecosystem with a good number of other thriving members. Agda[1] and Epigram[2] are the most developed tools among the alternatives to Coq, and there are others that are earlier in their life cycles. All the languages in this family are like different historical offshoots of Latin. The hardest conceptual epiphanies are, for the most part, portable among all the languages. Given this, why choose Coq for certified programming?

I think the answer is simple. None of the others has a well-developed system for tactic-based theorem proving. Agda and Epigram are designed and marketed more as programming languages than as proof assistants. Dependent types are helpful for proving deep theorems without needing anything that feels like proving. Nonetheless, almost any interesting certified programming project will benefit from some activity that deserves to be called proving, and many interesting projects absolutely require semiautomated proving to protect the sanity of the programmer. Informally, proving is unavoidable when any correctness

---

1. http://appserv.cs.chalmers.se/users/ulfn/wiki/agda.php
2. http://www.e-pig.org/

proof for a program has a structure that does not mirror the structure of the program itself. An example is a compiler correctness proof, which probably proceeds by induction on program execution traces, which have no simple relation with the structure of the compiler or the structure of the programs it compiles. In building such proofs, a mature system for scripted proof automation is invaluable.

On the other hand, Agda, Epigram, and similar tools have less implementation baggage associated with them, so they tend to be the default first homes of innovations in practical type theory. Some kinds of dependently typed programs are much easier to write in Agda and Epigram than in Coq. The former tools may very well be superior choices for projects that do not involve any proving. Anecdotally, I have gotten the impression that manual proving is orders of magnitude more costly than manual coping with Coq's lack of programming bells and whistles. In this book, I devote substantial space to patterns for programming with dependent types in Coq as it is today. We can hope that the type theory community is tending toward convergence on the right set of features for practical programming with dependent types and that eventually a single tool will embody those features.

1.4   Engineering with a Proof Assistant

In comparisons with its competitors, Coq is often derided for promoting unreadable proofs. It is easy to write proof scripts that manipulate proof goals imperatively, with no structure to aid readers. Such developments are nightmares to maintain, and they certainly do not convey why the theorem is true to anyone but the original author. An additional purpose of this book is to show why it is unfair and unproductive to dismiss Coq based on the existence of such developments.

You may favor some programming language and may have taught that language to undergraduates. I want to propose an analogy between coming to a negative conclusion about Coq after reading common Coq developments and coming to a negative conclusion about your favorite language after looking at the programs undergraduates write in it in the first week of class. The pragmatics of mechanized proving and program verification have been under serious study for much less time than the pragmatics of programming have been. The computer theorem–proving community is still developing the key insights corresponding to those that programming texts and instructors impart to new learners. Most of the insights for Coq are barely disseminated among experts, let alone set down in tutorial form. I hope this book goes a long way toward remedying that.

This book should be of interest even to people who have participated in classes or tutorials specifically about Coq. It should also be useful to those who have been using Coq for years but whose Coq developments prove impenetrable to colleagues. This book emphasizes that there are design patterns for reliably avoiding the tedious parts of theorem proving and that consistent use of these patterns can get you over the hump to the point where it is worth using Coq to prove your theorems and certify your programs even if formal verification is not your main concern. I follow this theme by pursuing two main methods for replacing manual proofs with more understandable artifacts: dependently typed functions and custom Ltac decision procedures.

1.5 Prerequisites

I try to keep the required background knowledge to a minimum in this book. I assume familiarity with the material from usual discrete math and logic courses taken by undergraduate computer science majors. I also assume significant experience programming in one of the ML dialects, in Haskell, or in some other closely related language. Experience with only dynamically typed functional languages might lead to befuddlement in some places, but readers who have come to understand Scheme deeply will probably be fine.

My background is in programming languages, formal semantics, and program verification. I sometimes use examples from that domain. As a reference on these topics, I recommend *Types and Programming Languages* [36], by Benjamin C. Pierce; however, I have tried to choose examples so that they may be understood without background in semantics.

1.6 Using This Book

This book is generated automatically from Coq source files using the coqdoc program. The latest PDF version, with hyperlinks from identifier uses to the corresponding definitions, is available at

                    http://adam.chlipala.net/cpdt/cpdt.pdf

An online HTML version is available, which also provides hyperlinks:

                    http://adam.chlipala.net/cpdt/html/toc.html

The source code for the book is freely available at

`http://adam.chlipala.net/cpdt/cpdt.tgz`

There, you can find all the code appearing in this book, with prose interspersed in comments, in exactly the order that you find here. You can step through the code interactively with your chosen graphical Coq interface. The code also has special comments indicating which parts of the chapters make suitable starting points for interactive class sessions, in which the class works together to construct the programs and proofs. The included Makefile has a target `templates` for building a fresh set of class template files automatically from the book source. The online versions will remain available at no cost, and I intend to keep the source code up-to-date with bug fixes and compatibility changes to track new Coq releases.

I believe that a good graphical interface to Coq is crucial for using it productively. I use the Proof General[3] mode for Emacs, which supports a number of other proof assistants besides Coq. There is also the stand-alone CoqIDE program developed by the Coq team. I like being able to combine certified programming and proving with other kinds of work inside the same full-featured editor. In the initial part of this book, I reference Proof General procedures explicitly in introducing how to use Coq, but most of the book is interface-agnostic, so feel free to use CoqIDE if you prefer it. The one issue with CoqIDE before version 8.4, regarding running through the book source, is that I sometimes begin a proof attempt but cancel it with the Coq `Abort` or `Restart` commands, which CoqIDE did not support until recently. It would be bad form to leave such commands intact in a finished development, but I find these commands helpful in writing single source files that trace a user's thought process in designing a proof.

1.6.1 Reading This Book

For experts in functional programming or formal methods, learning to use Coq is not hard. The Coq manual [7], the textbook by Bertot and Castéran [1], and Pierce et al.'s *Software Foundations*[4] have helped many people become productive Coq users. However, I believe that the best ways to manage significant Coq developments are far from settled. In this book, I propose my own techniques, and I employ them from

---

3. `http://proofgeneral.inf.ed.ac.uk/`
4. `http://www.cis.upenn.edu/~bcpierce/sf/`

the very beginning. After a first chapter showing off what can be done with dependent types, I retreat into simpler programming styles for the first part of the book. The other main thrust of the book, Ltac proof automation, is adopted from the start of the technical exposition.

Readers new to Coq and experienced Coq hackers can both benefit from reading Part I, which devotes substantial space to basic concepts, because as I introduce these concepts, I also develop my preferred automated proof style. I hope that my heavy reliance on proof automation early on will seem like the most natural way to go.

Coq is a very complex system, with many different commands driven more by pragmatic concerns than by any overarching aesthetic principle. When I use some construct for the first time, I try to give a one-sentence intuition for what it accomplishes, but I leave the details to the Coq reference manual [7]. I expect that readers interested in complete understanding will consult that manual frequently. I often use constructs in code snippets without first introducing them, but explanations follow in succeeding paragraphs.

Previous versions of the book included some suggested exercises at the ends of chapters. Since then, I have decided to remove the exercises and focus on the main book exposition. A database of exercises proposed by readers is available on the Web.[5] I do want to suggest, though, that the best way to learn Coq is to get started applying it in a real project rather than focusing on artificial exercises.

1.6.2   The Tactic Library

To make it possible to start from fancy proof automation rather than working up to it, I have included with the book source a library of *tactics*, or programs that find proofs, since the built-in Coq tactics do not support a high enough level of automation. I use these tactics from the first chapter with code examples.

Some readers have asked about the pragmatics of using this tactic library in their own developments. My position is that this tactic library was designed with the specific examples of the book in mind; I do not recommend using it in other settings. Part III should impart the necessary skills to reimplement these tactics and beyond. One generally deals with undecidable problems in interactive theorem proving, so no tactic can solve all goals, though the *crush* tactic that we will meet soon may sometimes seem as if it can. There are still very useful tricks found

---

5. http://adam.chlipala.net/cpdt/ex/

in the implementations of *crush* and its cousins, so it may be useful to examine the commented source file `CpdtTactics.v`. I implement a new tactic library for each new project because each project involves a different mix of undecidable theories where a different set of heuristics turns out to work well, and that is what I recommend others do, too.

1.6.3 Installation and Emacs Setup

At the start of the next chapter, I assume that you have installed Coq and Proof General. The code in this book is tested with Coq versions 8.4, 8.4pl1, and 8.4pl2. Though parts may work with other versions, it is expected that the book source will fail to build with earlier versions.

To set up your Proof General environment to process the source to the next chapter, a few simple steps are required:

1. Get the book source from

    http://adam.chlipala.net/cpdt/cpdt.tgz

2. Unpack the tarball to some directory `DIR`.

3. Run `make` in `DIR` (ideally with a `-j` flag to use multiple processor cores, if you have them).

4. There are some minor headaches associated with getting Proof General to pass the proper command line arguments to the `coqtop` program, which provides the interactive Coq toplevel. One way to add settings that will be shared by many source files is to add a custom variable setting to your `.emacs` file, like this:

```
(custom-set-variables
  ...
  '(coq-prog-args '("-I" "DIR/src"))
  ...
)
```

The extra arguments demonstrated here are the proper choices for working with the code for this book. The ellipses stand for other Emacs customization settings you may already have. It can be helpful to save several alternative sets of flags in your `.emacs` file, with all but one commented out within the `custom-set-variables` block at any given time.

Alternatively, Proof General configuration can be set on a per-directory basis, using a `.dir-locals.el` file in the directory of the source files for which you want the settings to apply. Here is an example that could be written in such a file to enable use of the book source. Note the need to include an argument that starts Coq in Emacs support mode.

```
((coq-mode . ((coq-prog-args .
  ("-emacs-U" "-I" "DIR/src")))))
```

Every chapter of this book is generated from a commented Coq source file. You can load these files and run through them step-by-step in Proof General. Be sure to run the Coq binary `coqtop` with the command line argument `-I DIR/src`. If you have installed Proof General properly, the Coq mode should start automatically when you visit a `.v` buffer in Emacs, and the preceding advice on `.emacs` settings should ensure that the proper arguments are passed to `coqtop` by Emacs.

With Proof General, the portion of a buffer that Coq has processed is highlighted in some way, such as being given a blue background. You step through Coq source files by positioning the point at the position you want Coq to run to and pressing C-C C-RET. This can be used both for normal step-by-step coding, by placing the point inside some command past the end of the highlighted region, and for undoing, by placing the point inside the highlighted region.

The chapter source files are as follows:

Chapter	Source File
Some Quick Examples	StackMachine.v
Introducing Inductive Types	InductiveTypes.v
Inductive Predicates	Predicates.v
Infinite Data and Proofs	Coinductive.v
Subset Types and Variations	Subset.v
General Recursion	GeneralRec.v
More Dependent Types	MoreDep.v
Dependent Data Structures	DataStruct.v
Reasoning About Equality Proofs	Equality.v
Generic Programming	Generic.v
Universes and Axioms	Universes.v
Proof Search by Logic Programming	LogicProg.v
Proof Search in Ltac	Match.v
Proof by Reflection	Reflection.v
Proving in the Large	Large.v
Reasoning about Programming Language Syntax	ProgLang.v

2   Some Quick Examples

I start off with a fully worked set of examples, building certified compilers from increasingly complicated source languages to stack machines. We meet a few useful tactics and see how they can be used in manual proofs and also how easily these proofs can be automated instead. This chapter is not meant to give full explanations of the features that are employed. Rather, it is a survey of what is possible. Later chapters introduce all the concepts in bottom-up fashion. In other words, it is expected that most readers will not understand what exactly is going on here, but I hope this demo will whet their appetite for the remaining chapters.

You can step through the source file `StackMachine.v` for this chapter interactively in Proof General. Alternatively, to get a feel for the whole life cycle of creating a Coq development, you can enter the pieces of source code in this chapter in a new `.v` file in an Emacs buffer. If you do the latter, include these two lines at the start of the file:

```
Require Import Bool Arith List CpdtTactics.
Set Implicit Arguments.
```

In general, similar commands are hidden in the book rendering of each chapter's source code, so you will need to insert them in from-scratch replayings of the code that is presented. Every chapter begins with those two lines, with the import list tweaked as appropriate, considering which definitions the chapter uses. The second command affects the default behavior of definitions regarding type inference.

2.1   Arithmetic Expressions over Natural Numbers

We begin with that staple of compiler textbooks, arithmetic expressions over a single type of numbers.

2.1.1 Source Language

We begin with the syntax of the source language:

`Inductive` **binop** : Set := Plus | Times.

This first line of Coq code should be unsurprising to ML and Haskell programmers. An algebraic datatype **binop** is defined to stand for the binary operators of the source language. There are just two differences compared to ML and Haskell. First, we use the keyword `Inductive` in place of `data`, `datatype`, or `type`. This is not just a trivial surface syntax difference; inductive types in Coq are much more expressive than ordinary algebraic datatypes, essentially enabling us to encode all of mathematics. Second, there is the : `Set` fragment, which declares that we are defining a datatype that should be thought of as a constituent of programs. Later, we meet other options for defining datatypes in the universe of proofs or in an infinite hierarchy of universes, encompassing both programs and proofs, that is useful in higher-order constructions.

`Inductive` **exp** : Set :=
| Const : **nat** → **exp**
| Binop : **binop** → **exp** → **exp** → **exp**.

Now we define the type of arithmetic expressions. We write that a constant may be built from one argument, a natural number; and a binary operation may be built from a choice of operator and two operand expressions.

A note for readers who want to relate the book contents to Coq source code: coqdoc supports pretty-printing of tokens in LaTeX or HTML. Where you see a right arrow character, the source contains the ASCII text ->. Other examples of this substitution appearing in this chapter are a double right arrow for =>, the inverted A symbol for `forall`, and the Cartesian product X for *. When in doubt about the ASCII version of a symbol, consult the chapter source code.

Now we are ready to say what programs in the expression language mean. We do this by writing an interpreter that can be thought of as a trivial operational or denotational semantics. (If you are not familiar with these semantic techniques, no need to worry: I stick to common sense constructions.)

`Definition` binopDenote (b : **binop**) : **nat** → **nat** → **nat** :=
  match b with
    | Plus ⇒ plus
    | Times ⇒ mult
  end.

The meaning of a binary operator is a binary function over naturals, defined with pattern-matching notation analogous to the `case` and `match` of ML and Haskell, and referring to the functions **plus** and **mult** from the Coq standard library. The keyword `Definition` is Coq's all-purpose notation for binding a term of the programming language to a name, with some associated syntactic sugar, like the notation we see here for defining a function. That sugar could be expanded to yield this definition:

```
Definition binopDenote : binop → nat → nat → nat :=
  fun (b : binop) ⇒
    match b with
      | Plus ⇒ plus
      | Times ⇒ mult
    end.
```

In this example, we could also omit all the type annotations, arriving at

```
Definition binopDenote := fun b ⇒
  match b with
    | Plus ⇒ plus
    | Times ⇒ mult
  end.
```

Languages like Haskell and ML have a convenient *principal types* property, which gives strong guarantees about how effective type inference will be. Unfortunately, Coq's type system is so expressive that any kind of complete type inference is impossible, and the task even seems to be hard in practice. Nonetheless, Coq includes some very helpful heuristics, many of them copying the workings of Haskell and ML type checkers for programs that fall in simple fragments of Coq's language.

This is as good a time as any to mention the profusion of different languages associated with Coq. The theoretical foundation of Coq is a formal system called the *Calculus of Inductive Constructions* (CIC) [31], which is an extension of the older *Calculus of Constructions* (CoC) [9]. CIC is quite a spartan foundation, which is helpful for proving metatheory but not so helpful for real development. Still, it is nice to know that it has been proved that CIC enjoys properties like *strong normalization* [31], meaning that every program (and more important, every proof term) terminates; and *relative consistency* [48] with systems like versions of Zermelo-Fraenkel set theory, which roughly means that you can believe that Coq proofs mean that the corresponding propositions are "really true" if you believe in set theory.

Coq is actually based on an extension of CIC called Gallina. The text after the := and before the period in the last code example is a term of Gallina. Gallina includes several useful features that must be considered as extensions to CIC. The important metatheorems about CIC have not been extended to the full breadth of the features that go beyond the formalized language, but most Coq users do not seem concerned over this omission.

Next, there is Ltac, Coq's domain-specific language for writing proofs and decision procedures. I give some basic examples of Ltac later in this chapter, and much of this book is devoted to more elaborate Ltac examples.

Finally, commands like **Inductive** and **Definition** are part of the Vernacular, which includes all sorts of useful queries and requests to the Coq system. Every Coq source file is a series of vernacular commands, where many command forms take arguments that are Gallina or Ltac programs. (Actually, Coq source files are more like *trees* of vernacular commands, thanks to various nested scoping constructs.)

We can give a simple definition of the meaning of an expression.

```
Fixpoint expDenote (e : exp) : nat :=
  match e with
    | Const n ⇒ n
    | Binop b e1 e2 ⇒ (binopDenote b) (expDenote e1) (expDenote e2)
  end.
```

We declare explicitly that this is a recursive definition, using the keyword **Fixpoint**. The rest should be familiar to functional programmers.

It is convenient to be able to test definitions before starting to prove things about them. We can verify that the semantics is sensible by evaluating some sample uses, using the command **Eval**. This command takes an argument expressing a *reduction strategy*, or an order of evaluation. Unlike with ML, which hardcodes an *eager* reduction strategy, or Haskell, which hardcodes a *lazy* strategy, in Coq we are free to choose between these and many other orders of evaluation, because all Coq programs terminate. In fact, Coq silently checked termination of the last **Fixpoint** definition, using a simple heuristic based on monotonically decreasing size of arguments across recursive calls. Specifically, recursive calls must be made on arguments that were pulled out of the original recursive argument with **match** expressions. (Chapter 7 shows some ways of getting around this restriction, though simply removing the restriction would leave Coq useless as a theorem-proving tool.)

To return to the test evaluations, we run the `Eval` command using the `simpl` evaluation strategy that usually gets the job done.

Eval simpl in expDenote (Const 42).
  $= 42$: **nat**

Eval simpl in expDenote (Binop Plus (Const 2) (Const 2)).
  $= 4$: **nat**

Eval simpl in expDenote (Binop Times (Binop Plus (Const 2) (Const 2)) (Const 7)).
  $= 28$: **nat**

2.1.2   Target Language

We compile the source programs onto a simple stack machine, whose syntax is

```
Inductive instr : Set :=
| iConst : nat → instr
| iBinop : binop → instr.
Definition prog := list instr.
Definition stack := list nat.
```

An instruction either pushes a constant onto the stack or pops two arguments, applies a binary operator to them, and pushes the result onto the stack. A program is a list of instructions, and a stack is a list of natural numbers.

We can give instructions meanings as functions from stacks to optional stacks, where running an instruction results in **None** in case of a stack underflow and results in **Some** *s'* when the result of execution is the new stack *s'*. The infix operator :: is list cons from the Coq standard library.

```
Definition instrDenote (i : instr) (s : stack) : option stack :=
  match i with
    | iConst n ⇒ Some (n :: s)
    | iBinop b ⇒
      match s with
        | arg1 :: arg2 :: s' ⇒
          Some ((binopDenote b) arg1 arg2 :: s')
        | _ ⇒ None
      end
  end.
```

With instrDenote defined, it is easy to define a function progDenote, which iterates application of instrDenote through a whole program.

```
Fixpoint progDenote (p : prog) (s : stack) : option stack :=
  match p with
    | nil ⇒ Some s
    | i :: p' ⇒
      match instrDenote i s with
        | None ⇒ None
        | Some s' ⇒ progDenote p' s'
      end
  end.
```

With the two programming languages defined, we turn to the compiler definition.

2.1.3   Translation

The compiler itself is now unsurprising. The list concatenation operator ++ comes from the Coq standard library.

```
Fixpoint compile (e : exp) : prog :=
  match e with
    | Const n ⇒ iConst n :: nil
    | Binop b e1 e2 ⇒ compile e2 ++ compile e1 ++ iBinop b :: nil
  end.
```

Before we set about proving that this compiler is correct, we can try a few test runs, using the sample programs from earlier.

```
Eval simpl in compile (Const 42).
    = iConst 42 :: nil : prog
```

```
Eval simpl in compile (Binop Plus (Const 2) (Const 2)).
    = iConst 2 :: iConst 2 :: iBinop Plus :: nil : prog
```

```
Eval simpl in compile (Binop Times (Binop Plus (Const 2) (Const 2))
  (Const 7)).
    = iConst 7 :: iConst 2 :: iConst 2 :: iBinop Plus :: iBinop Times
    :: nil : prog
```

We can also run the compiled programs and check that they give the right results.

```
Eval simpl in progDenote (compile (Const 42)) nil.
    = Some (42 :: nil) : option stack
```

```
Eval simpl in progDenote (compile (Binop Plus (Const 2)
  (Const 2))) nil.
```

= Some (4 :: nil) : **option** stack

Eval simpl in progDenote (compile (Binop Times (Binop Plus (Const 2)
(Const 2)) (Const 7))) nil.
  = Some (28 :: nil) : **option** stack

So far, so good, but how can we be sure the compiler operates
correctly for *all* input programs?

2.1.4 Translation Correctness

We are ready to prove that the compiler is implemented correctly. We
can use a new vernacular command Theorem to start a correctness proof,
in terms of the semantics defined earlier.

Theorem compile_correct :
  $\forall$ *e*, progDenote (compile *e*) nil = Some (expDenote *e* :: nil).

Though a pencil-and-paper proof might clock out at this point, writing "by a routine induction on *e*," it turns out not to make sense to
attack this proof directly. We need to use the standard trick of *strengthening the induction hypothesis*. We do that by proving an auxiliary
lemma, using the command Lemma that is a synonym for Theorem, con-
ventionally used for less important theorems that appear in the proofs
of primary theorems.

Abort.

Lemma compile_correct' : $\forall$ *e p s*,
  progDenote (compile *e* ++ *p*) *s* = progDenote *p* (expDenote *e* :: *s*).

After the period in the Lemma command, we are in the *interactive
proof-editing mode* and see this screen of text:

1 subgoal

  ================================
  $\forall$ (*e* : **exp**) (*p* : **list instr**) (*s* : stack),
    progDenote (compile *e* ++ *p*) *s* = progDenote *p* (expDenote *e* :: *s*)

Coq seems to be restating the lemma. What we see is a limited case
of a more general protocol for describing where we are in a proof. We
are told that we have a single subgoal. In general, during a proof, we
can have many pending subgoals, each of which is a logical proposition
to prove. Subgoals can be proved in any order, but it usually works best
to prove them in the order that Coq chooses.

Next in the output, the single subgoal is described in full detail. Above the double-dashed line would be free variables and hypotheses if we had any. Below the line is the conclusion, which, in general, is to be proved from the hypotheses.

We manipulate the proof state by running commands called *tactics*. One of the most important tactics is

```
induction e.
```

We declare that this proof will proceed by induction on the structure of the expression e. This swaps out the initial subgoal for two new subgoals, one for each case of the inductive proof.

```
2 subgoals
```

  n : **nat**
  ============================
  $\forall$ (s : stack) (p : **list instr**),
    progDenote (compile (Const n) ++ p) s =
    progDenote p (expDenote (Const n) :: s)

```
subgoal 2 is
```

  $\forall$ (s : stack) (p : **list instr**),
    progDenote (compile (Binop b $e1$ $e2$) ++ p) s =
    progDenote p (expDenote (Binop b $e1$ $e2$) :: s)

The first (current) subgoal is displayed with the double-dashed line below free variables and hypotheses, whereas later subgoals are only summarized with their conclusions. In the first subgoal, n is a free variable of type **nat**. The conclusion is the original theorem statement with e replaced by Const n. In a similar manner, the second case has e replaced by a generalized invocation of the Binop expression constructor. Proving both cases corresponds to a standard proof by structural induction.

We begin the first case with another very common tactic.

```
intros.
```

The current subgoal changes to

n : **nat**
s : stack
p : **list instr**

```
=====================================
progDenote (compile (Const n) ++ p) s =
progDenote p (expDenote (Const n) :: s)
```

We see that `intros` changes ∀-bound variables at the beginning of a goal into free variables.

To progress further, we need to use the definitions of some of the functions appearing in the goal. The `unfold` tactic replaces an identifier with its definition.

`unfold compile.`

n : **nat**
s : stack
p : **list instr**

```
=====================================
progDenote ((iConst n :: nil) ++ p) s =
progDenote p (expDenote (Const n) :: s)
```

`unfold expDenote.`

n : **nat**
s : stack
p : **list instr**

```
=====================================
progDenote ((iConst n :: nil) ++ p) s = progDenote p (n :: s)
```

We only need to unfold the first occurrence of **progDenote** to prove the goal. An `at` clause used with `unfold` specifies a particular occurrence of an identifier to unfold, where occurrences are counted from left to right.

`unfold progDenote at 1.`

n : **nat**
s : stack
p : **list instr**

```
=====================================
(fix progDenote (p0 : prog) (s0 : stack) {struct p0} :
   option stack :=
     match p0 with
```

```
| nil ⇒ Some s0
| i :: p' ⇒
    match instrDenote i s0 with
    | Some s' ⇒ progDenote p' s'
    | None ⇒ None (A:=stack)
    end
end) ((iConst n :: nil) ++ p) s =
progDenote p (n :: s)
```

This last `unfold` has left an anonymous recursive definition of prog-Denote (similar to `fun` or lambda constructs that allow anonymous nonrecursive functions), which will generally happen when unfolding recursive definitions. Note that Coq has automatically renamed the `fix` arguments p and s to $p0$ and $s0$ to avoid clashes with local free variables. There is also a subterm None (A:=stack), which has an annotation specifying that the type of the term ought to be **option** stack. This is phrased as an explicit instantiation of a named type parameter A from the definition of **option**.

Fortunately, in this case, we can eliminate the complications of anonymous recursion right away, since the structure of the argument (iConst n :: nil) ++ p is known, allowing us to simplify the internal pattern match with the `simpl` tactic, which applies the same reduction strategy used earlier with `Eval`.

```
simpl.
```

```
n : nat
s : stack
p : list instr
============================
(fix progDenote (p0 : prog) (s0 : stack) {struct p0} :
 option stack :=
   match p0 with
   | nil ⇒ Some s0
   | i :: p' ⇒
       match instrDenote i s0 with
       | Some s' ⇒ progDenote p' s'
       | None ⇒ None (A:=stack)
       end
   end) p (n :: s) = progDenote p (n :: s)
```

Now we can unexpand the definition of progDenote.

```
fold progDenote.
```

n : **nat**
s : stack
p : **list instr**
==============================
progDenote p $(n :: s)$ = progDenote p $(n :: s)$

It looks like we are at the end of this case, since we have a trivial equality. Indeed, a single tactic finishes the case.

```
reflexivity.
```

On to the second inductive case.

b : **binop**
$e1$: **exp**
$IHe1$: $\forall$ $(s :$ stack$)$ $(p :$ **list instr**$)$,
       progDenote (compile $e1$ ++ p) s
       = progDenote p (expDenote $e1 :: s$)
$e2$: **exp**
$IHe2$: $\forall$ $(s :$ stack$)$ $(p :$ **list instr**$)$,
       progDenote (compile $e2$ ++ p) s
       = progDenote p (expDenote $e2 :: s$)
==============================
$\forall$ $(s :$ stack$)$ $(p :$ **list instr**$)$,
progDenote (compile (Binop b $e1$ $e2$) ++ p) s =
progDenote p (expDenote (Binop b $e1$ $e2$) $:: s$)

This is the first example of hypotheses above the double-dashed line. They are the inductive hypotheses *IHe1* and *IHe2*, corresponding to the subterms *e1* and *e2*, respectively.

We start out the same way as before, introducing new free variables and unfolding and folding the appropriate definitions. The seemingly frivolous `unfold`/`fold` pairs are actually accomplishing useful work, because `unfold` will sometimes perform easy simplifications.

```
intros.
unfold compile.
fold compile.
unfold expDenote.
```

```
fold expDenote.
```

The tactics we have seen so far are insufficient. No further definition unfoldings are useful, so we need to try something different.

b : **binop**
$e1$: **exp**
$IHe1$: $\forall$ (s : stack) (p : **list instr**),
　　　progDenote (compile $e1$ ++ p) s
　　　= progDenote p (expDenote $e1$ :: s)
$e2$: **exp**
$IHe2$: $\forall$ (s : stack) (p : **list instr**),
　　　progDenote (compile $e2$ ++ p) s
　　　= progDenote p (expDenote $e2$ :: s)
s : stack
p : **list instr**
　============================
　progDenote ((compile $e2$ ++ compile $e1$ ++ iBinop b :: nil) ++ p) s
　= progDenote p (binopDenote b (expDenote $e1$) (expDenote $e2$) :: s)

We need the associative law of list concatenation, which is available as a theorem `app_assoc_reverse` in the standard library. (It is possible to tell the difference between inputs and outputs to Coq by periods at the ends of the inputs.)

Check `app_assoc_reverse`.

app_assoc_reverse
　　: $\forall$ (A : Type) (l m n : **list** A), (l ++ m) ++ n = l ++ m ++ n

If we did not already know the name of the theorem, we could use the `SearchRewrite` command to find it, based on a pattern that we would like to rewrite.

SearchRewrite ((_ ++ _) ++ _).

app_assoc_reverse:
　$\forall$ (A : Type) (l m n : **list** A), (l ++ m) ++ n = l ++ m ++ n
app_assoc:
　$\forall$ (A : Type) (l m n : **list** A), l ++ m ++ n = (l ++ m) ++ n

We use `app_assoc_reverse` to perform a rewrite

```
rewrite app_assoc_reverse.
```

changing the conclusion to

progDenote (compile *e2* ++ (compile *e1* ++ iBinop *b* :: nil) ++ *p*) *s*
= progDenote *p* (binopDenote *b* (expDenote *e1*) (expDenote *e2*) :: *s*)

The left side of the equality matches the left side of the second inductive hypothesis, so we can rewrite with that hypothesis, too.

```
rewrite IHe2.
```

progDenote ((compile *e1* ++ iBinop *b* :: nil) ++ *p*)
   (expDenote *e2* :: *s*)
= progDenote *p* (binopDenote *b* (expDenote *e1*) (expDenote *e2*) :: *s*)

The same process lets us apply the remaining hypothesis.

```
rewrite app_assoc_reverse.
rewrite IHe1.
```

progDenote ((iBinop *b* :: nil) ++ *p*)
   (expDenote *e1* :: expDenote *e2* :: *s*)
= progDenote *p* (binopDenote *b* (expDenote *e1*) (expDenote *e2*) :: *s*)

Now we can apply a similar sequence of tactics to the one that ended the proof of the first case.

```
unfold progDenote at 1.
simpl.
fold progDenote.
reflexivity.
```

The proof is completed, as indicated by the message

```
Proof completed.
```

Even for simple theorems like this, the final proof script is unstructured and not very enlightening to readers. If we extend this approach to more serious theorems, we arrive at the unreadable proof scripts complained of by opponents of tactic-based proving. Fortunately, Coq has rich support for scripted automation, and we can take advantage of such a scripted tactic (defined elsewhere in the book source) to make short work of this lemma. We abort the old proof attempt and start again.

```
Abort.
```

Lemma compile_correct' : $\forall$ *e s p*, progDenote (compile *e* ++ *p*) *s* =
  progDenote *p* (expDenote *e* :: *s*).
  induction *e*; *crush*.
```
Qed.
```

We need only state the basic inductive proof scheme and call a tactic that automates the tedious reasoning in between. In contrast to the period tactic terminator from the last proof, the semicolon tactic separator supports structured, compositional proofs. The tactic *t1* ; *t2* has the effect of running *t1* and then running *t2* on each remaining subgoal. The semicolon is one of the most fundamental building blocks of effective proof automation. The period terminator is very useful for exploratory proving, when we need to see intermediate proof states, but final proofs of any serious complexity should have just one period, terminating a single compound tactic that probably uses semicolons.

The *crush* tactic comes from the library associated with this book and is not part of the Coq standard library. The book's library contains a number of other tactics that are especially helpful in highly automated proofs.

The `Qed` command checks that the proof is finished and, if so, saves it. The sequence of tactic commands we have used is an example of a *proof script*, or a series of Ltac programs; `Qed` uses the result of a script to generate a *proof term*, a well-typed term of Gallina. To believe that a theorem is true, we need only trust that the (relatively simple) checker for proof terms is correct; the use of proof scripts is immaterial. Part I of this book introduces the principles behind encoding all proofs as terms of Gallina.

The proof of the main theorem is now easy. We prove it with four period-terminated tactics, though separating them with semicolons would work as well; the version here is easier to step through.

Theorem compile_correct : $\forall$ *e*, progDenote (compile *e*) nil
  = Some (expDenote *e* :: nil).
  intros.

e : **exp**
================================
  progDenote (compile *e*) nil = Some (expDenote *e* :: nil)

At this point, we want to format the left side of the equality to match the statement of compile_correct'. A theorem from the standard library is useful.

Check app_nil_end.

app_nil_end
      : $\forall$ (A : Type) (l : **list** A), $l = l\ $++$\ $nil

    rewrite (app_nil_end (compile e)).

This time, we explicitly specify the value of the variable l from the theorem statement, since multiple expressions of list type appear in the conclusion. The rewrite tactic might choose the wrong place to rewrite if we did not specify which we want.

    e : **exp**
    ============================
    progDenote (compile e ++ nil) nil = Some (expDenote e :: nil)

Now we can apply the lemma.

    rewrite compile_correct'.

    e : **exp**
    ============================
    progDenote nil (expDenote e :: nil) = Some (expDenote e :: nil)

We are almost done. The left and right sides of the equality match by simple symbolic evaluation. That means we are in luck because Coq identifies any pair of terms as equal whenever they normalize to the same result by symbolic evaluation. By the definition of progDenote, that is the case here, but we do not need to worry about such details. A simple invocation of reflexivity does the normalization and checks that the two results are syntactically equal.

    reflexivity.
Qed.

This proof can be shortened and automated, but that task is left as an exercise for the reader.

2.2   Typed Expressions

This section builds on the initial example by adding expression forms that depend on static typing of terms for safety.

2.2.1   Source Language

We define a trivial language of types to classify expressions.

`Inductive` **type** : Set := Nat | Bool.

Like most programming languages, Coq uses case-sensitive variable names, so the user-defined type `type` is distinct from the `Type` keyword that appeared in the statement of a polymorphic theorem, and the constructor names Nat and Bool are distinct from the types **nat** and **bool** in the standard library.

Now we define an expanded set of binary operators.

`Inductive` **tbinop** : **type** → **type** → **type** → Set :=
| TPlus : **tbinop** Nat Nat Nat
| TTimes : **tbinop** Nat Nat Nat
| TEq : ∀ *t*, **tbinop** *t* *t* Bool
| TLe : **tbinop** Nat Nat Bool.

The definition of **tbinop** is different from **binop** in an important way. Where we declared that **binop** has type `Set`, here we declare that **tbinop** has type `type` → `type` → `type` → `Set`. We define **tbinop** as an *indexed type family*. Indexed inductive types are at the heart of Coq's expressive power; almost everything else of interest is defined in terms of them.

The intuitive explanation of **tbinop** is that a **tbinop** *t1* *t2* *t* is a binary operator whose operands should have types *t1* and *t2*, and whose result has type *t*. For instance, constructor TLe (for less-than-or-equal comparison of numbers) is assigned type **tbinop** Nat Nat Bool, meaning the operator's arguments are naturals and its result is Boolean. The type of TEq introduces a small bit of additional complication via polymorphism: we want to allow equality comparison of any two values of any type, as long as they have the same type.

ML and Haskell have indexed algebraic datatypes. For instance, their list types are indexed by the type of data that the list carries. However, compared to Coq, ML and Haskell 98 place two important restrictions on datatype definitions.

First, the indices of the range of each data constructor must be type variables bound at the top level of the datatype definition. There is no way in those languages to do what we did here, for instance, to say that TPlus is a constructor building a **tbinop** whose indices are all fixed at

Nat. *Generalized algebraic datatypes* (GADTs) [50] are a popular feature
in GHC Haskell, OCaml 4, and other languages that removes this first
restriction.

The second restriction is not lifted by GADTs. In ML and Haskell,
indices of types must be types and may not be *expressions*. In Coq,
types may be indexed by arbitrary Gallina terms. Type indices can live
in the same universe as programs, and we can compute with them just
as with regular programs. Haskell supports a hobbled form of computation in type indices based on multiparameter type classes, and recent
extensions like type functions bring Haskell programming even closer
to functional programming with types, but without dependent typing,
there must always be a gap between how one programs with types and
how one programs normally.

We can define a similar type family for typed expressions, where
a term of type **texp** *t* can be assigned object language type *t*. (It is
conventional in the world of interactive theorem proving to call the
language of the proof assistant the *metalanguage* and a language being
formalized the *object language*.)

```
Inductive texp : type → Set :=
| TNConst : nat → texp Nat
| TBConst : bool → texp Bool
| TBinop : ∀ t1 t2 t, tbinop t1 t2 t → texp t1 → texp t2 → texp t.
```

Thanks to the use of dependent types, every well-typed **texp** represents a well-typed source expression, by construction. This turns out to
be very convenient for many things we might want to do with expressions. For instance, it is easy to adapt the interpreter approach to
defining semantics. We start by defining a function mapping the types
of the object language into Coq types.

```
Definition typeDenote (t : type) : Set :=
  match t with
    | Nat ⇒ nat
    | Bool ⇒ bool
  end.
```

Set, the type of types of programs, is itself a first-class type, and
we can write functions that return Sets. Beyond that, the definition of
typeDenote is trivial, relying on the **nat** and **bool** types from the Coq
standard library. We can interpret binary operators by relying on the
standard library equality test functions eqb and beq_nat for Booleans
and naturals, respectively, along with a less-than-or-equal test leb.

```
Definition tbinopDenote arg1 arg2 res (b : tbinop arg1 arg2 res)
```

```
  : typeDenote arg1 → typeDenote arg2 → typeDenote res :=
  match b with
    | TPlus ⇒ plus
    | TTimes ⇒ mult
    | TEq Nat ⇒ beq_nat
    | TEq Bool ⇒ eqb
    | TLe ⇒ leb
  end.
```

This function has just a few differences from the denotation functions we saw earlier. First, **tbinop** is an indexed type, so its indices become additional arguments to **tbinopDenote**. Second, we need to perform a genuine *dependent pattern match*, where the necessary *type* of each case body depends on the *value* that has been matched. At this early stage, I do not go into detail on the many subtle aspects of Gallina that support dependent pattern matching, but the subject is central to Part II of the book.

The same tricks suffice to define an expression denotation function in an unsurprising way. Note that the `type` arguments to the TBinop constructor must be included explicitly in pattern matching, but here we write underscores because we do not need to refer to those arguments directly.

```
Fixpoint texpDenote t (e : texp t) : typeDenote t :=
  match e with
    | TNConst n ⇒ n
    | TBConst b ⇒ b
    | TBinop _ _ _ b e1 e2 ⇒
      (tbinopDenote b) (texpDenote e1) (texpDenote e2)
  end.
```

We can evaluate a few example programs to convince ourselves that this semantics is correct.

```
Eval simpl in texpDenote (TNConst 42).
  = 42 : typeDenote Nat
```

```
Eval simpl in texpDenote (TBConst true).
  = true : typeDenote Bool
```

```
Eval simpl in texpDenote (TBinop TTimes (TBinop TPlus (TNConst 2)
  (TNConst 2)) (TNConst 7)).
  = 28 : typeDenote Nat
```

```
Eval simpl in texpDenote (TBinop (TEq Nat)
  (TBinop TPlus (TNConst 2) (TNConst 2)) (TNConst 7)).
  = false : typeDenote Bool
```

Eval simpl in texpDenote (TBinop TLe (TBinop TPlus (TNConst 2)
  (TNConst 2)) (TNConst 7)).
  = true : typeDenote Bool

Now we are ready to define a suitable stack machine target for compilation.

2.2.2   Target Language

In the example of the untyped language, stack machine programs could encounter stack underflows and get stuck. We had to deal with this complication even though we proved that the compiler never produced underflowing programs. We could have used dependent types to force all stack machine programs to be underflow-free.

For the new languages, besides underflow, we also have the problem of stack slots with naturals instead of Booleans, or vice versa. Using indexed typed families will avoid the need to reason about potential failures.

We start by defining stack types, which classify sets of possible stacks.

Definition tstack := **list type**.

Any stack classified by a **tstack** must have exactly as many elements, and each stack element must have the type found in the same position of the stack type.

We can define instructions in terms of stack types, where every instruction's type indicates what initial stack type it expects and what final stack type it will produce.

Inductive **tinstr** : tstack → tstack → Set :=
| TiNConst : ∀ s, **nat** → **tinstr** s (Nat :: s)
| TiBConst : ∀ s, **bool** → **tinstr** s (Bool :: s)
| TiBinop : ∀ $arg1$ $arg2$ res s,
    tbinop $arg1$ $arg2$ res
    → **tinstr** ($arg1$ :: $arg2$ :: s) (res :: s).

Stack machine programs must be a similar inductive family, since if we again used the **list** type family, we would not be able to guarantee that intermediate stack types match within a program.

Inductive **tprog** : tstack → tstack → Set :=
| TNil : ∀ s, **tprog** s s
| TCons : ∀ $s1$ $s2$ $s3$,
    tinstr $s1$ $s2$
    → **tprog** $s2$ $s3$
    → **tprog** $s1$ $s3$.

Now, to define the semantics of the new target language, we need
a representation for stacks at run-time. We again take advantage of
type information to define types of value stacks that, by construction,
contain the right number and types of elements.

```
Fixpoint vstack (ts : tstack) : Set :=
  match ts with
    | nil ⇒ unit
    | t :: ts' ⇒ typeDenote t × vstack ts'
  end%type.
```

This is another Set-valued function. This time it is recursive, which is
perfectly valid, since Set is not treated specially in determining which
functions may be written. We say that the value stack of an empty
stack type is any value of type unit, which has just a single value, tt.
A nonempty stack type leads to a value stack that is a pair, whose
first element has the proper type and whose second element follows the
representation for the remainder of the stack type. We write %*type* as
an instruction to Coq's extensible parser. In particular, this directive
applies to the whole match expression, which we ask to be parsed as
though it were a type, so that the operator × is interpreted as Cartesian
product instead of, say, multiplication. (Note that this use of *type* has
no connection to the inductive type type that was defined earlier.)

This idea of programming with types can take a while to internal-
ize, but it enables a very simple definition of instruction denotation.
The definition is similar to what might be expected from a Lisp-like
version of ML that ignored type information. Nonetheless, the fact
that tinstrDenote passes the type checker guarantees that the stack
machine programs can never go wrong. We use a special form of let to
destructure a multilevel tuple.

```
Definition tinstrDenote ts ts' (i : tinstr ts ts')
  : vstack ts → vstack ts' :=
  match i with
    | TiNConst _ n ⇒ fun s ⇒ (n , s)
    | TiBConst _ b ⇒ fun s ⇒ (b , s)
    | TiBinop _ _ _ _ b ⇒ fun s ⇒
      let '(arg1 , (arg2 , s')) := s in
        ((tbinopDenote b) arg1 arg2 , s')
  end.
```

Why do we choose to use an anonymous function to bind the initial
stack in every case of the match? Consider this well-intentioned but
invalid alternative version:

Definition tinstrDenote *ts ts'* (*i* : **tinstr** *ts ts'*) (*s* : vstack *ts*)
  : vstack *ts'* :=
  match *i* with
    | TiNConst _ *n* ⇒ (*n*, *s*)
    | TiBConst _ *b* ⇒ (*b*, *s*)
    | TiBinop _ _ _ _ *b* ⇒
      let '(*arg1*, (*arg2*, *s'*)) := *s* in
        ((tbinopDenote *b*) *arg1 arg2*, *s'*)
  end.

The Coq type checker complains that

```
The term "(n, s)" has type "(nat * vstack ts)%type"
 while it is expected to have type "vstack ?119".
```

This and other mysteries of Coq dependent typing are explained in Part II of the book, which clarifies why it is often useful to push inside of match branches those function parameters whose types depend on the type of the value being matched. (That more complete treatment of Gallina's typing rules explains why this helps.)

We finish the semantics with a straightforward definition of program denotation.

Fixpoint tprogDenote *ts ts'* (*p* : **tprog** *ts ts'*)
  : vstack *ts* → vstack *ts'* :=
  match *p* with
    | TNil _ ⇒ fun *s* ⇒ *s*
    | TCons _ _ _ *i p'* ⇒ fun *s* ⇒ tprogDenote *p'* (tinstrDenote *i s*)
  end.

The same argument-postponing trick is crucial for this definition.

2.2.3   Translation

To define the compilation, it is useful to have an auxiliary function for concatenating two stack machine programs.

Fixpoint tconcat *ts ts' ts''* (*p* : **tprog** *ts ts'*)
  : **tprog** *ts' ts''* → **tprog** *ts ts''* :=
  match *p* with
    | TNil _ ⇒ fun *p'* ⇒ *p'*
    | TCons _ _ _ *i p1* ⇒ fun *p'* ⇒ TCons *i* (tconcat *p1 p'*)
  end.

With that function in place, the compilation is defined similarly to the way it was earlier, modulo the use of dependent typing.

```
Fixpoint tcompile t (e : texp t) (ts : tstack) : tprog ts (t :: ts) :=
  match e with
    | TNConst n ⇒ TCons (TiNConst _ n) (TNil _)
    | TBConst b ⇒ TCons (TiBConst _ b) (TNil _)
    | TBinop _ _ _ b e1 e2 ⇒ tconcat (tcompile e2 _)
      (tconcat (tcompile e1 _) (TCons (TiBinop _ b) (TNil _)))
  end.
```

One interesting feature of the definition is the underscores appearing
to the right of ⇒ arrows. Haskell and ML programmers are familiar with
compilers that infer type parameters to polymorphic values. In Coq, it
is possible to go even further and ask the system to infer arbitrary
terms, by writing underscores in place of specific values. You may have
noticed that we have been calling functions without specifying all their
arguments. For instance, the recursive calls here to **tcompile** omit the
t argument. Coq's *implicit argument* mechanism automatically inserts
underscores for arguments that it will probably be able to infer, but
inference of such values is far from complete; generally, it only works in
cases similar to those encountered with polymorphic type instantiation
in Haskell and ML.

The underscores here are being filled in with stack types. That is, the
Coq type inferencer is, in a sense, inferring something about the flow of
control in the translated programs. We can look at exactly which values
are filled in.

```
Print tcompile.
```

```
tcompile =
fix tcompile (t : type) (e : texp t) (ts : tstack) {struct e} :
  tprog ts (t :: ts) :=
  match e in (texp t0) return (tprog ts (t0 :: ts)) with
  | TNConst n ⇒ TCons (TiNConst ts n) (TNil (Nat :: ts))
  | TBConst b ⇒ TCons (TiBConst ts b) (TNil (Bool :: ts))
  | TBinop arg1 arg2 res b e1 e2 ⇒
      tconcat (tcompile arg2 e2 ts)
        (tconcat (tcompile arg1 e1 (arg2 :: ts))
          (TCons (TiBinop ts b) (TNil (res :: ts))))
  end
     : ∀ t : type, texp t → ∀ ts : tstack, tprog ts (t :: ts)
```

We can check that the compiler generates programs that behave
appropriately on the earlier sample programs.

```
Eval simpl in tprogDenote (tcompile (TNConst 42) nil) tt.
  = (42, tt) : vstack (Nat :: nil)
```

Eval simpl in tprogDenote (tcompile (TBConst true) nil) tt.
  = (true, tt) : vstack (Bool :: nil)

Eval simpl in tprogDenote (tcompile (TBinop TTimes
  (TBinop TPlus (TNConst 2) (TNConst 2)) (TNConst 7)) nil) tt.
  = (28, tt) : vstack (Nat :: nil)

Eval simpl in tprogDenote (tcompile (TBinop (TEq Nat)
  (TBinop TPlus (TNConst 2) (TNConst 2)) (TNConst 7)) nil) tt.
  = (false, tt) : vstack (Bool :: nil)

Eval simpl in tprogDenote (tcompile (TBinop TLe
  (TBinop TPlus (TNConst 2) (TNConst 2)) (TNConst 7)) nil) tt.
  = (true, tt) : vstack (Bool :: nil)

The compiler seems to be working, so let us turn to proving that it *always* works.

2.2.4 Translation Correctness

We can state a correctness theorem similar to the last one.

Theorem tcompile_correct : ∀ *t* (*e* : **texp** *t*),
  tprogDenote (tcompile *e* nil) tt = (texpDenote *e*, tt).

Again, we need to strengthen the theorem statement so that the induction will go through. This time, to provide an excuse to demonstrate different tactics, I develop an alternative approach to this kind of proof, stating the key lemma as

Lemma tcompile_correct' : ∀ *t* (*e* : **texp** *t*) *ts* (*s* : vstack *ts*),
  tprogDenote (tcompile *e ts*) *s* = (texpDenote *e*, *s*).

While lemma compile_correct' quantified over a program that is the continuation [39] for the expression we are considering, here we avoid drawing in any extra syntactic elements. In addition to the source expression and its type, we also quantify over an initial stack type and a stack compatible with it. Running the compilation of the program starting from that stack, we should arrive at a stack that differs only in having the program's denotation pushed onto it.

Let us try to prove this theorem in the same way as in the last section.

  induction *e*; *crush*.

We are left with this unproved conclusion:

tprogDenote
    (tconcat (tcompile *e2 ts*)

$$(\text{tconcat } (\text{tcompile } e1 \ (arg2 :: ts))$$
$$(\text{TCons } (\text{TiBinop } ts \ t) \ (\text{TNil } (res :: ts)))))) \ s =$$
$$(\text{tbinopDenote } t \ (\text{texpDenote } e1) \ (\text{texpDenote } e2), s)$$

We need an analogue to the `app_assoc_reverse` theorem that we used to rewrite the goal in the last section. We can abort this proof and prove such a lemma about `tconcat`.

`Abort.`

Lemma tconcat_correct : $\forall \ ts \ ts' \ ts''$ (p : **tprog** $ts \ ts'$)
  (p' : **tprog** $ts' \ ts''$) (s : vstack ts),
  tprogDenote (tconcat $p \ p'$) s
  = tprogDenote p' (tprogDenote $p \ s$).
  induction p; *crush*.
Qed.

This one goes through completely automatically.

Some code behind the scenes registers `app_assoc_reverse` for use by *crush*. We must register `tconcat_correct` similarly to get the same effect.

`Hint Rewrite tconcat_correct.`

Here we meet the pervasive concept of a *hint*. Many proofs can be found through exhaustive enumerations of combinations of possible proof steps; hints provide the set of steps to consider. The tactic *crush* is applying brute force search silently, and it will consider more possibilities as we add more hints. This particular hint asks that the lemma be used for left-to-right rewriting.

Now we are ready to return to `tcompile_correct`', proving it automatically this time.

Lemma tcompile_correct' : $\forall \ t$ (e : **texp** t) ts (s : vstack ts),
  tprogDenote (tcompile $e \ ts$) s = (texpDenote e, s).
  induction e; *crush*.
Qed.

We can register this main lemma as another hint, allowing us to prove the final theorem trivially.

`Hint Rewrite tcompile_correct'.`

Theorem tcompile_correct : $\forall \ t$ (e : **texp** t),
  tprogDenote (tcompile e nil) tt = (texpDenote e, tt).
  crush.
Qed.

It is worth emphasizing that we are doing more than building mathematical models. The compilers are functional programs that can be executed efficiently. One strategy for doing so is based on *program extraction*, which generates OCaml code from Coq developments. For instance, we run a command to output the OCaml version of tcompile.

`Extraction tcompile.`

```
let rec tcompile t e ts =
  match e with
  | TNConst n ->
    TCons (ts, (Cons (Nat, ts)), (Cons (Nat, ts)),
      (TiNConst (ts, n)), (TNil (Cons (Nat, ts))))
  | TBConst b ->
    TCons (ts, (Cons (Bool, ts)), (Cons (Bool, ts)),
      (TiBConst (ts, b)), (TNil (Cons (Bool, ts))))
  | TBinop (t1, t2, t0, b, e1, e2) ->
    tconcat ts (Cons (t2, ts)) (Cons (t0, ts))
      (tcompile t2 e2 ts) (tconcat (Cons (t2, ts))
      (Cons (t1, (Cons (t2, ts)))) (Cons (t0, ts))
      (tcompile t1 e1 (Cons (t2, ts))) (TCons ((Cons (t1,
      (Cons (t2, ts)))), (Cons (t0, ts)), (Cons (t0, ts)),
      (TiBinop (t1, t2, t0, ts, b)),
      (TNil (Cons (t0, ts))))))
```

We can compile this code with the usual OCaml compiler and obtain an executable program with reasonable performance.

This chapter has given two examples of the style of Coq development that I advocate. Parts II and III of the book focus on the key elements of that style, namely, dependent types and scripted proof automation. Part I deals with more standard foundational material, but it may still be of interest to seasoned Coq hackers, since I follow the highly automated proof style even at that early stage.

Basic Programming and Proving

3   Introducing Inductive Types

The logical foundation of Coq is the Calculus of Inductive Constructions, or CIC. In a sense, CIC is built from just two relatively straightforward features: function types and inductive types. From this modest foundation, we can prove essentially all the theorems of math and carry out effectively all program verifications. This chapter introduces induction and recursion for functional programming in Coq. Most of the examples reproduce functionality from the Coq standard library, and I have tried to copy the standard library's choices of identifiers where possible, so many of the definitions here are available in the default Coq environment.

Chapter 2 presented some of the more advanced Coq features to highlight the unusual approach that I advocate in this book. However, from this point on, we go back to basics and study the relevant features of Coq in a more bottom-up manner. A useful first step is a discussion of the differences and connections between proofs and programs in Coq.

3.1   Proof Terms

Mainstream presentations of mathematics treat proofs as objects that exist outside of the universe of mathematical objects. However, for a variety of reasoning tasks, it is convenient to encode proofs, traditional mathematical objects, and programs within a single formal language. Validity checks on mathematical objects are useful in any setting, to catch typos and other trivial errors. The benefits of static typing for programs are widely recognized, and Coq brings those benefits to both mathematical objects and programs via a uniform mechanism. In fact, from here on, we do not distinguish between programs and mathematical objects. Many mathematical formalisms are most easily encoded in terms of programs.

Proofs are fundamentally different from programs because any two proofs of a theorem are considered equivalent, from a formal standpoint if not from an engineering standpoint. However, we can use the same type-checking technology to check proofs as we use to validate programs. This is the *Curry-Howard correspondence* [10, 14], an approach for relating proofs and programs. We represent mathematical theorems as types, such that a theorem's proofs are exactly those programs that type-check at the corresponding type.

An example of Curry-Howard was already given in Chapter 2, when the token → was used to stand for both function types and logical implications. Although this might seem like overloading notations, function types and implications are in fact precisely identical according to Curry-Howard. That is, they are just two ways of describing the same computational phenomenon.

A short demonstration should explain this. The identity function over the natural numbers is certainly not a controversial program.

Check (fun x : nat $\Rightarrow$ x).
  : nat → nat

Consider this alternative program, which is almost identical to the last one:

Check (fun x : True $\Rightarrow$ x).
  : True → True

The identity program is interpreted as a proof that **True**, the always-true proposition, implies itself. Curry-Howard interprets implications as functions, where an input is a proposition being assumed and an output is a proposition being deduced. This intuition is not too far from a common one for informal theorem proving, where we might think of an implication proof as a process for transforming a hypothesis into a conclusion.

More primitive proof forms are also available. For instance, the term I is the single proof of **True**, applicable in any context.

Check I.
  : True

With I, we can prove another simple propositional theorem.

Check (fun _ : False $\Rightarrow$ I).
  : False → True

No proofs of **False** exist in the top-level context, but the implication-as-function analogy gives an easy way to, for example, show that **False** implies itself.

```
Check (fun x : False ⇒ x).
```
: **False** → **False**

Every one of these example programs whose type looks like a logical formula is a *proof term*. We use that name for any Gallina term of a logical type.

This chapter introduces different ways of defining types. Every example type can be interpreted alternatively as a type of programs or a type of proofs.

One of the first types introduced is **bool**, with constructors true and false. Newcomers to Coq often wonder about the distinction between **True** and true and the distinction between **False** and false. One answer is that **True** and **False** are types, but true and false are not. A more useful answer is that Coq's metatheory guarantees that any term of type **bool** *evaluates* to either true or false. This means that we have an *algorithm* for answering any question phrased as an expression of type **bool**. Conversely, most propositions do not evaluate to **True** or **False**; the language of inductively defined propositions is much richer than that. We ought to be glad that we have no algorithm for deciding the formalized version of mathematical truth, since otherwise it would be clear that we could not formalize undecidable properties, such as interesting properties of general-purpose programs.

3.2   Enumerations

Coq inductive types generalize the algebraic datatypes found in Haskell and ML. Confusingly enough, inductive types also generalize generalized algebraic datatypes (GADTs), by adding the possibility for type dependency. Even so, it is worth backing up from the examples of Chapter 2 and going over basic algebraic datatype uses of inductive datatypes, because the chance to prove things about the values of these types goes beyond usual practice in Haskell and ML.

The singleton type **unit** is an inductive type.

```
Inductive unit : Set :=
  | tt.
```

This vernacular command defines a new inductive type **unit** whose only value is tt. We can verify the types of the two identifiers.

```
Check unit.
```
  unit : Set

```
Check tt.
```
  tt : **unit**

We can prove that **unit** is a genuine singleton type.

`Theorem unit_singleton :` $\forall$ `x :` **unit**, x = `tt`.

The important thing about an inductive type is that we can do induction over its values, and induction is the key to proving this theorem. We ask to proceed by induction on the variable x.

    `induction` x.

The goal changes to

`tt` $=$ `tt`

which we can discharge trivially.

    `reflexivity`.
`Qed`.

It seems odd to write a proof by induction with no inductive hypotheses. We could have arrived at the same result by beginning the proof with

    `destruct` x.

which corresponds to proof by case analysis in classical math. For nonrecursive inductive types, the two tactics will always have identical behavior. Often case analysis is sufficient, even in proofs about recursive types, and it is nice to avoid introducing unneeded induction hypotheses.

What exactly *is* the induction principle for **unit**? We can ask Coq.

`Check unit_ind`.
    `unit_ind :` $\forall$ P `:` **unit** $\rightarrow$ `Prop`, P `tt` $\rightarrow$ $\forall$ u `:` **unit**, P u

Every `Inductive` command defining a type T also defines an induction principle named T_ind. Recall from the last section that the type, operations over it, and principles for reasoning about it all live in the same language and are described by the same type system. The key to telling what is a program and what is a proof lies in the distinction between the type `Prop`, which appears in the induction principle; and the type `Set`.

The convention goes like this: `Set` is the type of normal types used in programming, and the values of such types are programs. `Prop` is the type of logical propositions, and the values of such types are proofs. Thus, an induction principle has a type that shows it is a function for building proofs.

Specifically, `unit_ind` quantifies over a predicate P over **unit** values. If we can present a proof that P holds for `tt`, then we are rewarded with a proof that P holds for any value u of type **unit**. In the last proof, the predicate was (**fun** u : **unit** $\Rightarrow u = $ **tt**).

The definition of **unit** places the type in Set. By replacing Set with Prop, **unit** with **True**, and **tt** with I, we arrive at precisely the definition of **True** that the Coq standard library employs. The program type **unit** is the Curry-Howard equivalent of the proposition **True**. We might say that while philosophers have expended much ink on the nature of truth, we have now determined that truth is the **unit** type of functional programming.

We can define an inductive type even simpler than **unit**.

```
Inductive Empty_set : Set := .
```

Empty_set has no elements. We can prove amusing theorems about it.

```
Theorem the_sky_is_falling : ∀ x : Empty_set, 2 + 2 = 5.
  destruct 1.
Qed.
```

Because **Empty_set** has no elements, the fact of having an element of this type implies anything. We use destruct 1 instead of destruct x in the proof because unused quantified variables are relegated to being referred to by number. (There is a good reason for this, related to the unity of quantifiers and implication. At least within Coq's logical foundation of constructive logic, an implication is just a quantification over a proof, where the quantified variable is never used. It generally makes more sense to refer to implication hypotheses by number than by name, and Coq treats the quantifier over an unused variable as an implication in determining the proper behavior.)

We can see the induction principle that made this proof so easy.

```
Check Empty_set_ind.
  Empty_set_ind : ∀ (P : Empty_set → Prop) (e : Empty_set), P e
```

In other words, any predicate over values from the empty set holds vacuously of every such element. In the last proof, we chose the predicate (**fun** _ : **Empty_set** $\Rightarrow 2 + 2 = 5$).

We can also apply this get-out-of-jail-free card programmatically. Here is a lazy way of converting values of **Empty_set** to values of **unit**:

```
Definition e2u (e : Empty_set) : unit := match e with end.
```

We employ match pattern matching as in Chapter 2. Since we match on a value whose type has no constructors, there is no need to provide any branches. It turns out that **Empty_set** is the Curry-Howard equivalent of **False**. As for why **Empty_set** starts with a capital letter and not a lowercase letter as **unit** does, I must refer readers to the authors of the Coq standard library.

Moving up the ladder of complexity, we can define the Booleans.

```
Inductive bool : Set :=
| true
| false.
```

We can use less vacuous pattern matching to define Boolean negation.

```
Definition negb (b : bool) : bool :=
  match b with
    | true ⇒ false
    | false ⇒ true
  end.
```

An alternative definition desugars to the preceding one, thanks to an `if` notation overloaded to work with any inductive type that has exactly two constructors:

```
Definition negb' (b : bool) : bool :=
  if b then false else true.
```

We might want to prove that **negb** is its own inverse operation.

```
Theorem negb_inverse : ∀ b : bool, negb (negb b) = b.
  destruct b.
```

After we case-analyze on b, we are left with one subgoal for each constructor of **bool**.

```
2 subgoals
```

```
  ============================
   negb (negb true) = true
```

```
subgoal 2 is
```

```
 negb (negb false) = false
```

The first subgoal follows by Coq's rules of computation, so we can dispatch it easily.

```
  reflexivity.
```

The same holds for the second subgoal, so we can restart the proof and give a very compact justification.

```
Restart.
```

```
  destruct b; reflexivity.
```

Qed.

Another theorem about Booleans illustrates another useful tactic.

Theorem negb_ineq : ∀ b : **bool**, negb $b \neq b$.
  destruct b; discriminate.
Qed.

The discriminate tactic is used to prove that two values of an inductive type are not equal if the values are formed with different constructors. In this case, the different constructors are true and false.

At this point, it is probably not hard to guess what the underlying induction principle for **bool** is.

Check bool_ind.
  bool_ind : ∀ P : **bool** → Prop, P true → P false → ∀ b : **bool**, P b

That is, to prove that a property describes all **bool**s, prove that it describes both true and false.

There is no interesting Curry-Howard analogue of **bool**. Of course, we can define such a type by replacing Set by Prop, but the resulting proposition is not very useful. It is logically equivalent to **True**, but it provides two indistinguishable primitive proofs, true and false.

3.3 Simple Recursive Types

The natural numbers are the simplest common example of an inductive type that actually deserves the name.

Inductive **nat** : Set :=
| O : **nat**
| S : **nat** → **nat**.

The constructor O is zero, and S is the successor function, so 0 is syntactic sugar for O, 1 for S O, 2 for S (S O), and so on.

Pattern matching works as demonstrated in Chapter 2:

Definition isZero (n : **nat**) : **bool** :=
  match n with
    | O ⇒ true
    | S _ ⇒ false
  end.

Definition pred (n : **nat**) : **nat** :=
  match n with
    | O ⇒ O
    | S n' ⇒ n'

```
end.
```

We can prove theorems by case analysis with `destruct` as for simpler inductive types, but we can also now get into genuine inductive theorems. First, we need a recursive function.

Fixpoint plus $(n\ m : \mathbf{nat}) : \mathbf{nat} :=$
  match n with
    | O $\Rightarrow m$
    | S $n' \Rightarrow$ S (plus $n'\ m$)
  end.

Recall that `Fixpoint` is Coq's mechanism for recursive function definitions. Some theorems about plus can be proved without induction.

Theorem O_plus_n : $\forall n : \mathbf{nat}$, plus O $n = n$.
  `intro`; `reflexivity`.
Qed.

Coq's computation rules automatically simplify the application of plus, because unfolding the definition of plus yields a `match` expression where the branch to be taken is obvious from syntax alone. If we just reverse the order of the arguments, though, this no longer works, and we need induction.

Theorem n_plus_O : $\forall n : \mathbf{nat}$, plus n O $= n$.
  `induction` n.

The first subgoal is plus O O $=$ O, which is trivial by computation.

  `reflexivity`.

The second subgoal requires more work and also gives a first example of an inductive hypothesis.

  $n : \mathbf{nat}$
  $IHn :$ plus n O $= n$
  $============================$
  plus (S n) O $=$ S n

We can start by using computation to simplify the goal as far as we can.

  `simpl`.

Now the conclusion is S (plus n O) $=$ S n. Using the inductive hypothesis

  `rewrite` IHn.

we get a trivial conclusion S n = S n.

```
reflexivity.
```

Not much really went on in this proof, so the *crush* tactic from the CpdtTactics module can prove this theorem automatically.

```
Restart.
```

   induction n; *crush*.

```
Qed.
```

We can check out the induction principle at work here.

```
Check nat_ind.
```

   nat_ind : ∀ P : **nat** → Prop,
             P O → (∀ n : **nat**, P n → P (S n)) → ∀ n : **nat**, P n

Each of the two cases of the last proof came from the type of one of the arguments to nat_ind. We chose P to be (**fun** n : **nat** ⇒ plus n O = n). The first proof case corresponded to P O and the second case to (∀ n : **nat**, P n → P (S n)). The free variable n and inductive hypothesis *IHn* came from the argument types given here.

Since **nat** has a constructor that takes an argument, we may sometimes need to know that the constructor is injective.

Theorem S_inj : ∀ n m : **nat**, S n = S m → n = m.
   injection 1; trivial.

```
Qed.
```

The `injection` tactic refers to a premise by number, adding new equalities between the corresponding arguments of equated terms that are formed with the same constructor. We need to prove $n = m → n = m$, so it is unsurprising that a tactic named `trivial` is able to finish the proof. This tactic attempts a variety of single proof steps, drawn from a user-specified database that can be extended.

There is also a very useful tactic called `congruence` that can prove this theorem immediately. The `congruence` tactic generalizes `discriminate` and `injection`, and it also adds reasoning about the general properties of equality, such as that a function returns equal results on equal arguments. That is, `congruence` is a *complete decision procedure for the theory of equality and uninterpreted functions* plus some reasoning about inductive types.

We can define a type of lists of natural numbers.

```
Inductive nat_list : Set :=
| NNil : nat_list
```

| NCons : **nat** → **nat_list** → **nat_list**.

Recursive definitions over **nat_list** are straightforward extensions of what we have seen before.

```
Fixpoint nlength (ls : nat_list) : nat :=
  match ls with
    | NNil ⇒ O
    | NCons _ ls' ⇒ S (nlength ls')
  end.
```

```
Fixpoint napp (ls1 ls2 : nat_list) : nat_list :=
  match ls1 with
    | NNil ⇒ ls2
    | NCons n ls1' ⇒ NCons n (napp ls1' ls2)
  end.
```

Inductive theorem proving can again be automated quite effectively.

```
Theorem nlength_napp : ∀ ls1 ls2 : nat_list, nlength (napp ls1 ls2)
  = plus (nlength ls1) (nlength ls2).
  induction ls1; crush.
Qed.
```

```
Check nat_list_ind.
```

```
  nat_list_ind
     : ∀ P : nat_list → Prop,
        P NNil →
        (∀ (n : nat) (n0 : nat_list), P n0 → P (NCons n n0)) →
        ∀ n : nat_list, P n
```

In general, we can implement any tree type as an inductive type. For example, here are binary trees of naturals:

```
Inductive nat_btree : Set :=
| NLeaf : nat_btree
| NNode : nat_btree → nat → nat_btree → nat_btree.
```

Here are two functions whose intuitive explanations are not so important. The first one computes the size of a tree, and the second performs some sort of splicing of one tree into the leftmost available leaf node of another.

```
Fixpoint nsize (tr : nat_btree) : nat :=
  match tr with
    | NLeaf ⇒ S O
    | NNode tr1 _ tr2 ⇒ plus (nsize tr1) (nsize tr2)
```

```
    end.
Fixpoint nsplice (tr1 tr2 : nat_btree) : nat_btree :=
    match tr1 with
      | NLeaf ⇒ NNode tr2 O NLeaf
      | NNode tr1' n tr2' ⇒ NNode (nsplice tr1' tr2) n tr2'
    end.
Theorem plus_assoc : ∀ n1 n2 n3 : nat, plus (plus n1 n2) n3
    = plus n1 (plus n2 n3).
    induction n1; crush.
Qed.
Theorem nsize_nsplice : ∀ tr1 tr2 : nat_btree, nsize (nsplice tr1 tr2)
    = plus (nsize tr2) (nsize tr1).
    Hint Rewrite n_plus_O plus_assoc.

    induction tr1; crush.
Qed.
```

It is convenient that these proofs go through so easily, but it is still useful to look into the details of what happened, by checking the statement of the tree induction principle.

```
Check nat_btree_ind.
```

```
    nat_btree_ind
        : ∀ P : nat_btree → Prop,
          P NLeaf →
          (∀ n : nat_btree,
            P n → ∀ (n0 : nat) (n1 : nat_btree), P n1
              → P (NNode n n0 n1)) →
          ∀ n : nat_btree, P n
```

We have the usual two cases, one for each constructor of **nat_btree**.

3.4   Parameterized Types

We can also define polymorphic inductive types, as with algebraic datatypes in Haskell and ML.

```
Inductive list (T : Set) : Set :=
| nil : list T
| cons : T → list T → list T.
Fixpoint length T (ls : list T) : nat :=
    match ls with
      | nil ⇒ O
```

```
    | cons _ ls' ⇒ S (length ls')
  end.
Fixpoint app T (ls1 ls2 : list T) : list T :=
  match ls1 with
    | nil ⇒ ls2
    | cons x ls1' ⇒ cons x (app ls1' ls2)
  end.
Theorem length_app : ∀ T (ls1 ls2 : list T), length (app ls1 ls2)
  = plus (length ls1) (length ls2).
  induction ls1; crush.
Qed.
```

There is a useful shorthand for writing many definitions that share the same parameter, based on Coq's *section* mechanism. The following block of code is equivalent to the previous one.

```
Section list.
  Variable T : Set.

  Inductive list : Set :=
  | nil : list
  | cons : T → list → list.

  Fixpoint length (ls : list) : nat :=
    match ls with
      | nil ⇒ O
      | cons _ ls' ⇒ S (length ls')
    end.

  Fixpoint app (ls1 ls2 : list) : list :=
    match ls1 with
      | nil ⇒ ls2
      | cons x ls1' ⇒ cons x (app ls1' ls2)
    end.

  Theorem length_app : ∀ ls1 ls2 : list, length (app ls1 ls2)
    = plus (length ls1) (length ls2).
    induction ls1; crush.
  Qed.
End list.

Implicit Arguments nil [T].
```

After we end the section, the `Variables` we used are added as extra function parameters for each defined identifier, as needed. With an `Implicit Arguments` command, we ask that T be inferred when we use nil; Coq's heuristics already decided to apply a similar policy to cons, because of the Set Implicit Arguments command elided at the beginning of this chapter. We verify that our definitions have been saved properly using the Print command, a cousin of Check that shows the definition of a symbol rather than just its type.

Print list.

> Inductive **list** (T : Set) : Set :=
>   nil : **list** T | cons : $T \rightarrow$ **list** $T \rightarrow$ **list** T

The final definition is the same as what we wrote manually before. The other elements of the section are altered similarly, turning out exactly as they were before, though we wrote their definitions more succinctly.

Check length.

> length
>   : $\forall\ T$: Set, **list** $T \rightarrow$ **nat**

The parameter T is treated as a new argument to the induction principle, too.

Check list_ind.

> list_ind
>   : $\forall$ (T : Set) (P : **list** $T \rightarrow$ Prop),
> P (nil T) $\rightarrow$
>   ($\forall$ (t : T) (l : **list** T), $P\ l \rightarrow P$ (cons $t\ l$)) $\rightarrow$
> $\forall\ l$: **list** T, $P\ l$

Thus, despite a very real sense in which the type T is an argument to the constructor cons, the inductive case in the type of list_ind (the third line of the type) includes no quantifier for T, even though all the other arguments are quantified explicitly. Parameters in other inductive definitions are treated similarly in stating induction principles.

3.5 Mutually Inductive Types

We can define inductive types that refer to each other:

```
Inductive even_list : Set :=
| ENil : even_list
| ECons : nat → odd_list → even_list

with odd_list : Set :=
| OCons : nat → even_list → odd_list.
```

```
Fixpoint elength (el : even_list) : nat :=
  match el with
    | ENil ⇒ O
    | ECons _ ol ⇒ S (olength ol)
  end
```

```
with olength (ol : odd_list) : nat :=
  match ol with
    | OCons _ el ⇒ S (elength el)
  end.
```

```
Fixpoint eapp (el1 el2 : even_list) : even_list :=
  match el1 with
    | ENil ⇒ el2
    | ECons n ol ⇒ ECons n (oapp ol el2)
  end
```

```
with oapp (ol : odd_list) (el : even_list) : odd_list :=
  match ol with
    | OCons n el' ⇒ OCons n (eapp el' el)
  end.
```

Everything is roughly the same as in earlier examples until we try to prove a theorem similar to those that came before.

```
Theorem elength_eapp : ∀ el1 el2 : even_list,
  elength (eapp el1 el2) = plus (elength el1) (elength el2).
  induction el1; crush.
```

One goal remains:

```
n : nat
o : odd_list
el2 : even_list
============================
   S (olength (oapp o el2)) = S (plus (olength o) (elength el2))
```

We have no induction hypothesis, so we cannot prove this goal without starting another induction, which would reach a similar point, resulting in a futile infinite chain of inductions. The problem is that Coq's generation of *T_ind* principles is incomplete. We only get nonmutual induction principles generated by default.

```
Abort.
Check even_list_ind.
```

```
even_list_ind
  : ∀ P : even_list → Prop,
    P ENil →
    (∀ (n : nat) (o : odd_list), P (ECons n o)) →
    ∀ e : even_list, P  e
```

We see that no inductive hypotheses are included anywhere in the type. To get them, we must ask for mutual principles as we need them, using the `Scheme` command.

Scheme even_list_mut := Induction for **even_list** Sort Prop
with odd_list_mut := Induction for **odd_list** Sort Prop.

This invocation of `Scheme` asks for the creation of induction principles even_list_mut for the type **even_list** and odd_list_mut for the type **odd_list**. The `Induction` keyword says we want standard induction schemes, since `Scheme` supports more exotic choices. Finally, `Sort Prop` establishes that we really want induction schemes, not recursion schemes, which are the same according to Curry-Howard, save for the `Prop`/`Set` distinction.

Check even_list_mut.

```
even_list_mut
  : ∀ (P : even_list → Prop) (P0 : odd_list → Prop),
    P ENil →
    (∀ (n : nat) (o : odd_list), P0 o → P (ECons n o)) →
    (∀ (n : nat) (e : even_list), P e → P0 (OCons n e)) →
    ∀ e : even_list, P  e
```

This is the principle we wanted in the first place.

The `Scheme` command is for asking Coq to generate particular induction schemes that are mutual among a set of inductive types (possibly only one such type, in which case we get a normal induction principle). In a sense, it generalizes the induction scheme generation that goes on automatically for each inductive definition. Future Coq versions might make that automatic generation smarter so that `Scheme` will be needed in fewer places. Section 3.7 explains how induction principles are derived theorems in Coq so that there is no need to build in *any* automatic scheme generation.

There is one more consideration in using the even_list_mut induction principle: the `induction` tactic will not apply it automatically. It is helpful to look at how to prove one of the past examples without using `induction` so that we can then generalize the technique to mutual inductive types.

Theorem n_plus_O' : ∀ n : **nat**, plus n O = n.

`apply nat_ind.`

Here we use `apply`, which is one of the most essential basic tactics. When we are trying to prove fact P, and when *thm* is a theorem whose conclusion can be made to match P by proper choice of quantified variable values, the invocation `apply` *thm* will replace the current goal with one new goal for each premise of *thm*.

This use of `apply` may seem a bit too magical. To better see what is going on, we use a variant where we partially apply the theorem `nat_ind` to give an explicit value for the predicate that gives the induction hypothesis.

   `Undo.`
   `apply (nat_ind (fun` n `⇒ plus` n `O =` n`));` *crush.*
`Qed.`

From this example, we see that `induction` is not magic. It only does some bookkeeping for us to make it easy to apply a theorem, which we can do directly with the `apply` tactic.

This technique generalizes to the mutual example.

`Theorem elength_eapp :` $\forall$ *el1 el2* : **even_list**,
   `elength (eapp` *el1 el2*`) = plus (elength` *el1*`) (elength` *el2*`).`

   `apply (even_list_mut`
     `(fun` *el1* `:` **even_list** `⇒` $\forall$ *el2* : **even_list**,
      `elength (eapp` *el1 el2*`) = plus (elength` *el1*`) (elength` *el2*`))`
     `(fun` *ol* `:` **odd_list** `⇒` $\forall$ *el* : **even_list**,
      `olength (oapp` *ol el*`) = plus (olength` *ol*`) (elength` *el*`)));` *crush.*
`Qed.`

We simply need to specify two predicates, one for each of the mutually inductive types. In general, it is not a good idea to assume that a proof assistant can infer extra predicates, so this way of applying mutual induction is about as straightforward as we may hope for.

3.6 Reflexive Types

A kind of inductive type called a *reflexive type* includes at least one constructor that takes as an argument *a function returning the same type we are defining*. One very useful class of examples is in modeling variable binders. The example will be an encoding of the syntax of first-order logic. Since the idea of syntactic encodings of logic may require a bit of acclimation, let us first consider a simpler formula type for a subset of propositional logic. We are not yet using a reflexive type, but later we will extend the example reflexively.

```
Inductive pformula : Set :=
| Truth : pformula
| Falsehood : pformula
| Conjunction : pformula → pformula → pformula.
```

A key distinction here is between, for instance, the *syntax* **Truth** and its *semantics* **True**. We can make the semantics explicit with a recursive function. This function uses the infix operator ∧, which desugars to instances of the type family **and** from the standard library. The family **and** implements conjunction, the `Prop` Curry-Howard analogue of the usual pair type from functional programming (which is the type family **prod** in Coq's standard library).

```
Fixpoint pformulaDenote (f : pformula) : Prop :=
   match f with
      | Truth ⇒ True
      | Falsehood ⇒ False
      | Conjunction f1 f2 ⇒ pformulaDenote f1 ∧ pformulaDenote f2
   end.
```

This example does not use reflexive types, the new feature to be introduced. When we set our sights on first-order logic instead, it becomes very handy to give constructors recursive arguments that are functions.

```
Inductive formula : Set :=
| Eq : nat → nat → formula
| And : formula → formula → formula
| Forall : (nat → formula) → formula.
```

Formulas are equalities between naturals, conjunction, and universal quantification over natural numbers. We avoid needing to include a notion of variables in the type by using Coq functions to encode the syntax of quantification. For instance, here is the encoding of $\forall\, x : $ **nat**, $x = x$:

```
Example forall_refl : formula := Forall (fun x ⇒ Eq x x).
```

We can write recursive functions over reflexive types quite naturally. Here is one translating the formulas into native Coq propositions:

```
Fixpoint formulaDenote (f : formula) : Prop :=
   match f with
      | Eq n1 n2 ⇒ n1 = n2
      | And f1 f2 ⇒ formulaDenote f1 ∧ formulaDenote f2
      | Forall f' ⇒ ∀ n : nat, formulaDenote (f' n)
   end.
```

We can also encode a trivial formula transformation that swaps the order of equality and conjunction operands.

```
Fixpoint swapper (f : formula) : formula :=
  match f with
    | Eq n1 n2 ⇒ Eq n2 n1
    | And f1 f2 ⇒ And (swapper f2) (swapper f1)
    | Forall f' ⇒ Forall (fun n ⇒ swapper (f' n))
  end.
```

It is helpful to prove that this transformation does not make true formulas false.

```
Theorem swapper_preserves_truth : ∀ f, formulaDenote f
  → formulaDenote (swapper f).
  induction f; crush.
Qed.
```

We can take a look at the induction principle behind this proof.

```
Check formula_ind.
```

```
formula_ind
    : ∀ P : formula → Prop,
      (∀ n n0 : nat, P (Eq n n0)) →
      (∀ f0 : formula,
        P f0 → ∀ f1 : formula, P f1 → P (And f0 f1)) →
      (∀ f1 : nat → formula,
        (∀ n : nat, P (f1 n)) → P (Forall f1)) →
      ∀ f2 : formula, P f2
```

Focusing on the Forall case, which comes third, we see that we are allowed to assume that the theorem holds *for any application of the argument function f1*. That is, Coq induction principles do not follow a simple rule that the textual representations of induction variables must get shorter in appeals to induction hypotheses. Luckily, the people behind the metatheory of Coq have verified that this flexibility does not introduce unsoundness.

Up to this point, we have seen how to encode in Coq more and more of what is possible with algebraic datatypes in Haskell and ML. This may have given the inaccurate impression that inductive types are a strict extension of algebraic datatypes. In fact, Coq must rule out some types allowed by Haskell and ML, for reasons of soundness. Reflexive types provide the first good example of such a case; only some of them are legal.

Given the last example of an inductive type, readers may be eager to try encoding the syntax of lambda calculus. Indeed, the function-based representation technique just used, called *higher-order abstract syntax* (HOAS) [35], is the representation of choice for lambda calculi in Twelf and in many applications implemented in Haskell and ML. Let us try to import that choice to Coq.

```
Inductive term : Set :=
| App : term → term → term
| Abs : (term → term) → term.
```

```
Error: Non strictly positive occurrence of "term" in
"(term -> term) -> term"
```

We have run afoul of the *strict positivity requirement* for inductive definitions, which says that the type being defined may not occur to the left of an arrow in the type of a constructor argument. It is important that the type of a constructor is viewed in terms of a series of arguments and a result, since clearly we need recursive occurrences on the left sides of the outermost arrows if we are to have recursive occurrences at all. The candidate definition violates the positivity requirement because it involves an argument of type **term** → **term**, where the type **term** that we are defining appears to the left of an arrow. The candidate type of **App** is fine, however, since every occurrence of **term** is either a constructor argument or the final result type.

Why must Coq enforce this restriction? Imagine that the last definition had been accepted, allowing us to write this function:

```
Definition uhoh (t : term) : term :=
  match t with
    | Abs f ⇒ f t
    | _ ⇒ t
  end.
```

Using an informal idea of Coq's semantics, it is easy to verify that the application uhoh (Abs uhoh) will run forever. This would be a mere curiosity in OCaml and Haskell, where nontermination is commonplace, though the fact that we have a nonterminating program without explicit recursive function definitions is unusual.

For Coq, however, this would be a disaster. The possibility of writing such a function would destroy all confidence that proving a theorem means anything. Since Coq combines programs and proofs in one language, we would be able to prove every theorem with an infinite loop.

Nonetheless, the basic insight of HOAS is a very useful one, and there are ways to realize most benefits of HOAS in Coq. Chapter 17 describes a particular technique of this kind.

3.7   An Interlude on Induction Principles

As mentioned, Coq proofs are actually programs, written in the same language used in the examples so far. We can get a sense of what this means by looking at the definitions of some of the induction principles. Studying the details will help us construct induction principles manually, which is necessary for some more advanced inductive definitions.

`Print nat_ind.`

nat_ind =
fun P : **nat** $\rightarrow$ Prop $\Rightarrow$ nat_rect P
   : $\forall P$: **nat** $\rightarrow$ Prop,
      P O $\rightarrow$ ($\forall n$: **nat**, P n $\rightarrow$ P (S n)) $\rightarrow$ $\forall n$: **nat**, P n

This induction principle is defined in terms of a more general principle, nat_rect. The `rec` stands for *recursion principle*, and the `t` at the end stands for `Type`.

`Check nat_rect.`

nat_rect
     : $\forall P$: **nat** $\rightarrow$ Type,
       P O $\rightarrow$ ($\forall n$: **nat**, P n $\rightarrow$ P (S n)) $\rightarrow$ $\forall n$: **nat**, P n

The principle nat_rect gives P type **nat** $\rightarrow$ Type instead of **nat** $\rightarrow$ Prop. Type is another universe, like Set and Prop. In fact, it is a common supertype of both (see Chapter 12). Type can be used as a sort of meta-universe that may turn out to be either Set or Prop. We can see the symmetry inherent in the subtyping relation by printing the definition of another principle that was generated for **nat** automatically:

`Print nat_rec.`

nat_rec =
fun P : **nat** $\rightarrow$ Set $\Rightarrow$ nat_rect P
   : $\forall P$: **nat** $\rightarrow$ Set,
      P O $\rightarrow$ ($\forall n$: **nat**, P n $\rightarrow$ P (S n)) $\rightarrow$ $\forall n$: **nat**, P n

This is identical to the definition for nat_ind except that Set is substituted for Prop. For most inductive types T, then, we get not just induction principles *T_ind* but also recursion principles *T_rec*. We can use *T_rec* to write recursive definitions without explicit `Fixpoint` recursion. For instance, the following two definitions are equivalent.

```
Fixpoint plus_recursive (n : nat) : nat → nat :=
  match n with
    | O ⇒ fun m ⇒ m
    | S n' ⇒ fun m ⇒ S (plus_recursive n' m)
  end.
```

```
Definition plus_rec : nat → nat → nat :=
  nat_rec (fun _ : nat ⇒ nat → nat) (fun m ⇒ m)
  (fun _ r m ⇒ S (r m)).
```

```
Theorem plus_equivalent : plus_recursive = plus_rec.
  reflexivity.
Qed.
```

Finally, `nat_rect` itself is not even a primitive. It is a functional program that we can write manually.

```
Print nat_rect.
```

```
nat_rect =
fun (P : nat → Type) (f : P O) (f0 : ∀ n : nat, P n → P (S n)) ⇒
fix F (n : nat) : P n :=
  match n as n0 return (P n0) with
  | O ⇒ f
  | S n0 ⇒ f0 n0 (F n0)
  end
      : ∀ P : nat → Type,
          P O → (∀ n : nat, P n → P (S n)) → ∀ n : nat, P n
```

The only new items here are first, an anonymous recursive function definition using the `fix` keyword of Gallina (which is like `fun` with recursion supported), and second, the annotations on the `match` expression. This is a *dependently typed* pattern match, because the *type* of the expression depends on the *value* being matched on. (More complex examples are given in Part II.)

Type inference for dependent pattern matching is undecidable, which can be proved by reduction from higher-order unification [15]. Thus, we often need to annotate programs in a way that explains dependencies to the type checker. In the example of `nat_rect`, we have an `as` clause, which binds a name for the discriminee, and a `return` clause, which gives a way to compute the `match` result type as a function of the discriminee.

To prove that nat_rect is not extraordinary, we can reimplement it manually.

Fixpoint nat_rect' (P : **nat** $\rightarrow$ Type)
  (HO : P O)
  (HS : $\forall$ n, P n $\rightarrow$ P (S n)) (n : **nat**) :=
  match n return P n with
    | O $\Rightarrow$ HO
    | S n' $\Rightarrow$ HS n' (nat_rect' P HO HS n')
  end.

We can understand the definition of nat_rect better by reimplementing nat_ind using sections.

Section nat_ind'.

First, we have the property of natural numbers that we aim to prove.

Variable P : **nat** $\rightarrow$ Prop.

Then we require a proof of the O case, which we declare with the command Hypothesis, which is a synonym for Variable that, by convention, is used for variables whose types are propositions.

Hypothesis O_case : P O.

Next is a proof of the S case, which may assume an inductive hypothesis.

Hypothesis S_case : $\forall$ n : **nat**, P n $\rightarrow$ P (S n).

Finally, we define a recursive function to tie the pieces together.

Fixpoint nat_ind' (n : **nat**) : P n :=
  match n with
    | O $\Rightarrow$ O_case
    | S n' $\Rightarrow$ S_case (nat_ind' n')
  end.
End nat_ind'.

Closing the section adds the variables declared with Variable and Hypothesis as new fun-bound arguments to nat_ind', and, modulo the use of Prop instead of Type, we end up with the exact definition that was generated automatically for nat_rect.

We can also examine the definition of even_list_mut, which we generated with Scheme for a mutually recursive type.

Print even_list_mut.

  even_list_mut =
  fun (P : **even_list** $\rightarrow$ Prop) ($P0$: **odd_list** $\rightarrow$ Prop)

```
(f : P ENil)
(f0 : ∀ (n : nat) (o : odd_list), P0 o → P (ECons n o))
(f1 : ∀ (n : nat) (e : even_list), P e → P0 (OCons n e)) ⇒
fix F (e : even_list) : P e :=
  match e as e0 return (P e0) with
  | ENil ⇒ f
  | ECons n o ⇒ f0 n o (F0 o)
  end
with F0 (o : odd_list) : P0 o :=
  match o as o0 return (P0 o0) with
  | OCons n e ⇒ f1 n e (F e)
  end
for F
   : ∀ (P : even_list → Prop) (P0 : odd_list → Prop),
     P ENil →
     (∀ (n : nat) (o : odd_list), P0 o → P (ECons n o)) →
     (∀ (n : nat) (e : even_list), P e → P0 (OCons n e)) →
     ∀ e : even_list, P e
```

We see a mutually recursive `fix`, with the different functions separated by `with` in the same way that they would be separated by `and` in ML. A final `for` clause identifies which of the mutually recursive functions should be the final value of the `fix` expression. Using this definition as a template, we can reimplement `even_list_mut` directly.

`Section even_list_mut'.`

First, we need the properties that we are proving.

`Variable` *Peven* : **even_list** → Prop.
`Variable` *Podd* : **odd_list** → Prop.

Next, we need proofs of the three cases.

`Hypothesis` *ENil_case* : *Peven* ENil.
`Hypothesis` *ECons_case* : ∀ (*n* : **nat**) (*o* : **odd_list**),
   Podd o → *Peven* (ECons *n o*).
`Hypothesis` *OCons_case* : ∀ (*n* : **nat**) (*e* : **even_list**),
   Peven e → *Podd* (OCons *n e*).

Finally, we define the recursive functions.

```
Fixpoint even_list_mut' (e : even_list) : Peven e :=
  match e with
    | ENil ⇒ ENil_case
    | ECons n o ⇒ ECons_case n (odd_list_mut' o)
  end
with odd_list_mut' (o : odd_list) : Podd o :=
```

```
  match o with
    | OCons n e ⇒ OCons_case n (even_list_mut' e)
  end.
End even_list_mut'.
```

Even induction principles for reflexive types are easy to implement directly. For the **formula** type, we can use a recursive definition much like the earlier ones.

```
Section formula_ind'.
  Variable P : formula → Prop.
  Hypothesis Eq_case : ∀ n1 n2 : nat, P (Eq n1 n2).
  Hypothesis And_case : ∀ f1 f2 : formula,
    P f1 → P f2 → P (And f1 f2).
  Hypothesis Forall_case : ∀ f : nat → formula,
    (∀ n : nat, P (f n)) → P (Forall f).

  Fixpoint formula_ind' (f : formula) : P f :=
    match f with
      | Eq n1 n2 ⇒ Eq_case n1 n2
      | And f1 f2 ⇒ And_case (formula_ind' f1) (formula_ind' f2)
      | Forall f' ⇒ Forall_case f' (fun n ⇒ formula_ind' (f' n))
    end.
End formula_ind'.
```

It is apparent that induction principle implementations involve some tedium but not much creativity.

3.8   Nested Inductive Types

Suppose we want to extend the earlier type of binary trees to trees with arbitrary finite branching. We can use lists to give a simple definition.

```
Inductive nat_tree : Set :=
| NNode' : nat → list nat_tree → nat_tree.
```

This is an example of a *nested* inductive type definition, because we use the type we are defining as an argument to a parameterized type family. Coq will not allow all such definitions; it effectively pretends that we are defining **nat_tree** mutually with a version of **list** specialized to **nat_tree**, checking that the resulting expanded definition satisfies the usual rules. For instance, if we replaced **list** with a type family that used its parameter as a function argument, then the definition would be rejected as violating the positivity restriction.

As with mutual inductive types, we find that the automatically generated induction principle for **nat_tree** is too weak.

```
Check nat_tree_ind.
```

> nat_tree_ind
>   : ∀ P : **nat_tree** → Prop,
>   (∀ (n : **nat**) (l : **list nat_tree**), P (NNode' n l)) →
>   ∀ n : **nat_tree**, P n

There is no command like `Scheme` that will implement an improved principle. In general, it takes creativity to figure out good ways to incorporate nested uses of different type families. Now that we know how to implement induction principles manually, it is possible to apply just such creativity to this problem.

Many induction principles for types with nested used of **list** could benefit from a unified predicate capturing the idea that some property holds of every element in a list. By defining this generic predicate once, we facilitate reuse of library theorems about it. (Here, we are actually duplicating the standard library's **Forall** predicate, with a different implementation, for didactic purposes.)

```
Section All.
  Variable T : Set.
  Variable P : T → Prop.

  Fixpoint All (ls : list T) : Prop :=
    match ls with
      | nil ⇒ True
      | cons h t ⇒ P h ∧ All t
    end.
End All.
```

It will be useful to review the definitions of **True** and ∧, since we will want to write manual proofs of them.

```
Print True.
```

> Inductive **True** : Prop := I : **True**

That is, **True** is a proposition with exactly one proof, I, which we may always supply trivially.

Finding the definition of ∧ takes a little more work. Coq supports user registration of arbitrary parsing rules, and it is such a rule that lets us write ∧ instead of an application of some inductive type family. We can find the underlying inductive type with the `Locate` command, whose argument may be a parsing token.

```
Locate "/\".
```

> "A /\ B" := **and** A B : *type_scope* (*default interpretation*)

Print **and**.

> Inductive **and** $(A : \text{Prop})\ (B : \text{Prop}) : \text{Prop} :=$
>   conj $: A \to B \to A \wedge B$
>
> For conj: Arguments A, B are implicit

In addition to the definition of **and** itself, we get information on implicit arguments (and some other information, omitted here). The implicit argument information tells us that we build a proof of a conjunction by calling the constructor conj on proofs of the conjuncts, with no need to include the types of those proofs as explicit arguments.

Now we create a section for the induction principle, following the same basic plan as earlier.

Section nat_tree_ind'.
> Variable P : **nat_tree** $\to$ Prop.
>
> Hypothesis $NNode'\_case : \forall\ (n : \textbf{nat})\ (ls : \textbf{list nat\_tree}),$
>   All $P\ ls \to P$ (NNode' $n\ ls$).

A first attempt at writing the induction principle itself follows the intuition that nested inductive type definitions are expanded into mutual inductive definitions.

> Fixpoint nat_tree_ind' $(tr : \textbf{nat\_tree}) : P\ tr :=$
>   match tr with
> | NNode' $n\ ls \Rightarrow NNode'\_case\ n\ ls$ (list_nat_tree_ind ls)
>   end
>
> with list_nat_tree_ind $(ls : \textbf{list nat_tree}) : $ All $P\ ls :=$
>   match ls with
> | nil $\Rightarrow$ I
> | cons $tr\ rest \Rightarrow$ conj (nat_tree_ind' tr) (list_nat_tree_ind $rest$)
>   end.

Coq rejects this definition, saying

Recursive call to nat_tree_ind' has principal argument
equal to "tr" instead of rest.

There is no theoretical reason why this program should be rejected; Coq applies incomplete termination-checking heuristics, and it is necessary to learn a few of the most important rules. The term *nested inductive type* hints at the solution to this particular problem.

Just as mutually inductive types require mutually recursive induction principles, nested types require nested recursion.

```
Fixpoint nat_tree_ind' (tr : nat_tree) : P tr :=
  match tr with
    | NNode' n ls ⇒ NNode'_case n ls
        ((fix list_nat_tree_ind (ls : list nat_tree) : All P ls :=
            match ls with
              | nil ⇒ I
              | cons tr' rest ⇒
                  conj (nat_tree_ind' tr') (list_nat_tree_ind rest)
            end) ls)
  end.
```

We include an anonymous `fix` version of list_nat_tree_ind that is literally nested inside the definition of the recursive function corresponding to the inductive definition that had the nested use of **list**.

End nat_tree_ind'.

We can test the induction principle by defining some recursive functions on **nat_tree** and proving a theorem about them. First, we define some helper functions that operate on lists.

```
Section map.
  Variables T T' : Set.
  Variable F : T → T'.

  Fixpoint map (ls : list T) : list T' :=
    match ls with
      | nil ⇒ nil
      | cons h t ⇒ cons (F h) (map t)
    end.
End map.

Fixpoint sum (ls : list nat) : nat :=
  match ls with
    | nil ⇒ O
    | cons h t ⇒ plus h (sum t)
  end.
```

Now we can define a size function over the trees.

```
Fixpoint ntsize (tr : nat_tree) : nat :=
  match tr with
    | NNode' _ trs ⇒ S (sum (map ntsize trs))
  end.
```

Notice that Coq expanded the definition of map to verify that we are using proper nested recursion, even through a use of a higher-order function.

Fixpoint ntsplice (*tr1 tr2* : **nat_tree**) : **nat_tree** :=
  match *tr1* with
    | NNode' *n* nil ⇒ NNode' *n* (cons *tr2* nil)
    | NNode' *n* (cons *tr trs*) ⇒ NNode' *n* (cons (ntsplice *tr tr2*) *trs*)
  end.

We have defined another arbitrary notion of tree splicing, similar to before, and we can prove an analogous theorem about its relation to tree size. We start with a useful lemma about addition.

Lemma plus_S : ∀ *n1 n2* : **nat**,
  plus *n1* (S *n2*) = S (plus *n1 n2*).
  induction *n1*; *crush*.
Qed.

Now we begin the proof of the theorem, adding the lemma plus_S as a hint.

Theorem ntsize_ntsplice : ∀ *tr1 tr2* : **nat_tree**, ntsize (ntsplice *tr1 tr2*)
  = plus (ntsize *tr2*) (ntsize *tr1*).
  Hint Rewrite plus_S.

We know that the standard induction principle is insufficient for the task, so we need to provide a using clause for the induction tactic to specify the alternative principle.

  induction *tr1* using nat_tree_ind'; *crush*.

One subgoal remains.

n : **nat**
ls : **list nat_tree**
H : All
        (fun *tr1* : **nat_tree** ⇒
         ∀ *tr2* : **nat_tree**,
          ntsize (ntsplice *tr1 tr2*) = plus (ntsize *tr2*) (ntsize *tr1*)) *ls*
tr2 : **nat_tree**
  ============================
  ntsize
    match *ls* with
    | nil ⇒ NNode' *n* (cons *tr2* nil)
    | cons *tr trs* ⇒ NNode' *n* (cons (ntsplice *tr tr2*) *trs*)
    end = S (plus (ntsize *tr2*) (sum (map ntsize *ls*)))

Now we need to do a case analysis on the structure of *ls*. The rest is routine.

destruct *ls*; *crush.*

We can go further in automating the proof by exploiting the hint mechanism.

Restart.

Hint Extern 1 (ntsize (match ?*LS* with nil ⇒ _
                | cons _ _ ⇒ _ end) = _) ⇒
  destruct *LS*; *crush.*

induction *tr1* using nat_tree_ind'; *crush.*
Qed.

Note that with the hint we register a pattern that describes a conclusion we expect to encounter during the proof. The pattern may contain unification variables, whose names are prefixed with question marks, and we may refer to those bound variables in a tactic that we ask to have run whenever the pattern matches.

The advantage of using the hint is not very clear here because the original proof was so short. However, the hint has fundamentally improved the readability of the proof. Before, the proof referred to the local variable *ls*, which has an automatically generated name. To a human reading the proof script without stepping through it interactively, it was not clear where *ls* came from. The hint explains to the reader the process for choosing which variables to case-analyze, and the hint can continue working even if the rest of the proof structure changes significantly.

3.9   Manual Proofs about Constructors

It can be useful to understand how tactics like discriminate and injection work, so it is worth stepping through a manual proof of each kind. We start with a proof fit for discriminate.

Theorem true_neq_false : true ≠ false.

We begin with the tactic red, which is short for one step of reduction, to unfold the definition of logical negation.

red.

============================
true = false → **False**

The negation is replaced with an implication of falsehood. We use the tactic `intro H` to change the assumption of the implication into a hypothesis named *H*.

`intro H`.

H : true = false

═══════════════════════════════
False

This is the point in the proof where we apply some creativity. We define a function whose utility will become clear soon.

`Definition toProp` (*b* : **bool**) := if *b* then **True** else **False**.

It is worth recalling the difference between the lowercase and upper-case versions of truth and falsehood: **True** and **False** are logical propositions, whereas **true** and **false** are Boolean values that we can case-analyze. We have defined **toProp** such that the conclusion of **False** is computationally equivalent to **toProp false**. Thus, the `change` tactic lets us change the conclusion to toProp false. The general form `change` *e* replaces the conclusion with *e* whenever Coq's built-in computation rules suffice to establish the equivalence of *e* with the original conclusion.

`change` (toProp false).

H : true = false

═══════════════════════════════
  toProp false

Now the right side of *H*'s equality appears in the conclusion, so we can rewrite, using the notation ← to request to replace the right side of the equality with the left side.

`rewrite` ← *H*.

H : true = false

═══════════════════════════════
  toProp true

Some computational simplification reveals that we are almost done.

`simpl`.

H : true = false

═══════════════════════════════
  True

`trivial`.

Qed.

I have no trivial automated version of this proof to suggest, beyond using `discriminate` or `congruence` in the first place.

We can perform a similar manual proof of injectivity of the constructor S. I leave the details to readers who want to run the proof script interactively.

Theorem S_inj' : $\forall$ *n m* : **nat**, S *n* = S *m* $\rightarrow$ *n* = *m*.
   intros *n m H*.
   change (pred (S *n*) = pred (S *m*)).
   rewrite *H*.
   reflexivity.
Qed.

The key in this theorem comes in using the natural number predecessor function pred. Embodied in the implementation of `injection` is a generic recipe for writing such type-specific functions.

The examples in this section illustrate an important aspect of the design philosophy behind Coq. We could certainly design a Gallina replacement with built-in rules for constructor discrimination and injectivity, but a simpler alternative is to include a few carefully chosen rules that enable the desired reasoning patterns and many others. A key benefit of this philosophy is that the complexity of proof checking is minimized, which bolsters confidence that proved theorems are really true.

4 Inductive Predicates

The Curry-Howard correspondence [10, 14] states a formal connection between functional programs and mathematical proofs. Witness the close similarity between the types **unit** and **True** from the Coq standard library.

Print **unit**.

> Inductive **unit** : Set := tt : **unit**

Print **True**.

> Inductive **True** : Prop := I : **True**

Recall that **unit** is the type with only one value, and **True** is the proposition that always holds. Despite this superficial difference between the two concepts, in both cases we can use the same inductive definition mechanism. The connection goes further than this. We arrive at the definition of **True** by replacing **unit** by **True**, tt by I, and Set by Prop. The first two of these differences are superficial changes of names, but the third difference is the crucial one for separating programs from proofs. A term T of type Set is a type of programs, and a term of type T is a program. A term T of type Prop is a logical proposition, and its proofs are of type T. Chapter 12 goes into more detail about the theoretical differences between Prop and Set. For now, we simply follow common intuitions about what a proof is.

The type **unit** has one value, tt. The type **True** has one proof, I. Why distinguish between these two types? Many people who have read about Curry-Howard in an abstract context but who have not put it to use in proof engineering say that the two types in fact *should not* be distinguished. There is a certain aesthetic appeal to this point of view, but I argue that it is best to treat Curry-Howard very loosely in practical proving. There are Coq-specific reasons for preferring the distinction, involving efficient compilation and avoidance of paradoxes in the presence of classical math, but there is a more general principle that should lead us to avoid conflating programming and proving.

The essence of the argument is roughly this: to an engineer, not all functions of type $A \to B$ are created equal, but all proofs of a proposition $P \to Q$ are. This idea is known as *proof irrelevance*, and its formalizations in logics prevent us from distinguishing between alternative proofs of the same proposition. Proof irrelevance is compatible with, but not derivable in, Gallina. Apart from this theoretical concern, I argue that it is most effective to do engineering with Coq by employing different techniques for programs versus proofs. Most of this book is organized around that distinction, describing how to program by applying standard functional programming techniques in the presence of dependent types, and how to prove by writing custom Ltac decision procedures.

With that perspective in mind, this chapter is a kind of mirror image of the last chapter, introducing how to define predicates with inductive definitions. I point out similarities in places, but much of the effective Coq user's bag of tricks is disjoint for predicates versus datatypes. This chapter is also an implicit introduction to dependent types, which are the foundation on which interesting inductive predicates are built, though here we rely on tactics to build dependently typed proof terms. Chapter 6 begins our study of more manual application of dependent types.

4.1 Propositional Logic

Let us begin with a brief tour through the definitions of the connectives for propositional logic. We will work within a Coq section that provides a set of propositional variables. In Coq parlance, these are just variables of type `Prop`.

```
Section Propositional.
  Variables P Q R : Prop.
```

In Coq, the most basic propositional connective is implication, written $\to$, which we have already used in almost every proof. Rather than being defined inductively, implication is built into Coq as the function type constructor.

We have also seen the definition of **True**. For a demonstration of a lower-level way of establishing proofs of inductive predicates, we turn to this trivial theorem.

```
Theorem obvious : True.
```

```
    apply I.
Qed.
```

We may always use the `apply` tactic to take a proof step based on applying a particular constructor of the inductive predicate that we are trying to establish. Sometimes there is only one constructor that could possibly apply, in which case a shortcut is available:

```
Theorem obvious' : True.
    constructor.
Qed.
```

There is also a predicate **False**, which is the Curry-Howard mirror image of **Empty_set** (see Chapter 3).

```
Print False.
```

```
Inductive False : Prop :=
```

We can conclude anything from **False**, doing case analysis on a proof of **False** in the same way we might do case analysis on, say, a natural number. Since there are no cases to consider, any such case analysis succeeds immediately in proving the goal.

```
Theorem False_imp : False → 2 + 2 = 5.
    destruct 1.
Qed.
```

In a consistent context, we can never build a proof of **False**. In inconsistent contexts that appear in the courses of proofs, it is usually easiest to proceed by demonstrating the inconsistency with an explicit proof of **False**.

```
Theorem arith_neq : 2 + 2 = 5 → 9 + 9 = 835.
    intro.
```

At this point, we have an inconsistent hypothesis $2 + 2 = 5$, so the specific conclusion is not important. We use the `elimtype` tactic (for a full description, see the Coq manual). For our purposes, we only need the variant `elimtype False`, which lets us replace any conclusion formula with **False**, because any fact follows from an inconsistent context.

```
    elimtype False.
```

$H : 2 + 2 = 5$
============================
False

For now, we will leave the details of this proof about arithmetic to *crush*.

 crush.
Qed.

A related notion to **False** is logical negation.

Print not.

 not = fun A : Prop $\Rightarrow$ $A \rightarrow$ **False**
  : Prop $\rightarrow$ Prop

We see that not is just shorthand for implication of **False**. We can use that fact explicitly in proofs. The syntax $\neg P$ (written with a tilde in ASCII) expands to not P.

Theorem arith_neq' : $\neg$ (2 + 2 = 5).
 unfold not.

```
============================
```
 $2 + 2 = 5 \rightarrow$ **False**

 crush.
Qed.

We also have conjunction (see Chapter 3).

Print **and**.

 Inductive **and** $(A : \text{Prop})$ $(B : \text{Prop})$: Prop :=
  conj : $A \rightarrow B \rightarrow A \wedge B$

The reader can check that **and** has a Curry-Howard equivalent called **prod**, the type of pairs. However, it is generally most convenient to reason about conjunction using tactics. An explicit proof of commutativity of **and** illustrates how such tasks are usually done. The operator $\wedge$ is an infix shorthand for **and**.

Theorem and_comm : $P \wedge Q \rightarrow Q \wedge P$.

We start by case analysis on the proof of $P \wedge Q$.

 destruct 1.

$H : P$
$H0 : Q$
```
============================
```

$Q \land P$

Every proof of a conjunction provides proofs for both conjuncts, so
we get a single subgoal reflecting that. We can split this subgoal into a
case for each conjunct of $Q \land P$.

    split.

```
2 subgoals
```

$H : P$
$H0 : Q$
===================================
Q

```
subgoal 2 is
```

P

In each case, the conclusion is among the hypotheses, so the
`assumption` tactic finishes the process.

    assumption.
    assumption.
  Qed.

Coq disjunction is called **or** and abbreviated with the infix operator
$\lor$.

  Print **or**.

  Inductive **or** $(A : \text{Prop})$ $(B : \text{Prop})$: $\text{Prop} :=$
    or_introl : $A \rightarrow A \lor B$ | or_intror : $B \rightarrow A \lor B$

There are two ways to prove a disjunction: prove the first disjunct or
prove the second. The Curry-Howard analogue of this is the Coq **sum**
type. We can demonstrate the main tactics here with another proof of
commutativity.

  Theorem or_comm : $P \lor Q \rightarrow Q \lor P$.

As in the proof for **and**, we begin with case analysis, though this time
we are met by two cases instead of one.

    destruct 1.

```
2 subgoals
```

$H : P$
================================
$Q \vee P$

subgoal 2 is

$Q \vee P$

In the first subgoal, we want to prove the disjunction by proving its second disjunct. The `right` tactic telegraphs this intent.

    `right`; `assumption`.

The second subgoal has a symmetric proof.

1 subgoal

$H : Q$
================================
$Q \vee P$

    `left`; `assumption`.

Qed.

There is no need to plod manually through all proofs about propositional logic. One of the most basic Coq automation tactics is `tauto`, which is a complete decision procedure for constructive propositional logic. We can use `tauto` to dispatch all the purely propositional theorems we have proved so far.

    Theorem or_comm' : $P \vee Q \rightarrow Q \vee P$.
    `tauto`.
Qed.

Sometimes propositional reasoning is important for proving a theorem, but we still need to apply some other insights about, say, arithmetic. The tactic `intuition` is a generalization of `tauto` that proves everything it can using propositional reasoning. When some further facts must be established to finish the proof, `intuition` uses propositional laws to simplify them as far as possible. Consider this example, which uses the list concatenation operator `++` from the standard library:

    Theorem arith_comm : $\forall$ *ls1 ls2* : **list nat**,

```
length ls1 = length ls2 ∨ length ls1 + length ls2 = 6
→ length (ls1 ++ ls2) = 6 ∨ length ls1 = length ls2.
intuition.
```

A lot of the proof structure has been generated by `intuition`, but the final proof depends on a fact about lists. The remaining subgoal hints at what is needed.

```
ls1 : list nat
ls2 : list nat
H0 : length ls1 + length ls2 = 6
============================
 length (ls1 ++ ls2) = 6 ∨ length ls1 = length ls2
```

We need a theorem about lengths of concatenated lists (see Chapter 3 and the standard library).

```
rewrite app_length.
```

```
ls1 : list nat
ls2 : list nat
H0 : length ls1 + length ls2 = 6
============================
 length ls1 + length ls2 = 6 ∨ length ls1 = length ls2
```

Now the subgoal follows by purely propositional reasoning. That is, we could replace length $ls1$ + length $ls2$ = 6 with P and length $ls1$ = length $ls2$ with Q and arrive at a tautology of propositional logic.

```
tauto.
Qed.
```

The `intuition` tactic is one of the main elements in the implementation of *crush*, so we can get a short automated proof of the theorem.

```
Theorem arith_comm' : ∀ ls1 ls2 : list nat,
   length ls1 = length ls2 ∨ length ls1 + length ls2 = 6
   → length (ls1 ++ ls2) = 6 ∨ length ls1 = length ls2.
   Hint Rewrite app_length.

   crush.
Qed.
```

End Propositional.

Each of the propositional theorems in this section becomes universally quantified over the propositional variables that we used.

4.2   What Does It Mean to Be Constructive?

One potential point of confusion in the presentation so far is the distinction between **bool** and `Prop`. The datatype **bool** is built from two values `true` and `false`, whereas `Prop` is a more primitive type that includes among its members **True** and **False**. Why not collapse these two concepts into one, and why must there be more than two states of mathematical truth, **True** and **False**?

The answer comes from the fact that Coq implements *constructive logic* or *intuitionistic logic*, in contrast to the *classical logic* that we may be more familiar with. In constructive logic, classical tautologies like $\neg \neg P \to P$ and $P \lor \neg P$ do not always hold. In general, we can only prove these tautologies when P is *decidable*, in the sense of computability theory. The Curry-Howard encoding that Coq uses for **or** allows us to extract either a proof of P or a proof of $\neg P$ from any proof of $P \lor \neg P$. Since the proofs are just functional programs that we can run, a general law of the excluded middle would yield a decision procedure for the halting problem, where the instantiations of P would be formulas like "this particular Turing machine halts."

A similar paradoxical situation would result if every proposition evaluated to either **True** or **False**. Evaluation in Coq is decidable, so we would be limiting ourselves to decidable propositions only.

Hence the distinction between **bool** and `Prop`. Programs of type **bool** are computational by construction; we can always run them to determine their results. Many `Props` are undecidable, so we can write more expressive formulas with `Props` than with **bool**s, but we cannot simply run a `Prop` to determine its truth.

Constructive logic lets us define all the logical connectives in an aesthetically appealing way, with orthogonal inductive definitions. That is, each connective is defined independently using a simple shared mechanism. Constructivity also enables a trick called *program extraction*, where programming tasks are phrased as theorems to be proved. Since the proofs are just functional programs, we can extract executable programs from the final proofs, which we could not do as naturally with classical proofs.

Chapter 6 presents more about Coq's program extraction facility. However, I think it is worth interjecting another warning at this point, following up on the prior warning about taking the Curry-Howard correspondence too literally. It is possible to write programs by theorem-proving methods in Coq, but hardly anyone does it. It is almost always most useful to maintain the distinction between programs and proofs. If we write a program by proving a theorem, we are likely to run into algorithmic inefficiencies that we introduced into the proof to make it easier to prove. Extracting programs from proofs is mostly limited to theoretical studies.

4.3   First-Order Logic

The $\forall$ connective of first-order logic, used in many earlier examples, is built into Coq. It can be viewed as the dependent function type constructor. In fact, implication and universal quantification are just different syntactic shorthands for the same Coq mechanism. A formula $P \rightarrow Q$ is equivalent to $\forall\ x : P,\ Q$, where x does not appear in Q. That is, the real type of the implication says "for every proof of P, there exists a proof of Q."

Existential quantification is defined in the standard library.

Print **ex**.

Inductive **ex** $(A : \mathtt{Type})\ (P : A \rightarrow \mathtt{Prop}) : \mathtt{Prop} :=$
ex_intro $: \forall\ x : A,\ P\ x \rightarrow$ **ex** P

Note that here, as always, each $\forall$ quantifier has the largest possible scope; the type of ex_intro could also be written $\forall\ x : A,\ (P\ x \rightarrow$ **ex** $P)$.

The family **ex** is parameterized by the type A that we quantify over, and by a predicate P over As. We prove an existential by exhibiting some x of type A, along with a proof of $P\ x$. As usual, there are tactics that take care of low-level details most of the time.

Here is an example of a theorem statement with existential quantification. We use the equality operator $=$, which, depending on the settings in which they learned logic, different people will say either is or is not part of first-order logic. For our purposes, it is.

Theorem exist1 $: \exists\ x : \mathbf{nat},\ x + 1 = 2.$

We can start this proof with a tactic `exists`, which should not be confused with the formula constructor shorthand of the same name. The reverse E in formulas stands for the ASCII token `exists`.

exists 1.

The conclusion is replaced with a version using the existential witness that we announced.

```
===============================
```
$$1 + 1 = 2$$

```
reflexivity.
Qed.
```

We can also use tactics to reason about existential hypotheses.

Theorem exist2 : $\forall$ n m : **nat**, ($\exists$ x : **nat**, $n + x = m$) $\rightarrow$ $n \leq m$.
We start by case analysis on the proof of the existential fact.

```
destruct 1.
```

n : **nat**
m : **nat**
x : **nat**
H : $n + x = m$

```
===============================
```
$$n \leq m$$

The goal has been replaced by a form with a new free variable x and a new hypothesis that the body of the existential holds with x substituted for the old bound variable. From here, the proof is just about arithmetic and is easy to automate.

   crush.
```
Qed.
```

The tactic `intuition` has a first-order cousin called `firstorder`, which proves many formulas when only first-order reasoning is needed, and it tries to perform first-order simplifications in any case. First-order reasoning is much harder than propositional reasoning, so `firstorder` is much more likely than `intuition` to get stuck and run long enough to be useless.

4.4   Predicates with Implicit Equality

We start our exploration of a more complicated class of predicates with a simple example: an alternative way of characterizing when a natural number is zero.

```
Inductive isZero : nat → Prop :=
| IsZero : isZero 0.
```

```
Theorem isZero_zero : isZero 0.
  constructor.
Qed.
```

We can call **isZero** a *judgment*, in the sense often used in the semantics of programming languages. Judgments are typically defined in the style of *natural deduction*, where we write a number of *inference rules* with premises appearing above a solid line and a conclusion appearing below the line. In this example, the sole constructor IsZero of **isZero** can be thought of as the single inference rule for deducing **isZero**, with nothing above the line and **isZero** 0 below it. The proof of isZero_zero demonstrates how we can apply an inference rule. (Readers not familiar with formal semantics should not worry about not following this paragraph.)

The definition of **isZero** differs in an important way from all the earlier inductive definitions. Instead of writing just Set or Prop after the colon, here we write **nat** $\rightarrow$ Prop. We saw examples of parameterized types like **list**, but there the parameters appeared with names *before* the colon. Every constructor of a parameterized inductive type must have a range type that uses the same parameter, whereas the form we use here enables us to choose different arguments to the type for different constructors.

For instance, the definition **isZero** makes the predicate provable only when the argument is 0. We can see that the concept of equality is somehow implicit in the inductive definition mechanism. The way this is accomplished is similar to the way that logic variables are used in Prolog, and it is a very powerful mechanism that forms a foundation for formalizing all of mathematics. In fact, though it is natural to think of inductive types as folding in the functionality of equality, in Coq the true situation is reversed, with equality defined as just another inductive type.

```
Print eq.
```

```
  Inductive eq (A : Type) (x : A) : A → Prop := eq_refl : x = x
```

Behind the scenes, uses of infix = are expanded to instances of **eq**. We see that **eq** has both a parameter x that is fixed and an extra unnamed argument of the same type. The type of **eq** allows us to state any equalities, even those that are provably false. However, examining the type of equality's sole constructor eq_refl, we see that we can only *prove* equality when its two arguments are syntactically equal. This definition turns out to capture all the basic properties of equality, and the equality-manipulating tactics that we have seen so far, like `reflexivity` and rewrite, are implemented treating **eq** as just another inductive type with a well-chosen definition. Another way of stating that definition is, equality is defined as the least reflexive relation.

Returning to the example of **isZero**, we can see how to work with hypotheses that use this predicate.

Theorem isZero_plus : $\forall$ n m : **nat**, **isZero** m → n + m = n.

We want to proceed by cases on the proof of the assumption about **isZero**.

    destruct 1.

    n : **nat**
    ================================
    $n + 0 = n$

Since **isZero** has only one constructor, we are presented with only one subgoal. The argument m to **isZero** is replaced with that type's argument from the single constructor **IsZero**. From this point, the proof is trivial.

    crush.
Qed.

Another example seems at first like it should admit an analogous proof, but in fact it provides a demonstration of one of the most common mistakes in basic Coq proving.

Theorem isZero_contra : **isZero** 1 → **False**.

Let us try a proof by cases on the assumption, as in the last proof.

    destruct 1.

    ================================
    False

It seems that case analysis has not helped. The sole hypothesis disappears, leaving us worse off than before. What went wrong? We have met an important restriction in tactics like destruct and induction when applied to types with arguments. If the arguments are not already free variables, they will be replaced by new free variables internally before the case analysis or induction is done. Since the argument 1 to **isZero** is replaced by a fresh variable, we lose the crucial fact that it is not equal to 0.

Why does Coq use this restriction? Chapter 8 discusses the issue in detail, describing the dependently typed programming techniques to write this proof term manually. For now, I just say that the algorithmic problem of "logically complete case analysis" is undecidable when phrased in Coq's logic. A few tactics and design patterns presented later in this chapter suffice in almost all cases. For the current example, what we want is a tactic called `inversion`, which corresponds to the concept of inversion that is frequently used with natural deduction proof systems.

```
  Undo.
  inversion 1.
Qed.
```

What does `inversion` do? Think of it as a version of `destruct` that takes advantage of the structure of arguments to inductive types. In this case, `inversion` completed the proof immediately because it was able to detect that we were using **isZero** with an impossible argument.

Sometimes using `destruct` when we should have used `inversion` can lead to confusing results. To illustrate, consider another proof attempt for the last theorem with a different choice of contradictory conclusion.

```
Theorem isZero_contra' : isZero 1 → 2 + 2 = 5.
  destruct 1.
```

```
  ============================
   1 + 1 = 4
```

What happened here? Internally, `destruct` replaced 1 with a fresh variable, and trying to be helpful, it also replaced the occurrence of 1 within the unary representation of each number in the goal. Then, within the O case of the proof, the fresh variable was replaced with O. This had the net effect of decrementing each of these numbers.

```
Abort.
```

To see more clearly what happened, consider the type of **isZero**'s induction principle.

```
Check isZero_ind.
```

```
isZero_ind
     : ∀ P : nat → Prop, P 0 → ∀ n : nat, isZero n → P n
```

In the last proof script, `destruct` chose to instantiate P as $\text{fun } n \Rightarrow$ S n + S n = S (S (S (S n))). Readers can verify that this specialization of the principle applies to the goal and that the hypothesis P 0 then matches the subgoal that was generated. A strange transmutation like this while doing a proof likely indicates that `destruct` should be replaced with `inversion`.

4.5 Recursive Predicates

We have already seen all the ingredients needed to build interesting recursive predicates, like this predicate capturing evenness.

```
Inductive even : nat → Prop :=
| EvenO : even O
| EvenSS : ∀ n, even n → even (S (S n)).
```

Think of **even** as another judgment defined by natural deduction rules. The rule EvenO has nothing above the line and **even** O below the line, and EvenSS is a rule with **even** n above the line and **even** (S (S n)) below.

The proof techniques of the last section are easily adapted.

```
Theorem even_0 : even 0.
  constructor.
Qed.
```

```
Theorem even_4 : even 4.
  constructor; constructor; constructor.
Qed.
```

It is not hard to see that such sequences of constructor applications can get tedious. We can avoid them using Coq's hint facility, with a new `Hint` variant that asks to consider all constructors of an inductive type during proof search. The tactic `auto` performs exhaustive proof search up to a fixed depth, considering only the proof steps registered as hints.

```
Hint Constructors even.
```

```
Theorem even_4' : even 4.
  auto.
Qed.
```

We may also use `inversion` with **even**.

```
Theorem even_1_contra : even 1 → False.
  inversion 1.
Qed.
```

```
Theorem even_3_contra : even 3 → False.
```

```
inversion 1.
```

H : **even** 3
n : **nat**
$H1$: **even** 1
$H0$: $n = 1$
================================
  False

The `inversion` tactic can be overzealous at times, as here with the introduction of the unused variable n and an equality hypothesis about it. For more complicated predicates, though, adding such assumptions is critical to dealing with the undecidability of general inversion. More complex inductive definitions and theorems can cause `inversion` to generate equalities where neither side is a variable.

  `inversion H1.`
`Qed.`

  We can also do inductive proofs about **even**.

`Theorem even_plus` : $\forall$ n m, **even** n $\to$ **even** m $\to$ **even** $(n + m)$.
  It seems a reasonable first choice to proceed by induction on n.

  `induction` n; *crush*.

n : **nat**
IHn : $\forall$ m : **nat**, **even** n $\to$ **even** m $\to$ **even** $(n + m)$
m : **nat**
H : **even** (S n)
$H0$: **even** m
================================
  even (S $(n + m)$)

We need to use the hypotheses H and $H0$ somehow. The most natural choice is to invert H.

  `inversion` H.

n : **nat**
IHn : $\forall$ m : **nat**, **even** n $\to$ **even** m $\to$ **even** $(n + m)$
m : **nat**
H : **even** (S n)
$H0$: **even** m

$n0$: **nat**
$H2$: **even** $n0$
$H1$: S $n0 = n$
==================================
  even (S (S $n0 + m$))

Simplifying the conclusion brings us to a point where we can apply a constructor.

```
simpl.
```

==================================
  even (S (S ($n0 + m$)))

```
constructor.
```

==================================
  even ($n0 + m$)

At this point, we would like to apply the inductive hypothesis, which is

IHn : $\forall\ m$: **nat**, **even** $n \to$ **even** $m \to$ **even** $(n + m)$

Unfortunately, the goal mentions $n0$ where it would need to mention n to match IHn. We could keep looking for a way to finish this proof from here, but it is easier to change the basic strategy. Instead of inducting on the structure of n, we should induct *on the structure of one of the* **even** *proofs*. This technique is commonly called *rule induction* in programming language semantics. In the setting of Coq, we have already seen how predicates are defined using the same inductive type mechanism as datatypes, so the fundamental unity of rule induction with normal induction is apparent.

Recall that tactics like `induction` and `destruct` may be passed numbers to refer to unnamed left sides of implications in the conclusion, where the argument n refers to the nth such hypothesis.

```
Restart.
```

```
  induction 1.
```

m : **nat**

```
===============================
```
  even $m \rightarrow$ **even** $(0 + m)$

subgoal 2 is:

 even $m \rightarrow$ **even** $(S (S n) + m)$

The first case is easily discharged by *crush*, based on the hint to try the constructors of **even**.

  crush.

Now we focus on the second case.

  `intro.`

  m : **nat**
  n : **nat**
  H : **even** n
  IHeven : **even** $m \rightarrow$ **even** $(n + m)$
  H0 : **even** m
```
===============================
```
  even $(S (S n) + m)$

We simplify and apply a constructor, as in the last proof attempt.

  `simpl; constructor.`

```
===============================
```
  even $(n + m)$

Now we have an exact match with the inductive hypothesis, and the remainder of the proof is trivial.

  `apply` *IHeven*; `assumption.`

In fact, *crush* can handle all the details of the proof once we declare the induction strategy.

`Restart.`

  `induction 1;` *crush.*
`Qed.`

Induction on recursive predicates has similar pitfalls to those encountered with inversion in the last section.

`Theorem even_contra :` $\forall n,$ **even** $(S (n + n)) \rightarrow$ **False**.

```
induction 1.
```

n : **nat**
============================
  False
```
subgoal 2 is:
```
  False

We cannot prove the first subgoal, since the argument to **even** was replaced by a fresh variable internally. This time, it is easier to prove this theorem by way of a lemma. Instead of trusting `induction` to replace expressions with fresh variables, we do it ourselves, explicitly adding the appropriate equalities as new assumptions.

```
Abort.
```
Lemma even_contra' : $\forall$ n', **even** n' $\rightarrow$ $\forall$ n, n' = S $(n + n)$ $\rightarrow$ **False**.
    induction 1; *crush*.

At this point, it is useful to consider all cases of n and $n0$ as being zero or nonzero. Only one of these cases has any trickiness to it.

    destruct n; destruct $n0$; *crush*.

n : **nat**
H : **even** (S n)
$IHeven$: $\forall$ $n0$: **nat**, S n = S $(n0 + n0)$ $\rightarrow$ **False**
$n0$: **nat**
$H0$: S n = $n0$ + S $n0$
============================
  False

Now it is useful to use a theorem from the standard library, which we also proved with a different name in the last chapter. We can search for a theorem that allows us to rewrite terms of the form $x + $ S y.

    SearchRewrite (_ + S _).

    plus_n_Sm : $\forall$ n m : **nat**, S $(n + m)$ = $n + $ S m

    rewrite $\leftarrow$ plus_n_Sm in $H0$.

The induction hypothesis lets us complete the proof if we use a variant of `apply` that has a `with` clause to give instantiations of quantified variables.

apply *IHeven* with *n0*; assumption.

As usual, we can rewrite the proof to avoid referencing any locally generated names, which makes the proof script more readable and more robust to changes in the theorem statement. We use the notation ← to request a hint that does right-to-left rewriting, just as with the `rewrite` tactic.

```
Restart.
```

```
Hint Rewrite ← plus_n_Sm.
```

```
induction 1; crush;
  match goal with
    | [ H : S ?N = ?N0 + ?N0 ⊢ _ ] ⇒ destruct N; destruct N0
  end; crush.
```
Qed.

We write the proof in a way that avoids the use of local variable or hypothesis names, using the `match` tactic form to do pattern matching on the goal. We use unification variables prefixed by question marks in the pattern and take advantage of the possibility to mention a unification variable twice in one pattern, to enforce equality between occurrences. The hint to rewrite with plus_n_Sm in a particular direction saves us from having to figure out the right place to apply that theorem.

The original theorem now follows trivially from the lemma, using a new tactic `eauto`, a fancier version of `auto` (see Chapter 13).

```
Theorem even_contra : ∀ n, even (S (n + n)) → False.
  intros; eapply even_contra'; eauto.
```
Qed.

We use a variant `eapply` of `apply`, which has the same relation to `apply` as `eauto` has to `auto`. An invocation of `apply` only succeeds if all arguments to the rule being used can be determined from the form of the goal, whereas `eapply` introduces unification variables for undetermined arguments. In this case, `eauto` is able to determine the right values for those unification variables, using a variant of the classic algorithm for *unification* [41].

By considering an alternative way to prove the lemma, we see another common pitfall of inductive proofs in Coq. Imagine that we had tried to prove even_contra' with all the ∀ quantifiers moved to the front of the lemma statement.

```
Lemma even_contra'' : ∀ n' n, even n' → n' = S (n + n) → False.
  induction 1; crush;
```

```
match goal with
  | [ H : S ?N = ?N0 + ?N0 ⊢ _ ] ⇒ destruct N; destruct N0
end; crush.
```

One subgoal remains.

n : **nat**
H : **even** (S ($n + n$))
IHeven : S ($n + n$) = S (S (S ($n + n$))) → **False**
============================
  False

We are out of luck here. The inductive hypothesis is trivially true, since its assumption is false. In the version of this proof that succeeded, *IHeven* had an explicit quantification over n. This is because the quantification of n *appeared after the thing we are inducting on* in the theorem statement. In general, quantified variables and hypotheses that appear before the induction object in the theorem statement stay fixed throughout the inductive proof. Variables and hypotheses that are quantified after the induction object may be varied explicitly in uses of inductive hypotheses.

```
Abort.
```

Why should Coq implement `induction` this way? One answer is that it avoids burdening this basic tactic with additional heuristics, but that is not the whole picture. Imagine that `induction` analyzed dependencies among variables and reordered quantifiers to preserve as much freedom as possible in later uses of inductive hypotheses. That could make the inductive hypotheses more complex, which could in turn cause particular automation machinery to fail when it would have succeeded before. In general, we want to avoid quantifiers in proofs whenever we can, and that goal is furthered by the refactoring that the `induction` tactic forces us to do.

5   Infinite Data and Proofs

In lazy functional programming languages like Haskell, infinite data structures are everywhere [16]. Infinite lists and more exotic datatypes provide convenient abstractions for communication between parts of a program. Achieving similar convenience without infinite lazy structures would, in many cases, require acrobatic inversions of control flow.

Laziness is easy to implement in Haskell, where all the definitions in a program may be thought of as mutually recursive. In such an unconstrained setting, it is easy to implement an infinite loop when we really meant to build an infinite list, where any finite prefix of the list should be forceable in finite time. Haskell programmers learn how to avoid such slipups. In Coq, such a laissez-faire policy is not good enough.

Chapter 4 discussed the Curry-Howard isomorphism, where proofs are identified with functional programs. In such a setting, infinite loops, intended or otherwise, are disastrous. If Coq allowed the full breadth of definitions that Haskell does, we could code an infinite loop and use it to prove any proposition vacuously. That is, the addition of general recursion would make the Calculus of Inductive Constructions (CIC) *inconsistent*. For an arbitrary proposition P, we could write

```
Fixpoint bad (u : unit) : P := bad u.
```

This would leave us with **bad tt** as a proof of P.

There are also algorithmic considerations that make universal termination very desirable. We have seen how tactics like `reflexivity` compare terms up to equivalence under computational rules. Calls to recursive, pattern-matching functions are simplified automatically, with no need for explicit proof steps. It would be very hard to hold onto that kind of benefit if it became possible to write nonterminating programs; we would run into the halting problem.

One solution is to use types to contain the possibility of nontermination. For instance, we can create a nontermination monad, inside which we must write all general-recursive programs; several such approaches are surveyed in Chapter 7. This is a heavyweight solution, so we would like to avoid it whenever possible.

Luckily, Coq has special support for a class of lazy data structures that happens to contain most examples found in Haskell. That mechanism, *co-inductive types*, is the subject of this chapter.

5.1 Computing with Infinite Data

Let us begin with the most basic type of infinite data, *streams*, or lazy lists.

Section stream.
  Variable A : Type.

  CoInductive **stream** : Type :=
  | Cons : $A \to$ **stream** $\to$ **stream**.
End stream.

The definition is surprisingly simple. Starting from the definition of **list**, we just need to change the keyword Inductive to CoInductive. We could have left a Nil constructor in the definition, but we will leave it out to force all streams to be infinite.

How do we write a stream constant? The simple application of constructors is not good enough, since we could only denote finite objects that way. Rather, whereas recursive definitions were necessary to *use* values of recursive inductive types effectively, here we find that we need *co-recursive definitions* to *build* values of co-inductive types effectively.

We can define a stream consisting only of zeroes.

CoFixpoint zeroes : **stream nat** := Cons 0 zeroes.

We can also define a stream that alternates between **true** and **false**.

CoFixpoint trues_falses : **stream bool** := Cons true falses_trues
with falses_trues : **stream bool** := Cons false trues_falses.

Co-inductive values can be used as arguments to recursive functions, and we can use that fact to write a function to take a finite approximation of a stream.

Fixpoint approx A (s : **stream** A) (n : **nat**) : **list** A :=
  match n with
    | O $\Rightarrow$ nil
    | S n' $\Rightarrow$
      match s with

```
      | Cons h t ⇒ h :: approx t n'
   end
end.
```

`Eval simpl in approx zeroes 10.`

> $= 0 :: 0 :: 0 :: 0 :: 0 :: 0 :: 0 :: 0 :: 0 :: 0 ::$ nil
> : **list nat**

`Eval simpl in approx trues_falses 10.`

> $=$ true
>   :: false
>   :: true
>   :: false
>   :: true :: false :: true :: false :: true :: false :: nil
> : **list bool**

So far, it looks like co-inductive types might allow us to import all the
Haskeller's usual tricks. However, some important restrictions are dual
to the restrictions on the use of inductive types. Fixpoints *consume*
values of inductive types, with restrictions on which *arguments* may
be passed in recursive calls. Dually, co-fixpoints *produce* values of co-
inductive types, with restrictions on what may be done with the *results*
of co-recursive calls.

The restriction for co-inductive types shows up as the *guardedness
condition*. First, consider this stream definition, which would be legal
in Haskell:

`CoFixpoint` looper : **stream nat** $:=$ looper.

```
Error:
Recursive definition of looper is ill-formed.
In environment
looper : stream nat

unguarded recursive call in "looper"
```

The rule we have run afoul of here is that *every co-recursive call
must be guarded by a constructor*; that is, every co-recursive call must
be a direct argument to a constructor of the co-inductive type we are
generating. It is a good thing that this rule is enforced. If the definition
of looper were accepted, the approx function would run forever when
passed looper, and we would have fallen into inconsistency.

Some familiar functions are easy to write in co-recursive fashion.

```
Section map.
  Variables A B : Type.
  Variable f : A → B.

  CoFixpoint map (s : stream A) : stream B :=
    match s with
      | Cons h t ⇒ Cons (f h) (map t)
    end.
End map.
```

This code is a literal copy of that for the list **map** function, with the nil case removed and `Fixpoint` changed to `CoFixpoint`. Many other standard functions on lazy data structures can be implemented just as easily. Some, like **filter**, cannot be implemented. Since the predicate passed to **filter** may reject every element of the stream, we cannot satisfy the guardedness condition.

The implications of the condition can be subtle. To illustrate, we start off with another co-recursive function definition that *is* legal. The function **interleave** takes two streams and produces a new stream that alternates between their elements.

```
Section interleave.
  Variable A : Type.

  CoFixpoint interleave (s1 s2 : stream A) : stream A :=
    match s1, s2 with
      | Cons h1 t1, Cons h2 t2 ⇒ Cons h1 (Cons h2 (interleave t1 t2))
    end.
End interleave.
```

Now suppose we want to write a weird stuttering version of **map** that repeats elements in a particular way, based on interleaving.

```
Section map'.
  Variables A B : Type.
  Variable f : A → B.

  CoFixpoint map' (s : stream A) : stream B :=
    match s with
      | Cons h t ⇒
        interleave (Cons (f h) (map' t)) (Cons (f h) (map' t))
    end.
```

We get another error message about an unguarded recursive call.

```
End map'.
```

What went wrong here? Imagine that instead of interleave we had called some other, less well-behaved function on streams. Here is one simpler example demonstrating the pitfall. We start by defining a standard function for taking the tail of a stream. Since streams are infinite, this operation is total.

Definition tl A (s : **stream** A) : **stream** A :=
  match s with
    | Cons _ s' $\Rightarrow$ s'
  end.

Coq rejects the following definition that uses tl.

CoFixpoint bad : **stream nat** := tl (Cons 0 bad).

Imagine that Coq had accepted the definition, and consider how we might evaluate approx bad 1. We would be trying to calculate the first element in the stream bad. However, the definition of bad begs the question: unfolding the definition of tl, we see that we essentially say "define bad to equal itself." Of course such an equation admits no single well-defined solution, which does not fit well with the determinism of Gallina reduction.

Coq's complete rule for co-recursive definitions includes not just the basic guardedness condition but also a requirement about where co-recursive calls may occur. In particular, a co-recursive call must be a direct argument to a constructor, *nested only inside of other constructor calls or fun or match expressions*. In the definition of bad, we erroneously nested the co-recursive call inside a call to tl, and we nested inside a call to interleave in the definition of map'.

Coq helps the user by performing the guardedness check after using computation to simplify terms. For instance, any co-recursive function definition can be expanded by inserting extra calls to an identity function, and this change preserves guardedness. However, in other cases computational simplification can reveal why definitions are dangerous. Consider what happens when we inline the definition of tl in bad.

CoFixpoint bad : **stream nat** := bad.

This is the same looping definition we rejected earlier. A similar inlining process reveals a different view on the failed definition of map'.

CoFixpoint map' (s : **stream** A) : **stream** B :=
  match s with
    | Cons h t $\Rightarrow$ Cons (f h) (Cons (f h) (interleave (map' t) (map' t)))
  end.

Clearly in this case the map' calls are not immediate arguments to constructors, so we violate the guardedness condition.

A more interesting question is why that condition is the right one. We can make an intuitive argument that the original map' definition is perfectly reasonable and denotes a well-understood transformation on streams, such that every output would behave properly with approx. The guardedness condition is an example of a syntactic check for *productivity* of co-recursive definitions. A productive definition can be thought of as one whose outputs can be forced in finite time to any finite approximation level, as with approx. If we replaced the guardedness condition with more involved checks, we might be able to detect and allow a broader range of productive definitions. However, mistakes in these checks could cause inconsistency, and programmers would need to understand the new, more complex checks. Coq's design strikes a balance between consistency and simplicity with its choice of guard condition, though we can imagine other worthwhile balances being struck.

5.2   Infinite Proofs

Let us say we want to give two different definitions of a stream of all ones and then prove that they are equivalent.

```
CoFixpoint ones : stream nat := Cons 1 ones.
Definition ones' := map S zeroes.
```

The obvious statement of the equality is this:

```
Theorem ones_eq : ones = ones'.
```

However, with the initial subgoal, it is not at all clear how this theorem can be proved. In fact, it is unprovable. The **eq** predicate is fundamentally limited to equalities that can be demonstrated by finite, syntactic arguments. To prove this equivalence, we need to introduce a new relation.

```
Abort.
```

Co-inductive datatypes make sense by analogy from Haskell. What we need now is a *co-inductive proposition*. That is, we want to define a proposition whose proofs may be infinite, subject to the guardedness condition. The idea of infinite proofs does not show up in usual mathematics, but it can be very useful for reasoning about infinite data structures. Besides examples from Haskell, infinite data and proofs will also turn out to be useful for modeling inherently infinite mathematical objects, like program executions.

We are ready for our first co-inductive predicate.

```
Section stream_eq.
  Variable A : Type.

  CoInductive stream_eq : stream A → stream A → Prop :=
  | Stream_eq : ∀ h t1 t2,
      stream_eq t1 t2
      → stream_eq (Cons h t1) (Cons h t2).
End stream_eq.
```

We say that two streams are equal if and only if they have the same heads and their tails are equal. We use the normal finite-syntactic equality for the heads, and we refer to the new equality recursively for the tails.

We can try restating the theorem with **stream_eq**.

```
Theorem ones_eq : stream_eq ones ones'.
```

Coq does not support tactical co-inductive proofs as well as it supports tactical inductive proofs. The usual starting point is the `cofix` tactic, which asks to structure this proof as a co-fixpoint.

```
  cofix.
```

```
ones_eq : stream_eq ones ones'
============================
  stream_eq ones ones'
```

It looks like this proof might be easier than we expected.

```
  assumption.
```

```
Proof completed.
```

Unfortunately, we are due for some disappointment.

```
Qed.
```

```
Error:
Recursive definition of ones_eq is ill-formed.

In environment
ones_eq : stream_eq ones ones'

unguarded recursive call in "ones_eq"
```

Via the Curry-Howard correspondence, the same guardedness condition applies to co-inductive proofs as to co-inductive data structures. If it did not, the same proof structure could be used to prove any co-inductive theorem vacuously, by direct appeal to itself.

Thinking about how Coq would generate a proof term from the previous proof script, we see that the problem is that we are violating the guardedness condition. During proofs, Coq can help us check whether we have yet gone wrong in this way. We can run the command `Guarded` in any context to see if it is possible to finish the proof in a way that will yield a properly guarded proof term.

```
Guarded.
```

Running `Guarded` here gives the same error message that we got when we tried to run `Qed`. In larger proofs, `Guarded` can be helpful in detecting problems *before* we think we are ready to run `Qed`.

We need to start the co-induction by applying **stream_eq**'s constructor. To do that, we need to know that both arguments to the predicate are Conses. Informally, this is trivial, but `simpl` is not able to help.

```
Undo.
simpl.
```

```
ones_eq : stream_eq ones ones'
============================
  stream_eq ones ones'
```

It turns out that we are best served by proving an auxiliary lemma.

```
Abort.
```

First, we need to define a function that seems pointless at first glance.

```
Definition frob A (s : stream A) : stream A :=
  match s with
    | Cons h t ⇒ Cons h t
  end.
```

Next, we need to prove a theorem that seems equally pointless.

```
Theorem frob_eq : ∀ A (s : stream A), s = frob s.
  destruct s; reflexivity.
Qed.
```

But this theorem turns out to be just what we needed.

```
Theorem ones_eq : stream_eq ones ones'.
  cofix.
```

We can use the theorem to rewrite the two streams.

```
rewrite (frob_eq ones).
rewrite (frob_eq ones').
```

ones_eq : **stream_eq** ones ones'
==============================
 stream_eq (frob ones) (frob ones')

Now `simpl` is able to reduce the streams.

```
simpl.
```

ones_eq : **stream_eq** ones ones'
==============================
 stream_eq (Cons 1 ones)
   (Cons 1
      ((cofix map (s : **stream nat**) : **stream nat** :=
          match s with
          | Cons h t ⇒ Cons (S h) (map t)
          end) zeroes))

Note the `cofix` notation for anonymous co-recursion, which is analogous to the `fix` notation we have already seen for recursion. Since we have exposed the Cons structure of each stream, we can apply the constructor of **stream_eq**.

```
constructor.
```

ones_eq : **stream_eq** ones ones'
==============================
 stream_eq ones
   ((cofix map (s : **stream nat**) : **stream nat** :=
       match s with
       | Cons h t ⇒ Cons (S h) (map t)
       end) zeroes)

Now, modulo unfolding of the definition of **map**, we have matched the assumption.

```
   assumption.
Qed.
```

Why did this work-around help? The answer has to do with the constraints placed on Coq's evaluation rules by the need for termination. The `cofix`-related restriction that foiled the first attempt at using `simpl` is dual to a restriction for `fix`. In particular, an application of an anonymous `fix` only reduces when the top-level structure of the recursive argument is known. Otherwise, we would be unfolding the recursive definition ad infinitum.

Fixpoints only reduce when enough is known about the *definitions* of their arguments. Dually, co-fixpoints only reduce when enough is known about *how their results will be used*. In particular, a `cofix` is only expanded when it is the discriminee of a `match`. Rewriting with the new lemma wrapped new `match`es around the two `cofix`es, triggering reduction.

If `cofix`es reduced haphazardly, it would be easy to run into infinite loops in evaluation, since we are, after all, building infinite objects.

One common source of difficulty with co-inductive proofs is bad interaction with standard Coq automation machinery. If we try to prove `ones_eq` with automation, as with previous inductive proofs, we get an invalid proof.

Theorem ones_eq' : **stream_eq** ones ones'.
  cofix; *crush.*

  Guarded.
Abort.

The standard `auto` machinery sees that the goal matches an assumption and so applies that assumption, even though this violates guardedness. A correct proof strategy for a theorem like this usually starts by `destruct`ing some parameter and running a custom tactic to figure out the first proof rule to apply for each case. Alternatively, there are tricks for "hiding" the co-inductive hypothesis.

Induction seems to have dual versions of the same pitfalls inherent in it, which can be avoided by encapsulating safe Curry-Howard recursion schemes inside named induction principles. We can usually do the same with *co-induction principles*. Let us do that here, so that we can arrive at an `induction` x; *crush*-style proof for ones_eq'.

An induction principle is parameterized over a predicate characterizing what we mean to prove, *as a function of the inductive fact that we already know*. Dually, a co-induction principle ought to be parameterized over a predicate characterizing what we need to assume, *as a function of the arguments to the co-inductive predicate that we are trying to prove.*

To state a useful principle for **stream_eq**, it will be useful first to define the stream head function.

```
Definition hd A (s : stream A) : A :=
  match s with
    | Cons x _ ⇒ x
  end.
```

Now we enter a section for the co-induction principle, based on Park's principle as introduced in a tutorial by Giménez [12].

```
Section stream_eq_coind.
  Variable A : Type.
  Variable R : stream A → stream A → Prop.
```

This relation generalizes the theorem we want to prove, defining a set of pairs of streams that we must eventually prove contains the particular pair we care about.

```
  Hypothesis Cons_case_hd : ∀ s1 s2, R s1 s2 → hd s1 = hd s2.
  Hypothesis Cons_case_tl : ∀ s1 s2, R s1 s2 → R (tl s1) (tl s2).
```

Two hypotheses characterize what makes a good choice of R: it enforces equality of stream heads, and it is hereditary in the sense that an R stream pair passes on R-ness to its tails. An established technical term for such a relation is *bisimulation*.

Now it is straightforward to prove the principle, which says that any stream pair in R is equal. Readers may wish to step through the proof script to see what is going on.

```
  Theorem stream_eq_coind : ∀ s1 s2, R s1 s2 → stream_eq s1 s2.
    cofix; destruct s1; destruct s2; intro.
    generalize (Cons_case_hd H); intro Heq;
      simpl in Heq; rewrite Heq.
    constructor.
    apply stream_eq_coind.
    apply (Cons_case_tl H).
  Qed.
End stream_eq_coind.
```

To see why this proof is guarded, we can print it and verify that the one co-recursive call is an immediate argument to a constructor.

```
Print stream_eq_coind.
```

We omit the output and proceed to proving **ones_eq**' again. The only bit of ingenuity lies in choosing R, and in this case the most restrictive predicate works.

Theorem ones_eq' : **stream_eq** ones ones'.
  apply (stream_eq_coind (fun *s1 s2* ⇒ *s1* = ones ∧ *s2* = ones')); *crush.*
Qed.

Note that this proof achieves the proper reduction behavior via hd and tl rather than frob, as in the last proof. All three functions pattern-match on their arguments, catalyzing computation steps.

Compared to inductive proofs, it still seems unsatisfactory that we had to write a choice of *R* in the last proof. An alternative is to capture a common pattern of co-recursion in a more specialized co-induction principle. For the current example, that pattern is, prove **stream_eq** *s1 s2*, where *s1* and *s2* are defined as their own tails.

Section stream_eq_loop.
  Variable *A* : Type.
  Variables *s1 s2* : **stream** *A*.

  Hypothesis *Cons_case_hd* : hd *s1* = hd *s2*.
  Hypothesis *loop1* : tl *s1* = *s1*.
  Hypothesis *loop2* : tl *s2* = *s2*.

The proof of the principle includes a choice of *R* so that we no longer need to make such choices.

  Theorem stream_eq_loop : **stream_eq** *s1 s2*.
    apply (stream_eq_coind (fun *s1' s2'* ⇒ *s1'* = *s1* ∧ *s2'* = *s2*));
      crush.
  Qed.
End stream_eq_loop.

Theorem ones_eq'' : **stream_eq** ones ones'.
  apply stream_eq_loop; *crush.*
Qed.

Let us put stream_eq_coind through its paces a bit more, considering two different ways to compute infinite streams of all factorial values. First, we import the fact factorial function from the standard library.

Require Import Arith.
Print fact.

fact =
fix fact (*n* : **nat**) : **nat** :=
  match *n* with
  | 0 ⇒ 1
  | S *n0* ⇒ S *n0* × fact *n0*
  end
      : **nat** → **nat**

The simplest way to compute the factorial stream involves calling fact afresh at each position.

```
CoFixpoint fact_slow' (n : nat) := Cons (fact n) (fact_slow' (S n)).
Definition fact_slow := fact_slow' 1.
```

An optimized method maintains an accumulator of the previous factorial so that each new entry can be computed with a single multiplication.

```
CoFixpoint fact_iter' (cur acc : nat) :=
  Cons acc (fact_iter' (S cur) (acc × cur)).
Definition fact_iter := fact_iter' 2 1.
```

We can verify that the streams are equal up to particular finite bounds.

```
Eval simpl in approx fact_iter 5.
```

$$= 1 :: 2 :: 6 :: 24 :: 120 :: \text{nil}$$
: list nat

```
Eval simpl in approx fact_slow 5.
```

$$= 1 :: 2 :: 6 :: 24 :: 120 :: \text{nil}$$
: list nat

Now, to prove that the two versions are equivalent, it is helpful to prove (and add as a proof hint) a lemma about the computational behavior of fact.

```
Lemma fact_def : ∀ x n,
  fact_iter' x (fact n × S n) = fact_iter' x (fact (S n)).
  simpl; intros; f_equal; ring.
Qed.

Hint Resolve fact_def.
```

With the hint added, it is easy to prove an auxiliary lemma relating fact_iter' and fact_slow'. The key is introduction of an existential quantifier for the shared parameter n.

```
Lemma fact_eq' : ∀ n,
  stream_eq (fact_iter' (S n) (fact n)) (fact_slow' n).
  intro; apply (stream_eq_coind (fun s1 s2 ⇒ ∃ n,
    s1 = fact_iter' (S n) (fact n)
    ∧ s2 = fact_slow' n)); crush; eauto.
Qed.
```

The final theorem is a direct corollary of fact_eq'.

```
Theorem fact_eq : stream_eq fact_iter fact_slow.
```

```
   apply fact_eq'.
Qed.
```

As in the case of ones_eq', we may be unsatisfied that we need to write a choice of R that seems to duplicate information already present in a lemma statement. We can facilitate a simpler proof by defining a co-induction principle specialized to goals that begin with single universal quantifiers, and the strategy can be extended in a straightforward way to principles for other counts of quantifiers. (The stream_eq_loop principle is effectively the instantiation of this technique to zero quantifiers.)

```
Section stream_eq_onequant.
   Variables A B : Type.
```

We have the type A, the domain of the one quantifier; and type B, the type of data found in the streams.

```
   Variables f g : A → stream B.
```

The two streams we compare must be of the forms f x and g x, for some shared x. Note that this falls out naturally when x is a shared universally quantified variable in a lemma statement.

```
   Hypothesis Cons_case_hd : ∀ x, hd (f x) = hd (g x).
   Hypothesis Cons_case_tl : ∀ x, ∃ y, tl (f x) = f y ∧ tl (g x) = g y.
```

These conditions are inspired by the bisimulation requirements, with a more general version of the R choice we made for fact_eq' inlined into the hypotheses of stream_eq_coind.

```
   Theorem stream_eq_onequant : ∀ x, stream_eq (f x) (g x).
      intro; apply (stream_eq_coind (fun s1 s2 ⇒ ∃ x,
         s1 = f x ∧ s2 = g x)); crush; eauto.
   Qed.
End stream_eq_onequant.

Lemma fact_eq'' : ∀ n,
   stream_eq (fact_iter' (S n) (fact n)) (fact_slow' n).
   apply stream_eq_onequant; crush; eauto.
Qed.
```

We have arrived at a customary automated proof, thanks to the new principle.

5.3   Simple Modeling of Nonterminating Programs

This chapter closes with a brief example of more complex uses of co-inductive types. We define a co-inductive semantics for a simple imperative programming language and use that semantics to prove the correctness of a trivial optimization that removes spurious additions by 0. We follow the technique of *co-inductive big-step operational semantics* [20].

We define a suggestive synonym for **nat**, as we will consider programs over infinitely many variables, represented as **nat**s.

Definition var := **nat**.

We define a type vars of maps from variables to values. To define a function set for setting a variable's value in a map, we use the standard library function beq_nat for comparing natural numbers.

Definition vars := var → **nat**.
Definition set $(vs : \text{vars})$ $(v : \text{var})$ $(n : \textbf{nat})$: vars :=
   fun v' ⇒ if beq_nat v v' then n else vs v'.

We define a simple arithmetic expression language with variables and give it a semantics via an interpreter.

Inductive **exp** : Set :=
| Const : **nat** → **exp**
| Var : var → **exp**
| Plus : **exp** → **exp** → **exp**.

Fixpoint evalExp $(vs : \text{vars})$ $(e : \textbf{exp})$: **nat** :=
   match e with
      | Const n ⇒ n
      | Var v ⇒ vs v
      | Plus $e1$ $e2$ ⇒ evalExp vs $e1$ + evalExp vs $e2$
   end.

Finally, we define a language of commands. It includes variable assignment, sequencing, and a `while` form that repeats as long as its test expression evaluates to a nonzero value.

Inductive **cmd** : Set :=
| Assign : var → **exp** → **cmd**
| Seq : **cmd** → **cmd** → **cmd**
| While : **exp** → **cmd** → **cmd**.

We could define an inductive relation to characterize the results of command evaluation. However, such a relation would not capture *nonterminating* executions. With a co-inductive relation, we can capture both cases. The parameters of the relation are an initial state, a command, and a final state. A program that does not terminate in a particular initial state is related to *any* final state. For more realistic languages than this one, it is often possible for programs to *crash*, in which case a semantics would generally relate their executions to no final states. Thus, relating safely nonterminating programs to all final states provides a crucial distinction.

```
CoInductive evalCmd : vars → cmd → vars → Prop :=
| EvalAssign : ∀ vs v e,
    evalCmd vs (Assign v e) (set vs v (evalExp vs e))
| EvalSeq : ∀ vs1 vs2 vs3 c1 c2, evalCmd vs1 c1 vs2
    → evalCmd vs2 c2 vs3
    → evalCmd vs1 (Seq c1 c2) vs3
| EvalWhileFalse : ∀ vs e c, evalExp vs e = 0
    → evalCmd vs (While e c) vs
| EvalWhileTrue : ∀ vs1 vs2 vs3 e c, evalExp vs1 e ≠ 0
    → evalCmd vs1 c vs2
    → evalCmd vs2 (While e c) vs3
    → evalCmd vs1 (While e c) vs3.
```

Before proceeding, we build a co-induction principle for **evalCmd**.

```
Section evalCmd_coind.
    Variable R : vars → cmd → vars → Prop.

    Hypothesis AssignCase : ∀ vs1 vs2 v e, R vs1 (Assign v e) vs2
        → vs2 = set vs1 v (evalExp vs1 e).

    Hypothesis SeqCase : ∀ vs1 vs3 c1 c2, R vs1 (Seq c1 c2) vs3
        → ∃ vs2, R vs1 c1 vs2 ∧ R vs2 c2 vs3.

    Hypothesis WhileCase : ∀ vs1 vs3 e c, R vs1 (While e c) vs3
        → (evalExp vs1 e = 0 ∧ vs3 = vs1)
        ∨ ∃ vs2, evalExp vs1 e ≠ 0 ∧ R vs1 c vs2
            ∧ R vs2 (While e c) vs3.
```

The proof is routine. We make use of a form of destruct that takes an *intro pattern* in an as clause. These patterns control how deeply we break apart the components of an inductive value (see the Coq manual for more details).

```
    Theorem evalCmd_coind : ∀ vs1 c vs2, R vs1 c vs2
        → evalCmd vs1 c vs2.
        cofix; intros; destruct c.
        rewrite (AssignCase H); constructor.
        destruct (SeqCase H) as [? [? ?]]; econstructor; eauto.
        destruct (WhileCase H) as [[? ?] | [? [? [? ?]]]];
            subst; econstructor; eauto.
    Qed.
End evalCmd_coind.
```

Now that we have a co-induction principle, we should use it to prove something. The example is a trivial program optimizer that finds places to replace $0 + e$ with e.

```
Fixpoint optExp (e : exp) : exp :=
  match e with
    | Plus (Const 0) e ⇒ optExp e
    | Plus e1 e2 ⇒ Plus (optExp e1) (optExp e2)
    | _ ⇒ e
  end.

Fixpoint optCmd (c : cmd) : cmd :=
  match c with
    | Assign v e ⇒ Assign v (optExp e)
    | Seq c1 c2 ⇒ Seq (optCmd c1) (optCmd c2)
    | While e c ⇒ While (optExp e) (optCmd c)
  end.
```

Before proving correctness of **optCmd**, we prove a lemma about optExp. This is where we have to do the most work, choosing pattern-matching opportunities automatically.

```
Lemma optExp_correct : ∀ vs e, evalExp vs (optExp e) = evalExp vs e.
  induction e; crush;
    repeat (match goal with
              | [ ⊢ context[match ?E with Const _ ⇒ _
                              | _ ⇒ _ end] ] ⇒ destruct E
              | [ ⊢ context[match ?E with O ⇒ _
                              | S _ ⇒ _ end] ] ⇒ destruct E
            end; crush).
Qed.

Hint Rewrite optExp_correct.
```

The final theorem is easy to establish using the co-induction principle and a bit of Ltac proof automation (see Chapter 14). At a high level, we show inclusions between behaviors, going in both directions between original and optimized programs.

```
Ltac finisher := match goal with
                   | [ H : evalCmd _ _ _ ⊢ _ ] ⇒ ((inversion H; [])
                       || (inversion H; [|])); subst
                 end; crush; eauto 10.

Lemma optCmd_correct1 : ∀ vs1 c vs2, evalCmd vs1 c vs2
  → evalCmd vs1 (optCmd c) vs2.
  intros; apply (evalCmd_coind (fun vs1 c' vs2 ⇒
```

$\exists\ c,\ $ **evalCmd** $vs1\ c\ vs2 \land c' = $ optCmd c));
eauto; *crush*;
match goal with
  | [H : _ = optCmd ?$E \vdash$ _] $\Rightarrow$
      destruct E; simpl in *; discriminate
      || injection H; intros; subst
  end; *finisher*.
Qed.

Lemma optCmd_correct2 : $\forall\ vs1\ c\ vs2,$ **evalCmd** $vs1$ (optCmd c) $vs2$
  $\rightarrow$ **evalCmd** $vs1\ c\ vs2.$
  intros; apply (evalCmd_coind (fun $vs1\ c\ vs2 \Rightarrow$
    evalCmd $vs1$ (optCmd c) $vs2$)); *crush*; *finisher*.
Qed.

Theorem optCmd_correct : $\forall\ vs1\ c\ vs2,$ **evalCmd** $vs1$ (optCmd c) $vs2$
  $\leftrightarrow$ **evalCmd** $vs1\ c\ vs2.$
  intuition; apply optCmd_correct1 || apply optCmd_correct2;
    assumption.
Qed.

In this form, the theorem tells us that the optimizer preserves observable behavior of both terminating and nonterminating programs, but we did not have to do more work than for the case of terminating programs alone. We merely took the natural inductive definition for terminating executions, made it co-inductive, and applied the appropriate co-induction principle. Readers might want to experiment with adding command constructs like if; the same proof script should continue working after the co-induction principle is extended to the new evaluation rules.

PART II

Programming with Dependent Types

6   Subset Types and Variations

So far, we have seen many examples of what might be called classical program verification. We write programs, write their specifications, and then prove that the programs satisfy their specifications. The programs that we have written in Coq have been normal functional programs that we could just as well have written in Haskell or ML. In this chapter, we start investigating uses of dependent types to integrate programming, specification, and proving into a single phase. These techniques make it possible to reduce the cost of program verification dramatically.

6.1   Introducing Subset Types

Let us consider several ways of implementing the natural number predecessor function. We start by displaying the definition from the standard library.

```
Print pred.
```

$$\text{pred} = \text{fun } n : \textbf{nat} \Rightarrow \text{match } n \text{ with}$$
$$| \ 0 \Rightarrow 0$$
$$| \ \textsf{S} \ u \Rightarrow u$$
$$\text{end}$$
$$: \textbf{nat} \rightarrow \textbf{nat}$$

We can use a new command, `Extraction`, to produce an OCaml version of this function.

```
Extraction pred.

(** val pred : nat -> nat **)

let pred = function
  | 0 -> 0
```

```
| S u -> u
```

Returning 0 as the predecessor of 0 can come across as somewhat of a hack. In some situations, we might like to be sure that we never try to take the predecessor of 0. We can enforce this by giving **pred** a stronger, dependent type.

Lemma zgtz : $0 > 0 \rightarrow$ **False**.
  crush.
Qed.

Definition pred_strong1 $(n :$ **nat**$) : n > 0 \rightarrow$ **nat** $:=$
  match n with
    $| \ O \Rightarrow$ fun $pf : 0 > 0 \Rightarrow$ match zgtz pf with end
    $| \ S \ n' \Rightarrow$ fun $\_ \Rightarrow n'$
  end.

We expand the type of **pred** to include a proof that its argument n is greater than 0. When n is 0, we use the proof to derive a contradiction, which we can use to build a value of any type via a vacuous pattern match. When n is a successor, we have no need for the proof and just return the answer. The proof argument can be said to have a dependent type because its type *depends* on the value of the argument n.

Coq's Eval command can execute particular invocations of pred_strong1 just as easily as it can execute more traditional functional programs. Note that Coq has decided that argument n of pred_strong1 can be made *implicit,* since it can be deduced from the type of the second argument, so we need not write n in function calls.

Theorem two_gt0 : $2 > 0$.
  crush.
Qed.

Eval compute in pred_strong1 two_gt0.

    $= 1$
    : **nat**

One aspect in particular of the definition of **pred_strong1** may be surprising. We took advantage of Definition's syntactic sugar for defining function arguments in the case of n, but we bound the proofs later with explicit fun expressions. Let us see what happens if we write this function in the way that at first seems most natural.

Definition pred_strong1' $(n :$ **nat**$) \ (pf : n > 0) :$ **nat** $:=$
  match n with
    $| \ O \Rightarrow$ match zgtz pf with end

```
   | S n' ⇒ n'
 end.
```

```
Error: In environment
n : nat
pf : n > 0
The term "pf" has type "n > 0" while it is expected to have
type "0 > 0"
```

The term zgtz *pf* fails to type-check. Somehow the type checker has failed to take into account information that follows from which match branch that term appears in. The problem is that, by default, match does not let us use such implied information. To get refined typing, we must always rely on match annotations, either written explicitly or inferred.

In this case, we must use a return annotation to declare the relation between the *value* of the match discriminee and the *type* of the result. There is no annotation that lets us declare a relation between the discriminee and the type of a variable that is already in scope; hence, we delay the binding of *pf* so that we can use the return annotation to express the needed relation.

Coq's heuristics infer the return clause (specifically, return $n >$ $0 \rightarrow$ **nat**) in the definition of pred_strong1, leading to the following elaborated code.

```
Definition pred_strong1' (n : nat) : n > 0 → nat :=
   match n return n > 0 → nat with
     | O ⇒ fun pf : 0 > 0 ⇒ match zgtz pf with end
     | S n' ⇒ fun _ ⇒ n'
   end.
```

By making explicit the functional relation between value n and the result type of the match, we guide Coq toward proper type checking. The clause for this example follows by simple copying of the original annotation on the definition. In general, however, the match annotation inference problem is undecidable. The known undecidable problem of *higher-order unification* [15] reduces to the match type inference problem. Over time, Coq is enhanced with more and more heuristics to get around this problem, but there must always exist matches whose types Coq cannot infer without annotations.

Let us now take a look at the OCaml code Coq generates for pred_strong1.

```
Extraction pred_strong1.
```

```
(** val pred_strong1 : nat -> nat **)

let pred_strong1 = function
  | 0 -> assert false (* absurd case *)
  | S n' -> n'
```

The proof argument has disappeared. We get exactly the OCaml code we would have written manually. This is the first demonstration of the main technically interesting feature of Coq program extraction: proofs are erased systematically.

We can reimplement the dependently typed **pred** based on *subset types*, defined in the standard library with the type family **sig**.

Print **sig**.

Inductive **sig** $(A : \text{Type})\ (P : A \to \text{Prop}) : \text{Type} :=$
    exist $: \forall\ x : A,\ P\ x \to$ **sig** P

The family **sig** is a Curry-Howard twin of **ex**, except that **sig** is in Type, whereas **ex** is in Prop. That means that **sig** values can survive extraction, but **ex** proofs will always be erased. The actual details of extraction of **sig**s are more subtle.

We rewrite pred_strong1, using some syntactic sugar for subset types.

Locate "{ _: _| _}".

    Notation
    "{ x : A | P }" := **sig** (fun $x : A \Rightarrow P$)

Definition pred_strong2 $(s : \{n :$ **nat** $\mid n > 0\})$: **nat** :=
    match s with
      | exist O $pf \Rightarrow$ match zgtz pf with end
      | exist (S n') _ $\Rightarrow n'$
    end.

To build a value of a subset type, we use the **exist** constructor; the details of how to do that follow from the output of the earlier Print **sig** command, where we elided the extra information that parameter A is implicit. We need an extra _ here and not in the definition of pred_strong2 because *parameters* of inductive types (like the predicate P for **sig**) are not mentioned in pattern matching but *are* mentioned in construction of terms (if they are not marked as implicit arguments).

Eval compute in pred_strong2 (exist _ 2 two_gt0).

      $= 1$
      : **nat**

```
Extraction pred_strong2.
```

```
(** val pred_strong2 : nat -> nat **)
```

```
let pred_strong2 = function
  | 0 -> assert false (* absurd case *)
  | S n' -> n'
```

We arrive at the same OCaml code as was extracted from pred_strong1. The reason is that a value of **sig** is a pair of two pieces, a value and a proof about it. Extraction erases the proof, which reduces the constructor exist of **sig** to taking just a single argument. An optimization eliminates uses of datatypes with single constructors taking single arguments, and we arrive back where we started.

We can continue the process of refining pred's type. Let us change its result type to capture that the output is really the predecessor of the input.

Definition pred_strong3 $(s : \{n : \textbf{nat} \mid n > 0\})$
  $: \{m : \textbf{nat} \mid \text{proj1\_sig } s = \text{S } m\} :=$
  match s return $\{m : \textbf{nat} \mid \text{proj1\_sig } s = \text{S } m\}$ with
    | exist 0 pf $\Rightarrow$ match zgtz pf with end
    | exist (S n') pf $\Rightarrow$ exist _ n' eq_refl
  end.

Eval compute in pred_strong3 (exist _ 2 two_gt0).

  $=$ exist (fun m : **nat** $\Rightarrow$ $2 = $ S m) 1 eq_refl
  $: \{m : \textbf{nat} \mid \text{proj1\_sig (exist (lt 0) 2 two\_gt0)} = \text{S } m\}$

A value in a subset type can be thought of as a *dependent pair* (or *sigma type*) of a base value and a proof about it. The function proj1_sig extracts the first component of the pair, but we need to include an explicit **return** clause, since Coq's heuristics do not propagate the result type that we wrote earlier.

The new pred_strong leads to the same OCaml code we have seen several times so far.

```
Extraction pred_strong3.
```

```
(** val pred_strong3 : nat -> nat **)
```

```
let pred_strong3 = function
  | 0 -> assert false (* absurd case *)
  | S n' -> n'
```

We have managed to reach a type that is, in a formal sense, the most expressive possible for pred. Any other implementation of the same type must have the same input-output behavior. However, there is still room for improvement in making this kind of code easier to write. Here is a version that takes advantage of tactic-based theorem proving. We switch back to passing a separate proof argument instead of using a subset type for the function's input because this leads to cleaner code. (Recall that False_rec is the Set-level induction principle for **False**, which can be used to produce a value in any Set given a proof of **False**.)

Definition pred_strong4 : $\forall$ n : **nat**, $n > 0 \rightarrow \{m$: **nat** $\mid n = $ S $m\}$.
  refine (fun $n \Rightarrow$
    match n with
      | O $\Rightarrow$ fun _ $\Rightarrow$ False_rec _ _
      | S n' $\Rightarrow$ fun _ $\Rightarrow$ exist _ n' _
    end).

We build pred_strong4 using tactic-based proving, beginning with a Definition command that ends in a period before a definition is given. Such a command enters the interactive proving mode, with the type given for the new identifier as the proof goal. It may seem strange to change perspective so implicitly between programming and proving, but recall that programs and proofs are two sides of the same coin in Coq, thanks to the Curry-Howard correspondence.

We do most of the work with the refine tactic, to which we pass a partial "proof" of the type we are trying to prove. There may be some pieces left to fill in, indicated by underscores. Any underscore that Coq cannot reconstruct with type inference is added as a proof subgoal. In this case, we have two subgoals.

2 subgoals

  n : **nat**
  _ : $0 > 0$
  ============================
  False

subgoal 2 is

  S $n' = $ S n'

The first subgoal comes from the second underscore passed to False_rec, and the second subgoal comes from the second underscore

passed to exist. In the first case, we see that though we bound the
proof variable with an underscore, it is still available in the proof context. It is hard to refer to underscore-named variables in manual proofs,
but automation makes short work of them. Both subgoals are easy to
discharge that way, so let us back up and ask to prove all subgoals
automatically.

```
Undo.
refine (fun n ⇒
    match n with
        | O ⇒ fun _ ⇒ False_rec _ _
        | S n' ⇒ fun _ ⇒ exist _ n' _
    end); crush.
Defined.
```

We end the "proof" with Defined instead of Qed, so that the definition
we constructed remains visible. This contrasts with the case of ending
a proof with Qed, where the details of the proof are hidden afterward.
(More formally, Defined marks an identifier as *transparent*, allowing it
to be unfolded, whereas Qed marks an identifier as *opaque*, preventing
unfolding.) Let us see what the proof script constructed.

```
Print pred_strong4.
```

```
pred_strong4 =
fun n : nat ⇒
match n as n0 return (n0 > 0 → {m : nat | n0 = S m}) with
| 0 ⇒
    fun _ : 0 > 0 ⇒
    False_rec {m : nat | 0 = S m}
        (Bool.diff_false_true
            (Bool.absurd_eq_true false
                (Bool.diff_false_true
                    (Bool.absurd_eq_true false
                        (pred_strong4_subproof n _)))))
| S n' ⇒
    fun _ : S n' > 0 ⇒
    exist (fun m : nat ⇒ S n' = S m) n' eq_refl
end
        : ∀ n : nat, n > 0 → {m : nat | n = S m}
```

We see the code we entered, with some proofs filled in. The first proof
obligation, the second argument to False_rec, is filled in with a proof
term that we can be glad we did not enter by hand. The second proof
obligation is a simple reflexivity proof.

Eval compute in pred_strong4 two_gt0.

> = exist (fun m : **nat** $\Rightarrow$ $2 = $ S m) 1 eq_refl
> : $\{m$: **nat** $\mid 2 = $ S $m\}$

A tactic modifier called `abstract` can be helpful for producing shorter terms, by automatically abstracting subgoals into named lemmas.

Definition pred_strong4' : $\forall$ n : **nat**, $n > 0 \rightarrow \{m$: **nat** $\mid n = $ S $m\}$.
  refine (fun $n \Rightarrow$
    match n with
      | O $\Rightarrow$ fun _ $\Rightarrow$ False_rec _ _
      | S n' $\Rightarrow$ fun _ $\Rightarrow$ exist _ n' _
    end); abstract *crush*.
Defined.

Print pred_strong4'.

pred_strong4' $=$
fun n : **nat** $\Rightarrow$
match n as $n0$ return ($n0 > 0 \rightarrow \{m$: **nat** $\mid n0 = $ S $m\}$) with
| 0 $\Rightarrow$
    fun _H : $0 > 0 \Rightarrow$
    False_rec $\{m$: **nat** $\mid 0 = $ S $m\}$ (*pred_strong4'_subproof* n _H)
| S n' $\Rightarrow$
    fun _H : S $n' > 0 \Rightarrow$
    exist (fun m : **nat** $\Rightarrow$ S $n' = $ S m) n'
      (*pred_strong4'_subproof0* n _H)
end
     : $\forall$ n : **nat**, $n > 0 \rightarrow \{m$: **nat** $\mid n = $ S $m\}$

We are almost done with the ideal implementation of dependent predecessor. We can use Coq's syntax extension facility to arrive at code with almost no complexity beyond a Haskell or ML program with a complete specification in a comment. In this book, I do not dwell on the details of syntax extensions; the Coq manual gives a straightforward introduction to them.

Notation "!" := (False_rec _ _).
Notation "[e]" := (exist _ e _).

Definition pred_strong5 : $\forall$ n : **nat**, $n > 0 \rightarrow \{m$: **nat** $\mid n = $ S $m\}$.
  refine (fun $n \Rightarrow$
    match n with
      | O $\Rightarrow$ fun _ $\Rightarrow$!
      | S n' $\Rightarrow$ fun _ $\Rightarrow$ [n']
    end); *crush*.

`Defined.`

By default, notations are also used in pretty-printing terms, including results of evaluation.

`Eval compute in pred_strong5 two_gt0.`

$$= [1]$$
$$: \{m : \textbf{nat} \mid 2 = \textsf{S}\ m\}$$

One other alternative is worth demonstrating. Recent Coq versions include a facility called `Program` that streamlines this style of definition. Here is a complete implementation using `Program`:

`Obligation Tactic :=` *crush.*

`Program Definition pred_strong6` $(n : \textbf{nat})\ (\_ : n > 0)$
   $: \{m : \textbf{nat} \mid n = \textsf{S}\ m\} :=$
  `match` n `with`
    $\mid \textsf{O} \Rightarrow \_$
    $\mid \textsf{S}\ n' \Rightarrow n'$
  `end.`

Printing the resulting definition of **pred_strong6** yields a term very similar to what we built with `refine`. `Program` can save time in writing programs that use subset types. Nonetheless, `refine` is often just as effective, and `refine` gives more control over the form of the final term, which can be useful to prove additional theorems about the definition. `Program` will sometimes insert type casts that can complicate theorem proving.

`Eval compute in pred_strong6 two_gt0.`

$$= [1]$$
$$: \{m : \textbf{nat} \mid 2 = \textsf{S}\ m\}$$

In this case, we see that the new definition yields the same computational behavior as before.

6.2 Decidable Proposition Types

Another type in the standard library captures the idea of program values that indicate which of two propositions is true.

`Print` **sumbool**.

`Inductive` **sumbool** $(A : \textsf{Prop})\ (B : \textsf{Prop}) : \textsf{Set} :=$
    `left` $: A \rightarrow \{A\} + \{B\} \mid$ `right` $: B \rightarrow \{A\} + \{B\}$

Here, the constructors of **sumbool** have types written in terms of a registered notation for **sumbool**, such that the result type of each constructor desugars to **sumbool** *A B*. We can define some notations to make working with **sumbool** more convenient.

```
Notation "'Yes'" := (left _ _).
Notation "'No'" := (right _ _).
Notation "'Reduce' x" := (if x then Yes else No) (at level 50).
```

The `Reduce` notation is notable because it demonstrates how `if` is overloaded in Coq. The `if` form actually works when the test expression has any two-constructor inductive type. Moreover, in the `then` and `else` branches, the appropriate constructor arguments are bound. This is important when working with **sumbool**s, when we want to have the proof stored in the test expression available when proving the proof obligations generated in the appropriate branch.

Now we can write `eq_nat_dec`, which compares two natural numbers, returning either a proof of their equality or a proof of their inequality.

```
Definition eq_nat_dec : ∀ n m : nat, {n = m} + {n ≠ m}.
  refine (fix f (n m : nat) : {n = m} + {n ≠ m} :=
    match n, m with
      | O, O ⇒ Yes
      | S n', S m' ⇒ Reduce (f n' m')
      | _, _ ⇒ No
    end); congruence.
Defined.

Eval compute in eq_nat_dec 2 2.
```

$$= Yes$$
$$: \{2 = 2\} + \{2 \neq 2\}$$

```
Eval compute in eq_nat_dec 2 3.
```

$$= No$$
$$: \{2 = 3\} + \{2 \neq 3\}$$

Note that the `Yes` and `No` notations are hiding proofs establishing the correctness of the outputs.

The definition extracts to reasonable OCaml code.

```
Extraction eq_nat_dec.

(** val eq_nat_dec : nat -> nat -> sumbool **)

let rec eq_nat_dec n m =
  match n with
```

```
  | O -> (match m with
          | O -> Left
          | S n0 -> Right)
  | S n' -> (match m with
            | O -> Right
            | S m' -> eq_nat_dec n' m')
```

Proving this kind of decidable equality result is so common that Coq comes with a tactic for automating it.

Definition eq_nat_dec' $(n\ m : \mathbf{nat}) : \{n = m\} + \{n \neq m\}$.
    decide equality.
Defined.

Readers can verify that the `decide equality` version extracts to the same OCaml code as the more manual version does. That OCaml code had one undesirable property, which is that it uses `Left` and `Right` constructors instead of the Boolean values built into OCaml. We can fix this by using Coq's facility for mapping Coq inductive types to OCaml variant types.

Extract Inductive **sumbool** $\Rightarrow$ "bool" ["true" "false"].
Extraction eq_nat_dec'.

```
(** val eq_nat_dec' : nat -> nat -> bool **)

let rec eq_nat_dec' n m0 =
  match n with
    | O -> (match m0 with
            | O -> true
            | S n0 -> false)
    | S n0 -> (match m0 with
              | O -> false
              | S n1 -> eq_nat_dec' n0 n1)
```

We can build smart versions of the usual Boolean operators and put them to good use in certified programming. For instance, here is a **sumbool** version of Boolean "or":

Notation "x || y" := (if x then Yes else Reduce y).

Let us use it for building a function that decides list membership. We need to assume the existence of an equality decision procedure for the type of list elements.

Section In_dec.

Variable A : Set.
Variable A_eq_dec : $\forall x \ y : A, \{x = y\} + \{x \neq y\}$.

The final function is easy to write using the techniques we have developed so far.

Definition In_dec : $\forall (x : A) (ls : \textbf{list } A), \{\text{In } x \ ls\} + \{\neg \text{ In } x \ ls\}$.
   refine (fix f $(x : A)$ $(ls : \textbf{list } A)$: $\{\text{In } x \ ls\} + \{\neg \text{ In } x \ ls\}$:=
      match ls with
      | nil $\Rightarrow$ No
      | x' :: ls' $\Rightarrow$ A_eq_dec x x' || f x ls'
      end); *crush*.
   Defined.
End In_dec.

Eval compute in In_dec eq_nat_dec 2 (1 :: 2 :: nil).

   $= Yes$
   : $\{\text{In } 2 \ (1 :: 2 :: \text{nil})\} + \{ \neg \text{ In } 2 \ (1 :: 2 :: \text{nil})\}$

Eval compute in In_dec eq_nat_dec 3 (1 :: 2 :: nil).

   $= No$
   : $\{\text{In } 3 \ (1 :: 2 :: \text{nil})\} + \{ \neg \text{ In } 3 \ (1 :: 2 :: \text{nil})\}$

The In_dec function has a reasonable extraction to OCaml.

Extraction In_dec.

```
(** val in_dec : ('a1 -> 'a1 -> bool) -> 'a1
    -> 'a1 list -> bool **)
```

```
let rec in_dec a_eq_dec x = function
  | Nil -> false
  | Cons (x', ls') ->
      (match a_eq_dec x x' with
         | true -> true
         | false -> in_dec a_eq_dec x ls')
```

This is more or less the code for the corresponding function from the OCaml standard library.

6.3 Partial Subset Types

The final implementation of dependent predecessor used a very specific argument type to ensure that execution could always complete normally. Sometimes we want to allow execution to fail, and we want a more principled way of signaling failure than returning a default value, as pred does for 0. One approach is to define the type family **maybe**, which is a version of **sig** that allows obligation-free failure.

Inductive **maybe** $(A : \mathsf{Set})\ (P : A \to \mathsf{Prop}) : \mathsf{Set} :=$
| Unknown : **maybe** P
| Found : $\forall\ x : A,\ P\ x \to$ **maybe** P.

We can define some new notations, analogous to those we defined for subset types.

Notation "{{ x | P }}" := (**maybe** (fun $x \Rightarrow P$)).
Notation "??" := (Unknown _).
Notation "|| x ||" := (Found _ x _).

Now the next version of pred is trivial to write.

Definition pred_strong7 : $\forall\ n :$ **nat**, {{$m\ |\ n = \mathsf{S}\ m$}}.
  refine (fun $n \Rightarrow$
    match n return {{$m\ |\ n = \mathsf{S}\ m$}} with
      | O $\Rightarrow$??
      | S $n' \Rightarrow [|n'|]$
    end); trivial.
Defined.

Eval compute in pred_strong7 2.

   $= [|1|]$
   $: \{\{m\ |\ 2 = \mathsf{S}\ m\}\}$

Eval compute in pred_strong7 0.

   $= {}$??
   $: \{\{m\ |\ 0 = \mathsf{S}\ m\}\}$

Because we used **maybe**, one valid implementation of the type we gave pred_strong7 would return ?? in every case. We can strengthen the type to rule out such vacuous implementations; the type family **sumor** from the standard library provides the easiest starting point. For type A and proposition B, $A + \{B\}$ desugars to **sumor** $A\ B$, whose values are either values of A or proofs of B.

Print **sumor**.

Inductive **sumor** $(A : \mathsf{Type})\ (B : \mathsf{Prop}) : \mathsf{Type} :=$
   inleft : $A \to A + \{B\}$ | inright : $B \to A + \{B\}$

We add notations for easy use of the **sumor** constructors. The second notation is specialized to **sumor**s whose A parameters are instantiated with regular subset types, since this is how we will use **sumor**.

```
Notation "!!" := (inright _ _).
Notation "[|| x ||]" := (inleft _ [x]).
```

Now we are ready to give the final version of possibly failing prede-cessor. The **sumor**-based type that we use is maximally expressive; any implementation of the type has the same input-output behavior.

```
Definition pred_strong8 : ∀ n : nat, {m : nat | n = S m} + {n = 0}.
  refine (fun n ⇒
    match n with
      | O ⇒ !!
      | S n' ⇒ [||n'||]
    end); trivial.
Defined.
```

```
Eval compute in pred_strong8 2.
```

$$= [||1||]$$
$$: \{m : \mathbf{nat} \mid 2 = \mathsf{S}\ m\} + \{2 = 0\}$$

```
Eval compute in pred_strong8 0.
```

$$= {!!}$$
$$: \{m : \mathbf{nat} \mid 0 = \mathsf{S}\ m\} + \{0 = 0\}$$

As with the other maximally expressive **pred** function, we arrive at quite simple output values, thanks to notations.

6.4   Monadic Notations

We can treat **maybe** like a monad [44], in the same way that the Haskell Maybe type is interpreted as a failure monad. **maybe** has the wrong type to be a literal monad, but a bind-like notation will still be helpful. Note that the notation definition uses an ASCII <-, whereas later code uses (in this rendering) a nicer left arrow ←.

```
Notation "x <- e1 ; e2" := (match e1 with
                             | Unknown ⇒ ??
                             | Found x _ ⇒ e2
                           end)
(right associativity, at level 60).
```

The meaning of $x \leftarrow e1;\ e2$ is the following: First run *e1*. If it fails to find an answer, then announce failure for the derived computation, too. If *e1* *does* find an answer, pass that answer on to *e2* to find the final result. The variable x can be considered bound in *e2*.

This notation is very helpful for composing richly typed procedures. For instance, here is a very simple implementation of a function to take the predecessors of two naturals at once:

```
Definition doublePred : ∀ n1 n2 : nat,
  {{p | n1 = S (fst p) ∧ n2 = S (snd p)}}.
  refine (fun n1 n2 ⇒
    m1 ← pred_strong7 n1 ;
    m2 ← pred_strong7 n2 ;
    [|(m1 , m2)|]); tauto.
Defined.
```

We can build a **sumor** version of the bind notation and use it to write a similarly straightforward version of this function. Again, the notation definition exposes the ASCII syntax with an operator <--, and the later code uses a nicer long left arrow ⟵.

```
Notation "x <- e1 ; e2" := (match e1 with
                            | inright _ ⇒ !!
                            | inleft (exist x _) ⇒ e2
                           end)
(right associativity, at level 60).
```

```
Definition doublePred' : ∀ n1 n2 : nat,
  {p : nat × nat | n1 = S (fst p) ∧ n2 = S (snd p)}
  + {n1 = 0 ∨ n2 = 0}.
  refine (fun n1 n2 ⇒
    m1 ⟵ pred_strong8 n1 ;
    m2 ⟵ pred_strong8 n2 ;
    [||(m1 , m2)||]); tauto.
Defined.
```

This example demonstrates how judicious selection of notations can hide complexities in the rich types of programs.

6.5 A Type-Checking Example

We can apply these specification types to build a certified type checker for a simple expression language.

```
Inductive exp : Set :=
| Nat : nat → exp
| Plus : exp → exp → exp
| Bool : bool → exp
```

| And : **exp** → **exp** → **exp**.

We define a simple language of types and its typing rules in the style introduced in Chapter 4.

Inductive **type** : Set := TNat | TBool.

Inductive **hasType** : **exp** → **type** → Prop :=
| HtNat : ∀ *n*,
  hasType (Nat *n*) TNat
| HtPlus : ∀ *e1 e2*,
  hasType *e1* TNat
  → **hasType** *e2* TNat
  → **hasType** (Plus *e1 e2*) TNat
| HtBool : ∀ *b*,
  hasType (Bool *b*) TBool
| HtAnd : ∀ *e1 e2*,
  hasType *e1* TBool
  → **hasType** *e2* TBool
  → **hasType** (And *e1 e2*) TBool.

It will be helpful to have a function for comparing two types. We build one using decide equality.

Definition eq_type_dec : ∀ *t1 t2* : **type**, {*t1* = *t2*} + {*t1* ≠ *t2*}.
  decide equality.
Defined.

Another notation complements the monadic notation for **maybe**, defined earlier. Sometimes we want to include assertions in a procedure. That is, we want to run a decision procedure and fail if it fails; otherwise, we want to continue, with the proof that it produced made available to us. This infix notation captures that idea for a procedure that returns an arbitrary two-constructor type.

Notation "e1 ;; e2" := (if *e1* then *e2* else ??)
  (right associativity, at level 60).

With that notation defined, we can implement a **typeCheck** function, whose code is only more complex than what we would write in ML because it needs to include some extra type annotations. Every $[|e|]$ expression adds a **hasType** proof obligation, and *crush* makes short work of them when we add **hasType**'s constructors as hints.

Definition typeCheck : ∀ *e* : **exp**, {{*t* | **hasType** *e t*}}.
  Hint Constructors **hasType**.

  refine (fix *F* (*e* : **exp**) : {{*t* | **hasType** *e t*}} :=
    match *e* return {{*t* | **hasType** *e t*}} with

```
    | Nat _ ⇒ [|TNat|]
    | Plus e1 e2 ⇒
        t1 ← F e1;
        t2 ← F e2;
        eq_type_dec t1 TNat;;
        eq_type_dec t2 TNat;;
        [|TNat|]
    | Bool _ ⇒ [|TBool|]
    | And e1 e2 ⇒
        t1 ← F e1;
        t2 ← F e2;
        eq_type_dec t1 TBool;;
        eq_type_dec t2 TBool;;
        [|TBool|]
  end); crush.
Defined.
```

Despite manipulating proofs, this type checker is easy to run.

Eval simpl in typeCheck (Nat 0).

```
    = [|TNat|]
    : {{t | hasType (Nat 0) t}}
```

Eval simpl in typeCheck (Plus (Nat 1) (Nat 2)).

```
    = [|TNat|]
    : {{t | hasType (Plus (Nat 1) (Nat 2)) t}}
```

Eval simpl in typeCheck (Plus (Nat 1) (Bool false)).

```
    = ??
    : {{t | hasType (Plus (Nat 1) (Bool false)) t}}
```

The type checker also extracts to some reasonable OCaml code.

Extraction typeCheck.

```
(** val typeCheck : exp -> type0 maybe **)

let rec typeCheck = function
  | Nat n -> Found TNat
  | Plus (e1, e2) ->
      (match typeCheck e1 with
          | Unknown -> Unknown
          | Found t1 ->
              (match typeCheck e2 with
```

```
                    | Unknown -> Unknown
                    | Found t2 ->
                       (match eq_type_dec t1 TNat with
                          | true ->
                             (match eq_type_dec t2 TNat with
                                | true -> Found TNat
                                | false -> Unknown)
                          | false -> Unknown)))
    | Bool b -> Found TBool
    | And (e1, e2) ->
       (match typeCheck e1 with
          | Unknown -> Unknown
          | Found t1 ->
             (match typeCheck e2 with
                | Unknown -> Unknown
                | Found t2 ->
                   (match eq_type_dec t1 TBool with
                      | true ->
                         (match eq_type_dec t2 TBool with
                            | true -> Found TBool
                            | false -> Unknown)
                      | false -> Unknown)))
```

We can adapt this implementation to use **sumor**, so that we know the type checker only fails on ill-typed inputs. First, we define an analogue to the assertion notation.

Notation "e1 ;;; e2" := (if *e1* then *e2* else !!)
   (right associativity, at level 60).

Next, we prove a helpful lemma, which states that a given expression can have at most one type.

Lemma hasType_det : $\forall$ *e t1*,
   hasType *e t1*
   $\rightarrow$ $\forall$ *t2*, **hasType** *e t2*
      $\rightarrow$ *t1* = *t2*.
   induction 1; inversion 1; *crush*.
Qed.

Now we can define the type checker. Its type expresses that it only fails on untypable expressions.

Definition typeCheck' : $\forall$ *e* : **exp**,
   {*t* : **type** | **hasType** *e t*} + {$\forall$ *t*, $\neg$ **hasType** *e t*}.

```
Hint Constructors hasType.
```

We register all the typing rules as hints.

```
Hint Resolve hasType_det.
```

The lemma hasType_det will also be useful for proving proof obligations with contradictory contexts. Since its statement includes ∀-bound variables that do not appear in its conclusion, only `eauto` will apply this hint.

Finally, the implementation of typeCheck can be transcribed literally, simply switching notations as needed.

```
refine (fix F (e : exp) : {t : type | hasType e t}
  + {∀ t, ¬ hasType e t} :=
 match e return {t : type | hasType e t}
     + {∀ t, ¬ hasType e t} with
   | Nat _ ⇒ [||TNat||]
   | Plus e1 e2 ⇒
       t1 ←— F e1;
       t2 ←— F e2;
       eq_type_dec t1 TNat;;;
       eq_type_dec t2 TNat;;;
       [||TNat||]
   | Bool _ ⇒ [||TBool||]
   | And e1 e2 ⇒
       t1 ←— F e1;
       t2 ←— F e2;
       eq_type_dec t1 TBool;;;
       eq_type_dec t2 TBool;;;
       [||TBool||]
 end); clear F; crush' tt hasType; eauto.
```

We clear F, the local name for the recursive function, to avoid strange proofs that refer to recursive calls that we never make. Such a step is usually warranted when defining a recursive function with `refine`. The *crush* variant *crush'* performs automatic inversion on instances of the predicates specified in its second argument. Once we include `eauto` to apply hasType_det, we have discharged all the subgoals.

```
Defined.
```

The short implementation here hides just how time-saving automation is. Every use of one of the notations adds a proof obligation, giving us twelve in total. Most of these obligations require multiple inversions and either uses of hasType_det or applications of **hasType** rules.

The new function remains easy to test.

Eval simpl in typeCheck' (Nat 0).

> = [||TNat||]
> : {t : type | **hasType** (Nat 0) t} +
> {($\forall$ t : type, $\neg$ **hasType** (Nat 0) t)}

Eval simpl in typeCheck' (Plus (Nat 1) (Nat 2)).

> = [||TNat||]
> : {t : type | **hasType** (Plus (Nat 1) (Nat 2)) t} +
> {($\forall$ t : type, $\neg$ **hasType** (Plus (Nat 1) (Nat 2)) t)}

Eval simpl in typeCheck' (Plus (Nat 1) (Bool false)).

> = !!
> : {t : type | **hasType** (Plus (Nat 1) (Bool false)) t} +
> {($\forall$ t : type, $\neg$ **hasType** (Plus (Nat 1) (Bool false)) t)}

The results of simplifying calls to typeCheck' look deceptively similar to the results for typeCheck, but now the types of the results provide more information.

7 General Recursion

Termination of all programs is a crucial property of Gallina. Nonterminating programs introduce logical inconsistency, that is, any theorem can be proved with an infinite loop. Coq uses a small set of conservative, syntactic criteria to check termination of all recursive definitions. These criteria are insufficient to support the natural encodings of a variety of important programming idioms. Further, since Coq makes it so convenient to encode mathematics computationally, with functional programs, we may want to employ more complicated recursion in mathematical definitions.

What exactly are the Coq criteria for checking termination? For *recursive* definitions, recursive calls are only allowed on *syntactic subterms* of the original primary argument, a restriction known as *primitive recursion*. In fact, Coq's handling of reflexive inductive types (those defined in terms of functions returning the same type) gives a bit more flexibility than in traditional primitive recursion, but the term is still applied commonly. Chapter 5 showed how *co-recursive* definitions are checked against a syntactic guardedness condition that guarantees productivity.

Many natural recursion patterns satisfy neither condition. For instance, in the simple running example in this chapter, we will study three different approaches to more flexible recursion, two of which support definitions that may fail to terminate on certain inputs without any up-front characterization of which inputs those may be.

The problem here is not as fundamental as it may appear. The final example of Chapter 5 demonstrated *deep embedding* of the syntax and semantics of a programming language. That is, it gave a mathematical definition of a language of programs and their meanings. This language clearly admitted nontermination, and we could think of writing all sophisticated recursive functions with such explicit syntax types. However, that would forfeit Coq's very good built-in support for reasoning about Gallina programs. It is preferable to use *shallow embedding*,

where informal constructs are modeled by encoding them as normal
Gallina programs. Each of the three techniques of this chapter follows
that style.

7.1 Well-Founded Recursion

The essence of terminating recursion is that there are no infinite
chains of nested recursive calls. This intuition is commonly mapped
to the mathematical idea of a *well-founded relation*, and the associated standard technique in Coq is *well-founded recursion*. The syntactic
subterm relation that Coq applies by default is well-founded, but
many cases demand alternative well-founded relations. To demonstrate,
let us see where we get stuck on attempting a standard merge sort
implementation.

Section mergeSort.
  Variable A : Type.
  Variable $le : A \to A \to$ **bool**.

We have a set equipped with some less-than-or-equal-to test.

A standard function inserts an element into a sorted list, preserving
sortedness.

  Fixpoint insert $(x : A)$ $(ls : $ **list** $A)$: **list** $A :=$
    match ls with
      | nil $\Rightarrow x ::$ nil
      | $h :: ls' \Rightarrow$
        if $le\ x\ h$
          then $x :: ls$
          else $h ::$ insert $x\ ls'$
    end.

We also need a function to merge two sorted lists. (We use a less
efficient implementation than usual because the more efficient implementation already forces us to think about well-founded recursion,
whereas here we are only interested in setting up the example of merge
sort.)

  Fixpoint merge $(ls1\ ls2 : $ **list** $A)$: **list** $A :=$
    match $ls1$ with
      | nil $\Rightarrow ls2$
      | $h :: ls' \Rightarrow$ insert h (merge $ls'\ ls2$)
    end.

The last helper function for classic merge sort is the one that follows,
to split a list arbitrarily into two pieces of approximately equal length.

```
Fixpoint split (ls : list A) : list A × list A :=
  match ls with
    | nil ⇒ (nil, nil)
    | h :: nil ⇒ (h :: nil, nil)
    | h1 :: h2 :: ls' ⇒
      let (ls1, ls2) := split ls' in
        (h1 :: ls1, h2 :: ls2)
  end.
```

Now, let us try to write the final sorting function, using a natural number ≤ test leb from the standard library.

```
Fixpoint mergeSort (ls : list A) : list A :=
  if leb (length ls) 1
    then ls
    else let lss := split ls in
      merge (mergeSort (fst lss)) (mergeSort (snd lss)).
```

```
Recursive call to mergeSort has principal argument equal to
"fst (split ls)" instead of a subterm of "ls".
```

The definition is rejected for not following the simple primitive recursion criterion. In particular, it is not apparent that recursive calls to mergeSort are syntactic subterms of the original argument ls; indeed, they are not, yet we know this is a well-founded recursive definition.

To produce an acceptable definition, we need to choose a well-founded relation and prove that mergeSort respects it. A good starting point is an examination of how well-foundedness is formalized in the Coq standard library.

```
Print well_founded.
```

well_founded =
fun (A : Type) (R : A → A → Prop) ⇒ ∀ a : A, **Acc** R a

The bulk of the definitional work devolves to the *accessibility* relation **Acc**, whose definition we may also examine.

```
Print Acc.
```

Inductive **Acc** (A : Type) (R : A → A → Prop) (x : A) : Prop :=
  Acc_intro : (∀ y : A, R y x → **Acc** R y) → **Acc** R x

In prose, an element x is accessible for a relation R if every element "less than" x according to R is also accessible. Since **Acc** is defined inductively, we know that any accessibility proof involves a finite chain of invocations, in a certain sense that we can make formal. Building on the examples from Chapter 5, let us define a co-inductive relation that is closer to the usual informal notion of "absence of infinite decreasing chains."

> CoInductive **infiniteDecreasingChain** A ($R : A \to A \to$ Prop)
>   : **stream** $A \to$ Prop :=
> | ChainCons : $\forall\ x\ y\ s$, **infiniteDecreasingChain** R (Cons $y\ s$)
> $\to R\ y\ x$
> $\to$ **infiniteDecreasingChain** R (Cons x (Cons $y\ s$)).

We can now prove that any accessible element cannot be the beginning of any infinite decreasing chain.

> Lemma noBadChains' : $\forall\ A$ ($R : A \to A \to$ Prop) x, **Acc** $R\ x$
> $\to \forall\ s$, ¬**infiniteDecreasingChain** R (Cons $x\ s$).
>   induction 1; *crush*;
>   match goal with
> | [H : **infiniteDecreasingChain** _ _ $\vdash$ _] $\Rightarrow$
>   inversion H; eauto
>   end.
> Qed.

From here, the absence of infinite decreasing chains in well-founded sets is immediate.

> Theorem noBadChains : $\forall\ A$ ($R : A \to A \to$ Prop), well_founded R
> $\to \forall\ s$, ¬**infiniteDecreasingChain** $R\ s$.
>   destruct s; apply noBadChains'; auto.
> Qed.

Absence of infinite decreasing chains implies absence of infinitely nested recursive calls, for any recursive definition that respects the well-founded relation. The Fix combinator from the standard library formalizes that intuition.

> Check Fix.

Fix
    : $\forall$ ($A :$ Type) ($R : A \to A \to$ Prop),
      well_founded $R \to$
      $\forall\ P : A \to$ Type,
      ($\forall\ x : A$, ($\forall\ y : A$, $R\ y\ x \to P\ y$) $\to P\ x$) $\to$
      $\forall\ x : A$, $P\ x$

A call to Fix must present a relation R and a proof of its well-foundedness. The next argument, P, is the possibly dependent range type of the function we build; the domain A of R is the function's domain. The subsequent argument has this type:

$$\forall\ x : A,\ (\forall\ y : A,\ R\ y\ x \to P\ y) \to P\ x$$

This is an encoding of the function body. The input x stands for the function argument, and the next input stands for the function we are defining. Recursive calls are encoded as calls to the second argument, whose type tells us it expects a value y and a proof that y is "less than" x, according to R. In this way, we enforce the well-foundedness restriction on recursive calls.

The rest of `Fix`'s type tells us that it returns a function of exactly the type we expect, so we are now ready to use it to implement mergeSort. Notice that `Fix` has a dependent type of the sort shown in Chapter 6.

Before writing mergeSort, we need to settle on a well-founded relation. The right one for this example is based on lengths of lists.

Definition lengthOrder (*ls1 ls2* : **list** A) :=
   length *ls1* < length *ls2*.

We must prove that the relation is truly well-founded. To save space, we skip right to automated proof scripts; the details of the principles behind such scripts are given in Part III of the book. (Readers may still replace semicolons with periods and newlines to step through these scripts interactively.)

Hint Constructors **Acc**.

Lemma lengthOrder_wf' : $\forall$ *len*, $\forall$ *ls*, length *ls* $\le$ *len*
   $\to$ **Acc** lengthOrder *ls*.
    unfold lengthOrder; induction *len*; *crush*.
Defined.

Theorem lengthOrder_wf : well_founded lengthOrder.
   red; intro; eapply lengthOrder_wf'; eauto.
Defined.

Notice that these proofs end with `Defined`, not `Qed`. Recall that `Defined` marks the theorems as transparent, so that the details of their proofs may be used during program execution. Why could such details possibly matter for computation? It turns out that `Fix` satisfies the primitive recursion restriction by declaring itself as *recursive in the structure of* **Acc** *proofs*. This is possible because **Acc** proofs follow a predictable inductive structure. We must do work, as in the last theorem's proof, to establish that all elements of a type belong to **Acc**, but the automatic unwinding of those proofs during recursion is straightforward. If the proof ended with `Qed`, the proof details would be hidden from computation, in which case the unwinding process would get stuck.

To justify the two recursive mergeSort calls, we also need to prove that `split` respects the lengthOrder relation. These proofs, too, must be kept transparent, to avoid the stuckness of `Fix` evaluation. We use the syntax @*foo* to reference identifier *foo* with its implicit argument behavior turned off. The following proof uses Ltac features that are explained in Chapter 14.

```
Lemma split_wf : ∀ len ls, 2 ≤ length ls ≤ len
    → let (ls1, ls2) := split ls in
      lengthOrder ls1 ls ∧ lengthOrder ls2 ls.
    unfold lengthOrder; induction len; crush;
      do 2 (destruct ls; crush);
      destruct (le_lt_dec 2 (length ls));
        repeat (match goal with
                  | [ _ : length ?E < 2 ⊢ _ ] ⇒ destruct E
                  | [ _ : S (length ?E) < 2 ⊢ _ ] ⇒ destruct E
                  | [ IH : _ ⊢ context[split ?L] ] ⇒
                    specialize (IH L);
                      destruct (split L); destruct IH
                end; crush).
Defined.

Ltac split_wf := intros ls ?; intros;
  generalize (@split_wf (length ls) ls);
  destruct (split ls); destruct 1; crush.

Lemma split_wf1 : ∀ ls, 2 ≤ length ls
    → lengthOrder (fst (split ls)) ls.
    split_wf.
Defined.

Lemma split_wf2 : ∀ ls, 2 ≤ length ls
    → lengthOrder (snd (split ls)) ls.
    split_wf.
Defined.

Hint Resolve split_wf1 split_wf2.
```

To write the function definition itself, we use the `refine` tactic as a convenient way to write a program that needs to manipulate proofs, without writing out those proofs manually. We also use a replacement le_lt_dec for leb that has a more interesting dependent type. (Note that we would not be able to complete the definition without this change, since `refine` will generate subgoals for the if branches based only on the *type* of the test expression, not its *value*.)

```
Definition mergeSort : list A → list A.
  refine (Fix lengthOrder_wf (fun _ ⇒ list A)
    (fun (ls : list A)
```

```
      (mergeSort : ∀ ls' : list A, lengthOrder ls' ls → list A) ⇒
      if le_lt_dec 2 (length ls)
        then let lss := split ls in
          merge (mergeSort (fst lss) _) (mergeSort (snd lss) _)
        else ls)); subst lss; eauto.
  Defined.
End mergeSort.
```

The important thing is that it is now easy to evaluate calls to mergeSort.

```
Eval compute in mergeSort leb (1 :: 2 :: 36 :: 8 :: 19 :: nil).
  = 1 :: 2 :: 8 :: 19 :: 36 :: nil
```

Since the subject of this chapter is how to define functions with unusual recursion structure, we do not prove any further correctness theorems about mergeSort, instead proving only that mergeSort has the expected computational behavior for all inputs, not merely the one just tested.

```
Theorem mergeSort_eq : ∀ A (le : A → A → bool) ls,
    mergeSort le ls = if le_lt_dec 2 (length ls)
      then let lss := split ls in
        merge le (mergeSort le (fst lss)) (mergeSort le (snd lss))
      else ls.
  intros; apply (Fix_eq (@lengthOrder_wf A) (fun _ ⇒ list A));
    intros.
```

The library theorem Fix_eq imposes one more subgoal. We must prove that the function body is unable to distinguish between "self" arguments that map equal inputs to equal outputs. One might think this should be true of any Gallina code, but in fact this general *function extensionality* property is neither provable nor disprovable within Coq. The type of Fix_eq makes clear what we must show manually:

```
  Check Fix_eq.
```

```
Fix_eq
    : ∀ (A : Type) (R : A → A → Prop) (Rwf : well_founded R)
      (P : A → Type)
      (F : ∀ x : A, (∀ y : A, R y x → P y) → P x),
    (∀ (x : A) (f g : ∀ y : A, R y x → P y),
      (∀ (y : A) (p : R y x), f y p = g y p) → F x f = F x g) →
    ∀ x : A,
    Fix Rwf P F x
    = F x (fun (y : A) (_ : R y x) ⇒ Fix Rwf P F y)
```

Most such obligations are dischargeable with straightforward proof automation, and this example is no exception.

```
match goal with
  | [ ⊢ context[match ?E with left _ ⇒ _ | right _ ⇒ _ end] ] ⇒
    destruct E
end; simpl; f_equal; auto.
Qed.
```

As a final test of the definition's suitability, we can extract to OCaml.

Extraction mergeSort.

```
let rec mergeSort le x =
  match le_lt_dec (S (S O)) (length x) with
  | Left ->
    let lss = split x in
    merge le (mergeSort le (fst lss)) (mergeSort le (snd lss))
  | Right -> x
```

We get almost the same definition we would have written manually in OCaml. Readers could use the commands we saw in the previous chapter to clean up some remaining differences from idiomatic OCaml.

One more piece of the full picture is missing. To prove correctness of mergeSort, we would need more than a way of unfolding its definition. We also need an appropriate induction principle matched to the well-founded relation. Such a principle is available in the standard library.

Check well_founded_induction.

```
well_founded_induction
     : ∀ (A : Type) (R : A → A → Prop),
       well_founded R →
       ∀ P : A → Set,
       (∀ x : A, (∀ y : A, R y x → P y) → P x) →
       ∀ a : A, P a
```

Some recent Coq features provide more convenient syntax for defining recursive functions. Interested readers can consult the Coq manual about the commands Function and Program Fixpoint.

7.2 A Nontermination Monad Inspired by Domain Theory

The key insights of domain theory [49] inspire the next approach to modeling nontermination. Domain theory is based on *information orders* that relate values representing computation results according to how much information these values convey. For instance, a simple domain might include values "the program does not terminate" and "the program terminates with the answer 5." The former is considered to be an *approximation* of the latter, whereas the latter is *not* an approximation of "the program terminates with the answer 6." The details of domain theory are not important in what follows; we merely borrow the notion of an approximation ordering on computation results.

Consider this definition of a type of computations.

```
Section computation.
  Variable A : Type.
```

The type A describes the result a computation will yield if it terminates.

We give a rich dependent type to computations themselves.

```
Definition computation :=
  {f : nat → option A
    | ∀ (n : nat) (v : A),
      f n = Some v
      → ∀ (n' : nat), n' ≥ n
        → f n' = Some v}.
```

A computation is fundamentally a function f from an *approximation level* n to an optional result. Intuitively, higher n values enable termination in more cases than lower values. A call to f may return None to indicate that n was not high enough to run the computation to completion; higher n values may yield Some. Further, the proof obligation within the subset type asserts that f is *monotone* in an appropriate sense: when some n is sufficient to produce termination, so are all higher n values, and they all yield the same program result v.

It is easy to define a relation characterizing when a computation runs to a particular result at a particular approximation level.

```
Definition runTo (m : computation) (n : nat) (v : A) :=
  proj1_sig m n = Some v.
```

On top of runTo, we also define run, which is the most abstract notion of when a computation runs to a value.

```
Definition run (m : computation) (v : A) :=
  ∃ n, runTo m n v.
End computation.
```

The book source code contains at this point some tactics, lemma proofs, and hint commands to be used in proving facts about computations.

As a simple first example of a computation, we can define Bottom, which corresponds to an infinite loop. For any approximation level, it fails to terminate (returns None). Note the use of `abstract` to create a new opaque lemma for the proof found by the *run* tactic. In contrast to the previous section, opaque proofs are fine here, since the proof components of computations do not influence evaluation behavior. It is generally preferable to make proofs opaque when possible, as this enforces a kind of modularity in the code to follow, preventing it from depending on any details of the proof.

Section Bottom.
  Variable A : Type.

  Definition Bottom : computation A.
    exists (fun _ : **nat** $\Rightarrow$ @None A); `abstract` *run*.
  Defined.

  Theorem run_Bottom : $\forall$ v, ¬run Bottom v.
    run.
  Qed.
End Bottom.

A slightly more complicated example is Return, which gives the same terminating answer at every approximation level.

Section Return.
  Variable A : Type.
  Variable v : A.

  Definition Return : computation A.
    exists (fun _ : **nat** $\Rightarrow$ Some v); `abstract` *run*.
  Defined.

  Theorem run_Return : run Return v.
    run.
  Qed.
End Return.

The name Return was meant to suggest the standard operations of monads [44]. The other standard operation is Bind, which lets us run one computation and, if it terminates, pass its result off to another computation. We implement bind using the notation `let` $(x, y) := e1$ `in` $e2$, for pulling apart the value $e1$, which may be thought of as a pair. The second component of a computation is a proof, which we do not need to mention directly in the definition of Bind.

Section Bind.
  Variables A B : Type.

```
  Variable m1 : computation A.
  Variable m2 : A → computation B.

  Definition Bind : computation B.
    exists (fun n ⇒
      let (f1, _) := m1 in
      match f1 n with
        | None ⇒ None
        | Some v ⇒
          let (f2, _) := m2 v in
            f2 n
      end); abstract run.
  Defined.

  Theorem run_Bind : ∀ (v1 : A) (v2 : B),
    run m1 v1
    → run (m2 v1) v2
    → run Bind v2.
    run; match goal with
           | [ x : nat, y : nat ⊢ _ ] ⇒ exists (max x y)
         end; run.
  Qed.
End Bind.
```

A simple notation lets us write `Bind` calls the way they appear in Haskell.

```
Notation "x <- m1 ; m2" :=
  (Bind m1 (fun x ⇒ m2)) (right associativity, at level 70).
```

We can verify that we have indeed defined a monad, by proving the standard monad laws. Part of the exercise is choosing an appropriate notion of equality between computations. We use "equality at all approximation levels."

```
Definition meq A (m1 m2 : computation A) :=
  ∀ n, proj1_sig m1 n = proj1_sig m2 n.

Theorem left_identity : ∀ A B (a : A) (f : A → computation B),
  meq (Bind (Return a) f) (f a).
  run.
Qed.

Theorem right_identity : ∀ A (m : computation A),
  meq (Bind m (@Return _)) m.
  run.
Qed.
```

Theorem associativity : $\forall$ A B C (m : computation A)
  ($f : A \rightarrow$ computation B) ($g : B \rightarrow$ computation C),
  meq (Bind (Bind m f) g) (Bind m (fun $x \Rightarrow$ Bind (f x) g)).
  run.
Qed.

Now we come to the piece most directly inspired by domain theory. We want to support general recursive function definitions, but domain theory says that not all definitions are reasonable; some fail to be *continuous* and thus represent unrealizable computations. To formalize an analogous notion of continuity for the nontermination monad, we write down the approximation relation on computation results that we have had in mind all along.

Section lattice.
  Variable A : Type.

  Definition leq (x y : **option** A) :=
    $\forall$ v, x = Some $v \rightarrow y$ = Some v.
End lattice.

We now have the tools we need to define a new Fix combinator that, unlike the one in Section 7.1, does not require a termination proof, and in fact admits recursive definition of functions that fail to terminate on some or all inputs.

Section Fix.

First, we have the function domain and range types.

  Variables A B : Type.

Next comes the function body, which is written as though it can be parameterized over itself, for recursive calls.

  Variable $f : (A \rightarrow$ computation $B) \rightarrow (A \rightarrow$ computation B).

Finally, we impose an obligation to prove that the body f is continuous. That is, when f terminates according to one recursive version of itself, it also terminates with the same result at the same approximation level when passed a recursive version that refines the original, according to leq.

  Hypothesis $f\_continuous$: $\forall$ n v $v1$ x,
    runTo (f $v1$ x) n v
    $\rightarrow$ $\forall$ ($v2 : A \rightarrow$ computation B),
      ($\forall$ x, leq (proj1_sig ($v1$ x) n) (proj1_sig ($v2$ x) n))
      $\rightarrow$ runTo (f $v2$ x) n v.

The computational part of the `Fix` combinator is easy to define. At approximation level 0, we diverge; at higher levels, we run the body with a functional argument drawn from the next lower level.

```
Fixpoint Fix' (n : nat) (x : A) : computation B :=
  match n with
    | O ⇒ Bottom _
    | S n' ⇒ f (Fix' n') x
  end.
```

Now it is straightforward to package `Fix'` as a computation combinator `Fix`.

```
Hint Extern 1 (_ ≥ _) ⇒ omega.
Hint Unfold leq.

Lemma Fix'_ok : ∀ steps n x v, proj1_sig (Fix' n x) steps = Some v
  → ∀ n', n' ≥ n
    → proj1_sig (Fix' n' x) steps = Some v.
  unfold runTo in *; induction n; crush;
    match goal with
      | [ H : _ ≥ _ ⊢ _ ] ⇒ inversion H; crush; eauto
    end.
Qed.

Hint Resolve Fix'_ok.

Hint Extern 1 (proj1_sig _ _ = _) ⇒ simpl;
  match goal with
    | [ ⊢ proj1_sig ?E _ = _ ] ⇒ eapply (proj2_sig E)
  end.

Definition Fix : A → computation B.
  intro x; exists (fun n ⇒ proj1_sig (Fix' n x) n); abstract run.
Defined.
```

Finally, we can prove that `Fix` obeys the expected computation rule.

```
Theorem run_Fix : ∀ x v,
  run (f Fix x) v
  → run (Fix x) v.
  run; match goal with
         | [ n : nat ⊢ _ ] ⇒ exists (S n); eauto
       end.
Qed.
End Fix.
```

After all that work, it is now fairly painless to define a version of mergeSort that requires no proof of termination. We appeal to a program-specific tactic (its definition is in the book source code).

Definition mergeSort' : ∀ A, (A → A → **bool**) → **list** A
  → computation (**list** A).
  refine (fun A le ⇒ Fix
    (fun ($mergeSort$: **list** A → computation (**list** A))
      (ls : **list** A) ⇒
      if le_lt_dec 2 (length ls)
        then let lss := split ls in
          $ls1$ ← $mergeSort$ (fst lss);
          $ls2$ ← $mergeSort$ (snd lss);
          Return (merge le $ls1$ $ls2$)
        else Return ls) _); abstract $mergeSort'$.
Defined.

Running mergeSort' on concrete inputs is as easy as choosing a sufficiently high approximation level and letting Coq's computation rules do the rest. Contrast this with the proof work that goes into deriving an evaluation fact for a deeply embedded language, with one explicit proof rule application per execution step.

Lemma test_mergeSort' : run (mergeSort' leb
  (1 :: 2 :: 36 :: 8 :: 19 :: nil))
  (1 :: 2 :: 8 :: 19 :: 36 :: nil).
  exists 4; reflexivity.
Qed.

There is another benefit of the new Fix compared with the one in Section 7.1: we can now write recursive functions that sometimes fail to terminate without losing easy reasoning principles for the terminating cases. Consider this simple example (which appeals to another tactic whose definition we elide here).

Definition looper : **bool** → computation **unit**.
  refine (Fix (fun $looper$ (b : **bool**) ⇒
    if b then Return tt else $looper$ b) _); abstract $looper$.
Defined.

Lemma test_looper : run (looper true) tt.
  exists 1; reflexivity.
Qed.

As before, proving outputs for specific inputs is as easy as demonstrating a high enough approximation level.

There are other theorems that are important to prove about combinators like Return, Bind, and Fix. In general, for a computation c, we sometimes have a hypothesis proving run c v for some v, and we want to perform inversion to deduce what v must be. Each combinator should ideally have a theorem of that kind, for c built directly from that combinator. Such theorems are omitted here, but they are not hard to prove. In general, the approach inspired by domain theory avoids the type-theoretic problems in approaches that try to mix normal Coq computation with explicit syntax types.

The next section of this chapter demonstrates two alternative approaches of that sort. The final section reviews the pros and cons of the different choices, concluding that none is better than any other for all situations.

7.3 Co-inductive Nontermination Monads

There are two key downsides to both of the previous approaches: both require unusual syntax based on explicit calls to fixpoint combinators, and both generate immediate proof obligations about the bodies of recursive definitions. Chapter 5 showed how co-inductive types support recursive definitions that exhibit certain well-behaved varieties of nontermination. We can leverage that co-induction support for encoding of general recursive definitions, by adding layers of co-inductive syntax. In effect, we mix elements of shallow and deep embeddings.

Our first example of this kind, proposed by Capretta [4], defines a type of thunks; that is, computations that may be forced to yield results if they terminate.

```
CoInductive thunk (A : Type) : Type :=
| Answer : A → thunk A
| Think : thunk A → thunk A.
```

A computation is either an immediate Answer or another computation wrapped inside Think. Since **thunk** is co-inductive, every **thunk** type is inhabited by an infinite nesting of Thinks, standing for nontermination. Terminating results are Answer wrapped inside some finite number of Thinks.

Why bother to write such an odd definition? The definition of **thunk** is motivated by the ability it gives to define a bind operation similar to the one defined in Section 7.2.

```
CoFixpoint TBind A B (m1 : thunk A) (m2 : A → thunk B)
  : thunk B :=
```

```
match m1 with
  | Answer x ⇒ m2 x
  | Think m1' ⇒ Think (TBind m1' m2)
end.
```

Note that the definition would violate the co-recursion guardedness restriction if we left out the seemingly superfluous Think on the right side of the second `match` branch.

We can prove that Answer and TBind form a monad for **thunk** (the proof is in the book source code). As usual for this sort of proof, a key element is choosing an appropriate notion of equality for **thunk**s.

In the following proofs, we need a function similar to one in Chapter 5, to pull apart and reassemble a **thunk** in a way that provokes reduction of co-recursive calls.

```
Definition frob A (m : thunk A) : thunk A :=
  match m with
    | Answer x ⇒ Answer x
    | Think m' ⇒ Think m'
  end.
Theorem frob_eq : ∀ A (m : thunk A), frob m = m.
  destruct m; reflexivity.
Qed.
```

As a simple example, here is how we might define a tail-recursive factorial function:

```
CoFixpoint fact (n acc : nat) : thunk nat :=
  match n with
    | O ⇒ Answer acc
    | S n' ⇒ Think (fact n' (S n' × acc))
  end.
```

To test the definition, we need an evaluation relation that characterizes results of evaluating **thunk**s.

```
Inductive eval A : thunk A → A → Prop :=
| EvalAnswer : ∀ x, eval (Answer x) x
| EvalThink : ∀ m x, eval m x → eval (Think m) x.

Hint Rewrite frob_eq.

Lemma eval_frob : ∀ A (c : thunk A) x,
  eval (frob c) x
  → eval c x.
  crush.
```

```
Qed.
```

```
Theorem eval_fact : eval (fact 5 1) 120.
  repeat (apply eval_frob; simpl; constructor).
Qed.
```

We need to apply constructors of `eval` explicitly, but the process is easy to automate completely for concrete input programs.

Now consider another very similar definition, this time of a Fibonacci number function.

```
Notation "x <- m1 ; m2" :=
  (TBind m1 (fun x ⇒ m2)) (right associativity, at level 70).
```

```
CoFixpoint fib (n : nat) : thunk nat :=
  match n with
    | 0 ⇒ Answer 1
    | 1 ⇒ Answer 1
    | _ ⇒ n1 ← fib (pred n);
      n2 ← fib (pred (pred n));
      Answer (n1 + n2)
  end.
```

Coq complains that the guardedness condition is violated. The two recursive calls are immediate arguments to TBind, but TBind is not a constructor of **thunk**. Rather, it is a defined function. This example shows a very serious limitation of **thunk** for traditional functional programming: it is not, in general, possible to make recursive calls and then make further recursive calls, depending on the first call's result. The fact example succeeded because it was already tail-recursive, meaning no further computation is needed after a recursive call.

I know no easy fix for this problem of **thunk**, but we can define a different co-inductive monad that avoids the problem, based on a proposal by Megacz [24]. We ran into trouble because TBind was not a constructor of **thunk**, so let us define a new type family where "bind" is a constructor.

```
CoInductive comp (A : Type) : Type :=
| Ret : A → comp A
| Bnd : ∀ B, comp B → (B → comp A) → comp A.
```

This example shows off Coq's support for *recursively nonuniform parameters*, as in the case of the parameter A, where each constructor's type ends in **comp** A but there is a recursive use of **comp** with a different parameter B. Beside that technical wrinkle, we see the simplest possible definition of a monad, via a type whose two constructors are precisely the monad operators.

It is easy to define the semantics of terminating **comp** computations.

```
Inductive exec A : comp A → A → Prop :=
| ExecRet : ∀ x, exec (Ret x) x
| ExecBnd : ∀ B (c : comp B) (f : B → comp A) x1 x2,
  exec (A := B) c x1
  → exec (f x1) x2
  → exec (Bnd c f) x2.
```

We can also prove that Ret and Bnd form a monad according to a notion of **comp** equality based on **exec** (the proof is in the book source code).

Not only can we define the Fibonacci function with the new monad but even the running example of merge sort becomes definable. By shadowing the previous notation for "bind," we can write almost exactly the same code as in the previous mergeSort' definition, but with less syntactic clutter.

```
Notation "x <- m1 ; m2" := (Bnd m1 (fun x ⇒ m2)).
```

```
CoFixpoint mergeSort'' A (le : A → A → bool) (ls : list A)
  : comp (list A) :=
  if le_lt_dec 2 (length ls)
    then let lss := split ls in
      ls1 ← mergeSort'' le (fst lss);
      ls2 ← mergeSort'' le (snd lss);
      Ret (merge le ls1 ls2)
    else Ret ls.
```

To execute this function, we go through the usual exercise of writing a function to catalyze evaluation of co-recursive calls.

```
Definition frob' A (c : comp A) :=
  match c with
    | Ret x ⇒ Ret x
    | Bnd _ c' f ⇒ Bnd c' f
  end.
```

```
Lemma exec_frob : ∀ A (c : comp A) x,
  exec (frob' c) x
  → exec c x.
  destruct c; crush.
Qed.
```

Now the same sort of proof script that we applied for testing **thunk** will get the job done.

Lemma test_mergeSort″ : **exec** (mergeSort″ leb
  $(1 :: 2 :: 36 :: 8 :: 19 :: nil))$
  $(1 :: 2 :: 8 :: 19 :: 36 :: nil)$.
  repeat (apply exec_frob; simpl; econstructor).
Qed.

Have we finally reached the ideal solution for encoding general recursive definitions, with minimal hassle in syntax and proof obligations? Unfortunately, we have not, as **comp** has a serious expressivity weakness. Consider the following definition of a curried addition function.

Definition curriedAdd $(n : \textbf{nat})$:= Ret (fun $m : \textbf{nat} \Rightarrow$ Ret $(n + m))$.

This definition works fine, but we run into trouble when we try to apply it in a trivial way.

Definition testCurriedAdd := Bnd (curriedAdd 2) (fun $f \Rightarrow f$ 3).

Error: Universe inconsistency.

The problem has to do with rules for inductive definitions (see Chapter 12). Briefly, recall that the type of the constructor Bnd quantifies over a type B. To make testCurriedAdd work, we would need to instantiate B as **nat** $\rightarrow$ **comp nat**. However, Coq enforces a *predicativity restriction* that (roughly) no quantifier in an inductive or co-inductive type's definition may ever be instantiated with a term that contains the type being defined. Chapter 12 presents the exact mechanism by which this restriction is enforced, but for now our conclusion is that **comp** is fatally flawed as a way of encoding higher-order functional programs that use general recursion.

7.4 Comparing the Alternatives

We have seen four different approaches to encoding general recursive definitions in Coq. Among them there is no clear champion that dominates the others in every important way. Instead, we close the chapter by comparing the techniques along a number of dimensions. Every technique allows recursive definitions with termination arguments that go beyond Coq's built-in termination checking, so we must turn to subtler points to highlight differences.

One useful property is automatic integration with normal Coq programming. That is, we would like the type of a function to be the same, whether or not that function is defined using an interesting recursion pattern. Only the first of the four techniques, well-founded recursion, meets this criterion. It is also the only one of the four to meet the related criterion that evaluation of function calls can take place entirely inside Coq's built-in computation machinery. The monad inspired by domain theory occupies some middle ground in this dimension, since generally standard computation is enough to evaluate a term once a high enough approximation level is provided.

Another useful property is that a function and its termination argument may be developed separately. We may even want to define functions that fail to terminate on some or all inputs. The well-founded recursion technique does not have this property, but the other three do.

One minor plus is the ability to write recursive definitions in natural syntax rather than with calls to higher-order combinators. This downside of the first two techniques is actually easy to get around using Coq's notation mechanism, though I leave the details as an exercise for the reader. (For this and other details of notations, see Chapter 12 of the Coq 8.4 manual.)

The first two techniques impose proof obligations that are more basic than termination arguments, where well-founded recursion requires a proof of extensionality and domain-theoretic recursion requires a proof of continuity. A function may not be defined, and thus may not be computed with, until these obligations are proved. The co-inductive techniques avoid this problem, as recursive definitions may be made without any proof obligations.

We can also consider support for common idioms in functional programming. For instance, the **thunk** monad effectively only supports recursion that is tail recursion, whereas the others allow arbitrary recursion schemes.

On the other hand, the **comp** monad does not support the effective mixing of higher-order functions and general recursion, whereas all the other techniques do. For instance, we can finish the failed curriedAdd example in the domain-theoretic monad.

```
Definition curriedAdd' (n : nat) :=
  Return (fun m : nat ⇒ Return (n + m)).

Definition testCurriedAdd := Bind (curriedAdd' 2) (fun f ⇒ f 3).
```

The same techniques also apply to more interesting higher-order functions like list map, and as in all four techniques, we can mix primitive and general recursion, preferring the former when possible to avoid proof obligations.

Fixpoint map A B $(f : A \rightarrow$ computation $B)$ $(ls :$ **list** $A)$
  : computation (**list** B) :=
  match ls with
    | nil $\Rightarrow$ Return nil
    | x :: ls' $\Rightarrow$ Bind $(f$ $x)$ (fun x' $\Rightarrow$
      Bind (map f ls') (fun ls'' $\Rightarrow$
        Return $(x'$ :: $ls'')))$
  end.

Theorem test_map : run (map (fun x $\Rightarrow$ Return (S x))
  $(1$ :: 2 :: 3 :: nil))
  $(2$ :: 3 :: 4 :: nil).
  exists 1; reflexivity.
Qed.

One further disadvantage of **comp** is that we cannot prove an inversion lemma for executions of Bind without appealing to an axiom (see Chapter 12). The other three techniques allow proof of all the important theorems within the normal logic of Coq.

Perhaps one theme of this comparison is that one must trade off between, on one hand, functional programming expressiveness and compatibility with normal Coq types and computation; and, on the other hand, the level of proof obligations one is willing to handle at function definition time.

8   More Dependent Types

Subset types and their relatives help us integrate verification with programming. Though they reorganize the programmer's work flow, they tend not to have deep effects on proofs. We write largely the same proofs as we would for classical verification, with some of the structure moved into the programs themselves. It turns out that when we use dependent types to their full potential, we warp the development and proving process even more, picking up "free theorems" to the extent that often a certified program is hardly more complex than its uncertified counterpart in Haskell or ML.

In particular, we have only scratched the surface of Coq's inductive definition mechanism. The inductive types we have seen so far have their counterparts in the other proof assistants that we surveyed in Chapter 1. This chapter explores the world of dependent inductive datatypes outside `Prop`, a possibility that sets Coq apart from all of the competition not based on type theory.

8.1   Length-Indexed Lists

Many introductions to dependent types start out by showing how to use them to eliminate array bounds checks. When the type of an array reveals how many elements it has, the compiler can detect out-of-bounds dereferences statically. Since we are working in a pure functional language, the next best thing is length-indexed lists, which the following code defines.

```
Section ilist.
  Variable A : Set.

  Inductive ilist : nat → Set :=
  | Nil : ilist O
  | Cons : ∀ n, A → ilist n → ilist (S n).
```

We see that, within its section, **ilist** is given type **nat** → **Set**. Previously, every inductive type had either plain **Set** as its type or was a predicate with some type ending in **Prop**. The full generality of inductive definitions lets us integrate the expressivity of predicates directly into normal programming.

The **nat** argument to **ilist** tells us the length of the list. The types of **ilist**'s constructors tell us that a Nil list has length O and that a Cons list has length one greater than the length of its tail. We may apply **ilist** to any natural number, even natural numbers that are only known at run-time. It is this breaking of the *phase distinction* that characterizes **ilist** as dependently typed.

In expositions of list types, we usually see the length function defined first, but here that would not be a very productive function to code. Instead, let us implement list concatenation.

```
Fixpoint app n1 (ls1 : ilist n1) n2 (ls2 : ilist n2)
  : ilist (n1 + n2) :=
  match ls1 with
    | Nil ⇒ ls2
    | Cons _ x ls1' ⇒ Cons x (app ls1' ls2)
  end.
```

Past Coq versions signaled an error for this definition. The code is still invalid within Coq's core language, but current Coq versions automatically add annotations to the original program, producing a valid core program. These are the annotations on **match** discriminees introduced in Chapter 6. We can rewrite **app** to give the annotations explicitly.

```
Fixpoint app' n1 (ls1 : ilist n1) n2 (ls2 : ilist n2)
  : ilist (n1 + n2) :=
  match ls1 in (ilist n1) return (ilist (n1 + n2)) with
    | Nil ⇒ ls2
    | Cons _ x ls1' ⇒ Cons x (app' ls1' ls2)
  end.
```

Using **return** alone allowed us to express a dependency of the **match** result type on the *value* of the discriminee. What **in** adds is a way of expressing a dependency on the *type* of the discriminee. Specifically, the *n1* in the **in** clause is a *binding occurrence* whose scope is the **return** clause.

We may use **in** clauses only to bind names for the arguments of an inductive type family. That is, each **in** clause must be an inductive type family name applied to a sequence of underscores and variable names of the proper length. The positions for *parameters* to the type family must all be underscores. Parameters are those arguments declared with section variables or with entries to the left of the first colon in an inductive definition. They cannot vary depending on which constructor was used to build the discriminee, so Coq prohibits pointless matches on them. It is those arguments defined in the type to the right of the colon that we may name with **in** clauses.

Our **app** function could be typed in *stratified* type systems, which avoid true dependency. That is, we could consider the length indices to lists to live in a separate, compile-time-only universe from the lists themselves. Compile-time data may be *erased* such that we can still execute a program. As an example where erasure would not work, consider an injection function from regular lists to length-indexed lists. Here the run-time computation actually depends on details of the compile-time argument, if we decide that the list to inject can be considered compile-time. More commonly, we think of lists as run-time data. Neither case will work with naïve erasure. (It is not too important to grasp the details of this run-time/compile-time distinction, since Coq's expressive power comes from avoiding such restrictions.)

```
Fixpoint inject (ls : list A) : ilist (length ls) :=
  match ls with
    | nil ⇒ Nil
    | h :: t ⇒ Cons h (inject t)
  end.
```

We can define an inverse conversion and prove that it really is an inverse.

```
Fixpoint unject n (ls : ilist n) : list A :=
  match ls with
    | Nil ⇒ nil
    | Cons _ h t ⇒ h :: unject t
  end.

Theorem inject_inverse : ∀ ls, unject (inject ls) = ls.
  induction ls; crush.
Qed.
```

Now let us attempt a function that is surprisingly tricky to write. In ML, the list head function raises an exception when passed an empty list. With length-indexed lists, we can rule out such invalid calls statically. Here is a first attempt. We write ??? as a placeholder for a term that we do not know how to write, not for any real Coq notation.

```
Definition hd n (ls : ilist (S n)) : A :=
```

```
match ls with
  | Nil ⇒ ???
  | Cons _ h _ ⇒ h
end.
```

It is not clear what to write for the Nil case, so we are stuck before we even turn the function over to the type checker. We could try omitting the Nil case.

```
Definition hd n (ls : ilist (S n)) : A :=
  match ls with
    | Cons _ h _ ⇒ h
  end.
```

`Error: Non exhaustive pattern-matching: no clause found for pattern Nil`

Unlike in ML, we cannot use inexhaustive pattern matching, because there is no conception of a `Match` exception to be thrown. In fact, recent versions of Coq *do* allow this, by implicit translation to a `match` that considers all constructors; the error message was generated by an older Coq version. It is educational to discover the encoding that the most recent Coq versions use. We might try using an **in** clause.

```
Definition hd n (ls : ilist (S n)) : A :=
  match ls in (ilist (S n)) with
    | Cons _ h _ ⇒ h
  end.
```

`Error: The reference n was not found in the current environment`

In this and other cases, we want **in** clauses with type family arguments that are not variables. Unfortunately, Coq only supports variables in those positions. A completely general mechanism could only be supported with a solution to the problem of higher-order unification [15], which is undecidable. There *are* useful heuristics for handling nonvariable indices that are gradually making their way into Coq, but we will use only the primitive `match` annotations in this and the next few chapters on effective pattern matching on dependent types.

The final working attempt at hd uses an auxiliary function and a surprising `return` annotation.

```
Definition hd' n (ls : ilist n) :=
  match ls in (ilist n)
```

```
      return (match n with O ⇒ unit | S _ ⇒ A end) with
      | Nil ⇒ tt
      | Cons _ h _ ⇒ h
   end.
```

   Check hd'.

hd'

   : ∀ n : **nat**, **ilist** n → match n with
                                | 0 ⇒ **unit**
                                | S _ ⇒ A
                                end

   Definition hd n (ls : **ilist** (S n)) : A := hd' ls.

End ilist.

We annotate the main `match` with a type that is itself a `match`. We write that the function hd' returns **unit** when the list is empty and returns the carried type A in all other cases. In the definition of hd, we just call hd'. Because the index of *ls* is known to be nonzero, the type checker reduces the `match` in the type of hd' to A.

8.2   The One Rule of Dependent Pattern Matching in Coq

The rest of this chapter demonstrates a few other elegant applications of dependent types in Coq. Readers encountering such ideas for the first time often feel overwhelmed, concluding that there is some magic at work whereby Coq sometimes solves the halting problem for the programmer and sometimes does not, applying automated program understanding in a way far beyond what is found in conventional languages. The point of this section is to preempt that sort of thinking. Dependent type checking in Coq follows just a few algorithmic rules. Chapters 10 and 12 introduce many of those rules more formally, and the main additional rule is centered on dependent pattern matching of the kind discussed in Section 8.1.

A dependent pattern match is a `match` expression where the type of the overall `match` is a function of the value and/or the type of the *discriminee*, the value being matched on. In other words, the `match` type *depends* on the discriminee.

When exactly will Coq accept a dependent pattern match as well-typed? Some other dependently typed languages employ elaborate decision procedures to determine when programs satisfy their very expressive types. The situation in Coq is just the opposite. Only very straightforward symbolic rules are applied. Such a design choice has its drawbacks, as it forces programmers to do more work to convince the type checker of program validity. However, the great advantage of a simple type-checking algorithm is that its action on *invalid* programs is easier to understand.

We come now to the one rule of dependent pattern matching in Coq. A general dependent pattern match assumes this form (with unnecessary parentheses included to make the syntax easier to parse):

```
match E as y in (T x1 ... xn) return U with
  | C z1 ... zm ⇒ B
  | ...
end
```

The discriminee is a term E, a value in some inductive type family T, which takes n arguments. An `as` clause binds the name y to refer to the discriminee E. An `in` clause binds an explicit name xi for the ith argument passed to T in the type of E.

We bind these new variables y and xi so that they may be referred to in U, a type given in the `return` clause. The overall type of the `match` will be U, with E substituted for y, and with each xi substituted by the actual argument appearing in that position within E's type.

In general, each case of a `match` may have a pattern built up in several layers from the constructors of various inductive type families. To keep this exposition simple, we focus on patterns that are just single applications of inductive type constructors to lists of variables. Coq actually compiles the more general kind of pattern matching into this more restricted kind automatically, so understanding the typing of `match` requires understanding the typing of `match`es lowered to match one constructor at a time.

The last piece of the typing rule tells how to type-check a `match` case. A generic constructor application $C\ z1\ ...\ zm$ has some type $T\ x1'\ ...$ xn', an application of the type family used in E's type, probably with occurrences of the zi variables. From here, a simple recipe determines what type is required for the case body B. The type of B should be U with the following two substitutions applied: replace y (the `as` clause variable) with $C\ z1\ ...\ zm$, and replace each xi (the `in` clause variables) with xi'. In other words, we specialize the result type based on what we learn based on which pattern has matched the discriminee.

This is an exhaustive description of the ways to specify how to take advantage of which pattern has matched. No other mechanisms come into play. For instance, there is no way to specify that the types of certain free variables should be refined based on which pattern has matched. Later chapters present design patterns for achieving similar effects, where each technique leads to an encoding only in terms of in, as, and return clauses.

A few details have been omitted here. Chapter 3 showed that inductive type families may have both parameters and regular arguments. Within an in clause, a parameter position must have the wildcard _ written instead of a variable. (In general, Coq uses the wildcard _ either to indicate pattern variables that will not be mentioned again or to indicate positions where we would like type inference to infer the appropriate terms.) Recent Coq versions are adding more and more heuristics to infer dependent match annotations in certain conditions. The general annotation inference problem is undecidable, so there will always be serious limitations on how much work these heuristics can do. When in doubt about why a particular dependent match is failing to type-check, add an explicit return annotation. At that point, the mechanical rule sketched in this section will provide a complete account of "what the type checker is thinking." Be sure to avoid the common pitfall of writing a return annotation that does not mention any variables bound by in or as; such a match will never refine typing requirements based on which pattern has matched. (One simple exception to this rule, when the discriminee is a variable, is that the same variable may be treated as if it were repeated as an as clause.)

8.3 A Tagless Interpreter

A favorite example for motivating the power of functional programming is implementation of a simple expression language interpreter. In ML and Haskell, such interpreters are often implemented using an algebraic datatype of values, where at many points it is checked that a value was built with the right constructor of the value type. With dependent types, we can implement a *tagless* interpreter that both removes this source of run-time inefficiency and gives more confidence that the implementation is correct.

```
Inductive type : Set :=
| Nat : type
| Bool : type
| Prod : type → type → type.

Inductive exp : type → Set :=
| NConst : nat → exp Nat
| Plus : exp Nat → exp Nat → exp Nat
```

| Eq : **exp** Nat → **exp** Nat → **exp** Bool

| BConst : **bool** → **exp** Bool
| And : **exp** Bool → **exp** Bool → **exp** Bool
| If : ∀ t, **exp** Bool → **exp** t → **exp** t → **exp** t

| Pair : ∀ $t1$ $t2$, **exp** $t1$ → **exp** $t2$ → **exp** (Prod $t1$ $t2$)
| Fst : ∀ $t1$ $t2$, **exp** (Prod $t1$ $t2$) → **exp** $t1$
| Snd : ∀ $t1$ $t2$, **exp** (Prod $t1$ $t2$) → **exp** $t2$.

We have a standard algebraic datatype **type**, defining a type language of naturals, Booleans, and product (pair) types. Then we have the indexed inductive type **exp**, where the argument to **exp** reveals the encoded type of an expression. In effect, we are defining the typing rules for expressions simultaneously with the syntax.

We can give types and expressions semantics in a new style, based critically on the chance for *type-level computation*.

```
Fixpoint typeDenote (t : type) : Set :=
  match t with
    | Nat ⇒ nat
    | Bool ⇒ bool
    | Prod t1 t2 ⇒ typeDenote t1 × typeDenote t2
  end%type.
```

The typeDenote function compiles types of the object language into native Coq types. It is deceptively easy to implement. The only new thing is the %*type* annotation, which tells Coq to parse the match expression using the notations associated with types. Without this annotation, the × would be interpreted as multiplication on naturals rather than as the product type constructor. The token *type* is one example of an identifier bound to a *notation scope delimiter* (see the Coq manual).

We can define a function expDenote that is typed in terms of typeDenote.

```
Fixpoint expDenote t (e : exp t) : typeDenote t :=
  match e with
    | NConst n ⇒ n
    | Plus e1 e2 ⇒ expDenote e1 + expDenote e2
    | Eq e1 e2 ⇒
      if eq_nat_dec (expDenote e1) (expDenote e2)
        then true else false
```

```
  | BConst b ⇒ b
  | And e1 e2 ⇒ expDenote e1 && expDenote e2
  | If _ e' e1 e2 ⇒
    if expDenote e' then expDenote e1 else expDenote e2

  | Pair _ _ e1 e2 ⇒ (expDenote e1 , expDenote e2)
  | Fst _ _ e' ⇒ fst (expDenote e')
  | Snd _ _ e' ⇒ snd (expDenote e')
end.
```

The function definition is routine. In fact, it is less complicated than what we would write in ML or Haskell 98, since we do not need to worry about pushing final values in and out of an algebraic datatype. The only unusual thing is the use of an expression of the form if E then true else false in the Eq case. Remember that eq_nat_dec has a rich dependent type rather than a simple Boolean type. Coq's native if is overloaded to work on a test of any two-constructor type, so we can use if to build a simple Boolean from the **sumbool** that eq_nat_dec returns.

We can implement a constant folding function and prove it correct. It will be useful to write a function pairOut that checks if an **exp** of Prod type is a pair, returning its two components if so. Unsurprisingly, a first attempt leads to a type error.

```
Definition pairOut t1 t2 (e : exp (Prod t1 t2))
  : option (exp t1 × exp t2) :=
  match e in (exp (Prod t1 t2)) return option (exp t1 × exp t2) with
    | Pair _ _ e1 e2 ⇒ Some (e1, e2)
    | _ ⇒ None
  end.
```

```
Error: The reference t2 was not found in the current
environment
```

We run again into the problem of not being able to specify nonvariable arguments in in clauses. The problem would be unsolvable without the use of an in clause, since the result type of the match depends on an argument to **exp**. The solution is to use a more general type, as we did for hd. First, we define a type-valued function to use in assigning a type to pairOut.

```
Definition pairOutType (t : type) :=
  option (match t with
            | Prod t1 t2 ⇒ exp t1 × exp t2
```

```
      | _ ⇒ unit
   end).
```

When passed a type that is a product, pairOutType returns the final desired type. On any other input type, pairOutType returns the harmless **option unit**, since we do not care about extracting components of nonpairs. Now pairOut is easy to write.

```
Definition pairOut t (e : exp t) :=
  match e in (exp t) return (pairOutType t) with
    | Pair _ _ e1 e2 ⇒ Some (e1 , e2)
    | _ ⇒ None
  end.
```

With pairOut available, we can write cfold in a straightforward way. There are really no surprises beyond that Coq verifies that this code has such an expressive type, given the small annotation burden. In some places, we see that Coq's `match` annotation inference is too smart for its own good, and we have to turn that inference off with explicit `return` clauses.

```
Fixpoint cfold t (e : exp t) : exp t :=
  match e with
    | NConst n ⇒ NConst n
    | Plus e1 e2 ⇒
      let e1' := cfold e1 in
      let e2' := cfold e2 in
      match e1', e2' return exp Nat with
        | NConst n1, NConst n2 ⇒ NConst (n1 + n2)
        | _, _ ⇒ Plus e1' e2'
      end
    | Eq e1 e2 ⇒
      let e1' := cfold e1 in
      let e2' := cfold e2 in
      match e1', e2' return exp Bool with
        | NConst n1, NConst n2 ⇒
          BConst (if eq_nat_dec n1 n2 then true else false)
        | _, _ ⇒ Eq e1' e2'
      end

    | BConst b ⇒ BConst b
    | And e1 e2 ⇒
      let e1' := cfold e1 in
      let e2' := cfold e2 in
```

```
      match e1', e2' return exp Bool with
        | BConst b1, BConst b2 ⇒ BConst (b1 && b2)
        | _, _ ⇒ And e1' e2'
      end
  | If _ e e1 e2 ⇒
    let e' := cfold e in
    match e' with
      | BConst true ⇒ cfold e1
      | BConst false ⇒ cfold e2
      | _ ⇒ If e' (cfold e1) (cfold e2)
    end

  | Pair _ _ e1 e2 ⇒ Pair (cfold e1) (cfold e2)
  | Fst _ _ e ⇒
    let e' := cfold e in
    match pairOut e' with
      | Some p ⇒ fst p
      | None ⇒ Fst e'
    end
  | Snd _ _ e ⇒
    let e' := cfold e in
    match pairOut e' with
      | Some p ⇒ snd p
      | None ⇒ Snd e'
    end
end.
```

The correctness theorem for cfold turns out to be easy to prove, once we get over one serious hurdle.

```
Theorem cfold_correct : ∀ t (e : exp t),
  expDenote e = expDenote (cfold e).
  induction e; crush.
```

The first remaining subgoal is

```
expDenote (cfold e1) + expDenote (cfold e2) =
  expDenote
    match cfold e1 with
    | NConst n1 ⇒
        match cfold e2 with
        | NConst n2 ⇒ NConst (n1 + n2)
        | Plus _ _ ⇒ Plus (cfold e1) (cfold e2)
```

```
      | Eq _ _ ⇒ Plus (cfold e1 ) (cfold e2 )
      | BConst _ ⇒ Plus (cfold e1 ) (cfold e2 )
      | And _ _ ⇒ Plus (cfold e1 ) (cfold e2 )
      | If _ _ _ _ ⇒ Plus (cfold e1 ) (cfold e2 )
      | Pair _ _ _ _ ⇒ Plus (cfold e1 ) (cfold e2 )
      | Fst _ _ _ ⇒ Plus (cfold e1 ) (cfold e2 )
      | Snd _ _ _ ⇒ Plus (cfold e1 ) (cfold e2 )
      end
  | Plus _ _ ⇒ Plus (cfold e1 ) (cfold e2 )
  | Eq _ _ ⇒ Plus (cfold e1 ) (cfold e2 )
  | BConst _ ⇒ Plus (cfold e1 ) (cfold e2 )
  | And _ _ ⇒ Plus (cfold e1 ) (cfold e2 )
  | If _ _ _ _ ⇒ Plus (cfold e1 ) (cfold e2 )
  | Pair _ _ _ _ ⇒ Plus (cfold e1 ) (cfold e2 )
  | Fst _ _ _ ⇒ Plus (cfold e1 ) (cfold e2 )
  | Snd _ _ _ ⇒ Plus (cfold e1 ) (cfold e2 )
  end
```

We would like to do a case analysis on cfold $e1$, and we attempt to do so in the way that has worked so far.

```
   destruct (cfold e1 ).
```

```
User error: e1 is used in hypothesis e
```

Coq gives us another cryptic error message. Like so many others, this one basically means that Coq is not able to build some proof about dependent types. It is hard to generate helpful and specific error messages for problems like this, since that would require some kind of understanding of the dependency structure of a piece of code. We will encounter many examples of case-specific tricks for recovering from errors like this one.

For the current proof, we can use a tactic *dep_destruct* defined in the CpdtTactics module from the source code to this book. General elimination/inversion of dependently typed hypotheses is undecidable, as shown by a simple reduction from the known-undecidable problem of higher-order unification, which has come up a few times already. The tactic *dep_destruct* makes a best effort to handle some common cases, relying upon the more primitive dependent destruction tactic that comes with Coq. Chapter 10 discusses the explicit manipulation of equality proofs that is behind dependent destruction's implementation, but for now we treat it as a useful black box. (Chapter 12 shows how `dependent destruction` forces us to make a larger philosophical commitment about our logic than we might like and gives some work-arounds.)

    dep_destruct (cfold *e1*).

This successfully breaks the subgoal into five new subgoals, one for each constructor of **exp** that could produce an **exp** Nat. Note that *dep_destruct* is successful in ruling out the other cases automatically, in effect automating some of the work that we did manually in implementing functions like hd and pairOut.

This is the only new technique we need to learn to complete the proof. A short automated proof uses Ltac features that are explained in Chapter 14.

    `Restart`.

    `induction` *e*; *crush*;
      `repeat (match goal with`
                    `| [ ⊢ context[match cfold ?E with NConst _ ⇒ _`
                                   `| _ ⇒ _ end] ] ⇒`
             dep_destruct (cfold *E*)
          `| [ ⊢ context[match pairOut (cfold ?E) with`
                        `Some _ ⇒ _ | None ⇒ _ end] ] ⇒`
             dep_destruct (cfold *E*)
          `| [ ⊢ (if ?E then _ else _) = _ ] ⇒ destruct` *E*
        `end;` *crush*).

`Qed`.

With this example, we get a first taste of how to build automated proofs that adapt automatically to changes in function definitions.

8.4 Dependently Typed Red-Black Trees

Red-black trees are a favorite purely functional data structure with an interesting invariant. We can use dependent types to guarantee that operations on red-black trees preserve the invariant. For simplicity, we specialize the red-black trees to represent sets of **nat**s.

`Inductive` **color** : **Set** := Red | Black.

`Inductive` **rbtree** : **color** → **nat** → **Set** :=
| Leaf : **rbtree** Black 0
| RedNode : ∀ *n*, **rbtree** Black *n* → **nat** → **rbtree** Black *n*
   → **rbtree** Red *n*
| BlackNode : ∀ *c1 c2 n*, **rbtree** *c1 n* → **nat** → **rbtree** *c2 n*

$\rightarrow$ **rbtree** Black (S n).

A value of type **rbtree** c d is a red-black tree with root of color c and a black depth d. The latter property means that there are exactly d black-colored nodes on any path from the root to a leaf.

At first, it can be unclear that this choice of type indices tracks any useful property, so we prove that every red-black tree is balanced. We phrase the theorem in terms of a depth-calculating function that ignores the extra information in the types. It is useful to parameterize this function over a combining operation so that we can reuse the same code to calculate the minimum or maximum height among all paths from root to leaf.

```
Require Import Max Min.

Section depth.
  Variable f : nat → nat → nat.

  Fixpoint depth c n (t : rbtree c n) : nat :=
    match t with
      | Leaf ⇒ 0
      | RedNode _ t1 _ t2 ⇒ S (f (depth t1) (depth t2))
      | BlackNode _ _ _ t1 _ t2 ⇒ S (f (depth t1) (depth t2))
    end.
End depth.
```

The proof of balancedness decomposes naturally into a lower bound and an upper bound. We prove the lower bound first. Unsurprisingly, a tree's black depth provides such a bound on the minimum path length. We use the richly typed procedure min_dec to do case analysis on whether min X Y equals X or Y.

```
Check min_dec.
```

min_dec
    : $\forall$ n m : **nat**, {min n m = n} + {min n m = m}

```
Theorem depth_min : ∀ c n (t : rbtree c n), depth min t ≥ n.
  induction t; crush;
    match goal with
      | [ ⊢ context[min ?X ?Y] ] ⇒ destruct (min_dec X Y)
    end; crush.
Qed.
```

There is an analogous upper-bound theorem based on black depth. Unfortunately, a symmetric proof script does not suffice to establish it.

```
Theorem depth_max : ∀ c n (t : rbtree c n), depth max t ≤ 2 × n + 1.
```

```
induction t; crush;
  match goal with
    | [ ⊢ context[max ?X ?Y] ] ⇒ destruct (max_dec X Y)
  end; crush.
```

Two subgoals remain. One of them is

n : **nat**
$t1$: **rbtree** Black n
$n0$: **nat**
$t2$: **rbtree** Black n
$IHt1$: depth max $t1 \leq n + (n + 0) + 1$
$IHt2$: depth max $t2 \leq n + (n + 0) + 1$
e : max (depth max $t1$) (depth max $t2$) = depth max $t1$
================================
  S (depth max $t1$) $\leq n + (n + 0) + 1$

We see that *IHt1* is almost the fact we need, but it is not quite strong enough. We need to strengthen the induction hypothesis to get the proof to go through.

```
Abort.
```

In particular, we prove a lemma that provides a stronger upper bound for trees with black root nodes. We got stuck in a case about a red root node. Since red nodes have only black children, our IH strengthening enables us to finish the proof.

```
Lemma depth_max' : ∀ c n (t : rbtree c n),
  match c with
    | Red ⇒ depth max t ≤ 2 × n + 1
    | Black ⇒ depth max t ≤ 2 × n
  end.
  induction t; crush;
    match goal with
      | [ ⊢ context[max ?X ?Y] ] ⇒ destruct (max_dec X Y)
    end; crush;
    repeat (match goal with
              | [ H : context[match ?C with Red ⇒ _
                                | Black ⇒ _ end] ⊢ _ ] ⇒
                destruct C
            end; crush).
Qed.
```

The original theorem follows easily from the lemma. We use the tactic **generalize** *pf*, which, when *pf* proves the proposition *P*, changes the goal from Q to $P \to Q$. This transformation is useful because it makes the truth of P manifest syntactically, so that automation machinery can rely on P, even if that machinery is not smart enough to establish P on its own.

```
Theorem depth_max : ∀ c n (t : rbtree c n), depth max t ≤ 2 × n + 1.
  intros; generalize (depth_max' t); destruct c; crush.
Qed.
```

The final balance theorem establishes that the minimum and maximum path lengths of any tree are within a factor of 2 of each other.

```
Theorem balanced : ∀ c n (t : rbtree c n),
  2 × depth min t + 1 ≥ depth max t.
  intros; generalize (depth_min t); generalize (depth_max t);
    crush.
Qed.
```

Now we are ready to implement an example operation on the trees, insertion. Insertion can be thought of as breaking the tree invariants locally but then rebalancing. In particular, in intermediate states we find red nodes that may have red children. The type **rtree** captures the idea of such a node, continuing to track black depth as a type index.

```
Inductive rtree : nat → Set :=
| RedNode' : ∀ c1 c2 n, rbtree c1 n → nat → rbtree c2 n → rtree n.
```

Before starting to define **insert**, we define predicates capturing when a data value is in the set represented by a normal or possibly invalid tree.

```
Section present.
  Variable x : nat.

  Fixpoint present c n (t : rbtree c n) : Prop :=
    match t with
      | Leaf ⇒ False
      | RedNode _ a y b ⇒ present a ∨ x = y ∨ present b
      | BlackNode _ _ _ a y b ⇒ present a ∨ x = y ∨ present b
    end.

  Definition rpresent n (t : rtree n) : Prop :=
    match t with
      | RedNode' _ _ _ a y b ⇒ present a ∨ x = y ∨ present b
    end.
End present.
```

Insertion relies on two balancing operations. It is useful to give types to these operations using a relative of the subset types discussed in Chapter 6. While subset types let us pair a value with a proof about that value, here we want to pair a value with another nonproof dependently typed value. The **sigT** type fills this role.

```
Locate "{ _: _& _}".
```

```
Notation Scope
"{ x : A & P }" := sigT (fun x : A ⇒ P)
```

```
Print sigT.
```

Inductive **sigT** $(A : \text{Type})$ $(P : A \to \text{Type}) : \text{Type} :=$
   existT : $\forall x : A, P\ x \to$ **sigT** P

It is helpful to define a concise notation for the constructor of **sigT**.

```
Notation "{< x >}" := (existT _ _ x).
```

Each balance function is used to construct a new tree whose keys include the keys of two input trees as well as a new key. One of the two input trees may violate the red-black alternation invariant (that is, it has an **rtree** type), while the other tree is known to be valid. Crucially, the two input trees have the same black depth.

A balance operation may return a tree whose root is of either color. Thus, we use a **sigT** type to package the result tree with the color of its root. Here is the definition of the first balance operation, which applies when the possibly invalid **rtree** belongs to the left of the valid **rbtree**.

A quick word of encouragement: After writing this code, even I do not understand the precise details of how balancing works. I consulted Chris Okasaki's paper "Red-Black Trees in a Functional Setting" [30] and transcribed the code to use dependent types. Luckily, the details are not so important here; types alone indicate that insertion preserves balancedness, and we will prove that insertion produces trees containing the right keys.

Definition balance1 n $(a : \text{\bf rtree}\ n)$ $(data : \text{\bf nat})$ $c2 :=$
  match a in **rtree** n return **rbtree** $c2\ n$
    → { c : **color** & **rbtree** c (S n) } with
    | RedNode' _ $c0$ _ $t1$ y $t2$ ⇒
      match $t1$ in **rbtree** $c\ n$ return **rbtree** $c0\ n$ → **rbtree** $c2\ n$
        → { c : **color** & **rbtree** c (S n) } with
        | RedNode _ a x b ⇒ fun c d ⇒
          {<RedNode (BlackNode a x b) y (BlackNode c $data$ d)>}
        | $t1'$ ⇒ fun $t2$ ⇒
          match $t2$ in **rbtree** $c\ n$ return **rbtree** Black n

```
        → rbtree c2 n → { c : color & rbtree c (S n) } with
        | RedNode _ b x c ⇒ fun a d ⇒
          {<RedNode (BlackNode a y b) x (BlackNode c data d)>}
        | b ⇒ fun a t ⇒ {<BlackNode (RedNode a y b) data t>}
      end t1'
    end t2
  end.
```

We apply a trick that I call the *convoy pattern*. Recall that `match` annotations only make it possible to describe a dependence of a `match` *result type* on the discriminee. There is no automatic refinement of the types of free variables. However, it is possible to effect such a refinement by finding a way to encode free variable type dependencies in the `match` result type, so that a `return` clause can express the connection.

In particular, we can extend the `match` to return *functions over the free variables whose types we want to refine*. In the case of balance1, we only want to refine the type of one tree variable at a time. We match on one subtree of a node, and we want the type of the other subtree to be refined based on what we learn. We indicate this with a `return` clause starting like **rbtree** _ n → ..., where n is bound in an **in** pattern. Such a `match` expression is applied immediately to the "old version" of the variable to be refined, and the type checker is satisfied.

Here is the symmetric function balance2, for cases where the possibly invalid tree appears on the right rather than on the left:

```
Definition balance2 n (a : rtree n) (data : nat) c2 :=
  match a in rtree n
    return rbtree c2 n → { c : color & rbtree c (S n) } with
    | RedNode' _ c0 _ t1 z t2 ⇒
      match t1 in rbtree c n return rbtree c0 n → rbtree c2 n
        → { c : color & rbtree c (S n) } with
      | RedNode _ b y c ⇒ fun d a ⇒
        {<RedNode (BlackNode a data b) y (BlackNode c z d)>}
      | t1' ⇒ fun t2 ⇒
        match t2 in rbtree c n return rbtree Black n
          → rbtree c2 n → { c : color & rbtree c (S n) } with
          | RedNode _ c z' d ⇒ fun b a ⇒
            {<RedNode (BlackNode a data b) z
              (BlackNode c z' d)>}
          | b ⇒ fun a t ⇒ {<BlackNode t data (RedNode a z b)>}
        end t1'
    end t2
  end.
```

Now we are almost ready to write an insert function. First, we enter a section that declares a variable x for the key we want to insert.

```
Section insert.
  Variable x : nat.
```

Most of the work of insertion is done by a helper function ins, whose return types are expressed using a type-level function insResult.

```
Definition insResult c n :=
  match c with
    | Red ⇒ rtree n
    | Black ⇒ { c' : color & rbtree c' n }
  end.
```

That is, inserting into a tree with root color c and black depth n, the variety of tree we get out depends on c. If we started with a red root, then we get back a possibly invalid tree of depth n. If we started with a black root, we get back a valid tree of depth n with a root node of an arbitrary color.

Here is the definition of ins. Again, we do not want to dwell on the functional details.

```
Fixpoint ins c n (t : rbtree c n) : insResult c n :=
  match t with
    | Leaf ⇒ {< RedNode Leaf x Leaf >}
    | RedNode _ a y b ⇒
      if le_lt_dec x y
        then RedNode' (projT2 (ins a)) y b
        else RedNode' a y (projT2 (ins b))
    | BlackNode c1 c2 _ a y b ⇒
      if le_lt_dec x y
        then
          match c1 return insResult c1 _ → _ with
            | Red ⇒ fun ins_a ⇒ balance1 ins_a y b
            | _ ⇒ fun ins_a ⇒ {< BlackNode (projT2 ins_a) y b >}
          end (ins a)
        else
          match c2 return insResult c2 _ → _ with
            | Red ⇒ fun ins_b ⇒ balance2 ins_b y a
            | _ ⇒ fun ins_b ⇒ {< BlackNode a y (projT2 ins_b) >}
          end (ins b)
  end.
```

The one new trick is a variation of the convoy pattern. In each of the last two pattern matches, we want to take advantage of the typing connection between the trees *a* and *b*. We might naïvely apply the convoy pattern directly on *a* in the first `match` and on *b* in the second. This satisfies the type checker per se, but it does not satisfy the termination checker. Inside each `match`, we would be calling ins recursively on a locally bound variable. The termination checker is not smart enough to trace the data flow into that variable, so the checker does not know that this recursive argument is smaller than the original argument. We make this fact clearer by applying the convoy pattern on *the result of a recursive call* rather than just on that call's argument.

We are almost done defining insert. We just need a few more definitions of nonrecursive functions. First, we need to give the final characterization of insert's return type. Inserting into a red-rooted tree gives a black-rooted tree whose black depth has increased, and inserting into a black-rooted tree gives a tree whose black depth has stayed the same and whose root is an arbitrary color.

```
Definition insertResult c n :=
  match c with
    | Red ⇒ rbtree Black (S n)
    | Black ⇒ { c' : color & rbtree c' n }
  end.
```

A simple cleanup procedure translates insResults into insertResults.

```
Definition makeRbtree c n : insResult c n → insertResult c n :=
  match c with
    | Red ⇒ fun r ⇒
      match r with
        | RedNode' _ _ _ a x b ⇒ BlackNode a x b
      end
    | Black ⇒ fun r ⇒ r
  end.
```

We modify Coq's default choice of implicit arguments for makeRbtree so that we do not need to specify the *c* and *n* arguments explicitly in later calls.

```
Implicit Arguments makeRbtree [c n].
```

Finally, we define insert as a simple composition of ins and makeRbtree.

```
Definition insert c n (t : rbtree c n) : insertResult c n :=
  makeRbtree (ins t).
```

As noted earlier, the type of insert guarantees that it outputs balanced trees whose depths have not increased too much. We also want to know that insert operates correctly on trees interpreted as finite sets, so we finish this section with a proof of that fact.

```
Section present.
    Variable z : nat.
```

The variable z stands for an arbitrary key. We reason about z's presence in particular trees. As usual, outside the section the theorems we prove quantify over all possible keys, giving us the facts we wanted.

We start by proving the correctness of the balance operations. It is useful to define a custom tactic *present_balance* that encapsulates the reasoning common to the two proofs. We use the keyword Ltac to assign a name to a proof script. This particular script just iterates between *crush* and identification of a tree that is being pattern-matched and should be destructed.

```
Ltac present_balance :=
    crush;
    repeat (match goal with
                | [ _ : context[match ?T with Leaf ⇒ _
                                    | _ ⇒ _ end] ⊢ _ ] ⇒
                    dep_destruct T
                | [ ⊢ context[match ?T with Leaf ⇒ _
                                    | _ ⇒ _ end] ] ⇒
                    dep_destruct T
            end; crush).
```

The balance correctness theorems are simple first-order logic equivalences, where we use the function projT2 to project the payload of a sigT value.

```
Lemma present_balance1 : ∀ n (a : rtree n) (y : nat) c2
    (b : rbtree c2 n),
    present z (projT2 (balance1 a y b))
    ↔ rpresent z a ∨ z = y ∨ present z b.
    destruct a; present_balance.
Qed.

Lemma present_balance2 : ∀ n (a : rtree n) (y : nat) c2
    (b : rbtree c2 n),
    present z (projT2 (balance2 a y b))
    ↔ rpresent z a ∨ z = y ∨ present z b.
    destruct a; present_balance.
Qed.
```

To state the theorem for ins, it is useful to define a new type-level function, since ins returns different result types based on the type indices passed to it. Recall that x is the section variable standing for the key we are inserting.

Definition present_insResult c n :=
  match c return (**rbtree** c n → insResult c n → Prop) with
   | Red ⇒ fun t r ⇒ rpresent z r ↔ z = x ∨ present z t
   | Black ⇒ fun t r ⇒ present z (projT2 r) ↔
    z = x ∨ present z t
  end.

Now the statement and proof of the ins correctness theorem are straightforward. We proceed by induction on the structure of a tree, followed by finding case analysis opportunities on expressions being analyzed in `if` or `match` expressions. After that, we pattern-match to find opportunities to use the theorems we proved about balancing. Finally, we identify two variables that are asserted by some hypothesis to be equal, and we use that hypothesis to replace one variable with the other everywhere.

Theorem present_ins : ∀ c n (t : **rbtree** c n),
  present_insResult t (ins t).
  induction t; *crush*;
   repeat (match goal with
        | [_ : context[if ?E then _ else _] ⊢ _] ⇒
         destruct E
        | [⊢ context[if ?E then _ else _]] ⇒
         destruct E
        | [_ : context[match ?C with Red ⇒ _
                 | Black ⇒ _ end]
          ⊢ _] ⇒ destruct C
      end; *crush*);
   try match goal with
     | [_ : context[balance1 ?A ?B ?C] ⊢ _] ⇒
      generalize (present_balance1 A B C)
   end;
   try match goal with
     | [_ : context[balance2 ?A ?B ?C] ⊢ _] ⇒
      generalize (present_balance2 A B C)
   end;
   try match goal with
     | [⊢ context[balance1 ?A ?B ?C]] ⇒
      generalize (present_balance1 A B C)

```
              end;
        try match goal with
              | [ ⊢ context[balance2 ?A ?B ?C] ] ⇒
                  generalize (present_balance2 A B C)
              end;
          crush;
            match goal with
              | [ z : nat, x : nat ⊢ _ ] ⇒
              match goal with
                | [ H : z = x ⊢ _ ] ⇒ rewrite H in *; clear H
              end
            end;
            tauto.
  Qed.
```

The hard work is done. The most readable way to state correctness
of insert involves splitting the property into two color-specific theorems. We write a tactic to encapsulate the reasoning steps that work
to establish both facts.

```
    Ltac present_insert :=
        unfold insert; intros n t; inversion t;
          generalize (present_ins t); simpl;
            dep_destruct (ins t); tauto.

    Theorem present_insert_Red : ∀ n (t : rbtree Red n),
        present z (insert t)
        ↔ (z = x ∨ present z t).
        present_insert.
    Qed.

    Theorem present_insert_Black : ∀ n (t : rbtree Black n),
        present z (projT2 (insert t))
        ↔ (z = x ∨ present z t).
        present_insert.
    Qed.
  End present.
End insert.
```

We can generate executable OCaml code with the command
Recursive Extraction insert, which also automatically outputs the
OCaml versions of all of insert's dependencies. In previous extractions,
we wound up with clean OCaml code. Here, we find uses of Obj.magic,
OCaml's unsafe cast operator for tweaking the apparent type of an
expression in an arbitrary way. Casts appear for this example because

the return type of insert depends on the *value* of the function's argument, a pattern that OCaml cannot handle. Coq's type system is much more expressive than OCaml's, so such casts are unavoidable in general. Since the OCaml type checker is no longer checking full safety of programs, we must rely on Coq's extractor to use casts only in provably safe ways.

8.5   A Certified Regular Expression Matcher

Another interesting example is regular expressions with dependent types that express which predicates over strings particular expressions implement. We can then assign a dependent type to a regular expression matching function, guaranteeing that it always decides the string property that we expect it to decide.

Before defining the syntax of expressions, it is helpful to define an inductive type capturing the meaning of the Kleene star. That is, a string s matches regular expression **star** e if and only if s can be decomposed into a sequence of substrings that all match e. We use Coq's string support, which comes through a combination of the String library and some parsing notations built into Coq. Operators like $++$ and functions like length that we know from lists are defined again for strings. Notation scopes help us control which versions we want to use in particular contexts.

Require Import Ascii String.
Open Scope *string_scope*.

Section star.
  Variable P : **string** → Prop.

  Inductive **star** : **string** → Prop :=
 | Empty : **star** ""
 | Iter : ∀ *s1 s2*,
   P *s1*
   → **star** *s2*
   → **star** (*s1* ++ *s2*).
End star.

Now we can make a first attempt at defining a **regexp** type that is indexed by predicates on strings, such that the index of a **regexp** tells us which language (string predicate) it recognizes. The following definition, which is restricted to constant characters and concatenation, seems reasonable. We use the constructor String, which is the analogue of list cons for the type **string**, where "" is like list nil.

```
Inductive regexp : (string → Prop) → Set :=
| Char : ∀ ch : ascii,
    regexp (fun s ⇒ s = String ch "")
| Concat : ∀ (P1 P2 : string → Prop) (r1 : regexp P1)
    (r2 : regexp P2),
    regexp (fun s ⇒ ∃ s1, ∃ s2, s = s1 ++ s2 ∧ P1 s1 ∧ P2 s2).
```

```
User error: Large non-propositional inductive types must be
in Type
```

What is a large inductive type? In Coq, it is an inductive type with a constructor that quantifies over some type of type **Type**. We have not worked with **Type** very much to this point. Every term of the Calculus of Inductive Constructions has a type, including **Set** and **Prop**, which are assigned type **Type**. The type **string** → **Prop** from the failed definition also has type **Type**.

It turns out that allowing large inductive types in **Set** leads to contradictions when combined with certain kinds of classical logic reasoning. Thus, by default, such types are ruled out. There is a simple fix for the **regexp** definition, which is to place the new type in **Type**. While fixing the problem, we also expand the list of constructors to cover the remaining regular expression operators.

```
Inductive regexp : (string → Prop) → Type :=
| Char : ∀ ch : ascii,
    regexp (fun s ⇒ s = String ch "")
| Concat : ∀ P1 P2 (r1 : regexp P1) (r2 : regexp P2),
    regexp (fun s ⇒ ∃ s1 , ∃ s2 , s = s1 ++ s2 ∧ P1 s1 ∧ P2 s2)
| Or : ∀ P1 P2 (r1 : regexp P1) (r2 : regexp P2),
    regexp (fun s ⇒ P1 s ∨ P2 s)
| Star : ∀ P (r : regexp P),
    regexp (star P).
```

Many theorems about strings are useful for implementing a certified regexp matcher, and few of them are in the **String** library. The book source includes statements, proofs, and hint commands for a handful of such omitted theorems.

A few auxiliary functions help in the final matcher definition. The function `split` is used to implement the regexp concatenation case.

```
Section split.
    Variables P1 P2 : string → Prop.
    Variable P1_dec : ∀ s, {P1 s} + {¬ P1 s}.
    Variable P2_dec : ∀ s, {P2 s} + {¬ P2 s}.
```

We require a choice of two arbitrary string predicates and functions for deciding them.

Variable s : **string**.

The computation takes place relative to a single fixed string, so it is easiest to make it a `Variable` rather than an explicit argument to the functions.

The function split' is the workhorse behind `split`. It searches through the possible ways of splitting s into two pieces, checking the two predicates against each such pair. The execution of split' progresses right to left, from splitting all of s into the first piece to splitting all of s into the second piece. It takes an extra argument, n, which specifies how far along we are in this search process.

```
Definition split' : ∀ n : nat, n ≤ length s
  → {∃ s1 , ∃ s2 , length s1 ≤ n ∧ s1 ++ s2 = s ∧ P1 s1 ∧ P2 s2}
 + {∀ s1 s2, length s1 ≤ n → s1 ++ s2 = s → ¬ P1 s1 ∨ ¬ P2 s2}.
  refine (fix F (n : nat) : n ≤ length s
    → {∃ s1 , ∃ s2 ,
      length s1 ≤ n ∧ s1 ++ s2 = s ∧ P1 s1 ∧ P2 s2}
   + {∀ s1 s2,
      length s1 ≤ n → s1 ++ s2 = s → ¬ P1 s1 ∨ ¬ P2 s2} :=
  match n with
    | O ⇒ fun _ ⇒ Reduce (P1_dec "" && P2_dec s)
    | S n' ⇒ fun _ ⇒ (P1_dec (substring 0 (S n') s)
        && P2_dec (substring (S n') (length s - S n') s))
      || F n' _
  end); clear F; crush; eauto 7;
  match goal with
    | [ _ : length ?S ≤ 0 ⊢ _ ] ⇒ destruct S
    | [ _ : length ?S' ≤ S ?N ⊢ _ ] ⇒
      destruct (eq_nat_dec (length S') (S N))
  end; crush.
Defined.
```

There is one subtle point in the split' code that is worth mentioning. The main body of the function is a `match` on n. In the case where n is known to be S n', we write S n' in several places where we might be tempted to write n. However, without further work to craft proper `match` annotations, the type checker does not use the equality between n and S n'. Thus, it is common to see patterns repeated in `match` case bodies in dependently typed Coq code. We can at least use a `let` expression to avoid copying the pattern more than once, replacing the first case body with

```
  | S n' ⇒ fun _ ⇒ let n := S n' in
    (P1_dec (substring 0 n s)
      && P2_dec (substring n (length s - n) s))
    || F n' _
```

The split function itself is trivial to implement in terms of split'. We just ask split' to begin its search with $n =$ length s.

```
  Definition split : {∃ s1 , ∃ s2 , s = s1 ++ s2 ∧ P1 s1 ∧ P2 s2}
    + {∀ s1 s2, s = s1 ++ s2 → ¬ P1 s1 ∨ ¬ P2 s2}.
    refine (Reduce (split' (n := length s) _)); crush; eauto.
  Defined.
End split.

Implicit Arguments split [P1 P2].
```

One more helper function will come in handy: dec_star, for implementing another linear search through ways of splitting a string, this time for implementing the Kleene star.

```
Section dec_star.
  Variable P : string → Prop.
  Variable P_dec : ∀ s, {P s} + {¬ P s}.
```

Some new lemmas and hints about the **star** type family are included in the book source at this point.

The function dec_star'' implements a single iteration of the star. That is, it tries to find a string prefix matching P, and it calls a parameter function on the remainder of the string.

```
  Section dec_star''.
    Variable n : nat.
```

Variable n is the length of the prefix of s that we have already processed.

```
    Variable P' : string → Prop.
    Variable P'_dec : ∀ n' : nat, n' > n
      → {P' (substring n' (length s - n') s)}
      + {¬ P' (substring n' (length s - n') s)}.
```

When we use dec_star'', we instantiate P'_dec with a function for continuing the search for more instances of P in s.

Now we come to dec_star'' itself. It takes as an input a natural l that records how much of the string has been searched so far, as we did for split'. The return type expresses that dec_star'' is looking for an index into s that splits s into a nonempty prefix and a suffix, such that the prefix satisfies P and the suffix satisfies P'.

```
Definition dec_star'' : ∀ l : nat,
  {∃ l', S l' ≤ l
    ∧ P (substring n (S l') s) ∧ P' (substring (n + S l')
      (length s - (n + S l')) s)}
  + {∀ l', S l' ≤ l
    → ¬ P (substring n (S l') s)
    ∨ ¬ P' (substring (n + S l') (length s - (n + S l')) s)}.
  refine (fix F (l : nat) : {∃ l', S l' ≤ l
    ∧ P (substring n (S l') s) ∧ P' (substring (n + S l')
      (length s - (n + S l')) s)}
    + {∀ l', S l' ≤ l
      → ¬ P (substring n (S l') s)
      ∨ ¬ P' (substring (n + S l') (length s - (n + S l')) s)} :=
    match l with
      | O ⇒ _
      | S l' ⇒
        (P_dec (substring n (S l') s)
          && P'_dec (n' := n + S l') _)
        || F l'
    end); clear F; crush; eauto 7;
    match goal with
      | [ H : ?X ≤ S ?Y ⊢ _ ] ⇒
        destruct (eq_nat_dec X (S Y)); crush
    end.
  Defined.
End dec_star''.
```

The work of dec_star'' is nested inside another linear search by dec_star', which provides the final functionality we need, but for arbitrary suffixes of s rather than just for s overall.

```
Definition dec_star' : ∀ n n' : nat, length s - n' ≤ n
  → {star P (substring n' (length s - n') s)}
  + {¬ star P (substring n' (length s - n') s)}.
  refine (fix F (n n' : nat) : length s - n' ≤ n
    → {star P (substring n' (length s - n') s)}
    + {¬ star P (substring n' (length s - n') s)} :=
    match n with
      | O ⇒ fun _ ⇒ Yes
      | S n'' ⇒ fun _ ⇒
        le_gt_dec (length s) n'
        || dec_star'' (n := n') (star P)
          (fun n0 _ ⇒ Reduce (F n'' n0 _)) (length s - n')
```

```
    end); clear F; crush; eauto;
  match goal with
    | [ H : star _ _ ⊢ _ ] ⇒ apply star_substring_inv in H;
      crush; eauto
  end;
  match goal with
    | [ H1 : _ < _ - _, H2 : ∀ l' : nat, _ ≤ _ - _ → _ ⊢ _ ] ⇒
      generalize (H2 _ (lt_le_S _ _ H1)); tauto
  end.
Defined.
```

Finally, we have dec_star, defined by straightforward reduction from dec_star'.

```
Definition dec_star : {star P s} + {¬ star P s}.
  refine (Reduce (dec_star' (n := length s) 0 _)); crush.
Defined.
End dec_star.
```

With these helper functions completed, the implementation of the matches function is straightforward. We only need one small piece of specific tactic work beyond *crush*.

```
Definition matches : ∀ P (r : regexp P) s, {P s} + {¬ P s}.
  refine (fix F P (r : regexp P) s : {P s} + {¬ P s} :=
    match r with
      | Char ch ⇒ string_dec s (String ch "")
      | Concat _ _ r1 r2 ⇒ Reduce (split (F _ r1) (F _ r2) s)
      | Or _ _ r1 r2 ⇒ F _ r1 s || F _ r2 s
      | Star _ r ⇒ dec_star _ _ _
    end); crush;
  match goal with
    | [ H : _ ⊢ _ ] ⇒ generalize (H _ _ (eq_refl _))
  end; tauto.
Defined.
```

It is interesting to consider alternative implementations of matches. Dependent types offer much latitude in how specific correctness properties may be encoded with types. For instance, we could have made **regexp** a nonindexed inductive type, along the lines of what is possible in traditional ML and Haskell. We could then have implemented a recursive function to map **regexp**s to their intended meanings, much as was done with types and programs in other examples. That style is compatible with the **refine**-based approach that we have used here, and it might be an interesting exercise to redo the code from this sub-section in that style or some other encoding of the reader's choice. The main advantage of indexed inductive types is that they generally lead to the least code.

Many regular expression-matching problems are easy to test. The reader could run each of the following queries to verify that it gives the correct answer. We use evaluation strategy `hnf` to reduce each term to *head-normal form*, where the datatype constructor used to build its value is known. (Further reduction would involve wasteful simplification of proof terms justifying the answers of the procedures.)

```
Example a_star := Star (Char "a"%char).
Eval hnf in matches a_star "".
Eval hnf in matches a_star "a".
Eval hnf in matches a_star "b".
Eval hnf in matches a_star "aa".
```

Evaluation inside Coq does not scale very well, so it is easy to build other tests that run for hours or more. Such cases are better suited to execution with the extracted OCaml code.

9   Dependent Data Structures

The red-black tree example in the last chapter illustrated how dependent types enable static enforcement of data structure invariants. To find interesting uses of dependent data structures, however, we need not look to the favorite examples of data structures and algorithms textbooks. More basic examples like length-indexed and heterogeneous lists come up again and again as the building blocks of dependent programs. There is a surprisingly large design space for this class of data structure, and this chapter explores it.

9.1   More Length-Indexed Lists

We begin with a deeper look at length-indexed lists.

```
Section ilist.
  Variable A : Set.

  Inductive ilist : nat → Set :=
  | Nil : ilist O
  | Cons : ∀ n, A → ilist n → ilist (S n).
```

We might like to have a certified function for selecting an element of an **ilist** by position. We could do this using subset types and explicit manipulation of proofs, but dependent types let us do it more directly. It is helpful to define a type family **fin**, where **fin** n is isomorphic to $\{m : \textbf{nat} \mid m < n\}$. The type family name stands for *finite*.

```
  Inductive fin : nat → Set :=
  | First : ∀ n, fin (S n)
  | Next : ∀ n, fin n → fin (S n).
```

An instance of **fin** is essentially a more richly typed copy of a prefix of the natural numbers. Every element is a **First** iterated through applying `Next` a number of times that indicates which number is being selected.

For instance, the three values of type **fin** 3 are First 2, Next (First 1), and Next (Next (First 0)).

Now it is easy to pick a Prop-free type for a selection function. As usual, the first implementation attempt will not satisfy the type checker, and we will attack the deficiencies one at a time.

```
Fixpoint get n (ls : ilist n) : fin n → A :=
  match ls with
    | Nil ⇒ fun idx ⇒ ?
    | Cons _ x ls' ⇒ fun idx ⇒
      match idx with
        | First _ ⇒ x
        | Next _ idx' ⇒ get ls' idx'
      end
  end.
```

We apply the usual wisdom of delaying arguments in **Fixpoint**s so that they may be included in **return** clauses. This still leaves us with a quandary in each of the **match** cases. First, we need to figure out how to take advantage of the contradiction in the Nil case. Every **fin** has a type of the form S n, which cannot unify with the O value that we learn for n in the Nil case. The solution we adopt is another case of **match**-within-**return**, with the **return** clause chosen carefully so that it returns the proper type A in case the **fin** index is O, which we know is true here, and so that it returns an easy-to-inhabit type **unit** in the remaining, impossible cases, which nonetheless appear explicitly in the body of the **match**.

```
Fixpoint get n (ls : ilist n) : fin n → A :=
  match ls with
    | Nil ⇒ fun idx ⇒
      match idx in fin n' return (match n' with
                                    | O ⇒ A
                                    | S _ ⇒ unit
                                  end) with
        | First _ ⇒ tt
        | Next _ _ ⇒ tt
      end
    | Cons _ x ls' ⇒ fun idx ⇒
      match idx with
        | First _ ⇒ x
        | Next _ idx' ⇒ get ls' idx'
      end
  end.
```

Now the first `match` case type-checks, and we see that the problem with the Cons case is that the pattern-bound variable *idx'* does not have an apparent type compatible with *ls'*. In fact, the error message Coq gives for this exact code can be confusing, thanks to an overenthusiastic type inference heuristic. We are told that the Nil case body has type `match X with | O ⇒ A | S _ ⇒ unit end` for a unification variable X, while it is expected to have type A. We can see that setting X to O resolves the conflict, but Coq is not yet smart enough to do this unification automatically. Repeating the function's type in a `return` annotation, used with an `in` annotation, leads us to a more informative error message saying that *idx'* has type **fin** *n1*, while it is expected to have type **fin** *n0*, where *n0* is bound by the Cons pattern and *n1* by the Next pattern. As the code is written, nothing forces these two natural numbers to be equal, though we know intuitively that they must be.

We need to use `match` annotations to make the relation explicit. Unfortunately, the usual trick of postponing argument binding will not help here. We need to match on both *ls* and *idx*; one or the other must be matched first. To get around this, we apply the convoy pattern (see Chapter 8). This application is a little more clever than those we saw before; we use the natural number predecessor function **pred** to express the relation between the types of these variables.

```
Fixpoint get n (ls : ilist n) : fin n → A :=
  match ls with
    | Nil ⇒ fun idx ⇒
      match idx in fin n' return (match n' with
                                    | O ⇒ A
                                    | S _ ⇒ unit
                                  end) with
        | First _ ⇒ tt
        | Next _ _ ⇒ tt
      end
    | Cons _ x ls' ⇒ fun idx ⇒
      match idx in fin n' return ilist (pred n') → A with
        | First _ ⇒ fun _ ⇒ x
        | Next _ idx' ⇒ fun ls' ⇒ get ls' idx'
      end ls'
  end.
```

There is just one problem left with this implementation. Though we know that the local *ls'* in the Next case is equal to the original *ls'*, the type checker is not satisfied that the recursive call to **get** does not

introduce nontermination. We solve the problem by convoy-binding the
partial application of get to *ls'* rather than *ls'* by itself.

```
Fixpoint get n (ls : ilist n) : fin n → A :=
  match ls with
    | Nil ⇒ fun idx ⇒
      match idx in fin n' return (match n' with
                                      | O ⇒ A
                                      | S _ ⇒ unit
                                    end) with
        | First _ ⇒ tt
        | Next _ _ ⇒ tt
      end
    | Cons _ x ls' ⇒ fun idx ⇒
      match idx in fin n' return (fin (pred n') → A) → A with
        | First _ ⇒ fun _ ⇒ x
        | Next _ idx' ⇒ fun get_ls' ⇒ get_ls' idx'
      end (get ls')
  end.
End ilist.
```

```
Implicit Arguments Nil [A].
Implicit Arguments First [n].
```

A few examples show how to make use of these definitions.

```
Check Cons 0 (Cons 1 (Cons 2 Nil)).
```

```
Cons 0 (Cons 1 (Cons 2 Nil))
   : ilist nat 3
```

```
Eval simpl in get (Cons 0 (Cons 1 (Cons 2 Nil))) First.
```

```
= 0
: nat
```

```
Eval simpl in get (Cons 0 (Cons 1 (Cons 2 Nil))) (Next First).
```

```
= 1
: nat
```

```
Eval simpl in get (Cons 0 (Cons 1 (Cons 2 Nil))) (Next (Next First)).
```

```
= 2
: nat
```

The get function is also quite easy to reason about. We look at a
short example about an analogue to the list map function.

```
Section ilist_map.
  Variables A B : Set.
  Variable f : A → B.

  Fixpoint imap n (ls : ilist A n) : ilist B n :=
    match ls with
      | Nil ⇒ Nil
      | Cons _ x ls' ⇒ Cons (f x) (imap ls')
    end.
```

It is easy to prove that **get** distributes over **imap** calls.

```
  Theorem get_imap : ∀ n (idx : fin n) (ls : ilist A n),
    get (imap ls) idx = f (get ls idx).
    induction ls; dep_destruct idx; crush.
  Qed.
End ilist_map.
```

The only tricky bit is remembering to use the *dep_destruct* tactic in place of plain destruct when faced with a baffling tactic error message.

9.2   Heterogeneous Lists

Programmers who move to statically typed functional languages from scripting languages often complain about the requirement that every element of a list have the same type. With more elaborate type systems, we can partially lift this requirement. We can index a list type with a type-level list that explains what type each element of the list should have. This has been done in a variety of ways in Haskell using type classes, and it can be done much more cleanly and directly in Coq.

```
Section hlist.
  Variable A : Type.
  Variable B : A → Type.
```

We parameterize the heterogeneous lists by a type A and an A-indexed type B.

```
  Inductive hlist : list A → Type :=
  | HNil : hlist nil
  | HCons : ∀ (x : A) (ls : list A), B x → hlist ls → hlist (x :: ls).
```

We can implement a variant of the **get** function for **hlist**s. To get the dependent typing to work out, we need to index the element selectors (in type family **member**) by the types of data that they point to.

```
  Variable elm : A.
```

```
Inductive member : list A → Type :=
| HFirst : ∀ ls, member (elm :: ls)
| HNext : ∀ x ls, member ls → member (x :: ls).
```

Because the element *elm* that we are searching for in a list does not change across the constructors of **member**, we simplify the definitions by making *elm* a local variable. In the definition of **member**, we say that *elm* is found in any list that begins with *elm*, and if removing the first element of a list leaves *elm* present, then *elm* is present in the original list, too. The form looks much like a predicate for list membership, but we purposely define **member** in Type so that we may decompose its values to guide computations.

We can use **member** to adapt the definition of get to **hlist**s. The same basic `match` techniques apply. In the HCons case, we form a two-element convoy, passing both the data element *x* and the recursor for the sublist *mls'* to the result of the inner `match`. We did not need to do that in get's definition because the types of list elements were not dependent there.

```
Fixpoint hget ls (mls : hlist ls) : member ls → B elm :=
  match mls with
    | HNil ⇒ fun mem ⇒
      match mem in member ls'
        return (match ls' with
                  | nil ⇒ B elm
                  | _ :: _ ⇒ unit
                end) with
        | HFirst _ ⇒ tt
        | HNext _ _ _ ⇒ tt
      end
    | HCons _ _ x mls' ⇒ fun mem ⇒
      match mem in member ls'
        return (match ls' with
                  | nil ⇒ Empty_set
                  | x' :: ls'' ⇒
                      B x' → (member ls'' → B elm) → B elm
                end) with
        | HFirst _ ⇒ fun x _ ⇒ x
        | HNext _ _ mem' ⇒ fun _ get_mls' ⇒ get_mls' mem'
      end x (hget mls')
  end.
End hlist.

Implicit Arguments HNil [A B].
```

Implicit Arguments HCons [*A B x ls*].

Implicit Arguments HFirst [*A elm ls*].
Implicit Arguments HNext [*A elm x ls*].

By putting the parameters A and B in Type, we enable more kinds of polymorphism than in mainstream functional languages. For instance, one use of **hlist** is for the simple heterogeneous lists referred to earlier.

Definition someTypes : list Set := **nat** :: **bool** :: nil.

Example someValues : **hlist** (fun T : Set $\Rightarrow T$) someTypes :=
  HCons 5 (HCons true HNil).

Eval simpl in hget someValues HFirst.

> $= 5$
> : (fun T : Set $\Rightarrow T$) **nat**

Eval simpl in hget someValues (HNext HFirst).

> $= \text{true}$
> : (fun T : Set $\Rightarrow T$) **bool**

We can also build indexed lists of pairs in this way.

Example somePairs : **hlist** (fun T : Set $\Rightarrow T \times T$)%type someTypes :=
  HCons (1, 2) (HCons (true, false) HNil).

There are many other useful applications of heterogeneous lists, based on different choices of the first argument to **hlist**.

9.2.1   A Lambda Calculus Interpreter

Heterogeneous lists are very useful in implementing interpreters for functional programming languages. Using the types and operations already defined, it is trivial to write an interpreter for simply typed lambda calculus. Those familiar with the terminology of semantics may find it helpful to think of the interpreter as a denotational semantics.

We start with an algebraic datatype for types.

Inductive **type** : Set :=
| Unit : **type**
| Arrow : **type** $\rightarrow$ **type** $\rightarrow$ **type**.

Now we can define a type family for expressions. An **exp** *ts t* stands for an expression that has type *t* and whose free variables have types in the list *ts*. We effectively use the de Bruijn index variable representation [11]. Variables are represented as **member** values; that is, a variable is more or less a constructive proof that a particular type is found in the type environment.

```
Inductive exp : list type → type → Set :=
| Const : ∀ ts, exp ts Unit
```

```
| Var : ∀ ts t, member t ts → exp ts t
| App : ∀ ts dom ran,
    exp ts (Arrow dom ran) → exp ts dom → exp ts ran
| Abs : ∀ ts dom ran, exp (dom :: ts) ran → exp ts (Arrow dom ran).
```

```
Implicit Arguments Const [ts].
```

We write a simple recursive function to translate types into Sets.

```
Fixpoint typeDenote (t : type) : Set :=
  match t with
    | Unit ⇒ unit
    | Arrow t1 t2 ⇒ typeDenote t1 → typeDenote t2
  end.
```

Now it is straightforward to write an expression interpreter. The type of the function, expDenote, tells us that we translate expressions into functions from properly typed environments to final values. An environment for a free variable list *ts* is simply an **hlist** typeDenote *ts*. That is, for each free variable, the heterogeneous list that is the environment must have a value of the variable's associated type. We use hget to implement the Var case, and we use HCons to extend the environment in the Abs case.

```
Fixpoint expDenote ts t (e : exp ts t)
  : hlist typeDenote ts → typeDenote t :=
  match e with
    | Const _ ⇒ fun _ ⇒ tt
```

```
    | Var _ _ mem ⇒ fun s ⇒ hget s mem
    | App _ _ _ e1 e2 ⇒ fun s ⇒ (expDenote e1 s) (expDenote e2 s)
    | Abs _ _ _ e' ⇒ fun s ⇒ fun x ⇒ expDenote e' (HCons x s)
  end.
```

As in previous examples, the interpreter is easy to run with `simpl`.

```
Eval simpl in expDenote Const HNil.
```

```
= tt
  : typeDenote Unit
```

```
Eval simpl in expDenote (Abs (dom := Unit) (Var HFirst)) HNil.
```

```
    = fun x : unit ⇒ x
    : typeDenote (Arrow Unit Unit)
```

Eval simpl in expDenote (Abs (*dom* := Unit)
  (Abs (*dom* := Unit) (Var (HNext HFirst)))) HNil.

```
      = fun x _ : unit ⇒ x
      : typeDenote (Arrow Unit (Arrow Unit Unit))
```

Eval simpl in expDenote (Abs (*dom* := Unit) (Abs (*dom* := Unit)
  (Var HFirst))) HNil.

```
      = fun _ x0 : unit ⇒ x0
      : typeDenote (Arrow Unit (Arrow Unit Unit))
```

Eval simpl in expDenote (App (Abs (Var HFirst)) Const) HNil.

```
    = tt
    : typeDenote Unit
```

We are starting to develop the tools underlying dependent typing's amazing advantage over alternative approaches in several important areas. Here, we have implemented complete syntax, typing rules, and evaluation semantics for simply typed lambda calculus without even needing to define a syntactic substitution operation. We did it all without a single line of proof, and the implementation is manifestly executable. Other, more common approaches to language formalization often state and prove explicit theorems about type safety of languages. In the preceding example, we established type safety, termination, and other metatheorems by reduction to the Calculus of Inductive Constructions, which we know has those properties.

9.3   Recursive Type Definitions

There is another style of datatype definition that leads to much simpler definitions of the get and hget functions. Because Coq supports type-level computation, we can redo the inductive definitions as *recursive* definitions. Here we preface type names with the letter f to indicate that they are based on explicit recursive *function* definitions.

```
Section filist.
  Variable A : Set.
  Fixpoint filist (n : nat) : Set :=
```

```
match n with
  | O ⇒ unit
  | S n' ⇒ A × filist n'
end%type.
```

We say that a list of length 0 has no contents, and a list of length S n' is a pair of a data value and a list of length n'.

```
Fixpoint ffin (n : nat) : Set :=
  match n with
    | O ⇒ Empty_set
    | S n' ⇒ option (ffin n')
  end.
```

We express that there are no index values when $n = $ O, by defining such indices as type **Empty_set**; and we express that at $n = $ S n' there is a choice between picking the first element of the list (represented as None) or choosing a later element (represented by Some idx, where idx is an index into the list tail). For instance, the three values of type ffin 3 are None, Some None, and Some (Some None).

```
Fixpoint fget (n : nat) : filist n → ffin n → A :=
  match n with
    | O ⇒ fun _ idx ⇒ match idx with end
    | S n' ⇒ fun ls idx ⇒
      match idx with
        | None ⇒ fst ls
        | Some idx' ⇒ fget n' (snd ls) idx'
      end
  end.
```

The new `get` implementation needs only one dependent `match`, and its annotation is inferred for us. Our choices of data structure implementations lead to just the right typing behavior for this new definition to work out.

End filist.

Heterogeneous lists are a little trickier to define with recursion, but we then reap similar benefits in simplicity of use.

```
Section fhlist.
  Variable A : Type.
  Variable B : A → Type.

  Fixpoint fhlist (ls : list A) : Type :=
    match ls with
      | nil ⇒ unit
```

```
    | x :: ls' ⇒ B x × fhlist ls'
  end%type.
```

The definition of fhlist follows the definition of filist, where some data elements now have more dependent types.

```
Variable elm : A.
```

```
Fixpoint fmember (ls : list A) : Type :=
  match ls with
    | nil ⇒ Empty_set
    | x :: ls' ⇒ (x = elm) + fmember ls'
  end%type.
```

The definition of fmember follows the definition of ffin. Empty lists have no members, and member types for nonempty lists are built by adding one new option to the type of members of the list tail. While for ffin we needed no new information associated with the option that we add, here we need to know that the head of the list equals the element we are searching for. We express that idea with a sum type whose left branch is the appropriate equality proposition. Since we define fmember to live in Type, we can insert Prop types as needed, because Prop is a subtype of Type.

Here is a first attempt to write a get function for fhlists.

```
Fixpoint fhget (ls : list A) : fhlist ls → fmember ls → B elm :=
  match ls with
    | nil ⇒ fun _ idx ⇒ match idx with end
    | _ :: ls' ⇒ fun mls idx ⇒
      match idx with
        | inl _ ⇒ fst mls
        | inr idx' ⇒ fhget ls' (snd mls) idx'
      end
  end.
```

Only one problem remains. The expression fst *mls* is not known to have the proper type. To demonstrate that it does, we need to use the proof available in the inl case of the inner `match`.

```
Fixpoint fhget (ls : list A) : fhlist ls → fmember ls → B elm :=
  match ls with
    | nil ⇒ fun _ idx ⇒ match idx with end
    | _ :: ls' ⇒ fun mls idx ⇒
      match idx with
        | inl pf ⇒ match pf with
                     | eq_refl ⇒ fst mls
```

```
                        end
        | inr idx' ⇒ fhget ls' (snd mls) idx'
    end
  end.
```

By pattern matching on the equality proof *pf*, we make that equality known to the type checker. Exactly why this works can be seen by studying the definition of equality.

> Print **eq**.

Inductive **eq** $(A : \mathtt{Type})\ (x : A) : A \to \mathtt{Prop} := \mathtt{eq\_refl} : x = x$

In a proposition $x = y$, we see that x is a parameter and y is a regular argument. The type of the constructor eq_refl shows that y can only ever be instantiated to x. Thus, within a pattern match with eq_refl, occurrences of y can be replaced with occurrences of x for typing purposes.

End fhlist.

Implicit Arguments fhget $[A\ B\ elm\ ls]$.

How does one choose between the two data structure encoding strategies presented so far? Before deciding, we study one further approach.

9.4 Data Structures as Index Functions

Indexed lists can be useful in defining other inductive types with constructors that take variable numbers of arguments. In this section, we consider parameterized trees with arbitrary branching factor.

```
Section tree.
  Variable A : Set.

  Inductive tree : Set :=
  | Leaf : A → tree
  | Node : ∀ n, ilist tree n → tree.
End tree.
```

Every Node of a **tree** has a natural number argument, which gives the number of child trees in the second argument, typed with **ilist**. We can define two operations on trees of naturals: summing their elements and incrementing their elements. It is useful to define a generic fold function on **ilist**s first.

Section ifoldr.

Variables A B : Set.
Variable $f : A \rightarrow B \rightarrow B$.
Variable $i : B$.

Fixpoint ifoldr n $(ls : \textbf{ilist } A \ n) : B :=$
    match ls with
        | Nil $\Rightarrow i$
        | Cons _ x ls' $\Rightarrow f$ x (ifoldr ls')
    end.
End ifoldr.

Fixpoint sum $(t : \textbf{tree nat}) : \textbf{nat} :=$
    match t with
        | Leaf $n \Rightarrow n$
        | Node _ $ls \Rightarrow$ ifoldr (fun t' $n \Rightarrow$ sum t' + n) O ls
    end.

Fixpoint inc $(t : \textbf{tree nat}) : \textbf{tree nat} :=$
    match t with
        | Leaf $n \Rightarrow$ Leaf (S n)
        | Node _ $ls \Rightarrow$ Node (imap inc ls)
    end.

Now we might like to prove that inc does not decrease a tree's sum.

Theorem sum_inc : $\forall$ t, sum (inc t) $\geq$ sum t.
    induction t; *crush*.

n : **nat**
i : **ilist** (**tree nat**) n
=================================
  ifoldr (fun $(t' : \textbf{tree nat})$ $(n0 : \textbf{nat}) \Rightarrow$ sum t' + $n0$) 0 (imap inc i)
  $\geq$ ifoldr (fun $(t' : \textbf{tree nat})$ $(n0 : \textbf{nat}) \Rightarrow$ sum t' + $n0$) 0 i

We are left with a single subgoal that does not seem provable directly. This is the same problem we encountered in Chapter 3 with other nested inductive types.

Check tree_ind.

tree_ind
    : $\forall$ $(A : \text{Set})$ $(P : \textbf{tree } A \rightarrow \text{Prop})$,
        $(\forall$ $a : A, P$ (Leaf a)) $\rightarrow$
        $(\forall$ $(n : \textbf{nat})$ $(i : \textbf{ilist} (\textbf{tree } A) \ n), P$ (Node i)) $\rightarrow$
        $\forall$ $t : \textbf{tree } A, P$ t

The automatically generated induction principle is too weak. For the Node case, it gives no inductive hypothesis. We could write an alternative induction principle, as in Chapter 3, but there is an easier way, if we alter the definition of **tree**.

```
Abort.
```

```
Reset tree.
```

First, let us try using the recursive definition of **ilist**s instead of the inductive version.

```
Section tree.
  Variable A : Set.

  Inductive tree : Set :=
  | Leaf : A → tree
  | Node : ∀ n, filist tree n → tree.
```

```
Error: Non strictly positive occurrence of "tree" in
  "forall n : nat, filist tree n -> tree"
```

The special-case rule for nested datatypes only works with nested uses of other inductive types, which could be replaced with uses of new mutually inductive types. We defined **filist** recursively, so it may not be used in nested inductive definitions.

The final solution uses yet another of the inductive definition techniques introduced in Chapter 3, reflexive types. Instead of merely using **fin** to get elements out of **ilist**, we can *define* **ilist** in terms of **fin**. For the reasons outlined in Section 9.3, it is easier to work with ffin in place of **fin**.

```
  Inductive tree : Set :=
  | Leaf : A → tree
  | Node : ∀ n, (ffin n → tree) → tree.
```

A Node is indexed by a natural number n, and the node's n children are represented as a function from ffin n to trees, which is isomorphic to the **ilist**-based representation used earlier.

```
End tree.
```

```
Implicit Arguments Node [A n].
```

We can redefine sum and inc for the new **tree** type. Again, it is useful to define a generic fold function first. This time, it takes in a function whose domain is some ffin type, and it folds another function over the results of calling the first function at every possible ffin value.

```
Section rifoldr.
```

```
  Variables A B : Set.
  Variable f : A → B → B.
  Variable i : B.

  Fixpoint rifoldr (n : nat) : (ffin n → A) → B :=
    match n with
      | O ⇒ fun _ ⇒ i
      | S n' ⇒ fun get ⇒ f (get None)
        (rifoldr n' (fun idx ⇒ get (Some idx)))
    end.
End rifoldr.

Implicit Arguments rifoldr [A B n].

Fixpoint sum (t : tree nat) : nat :=
  match t with
    | Leaf n ⇒ n
    | Node _ f ⇒ rifoldr plus O (fun idx ⇒ sum (f idx))
  end.

Fixpoint inc (t : tree nat) : tree nat :=
  match t with
    | Leaf n ⇒ Leaf (S n)
    | Node _ f ⇒ Node (fun idx ⇒ inc (f idx))
  end.
```

Now we are ready to prove the theorem. We do not need to define any new induction principle, but it will be helpful to prove some lemmas.

```
Lemma plus_ge : ∀ x1 y1 x2 y2,
  x1 ≥ x2
  → y1 ≥ y2
  → x1 + y1 ≥ x2 + y2.
  crush.
Qed.

Lemma sum_inc' : ∀ n (f1 f2 : ffin n → nat),
  (∀ idx, f1 idx ≥ f2 idx)
  → rifoldr plus O f1 ≥ rifoldr plus O f2.
  Hint Resolve plus_ge.

  induction n; crush.
Qed.

Theorem sum_inc : ∀ t, sum (inc t) ≥ sum t.
  Hint Resolve sum_inc'.

  induction t; crush.
Qed.
```

Even if Coq generated complete induction principles automatically for nested inductive definitions like the one we started with, there would still be advantages to using this style of reflexive encoding. We see one of those advantages in the definition of inc, where we did not need to use any kind of auxiliary function. In general, reflexive encodings often admit direct implementations of operations that would require recursion if performed with more traditional inductive data structures.

9.4.1   Another Interpreter Example

We develop another example of variable arity constructors, in the form of optimization of a small expression language with a construct like Scheme's cond. Each conditional expression takes a list of pairs of Boolean tests and bodies. The value of the conditional comes from the body of the first test in the list to evaluate to true. To simplify the interpreter, we force each conditional to include a final, default case.

Inductive **type'** : Type := Nat | Bool.

Inductive **exp'** : **type'** → Type :=
| NConst : **nat** → **exp'** Nat
| Plus : **exp'** Nat → **exp'** Nat → **exp'** Nat
| Eq : **exp'** Nat → **exp'** Nat → **exp'** Bool

| BConst : **bool** → **exp'** Bool

| Cond : ∀ n t, (ffin n → **exp'** Bool)
  → (ffin n → **exp'** t) → **exp'** t → **exp'** t.

A Cond is parameterized by a natural n, which tells us how many cases this conditional has. The test expressions are represented with a function of type ffin n → **exp'** Bool, and the bodies are represented with a function of type ffin n → **exp'** t, where t is the overall type. The final **exp'** t argument is the default case. For example, here is an expression that successively checks whether $2 + 2 = 5$ (returning 0 if so) or if $1 + 1 = 2$ (returning 1 if so), returning 2 otherwise:

Example ex1 := Cond 2
  (fun f ⇒ match f with
              | None ⇒ Eq (Plus (NConst 2) (NConst 2)) (NConst 5)
              | Some None ⇒ Eq (Plus (NConst 1) (NConst 1))
                (NConst 2)
              | Some (Some v) ⇒ match v with end
            end)
  (fun f ⇒ match f with

```
              | None ⇒ NConst 0
              | Some None ⇒ NConst 1
              | Some (Some v) ⇒ match v with end
            end)
    (NConst 2).
```

We start implementing the interpreter with a standard type denotation function.

```
Definition type'Denote (t : type') : Set :=
  match t with
    | Nat ⇒ nat
    | Bool ⇒ bool
  end.
```

To implement the expression interpreter, it is useful to have the following function that implements the functionality of Cond without involving any syntax.

```
Section cond.
  Variable A : Set.
  Variable default : A.

  Fixpoint cond (n : nat) : (ffin n → bool) → (ffin n → A) → A :=
    match n with
      | O ⇒ fun _ _ ⇒ default
      | S n' ⇒ fun tests bodies ⇒
        if tests None
          then bodies None
          else cond n'
            (fun idx ⇒ tests (Some idx))
            (fun idx ⇒ bodies (Some idx))
    end.
End cond.

Implicit Arguments cond [A n].
```

Now the expression interpreter is straightforward to write.

```
Fixpoint exp'Denote t (e : exp' t) : type'Denote t :=
  match e with
    | NConst n ⇒ n
    | Plus e1 e2 ⇒ exp'Denote e1 + exp'Denote e2
    | Eq e1 e2 ⇒
      if eq_nat_dec (exp'Denote e1) (exp'Denote e2) then true
        else false
```

```
    | BConst b ⇒ b
    | Cond _ _ tests bodies default ⇒
      cond
      (exp'Denote default)
      (fun idx ⇒ exp'Denote (tests idx))
      (fun idx ⇒ exp'Denote (bodies idx))
  end.
```

We implement a constant-folding function that optimizes conditionals, removing cases with known false tests and cases that come after known true tests. A function cfoldCond implements the heart of this logic. The convoy pattern is used again near the end of the implementation.

```
Section cfoldCond.
  Variable t : type'.
  Variable default : exp' t.

  Fixpoint cfoldCond (n : nat)
    : (ffin n → exp' Bool) → (ffin n → exp' t) → exp' t :=
    match n with
      | O ⇒ fun _ _ ⇒ default
      | S n' ⇒ fun tests bodies ⇒
        match tests None return _ with
          | BConst true ⇒ bodies None
          | BConst false ⇒ cfoldCond n'
            (fun idx ⇒ tests (Some idx))
            (fun idx ⇒ bodies (Some idx))
          | _ ⇒
            let e := cfoldCond n'
              (fun idx ⇒ tests (Some idx))
              (fun idx ⇒ bodies (Some idx)) in
            match e in exp' t return exp' t → exp' t with
              | Cond n _ tests' bodies' default' ⇒ fun body ⇒
                Cond
                (S n)
                (fun idx ⇒ match idx with
                               | None ⇒ tests None
                               | Some idx ⇒ tests' idx
                           end)
                (fun idx ⇒ match idx with
                               | None ⇒ body
                               | Some idx ⇒ bodies' idx
```

$$\begin{array}{l}
\quad\quad\quad\quad\quad\quad\quad\quad\quad\text{end)} \\
\quad\quad\quad\quad\quad\quad\textit{default'} \\
\quad\quad\quad\quad\mid e \Rightarrow \textsf{fun } \textit{body} \Rightarrow \\
\quad\quad\quad\quad\textsf{Cond} \\
\quad\quad\quad\quad 1 \\
\quad\quad\quad\quad (\textsf{fun } \_ \Rightarrow \textit{tests } \textsf{None}) \\
\quad\quad\quad\quad (\textsf{fun } \_ \Rightarrow \textit{body}) \\
\quad\quad\quad\quad e \\
\quad\quad\quad\text{end } (\textit{bodies } \textsf{None}) \\
\quad\quad\text{end} \\
\quad\text{end.}
\end{array}$$

End cfoldCond.

Implicit Arguments cfoldCond [*t n*].

As in the interpreters, most of the action was in this helper function, and cfold itself is easy to write.

Fixpoint cfold *t* (*e* : **exp'** *t*) : **exp'** *t* :=
  match *e* with
    | NConst *n* ⇒ NConst *n*
    | Plus *e1 e2* ⇒
      let *e1'* := cfold *e1* in
      let *e2'* := cfold *e2* in
      match *e1', e2'* return **exp'** Nat with
        | NConst *n1*, NConst *n2* ⇒ NConst (*n1* + *n2*)
        | _, _ ⇒ Plus *e1' e2'*
      end
    | Eq *e1 e2* ⇒
      let *e1'* := cfold *e1* in
      let *e2'* := cfold *e2* in
      match *e1', e2'* return **exp'** Bool with
        | NConst *n1*, NConst *n2* ⇒
          BConst (if eq_nat_dec *n1 n2* then true else false)
        | _, _ ⇒ Eq *e1' e2'*
      end

    | BConst *b* ⇒ BConst *b*
    | Cond _ _ *tests bodies default* ⇒
      cfoldCond
      (cfold *default*)
      (fun *idx* ⇒ cfold (*tests idx*))
      (fun *idx* ⇒ cfold (*bodies idx*))
  end.

To prove the final correctness theorem, it is useful to know that cfoldCond preserves expression meanings. The following lemma formalizes that property. The proof is a standard, mostly automated one, along with a guided instantiation of the quantifiers in the induction hypothesis.

Lemma cfoldCond_correct : $\forall$ t (*default* : **exp'** t)
   n (*tests* : ffin n $\rightarrow$ **exp'** Bool) (*bodies* : ffin n $\rightarrow$ **exp'** t),
   exp'Denote (cfoldCond *default tests bodies*)
   = exp'Denote (Cond n *tests bodies default*).
   induction n; *crush*;
     match goal with
        | [*IHn* : $\forall$ *tests bodies*, _, *tests* : _ $\rightarrow$ _, *bodies* : _ $\rightarrow$ _ $\vdash$ _] $\Rightarrow$
          specialize (*IHn* (fun idx $\Rightarrow$ *tests* (Some idx))
            (fun idx $\Rightarrow$ *bodies* (Some idx)))
     end;
     repeat (match goal with
             | [$\vdash$ context[match ?E with NConst _ $\Rightarrow$ _
                     | _ $\Rightarrow$ _ end]] $\Rightarrow$
              dep_destruct E
            | [$\vdash$ context[if ?B then _ else _]] $\Rightarrow$ destruct B
        end; *crush*).
Qed.

It is also useful to know that the result of a call to cond is not changed by substituting new tests and bodies functions, so long as the new functions have the same input-output behavior as the old. It turns out that, in Coq, it is not possible to prove in general that functions related in this way are equal (see Section 10.6). For now, it suffices to prove that the particular function cond is *extensional*; that is, it is unaffected by substitution of functions with input-output equivalents.

Lemma cond_ext : $\forall$ (A : Set) (*default* : A) n
   (*tests tests'* : ffin n $\rightarrow$ **bool**) (*bodies bodies'* : ffin n $\rightarrow$ A),
   ($\forall$ idx, *tests idx* = *tests' idx*)
   $\rightarrow$ ($\forall$ idx, *bodies idx* = *bodies' idx*)
   $\rightarrow$ cond *default tests bodies*
   = cond *default tests' bodies'*.
   induction n; *crush*;
     match goal with
        | [$\vdash$ context[if ?E then _ else _]] $\Rightarrow$ destruct E
     end; *crush*.
Qed.

Now the final theorem is easy to prove.

```
Theorem cfold_correct : ∀ t (e : exp' t),
  exp'Denote (cfold e) = exp'Denote e.
  Hint Rewrite cfoldCond_correct.
  Hint Resolve cond_ext.
```

> induction *e*; *crush*;
> > repeat (match goal with
> > > | [⊢ context[cfold ?*E*]] ⇒ *dep_destruct* (cfold *E*)
> > > end; *crush*).

```
Qed.
```

We add the two lemmas as hints and perform standard automation with pattern matching of subterms to destruct.

9.5   Choosing between Representations

It is not always clear which of these representation techniques to apply in a particular situation, but I summarize here the pros and cons of each.

Inductive types are often the most pleasant to work with, after someone has spent the time implementing some basic library functions for them using `match` annotations. Many aspects of Coq's logic and tactic support are specialized to deal with inductive types, and one may miss out with other encodings.

Recursive types usually involve much less initial effort, but they can be less convenient to use with proof automation. For instance, the `simpl` tactic (which is among the ingredients in *crush*) is sometimes overzealous in simplifying uses of functions over recursive types. Consider a call `get l f`, where variable *l* has type `filist` *A* (`S` *n*). The type of *l* would be simplified to an explicit pair type. In a proof involving many recursive types, this kind of unhelpful "simplification" can lead to rapid bloat in the sizes of subgoals. Even worse, it can prevent syntactic pattern matching, as in cases where `filist` is expected but a pair type is found in the "simplified" version. The same problem applies to applications of recursive functions to values in recursive types: the recursive function call may "simplify" when the top-level structure of the type index but not the recursive value is known, because such functions are generally defined by recursion on the index, not the value.

Another disadvantage of recursive types is that they only apply to type families whose indices determine their skeletons. This is not true for all data structures; a good counterexample comes from the richly typed programming language syntax types we have used several times so far. The fact that a piece of syntax has type Nat says nothing about the tree structure of that syntax.

It is also true that parameterized recursive types are hard to use within the definitions of nested inductive types, as we saw in Section 9.4. Coq's well-formedness check on inductive definitions will accept many definitions that use inductive or function-based nested types but reject similar definitions based on recursive types.

Finally, Coq type inference can be more helpful in constructing values in inductive types. Application of a particular constructor of that type tells Coq what to expect from the arguments, whereas, for instance, forming a generic pair does not make clear an intention to interpret the value as belonging to a particular recursive type. This downside can be mitigated to an extent by writing constructor functions for a recursive type, mirroring the definition of the corresponding inductive type.

Reflexive encodings of datatypes are seen relatively rarely. As the earlier examples demonstrated, manipulating index values manually can lead to hard-to-read code. A normal inductive type is generally easier to work with, once someone has gone through the trouble of implementing an induction principle manually with the techniques studied in Chapter 3. For small developments, avoiding that kind of coding can justify the use of reflexive data structures. There are also some useful instances of co-inductive definitions with nested data structures (e.g., lists of values in the co-inductive type) that can only be deconstructed effectively with reflexive encoding of the nested structures.

10   Reasoning about Equality Proofs

In traditional mathematics, the concept of equality is usually taken as a given, but in type theory, equality is a very contentious subject. There are at least three different notions of equality that are important in Coq, and researchers are actively investigating new definitions of what it means for two terms to be equal. Even once we fix a notion of equality, there are inevitably issues that arise in proving properties of programs that manipulate equality proofs explicitly. In this chapter, I introduce the different notions of equality and describe design patterns for manipulating equality proofs in programs.

10.1   The Definitional Equality

In many examples so far, proof goals followed by computation. That is, we applied computational reduction rules to reduce the goal to a normal form, at which point it followed trivially. Exactly when this works and when it does not depends on the details of Coq's *definitional equality*. This is an untyped binary relation appearing in the formal metatheory of the Calculus of Inductive Constructions (CIC), which contains a typing rule allowing the conclusion $E : T$ from the premise $E : T'$ and a proof that T and T' are definitionally equal.

The cbv tactic helps us illustrate the rules of Coq's definitional equality. We redefine the natural number predecessor function and construct a manual proof that it returns 0 when applied to 1.

```
Definition pred' (x : nat) :=
  match x with
    | O ⇒ O
    | S n' ⇒ let y := n' in y
  end.

Theorem reduce_me : pred' 1 = 0.
```

CIC follows the traditions of lambda calculus in associating reduction rules with Greek letters. Coq can certainly be said to support the familiar alpha reduction rule, which allows capture-avoiding renaming of bound variables, but we never need to apply alpha explicitly, since Coq uses a de Bruijn representation [11] that encodes terms canonically.

The delta rule is for unfolding global definitions. We can use it here to unfold the definition of pred′. We do this with the cbv tactic, which takes a list of reduction rules and makes as many call-by-value reduction steps as possible, using only those rules. There is an analogous tactic lazy for call-by-need reduction.

```
cbv delta.
```

```
==============================
```

$(\text{fun } x : \textsf{nat} \Rightarrow \texttt{match } x \texttt{ with}$
$\qquad\qquad |\ 0 \Rightarrow 0$
$\qquad\qquad |\ \textsf{S } n' \Rightarrow \texttt{let } y := n' \texttt{ in } y$
$\qquad\qquad \texttt{end})\ 1 = 0$

At this point, we apply the beta reduction of lambda calculus to simplify the application of a known function abstraction.

```
cbv beta.
```

```
==============================
```

$\texttt{match } 1 \texttt{ with}$
$|\ 0 \Rightarrow 0$
$|\ \textsf{S } n' \Rightarrow \texttt{let } y := n' \texttt{ in } y$
$\texttt{end} = 0$

Next is the iota reduction, which simplifies a single match term by determining which pattern matches.

```
cbv iota.
```

```
==============================
```

$(\texttt{fun } n' : \textsf{nat} \Rightarrow \texttt{let } y := n' \texttt{ in } y)\ 0 = 0$

Now we need another beta reduction.

```
cbv beta.
```

```
==============================
```

$(\texttt{let } y := 0 \texttt{ in } y) = 0$

The final reduction rule is zeta, which replaces a let expression by its body with the appropriate term substituted.

```
cbv zeta.
```

```
==============================
```

$$0 = 0$$

```
reflexivity.
Qed.
```

The `beta` reduction rule applies to recursive functions as well, and its behavior may be surprising in some instances. For instance, we can run some simple tests using the reduction strategy `compute`, which applies all applicable rules of the definitional equality.

Definition id $(n : \mathbf{nat}) := n$.

Eval compute in fun $x \Rightarrow$ id x.

    $=$ fun $x : \mathbf{nat} \Rightarrow x$

Fixpoint id' $(n : \mathbf{nat}) := n$.

Eval compute in fun $x \Rightarrow$ id' x.

    $=$ fun $x : \mathbf{nat} \Rightarrow (\mathtt{fix}$ id' $(n : \mathbf{nat}) : \mathbf{nat} := n)$ x

By running `compute`, we ask Coq to run reduction steps until no more apply, so why do we see an application of a known function where clearly no beta reduction has been performed? The answer has to do with ensuring termination of all Gallina programs. One candidate rule would say that we apply recursive definitions wherever possible. However, this would clearly lead to nonterminating reduction sequences, since the function may appear fully applied within its own definition, and we would naïvely "simplify" such applications immediately. Instead, Coq only applies the beta rule for a recursive function when *the top-level structure of the recursive argument is known*. For id', we have only one argument n, so clearly it is the recursive argument, and the top-level structure of n is known when the function is applied to O or to some S e term. The variable x is neither, so reduction is blocked.

What are recursive arguments in general? Every recursive function is compiled by Coq to a `fix` expression, for anonymous definition of recursive functions. Further, every `fix` with multiple arguments has one designated as the recursive argument via a `struct` annotation. The recursive argument is the one that must decrease across recursive calls, to appease Coq's termination checker. Coq will generally infer which argument is recursive, though we may also specify it manually, if we want to tweak reduction behavior. For instance, consider this definition of a function to add two lists of **nat**s elementwise:

Fixpoint addLists $(ls1 \; ls2 : \mathbf{list} \; \mathbf{nat}) : \mathbf{list} \; \mathbf{nat} :=$
  match $ls1, ls2$ with
    | $n1 :: ls1'$, $n2 :: ls2' \Rightarrow n1 + n2 ::$ addLists $ls1' \; ls2'$

```
    | _, _ ⇒ nil
  end.
```

By default, Coq chooses *ls1* as the recursive argument. We see that *ls2* would have been another valid choice. The choice has a critical effect on reduction behavior, as two examples illustrate.

Eval compute in fun *ls* ⇒ addLists nil *ls*.

```
    = fun _ : list nat ⇒ nil
```

Eval compute in fun *ls* ⇒ addLists *ls* nil.

```
    = fun ls : list nat ⇒
      (fix addLists (ls1 ls2 : list nat) : list nat :=
          match ls1 with
          | nil ⇒ nil
          | n1 :: ls1' ⇒
              match ls2 with
              | nil ⇒ nil
              | n2 :: ls2' ⇒
                  (fix plus (n m : nat) : nat :=
                      match n with
                      | 0 ⇒ m
                      | S p ⇒ S (plus p m)
                      end) n1 n2 :: addLists ls1' ls2'
              end
          end) ls nil
```

The outer application of the fix expression for addLists was only simplified in the first case, because in the second case the recursive argument is *ls*, whose top-level structure is not known.

The opposite behavior pertains to a version of addLists with *ls2* marked as recursive.

Fixpoint addLists' (*ls1 ls2* : list nat) {struct *ls2*} : list nat :=
```
  match ls1, ls2 with
    | n1 :: ls1' , n2 :: ls2' ⇒ n1 + n2 :: addLists' ls1' ls2'
    | _, _ ⇒ nil
  end.
```

Eval compute in fun *ls* ⇒ addLists' *ls* nil.

```
    = fun ls : list nat ⇒ match ls with
                          | nil ⇒ nil
                          | _ :: _ ⇒ nil
                          end
```

We see that all use of recursive functions has been eliminated, though the term has not quite simplified to nil. We could get it to do so by switching the order of the `match` discriminees in the definition of addLists'.

Recall that co-recursive definitions have a dual rule: a co-recursive call only simplifies when it is the discriminee of a `match`. This condition is built into the beta rule for `cofix`, the anonymous form of `CoFixpoint`.

The standard **eq** relation is critically dependent on the definitional equality. The relation **eq** is often called a *propositional equality*, because it reifies definitional equality as a proposition that may or may not hold. Standard axiomatizations of an equality predicate in first-order logic define equality in terms of properties it has, like reflexivity, symmetry, and transitivity. In contrast, for **eq** in Coq, those properties are implicit in the properties of the definitional equality, which are built into CIC's metatheory and the implementation of Gallina. We could add new rules to the definitional equality, and **eq** would keep its definition and methods of use.

This may sound like the choice of **eq**'s definition is unimportant. To the contrary, this chapter gives examples where alternative definitions may simplify proofs. Before that, I introduce proof methods for goals that use proofs of the standard propositional equality as data.

10.2 Heterogeneous Lists Revisited

An example dependent data structure was the heterogeneous list and its associated cursor type (see Section 9.2). The recursive version poses some special challenges related to equality proofs, since it uses such proofs in its definition of fmember types (see Section 9.3 or the code repeated below).

```
Section fhlist.
  Variable A : Type.
  Variable B : A → Type.

  Fixpoint fhlist (ls : list A) : Type :=
    match ls with
      | nil ⇒ unit
      | x :: ls' ⇒ B x × fhlist ls'
    end%type.

  Variable elm : A.

  Fixpoint fmember (ls : list A) : Type :=
```

```
  match ls with
    | nil ⇒ Empty_set
    | x :: ls’ ⇒ (x = elm) + fmember ls’
  end%type.
Fixpoint fhget (ls : list A) : fhlist ls → fmember ls → B elm :=
  match ls return fhlist ls → fmember ls → B elm with
    | nil ⇒ fun _ idx ⇒ match idx with end
    | _ :: ls’ ⇒ fun mls idx ⇒
      match idx with
        | inl pf ⇒ match pf with
                     | eq_refl ⇒ fst mls
                   end
        | inr idx’ ⇒ fhget ls’ (snd mls) idx’
      end
  end.
End fhlist.
Implicit Arguments fhget [A B elm ls].
```

We can define a map-like function for fhlists.

```
Section fhlist_map.
  Variables A : Type.
  Variables B C : A → Type.
  Variable f : ∀ x, B x → C x.
  Fixpoint fhmap (ls : list A) : fhlist B ls → fhlist C ls :=
    match ls return fhlist B ls → fhlist C ls with
      | nil ⇒ fun _ ⇒ tt
      | _ :: _ ⇒ fun hls ⇒ (f (fst hls), fhmap _ (snd hls))
    end.
  Implicit Arguments fhmap [ls].
```

For the inductive versions of the ilist definitions, we proved a lemma about the interaction of get and imap. It was a strategic choice not to attempt such a proof for the preceding definitions, which brings us to the problems that are the subject of this chapter.

```
  Variable elm : A.
  Theorem fhget_fhmap : ∀ ls (mem : fmember elm ls) (hls : fhlist B ls),
    fhget (fhmap hls) mem = f (fhget hls mem).
    induction ls; crush.
```

In Coq 8.2, one subgoal remains at this point. Coq 8.3 has added some tactic improvements that enable *crush* to complete all of both inductive cases. To introduce the basics of reasoning about equality, it is useful to review what was necessary in Coq 8.2.

Part of the single remaining subgoal is

$a0 : a = elm$

===============================

```
  match a0 in (_ = a2) return (C a2) with
  | eq_refl ⇒ f a1
  end = f match a0 in (_ = a2) return (B a2) with
          | eq_refl ⇒ a1
          end
```

This seems like a trivial obligation. The equality proof $a0$ must be eq_refl, the only constructor of **eq**. Therefore, both the `match`es reduce to the point where the conclusion follows by reflexivity.

    destruct $a0$.

`User error: Cannot solve a second-order unification problem`

This is one of Coq's standard error messages for indicating a failure in its heuristics for attempting an instance of an undecidable problem about dependent typing. We might try to nudge things in the right direction by stating the lemma that we believe makes the conclusion trivial.

    assert ($a0$ = eq_refl _).

```
The term "eq_refl ?98" has type "?98 = ?98"
while it is expected to have type "a = elm"
```

In retrospect, the problem is not hard to see. Reflexivity proofs only show $x = x$ for particular values of x, whereas here we are thinking in terms of a proof of $a = elm$, where the two sides of the equality are not equal syntactically. Thus, the essential lemma we need does not even type-check.

This chapter gives several useful patterns for proving obligations like this.

For this particular example, the solution is straightforward. The destruct tactic has a simpler sibling `case` that should behave identically for any inductive type with one constructor of no arguments.

    case $a0$.

===============================

$f\ a1 = f\ a1$

It seems that `destruct` was trying to be too smart.

    reflexivity.
Qed.

It is helpful to examine the proof terms generated by this sort of strategy. A simpler example illustrates this.

    Lemma lemma1 : ∀ x (pf : x = elm),
      O = match pf with eq_refl ⇒ O end.
      simple destruct pf; reflexivity.
    Qed.

The tactic `simple destruct` *pf* is a convenient form for applying case. It runs `intro` to bring into scope all quantified variables up to its argument.

    Print lemma1.

lemma1 =
fun (x : A) (pf : x = elm) ⇒
match pf as e in (_ = y) return (0 = match e with
                                    | eq_refl ⇒ 0
                                    end) with
| eq_refl ⇒ eq_refl 0
end
      : ∀ (x : A) (pf : x = elm), 0 = match pf with
                                      | eq_refl ⇒ 0
                                      end

Using what we know about shorthands for `match` annotations, we can write this proof in shorter form manually.

    Definition lemma1' (x : A) (pf : x = elm) :=
      match pf return (0 = match pf with
                           | eq_refl ⇒ 0
                          end) with
        | eq_refl ⇒ eq_refl 0
      end.

Surprisingly, what seems at first like a simpler lemma is harder to prove.

    Lemma lemma2 : ∀ (x : A) (pf : x = x),
      O = match pf with eq_refl ⇒ O end.
      simple destruct pf.

User error: Cannot solve a second-order unification problem

```
  Abort.
```

Nonetheless, we can adapt the last manual proof to handle this theorem.

```
  Definition lemma2 :=
    fun (x : A) (pf : x = x) ⇒
      match pf return (0 = match pf with
                              | eq_refl ⇒ 0
                            end) with
        | eq_refl ⇒ eq_refl 0
      end.
```

We can try to prove a lemma that would simplify proofs of many facts like lemma2.

```
  Lemma lemma3 : ∀ (x : A) (pf : x = x), pf = eq_refl x.
    simple destruct pf.
```

```
User error: Cannot solve a second-order unification problem
  Abort.
```

This time, even our manual attempt fails.

```
  Definition lemma3' :=
    fun (x : A) (pf : x = x) ⇒
      match pf as pf' in (_ = x') return (pf' = eq_refl x') with
        | eq_refl ⇒ eq_refl _
      end.
```

```
The term "eq_refl x'" has type "x' = x'"
while it is expected to have type "x = x'"
```

The type error comes from the **return** annotation. In that annotation, the **as**-bound variable pf' has type $x = x'$, referring to the **in**-bound variable x'. To do a dependent **match**, we must choose a fresh name for the second argument of **eq** and use the "real" value x for the first argument. Thus, within the **return** clause, the proof we are matching on must equate two nonmatching terms, which makes it impossible to equate that proof with reflexivity.

Nonetheless, it turns out that, with one catch, we can prove this lemma.

```
  Lemma lemma3 : ∀ (x : A) (pf : x = x), pf = eq_refl x.
    intros; apply UIP_refl.
  Qed.
```

```
  Check UIP_refl.
```

UIP_refl
  $: \forall \, (U : \mathsf{Type}) \, (x : U) \, (p : x = x), \, p = \mathsf{eq\_refl} \; x$

The theorem UIP_refl comes from the Eqdep module of the standard library. (Its name uses the acronym UIP for "unicity of identity proofs.") Do the Coq authors know some clever technique for building such proofs that we have not seen yet? If they do, they did not use it for this proof. Rather, the proof is based on an *axiom*, the term *eq_rect_eq*.

    Print *eq_rect_eq*.

*** [*eq_rect_eq* :
$\forall \, (U : \mathsf{Type}) \, (p : U) \, (Q : U \to \mathsf{Type}) \, (x : Q \; p) \, (h : p = p),$
$x = \mathsf{eq\_rect} \; p \; Q \; x \; p \; h$]

The axiom *eq_rect_eq* states a fact that seems like common sense, once the notation is deciphered. The term eq_rect is the automatically generated recursion principle for **eq**. Calling eq_rect is another way of matching on an equality proof. The proof we match on is the argument h, and x is the body of the match. The statement of *eq_rect_eq* says that matches on proofs of $p = p$, for any p, are superfluous and may be removed. We can see this intuition better in code by asking Coq to simplify the theorem statement with the compute reduction strategy.

    Eval compute in $(\forall \, (U : \mathsf{Type}) \, (p : U) \, (Q : U \to \mathsf{Type})$
      $(x : Q \; p) \, (h : p = p),$
      $x = \mathsf{eq\_rect} \; p \; Q \; x \; p \; h).$

        $= \forall \, (U : \mathsf{Type}) \, (p : U) \, (Q : U \to \mathsf{Type}) \, (x : Q \; p) \, (h : p = p),$
        $x = \mathsf{match} \; h \; \mathsf{in} \; (\_ = y) \; \mathsf{return} \; (Q \; y) \; \mathsf{with}$
          $| \; \mathsf{eq\_refl} \Rightarrow x$
        end

We cannot prove *eq_rect_eq* from within Coq. This proposition is introduced as an axiom; that is, a proposition asserted as true without proof. We cannot assert just any statement without proof. For instance, adding **False** as an axiom would allow us to prove any proposition, defeating the point of using a proof assistant. In general, we need to be sure that we never assert *inconsistent* sets of axioms. A set of axioms is inconsistent if its conjunction implies **False**. For the case of *eq_rect_eq*, consistency has been verified outside of Coq via informal metatheory [43], in a study that also established unprovability of the axiom in CIC.

This axiom is equivalent to another that is more commonly known and mentioned in type theory circles.

    Check Streicher_K.

Streicher_K
  : ∀ (U : Type) (x : U) (P : $x = x$ → Prop),
      P eq_refl → ∀ p : $x = x$, P p

This refers to Streicher's axiom K [43], which says that a predicate on properly typed equality proofs holds of all such proofs if it holds of reflexivity.

End fhlist_map.

It is possible to avoid axioms altogether for equalities on types with decidable equality. The Eqdep_dec module of the standard library contains a parametric proof of UIP_refl for such cases. To simplify presentation, we continue to work with the axiom version in the rest of this chapter.

10.3   Type Casts in Theorem Statements

Sometimes we need to use tricks with equality just to state the theorems that we care about. To illustrate, we start by defining a concatenation function for fhlists.

Section fhapp.
  Variable A : Type.
  Variable B : A → Type.

  Fixpoint fhapp ($ls1$ $ls2$: list A)
      : fhlist B $ls1$ → fhlist B $ls2$ → fhlist B ($ls1$ ++ $ls2$) :=
    match $ls1$ with
      | nil ⇒ fun _ $hls2$ ⇒ $hls2$
      | _ :: _ ⇒ fun $hls1$ $hls2$ ⇒ (fst $hls1$, fhapp _ _ (snd $hls1$) $hls2$)
    end.

  Implicit Arguments fhapp [$ls1$ $ls2$].

We might like to prove that fhapp is associative.

  Theorem fhapp_assoc : ∀ $ls1$ $ls2$ $ls3$
      ($hls1$: fhlist B $ls1$) ($hls2$: fhlist B $ls2$) ($hls3$: fhlist B $ls3$),
      fhapp $hls1$ (fhapp $hls2$ $hls3$) = fhapp (fhapp $hls1$ $hls2$) $hls3$.

```
The term
"fhapp (ls1:=ls1 ++ ls2) (ls2:=ls3)
  (fhapp (ls1:=ls1) (ls2:=ls2) hls1 hls2) hls3"
has type "fhlist B ((ls1 ++ ls2) ++ ls3)"
```

```
while it is expected to have type
"fhlist B (ls1 ++ ls2 ++ ls3)"
```

This first attempt at the theorem statement does not even type-check. We know that the two fhlist types appearing in the error message are always equal, by associativity of normal list append, but this fact is not apparent to the type checker. This stems from the fact that Coq's equality is *intensional*, in the sense that type equality theorems can never be applied after the fact to get a term to type-check. Instead, we need to make use of equality explicitly in the theorem statement.

> Theorem fhapp_assoc : ∀ *ls1 ls2 ls3*
>   (*pf* : (*ls1* ++ *ls2*) ++ *ls3* = *ls1* ++ (*ls2* ++ *ls3*))
>   (*hls1* : fhlist *B ls1*) (*hls2* : fhlist *B ls2*) (*hls3* : fhlist *B ls3*),
>   fhapp *hls1* (fhapp *hls2 hls3*)
>   = match *pf* in (_ = *ls*) return fhlist _ *ls* with
> | eq_refl ⇒ fhapp (fhapp *hls1 hls2*) *hls3*
>   end.
>   induction *ls1*; *crush*.

The first remaining subgoal looks trivial enough.

```
============================
```
> fhapp (*ls1*:=*ls2*) (*ls2*:=*ls3*) *hls2 hls3* =
> match *pf* in (_ = *ls*) return (fhlist *B ls*) with
> | eq_refl ⇒ fhapp (*ls1*:=*ls2*) (*ls2*:=*ls3*) *hls2 hls3*
> end

We can try what worked in previous examples.

> case *pf*.

```
User error: Cannot solve a second-order unification problem
```

It seems we have reached another case where it is unclear how to use a dependent match to implement case analysis on the proof. We can try the UIP_refl theorem again.

> rewrite (UIP_refl _ _ *pf*).

```
============================
```
> fhapp (*ls1*:=*ls2*) (*ls2*:=*ls3*) *hls2 hls3* =
> fhapp (*ls1*:=*ls2*) (*ls2*:=*ls3*) *hls2 hls3*

> reflexivity.

The second subgoal is trickier.

> *pf* : *a* :: (*ls1* ++ *ls2*) ++ *ls3* = *a* :: *ls1* ++ *ls2* ++ *ls3*

```
==============================
(a0,
fhapp (ls1:=ls1) (ls2:=ls2 ++ ls3) b
  (fhapp (ls1:=ls2) (ls2:=ls3) hls2 hls3)) =
match pf in (_ = ls) return (fhlist B ls) with
| eq_refl ⇒
      (a0,
      fhapp (ls1:=ls1 ++ ls2) (ls2:=ls3)
        (fhapp (ls1:=ls1) (ls2:=ls2) b hls2) hls3)
end
```

```
    rewrite (UIP_refl _ _ pf).
```

```
The term "pf" has type
"a :: (ls1 ++ ls2) ++ ls3 = a :: ls1 ++ ls2 ++ ls3"
while it is expected to have type "?556 = ?556"
```

We can only apply UIP_refl on proofs of equality with syntactically equal operands, which is not the case with *pf* here. We need to manipulate the form of this subgoal to get to a point where we may use UIP_refl. A first step is obtaining a proof suitable to use in applying the induction hypothesis. Inversion on the structure of *pf* is sufficient for that.

```
    injection pf; intro pf'.
```

```
pf : a :: (ls1 ++ ls2) ++ ls3 = a :: ls1 ++ ls2 ++ ls3
pf' : (ls1 ++ ls2) ++ ls3 = ls1 ++ ls2 ++ ls3
==============================
(a0,
fhapp (ls1:=ls1) (ls2:=ls2 ++ ls3) b
  (fhapp (ls1:=ls2) (ls2:=ls3) hls2 hls3)) =
match pf in (_ = ls) return (fhlist B ls) with
| eq_refl ⇒
      (a0,
      fhapp (ls1:=ls1 ++ ls2) (ls2:=ls3)
        (fhapp (ls1:=ls1) (ls2:=ls2) b hls2) hls3)
end
```

Now we can rewrite using the inductive hypothesis.

```
    rewrite (IHls1 _ _ pf').
```

```
==============================
```

```
(a0,
match pf' in (_ = ls) return (fhlist B ls) with
| eq_refl ⇒
      fhapp (ls1:=ls1 ++ ls2) (ls2:=ls3)
        (fhapp (ls1:=ls1) (ls2:=ls2) b hls2) hls3
end) =
match pf in (_ = ls) return (fhlist B ls) with
| eq_refl ⇒
      (a0,
      fhapp (ls1:=ls1 ++ ls2) (ls2:=ls3)
        (fhapp (ls1:=ls1) (ls2:=ls2) b hls2) hls3)
end
```

We have made progress, as now only a single call to fhapp appears in the conclusion, repeated twice. Trying case analysis on the proofs still will not work, but we can enable it. Not only does just one call to fhapp matter now but it also *does not matter what the result of the call is.* In other words, the subgoal should remain true if we replace this fhapp call with a fresh variable. The generalize tactic helps us do exactly that.

generalize (fhapp (fhapp b $hls2$) $hls3$).

```
∀ f : fhlist B ((ls1 ++ ls2) ++ ls3),
(a0,
match pf' in (_ = ls) return (fhlist B ls) with
| eq_refl ⇒ f
end) =
match pf in (_ = ls) return (fhlist B ls) with
| eq_refl ⇒ (a0, f)
end
```

The conclusion has gotten markedly simpler. It seems counterintuitive that proving a more general theorem is easier, but such is the case here and in many other proofs that use dependent types heavily. Speaking informally, the reason is that match annotations contain some positions where only variables are allowed. When more elements of a goal are reduced to variables, built-in tactics can have more success building match terms.

In this case, it is helpful to generalize over the two proofs as well.

generalize pf pf'.

$$\forall (pf0 : a :: (ls1 ++ ls2) ++ ls3 = a :: ls1 ++ ls2 ++ ls3)$$

$(pf\text{'}0 : (ls1 \mathbin{++} ls2) \mathbin{++} ls3 = ls1 \mathbin{++} ls2 \mathbin{++} ls3)$
$(f : \mathsf{fhlist}\ B\ ((ls1 \mathbin{++} ls2) \mathbin{++} ls3)),$
$(a0,$
match $pf\text{'}0$ in $(\_ = ls)$ return $(\mathsf{fhlist}\ B\ ls)$ with
$\mid \mathsf{eq\_refl} \Rightarrow f$
end$) =$
match $pf0$ in $(\_ = ls)$ return $(\mathsf{fhlist}\ B\ ls)$ with
$\mid \mathsf{eq\_refl} \Rightarrow (a0, f)$
end

To an experienced dependent types hacker, the appearance of this goal term calls for a celebration. The formula has a critical property that indicates that our problems are over. To get the proofs into the right form to apply $\mathsf{UIP\_refl}$, we need to use associativity of list append to rewrite their types. We could not do so before because other parts of the goal require the proofs to retain their original types. In particular, the call to fhapp that we generalized must have type $(ls1 \mathbin{++} ls2) \mathbin{++} ls3$, for some values of the list variables. If we rewrite the type of the proof used to type-cast this value to something like $ls1 \mathbin{++} ls2 \mathbin{++} ls3 = ls1 \mathbin{++} ls2 \mathbin{++} ls3$, then the left side of the equality would no longer match the type of the term we are trying to cast.

However, now that we have generalized over the fhapp call, the type of the term being type-cast appears explicitly in the goal and *may be rewritten as well*. In particular, the final masterstroke is rewriting everywhere in the goal using associativity of list append.

```
rewrite app_assoc.
```

===============================
$\forall\ (pf0 : a :: ls1 \mathbin{++} ls2 \mathbin{++} ls3 = a :: ls1 \mathbin{++} ls2 \mathbin{++} ls3)$
$(pf\text{'}0 : ls1 \mathbin{++} ls2 \mathbin{++} ls3 = ls1 \mathbin{++} ls2 \mathbin{++} ls3)$
$(f : \mathsf{fhlist}\ B\ (ls1 \mathbin{++} ls2 \mathbin{++} ls3)),$
$(a0,$
match $pf\text{'}0$ in $(\_ = ls)$ return $(\mathsf{fhlist}\ B\ ls)$ with
$\mid \mathsf{eq\_refl} \Rightarrow f$
end$) =$
match $pf0$ in $(\_ = ls)$ return $(\mathsf{fhlist}\ B\ ls)$ with
$\mid \mathsf{eq\_refl} \Rightarrow (a0, f)$
end

We have achieved the crucial property: the type of each generalized equality proof has syntactically equal operands. This makes it easy to finish the proof with $\mathsf{UIP\_refl}$.

```
    intros.
    rewrite (UIP_refl _ _ pf0).
    rewrite (UIP_refl _ _ pf'0).
    reflexivity.
  Qed.
End fhapp.
```

Implicit Arguments fhapp [*A B ls1 ls2*].

This proof strategy was cumbersome and unorthodox, from the perspective of mainstream mathematics. The next section explores an alternative that leads to simpler developments in some cases.

10.4   Heterogeneous Equality

There is another equality predicate, defined in the **JMeq** module of the standard library, implementing *heterogeneous equality*.

Print **JMeq**.

Inductive JMeq (A : Type) (x : A) : $\forall$ B : Type, $B \to$ Prop :=
    JMeq_refl : JMeq x x

The identifier **JMeq** stands for *John Major equality*, a name coined by Conor McBride [23] as an inside joke about British politics. The definition **JMeq** starts out looking a lot like the definition of **eq**. The crucial difference is that we may use **JMeq** *on arguments of different types*. For instance, a lemma that we failed to establish before is trivial with **JMeq**. It makes for prettier theorem statements to define some syntactic shorthand first.

Infix "==" := **JMeq** (at level 70, no associativity).

Definition UIP_refl' (A : Type) (x : A) (pf : x = x)
    : pf == eq_refl x :=
    match pf return (pf == eq_refl _) with
      | eq_refl $\Rightarrow$ JMeq_refl _
    end.

There is no quick way to write such a proof by tactics, but the underlying proof term that we want is trivial.

Suppose that we want to use UIP_refl' to establish another lemma of the kind seen earlier.

Lemma lemma4 : $\forall$ (A : Type) (x : A) (pf : x = x),
    O = match pf with eq_refl $\Rightarrow$ O end.
    intros; rewrite (UIP_refl' pf); reflexivity.

```
Qed.
```

This seems straightforward, but the `rewrite` is implemented in terms of an axiom.

```
Check JMeq_eq.
```

JMeq_eq
    : ∀ $(A : \mathsf{Type})$ $(x\ y : A)$, $x == y \rightarrow x = y$

We cannot prove that heterogeneous equality implies normal equality. The difficulties are based on limitations of `match` annotations. The *JMeq_eq* axiom has been proved consistent, but asserting it may still be considered to complicate the logic, so there is some motivation for avoiding it.

We can redo the fhapp associativity proof based on JMeq.

```
Section fhapp'.
  Variable A : Type.
  Variable B : A → Type.
```

This time, the naïve theorem statement type-checks.

```
Theorem fhapp_assoc' : ∀ ls1 ls2 ls3 (hls1 : fhlist B ls1)
  (hls2 : fhlist B ls2) (hls3 : fhlist B ls3),
  fhapp hls1 (fhapp hls2 hls3) == fhapp (fhapp hls1 hls2) hls3.
  induction ls1; crush.
```

Even better, *crush* discharges the first subgoal automatically. The second subgoal is

==============================
  $(a0, \mathsf{fhapp}\ b\ (\mathsf{fhapp}\ hls2\ hls3)) == (a0, \mathsf{fhapp}\ (\mathsf{fhapp}\ b\ hls2)\ hls3)$

It looks like one rewrite with the inductive hypothesis should be enough to make the goal trivial. Here is what happens when we try that in Coq 8.2:

```
  rewrite IHls1.
```

```
Error: Impossible to unify
"fhlist B ((ls1 ++ ?1572) ++ ?1573)" with
"fhlist B (ls1 ++ ?1572 ++ ?1573)"
```

Coq 8.4 currently gives an error message about an uncaught exception. Perhaps that will be fixed soon. In any case, it is educational to consider a more explicit approach.

We see that JMeq is not a silver bullet. We can use it to simplify the statements of equality facts, but the Coq type checker uses nontrivial heterogeneous equality facts no more readily than it uses standard equality facts. Here, the problem is that the form (*e1*, *e2*) is syntactic sugar for an explicit application of a constructor of an inductive type. That application mentions the type of each tuple element explicitly, and `rewrite` tries to change one of those elements without updating the corresponding type argument.

We can get around this problem by another multiple use of `generalize`. We want to bring into the goal the proper instance of the inductive hypothesis and also generalize the two relevant uses of fhapp.

```
generalize (fhapp b (fhapp hls2 hls3))
   (fhapp (fhapp b hls2) hls3)
   (IHls1 _ _ b hls2 hls3).
```

    ================================

$\forall$ (*f* : fhlist *B* (*ls1* ++ *ls2* ++ *ls3*))
   (*f0* : fhlist *B* ((*ls1* ++ *ls2*) ++ *ls3*)),
   f == *f0* → (*a0*, *f*) == (*a0*, *f0*)

Now we can rewrite with append associativity, as before.

```
rewrite app_assoc.
```

    ================================

$\forall$ *f f0* : fhlist *B* (*ls1* ++ *ls2* ++ *ls3*), *f* == *f0*
   → (*a0*, *f*) == (*a0*, *f0*)

From this point, the goal is trivial.

```
intros f f0 H; rewrite H; reflexivity.
Qed.
```

End fhapp'.

This example illustrates a general pattern: heterogeneous equality often simplifies theorem statements, but we still need to line up some dependent pattern matches that tactics will generate for us.

The proof we have found relies on the *JMeq_eq* axiom, which we can verify with a command `Print Assumptions`.

`Print Assumptions fhapp_assoc'.`

Axioms:
JMeq_eq : $\forall$ (*A* : Type) (*x y* : *A*), *x* == *y* → *x* = *y*

It was the `rewrite H` tactic that implicitly appealed to the axiom. By restructuring the proof, we can avoid axiom dependence. A general lemma about pairs provides the key element. (The use of `generalize` can be thought of as reducing the proof to another, more complex and specialized lemma.)

Lemma pair_cong : $\forall$ *A1 A2 B1 B2* $(x1 : A1)$ $(x2 : A2)$
  $(y1 : B1)$ $(y2 : B2)$,
  $x1 == x2$
  $\rightarrow y1 == y2$
  $\rightarrow (x1 , y1) == (x2 , y2)$.
  intros until $y2$; intros Hx Hy; rewrite Hx; rewrite Hy;
    reflexivity.
Qed.

Hint Resolve pair_cong.

Section fhapp''.
  Variable A : Type.
  Variable $B : A \rightarrow$ Type.

  Theorem fhapp_assoc'' : $\forall$ *ls1 ls2 ls3* $(hls1 :$ fhlist B *ls1*$)$
    $(hls2 :$ fhlist B *ls2*$)$ $(hls3 :$ fhlist B *ls3*$)$,
    fhapp *hls1* (fhapp *hls2* *hls3*) == fhapp (fhapp *hls1* *hls2*) *hls3*.
    induction *ls1*; *crush*.

  Qed.
End fhapp''.

Print Assumptions fhapp_assoc''.

Closed under the global context

One might wonder exactly which elements of a proof involving JMeq imply that *JMeq_eq* must be used. For instance, rewrite brought *JMeq_eq* into the proof of fhapp_assoc', yet we also used rewrite with JMeq hypotheses while avoiding axioms. One illuminating exercise is comparing the types of the lemmas that rewrite uses to implement the rewrites. Here is the normal lemma for **eq** rewriting:

Check eq_ind_r.

eq_ind_r
    : $\forall$ $(A :$ Type$)$ $(x : A)$ $(P : A \rightarrow$ Prop$)$,
      P $x \rightarrow \forall$ $y : A, y = x \rightarrow P$ y

The corresponding lemma used for JMeq in the proof of pair_cong is internal_JMeq_rew_r, which, confusingly, is defined by rewrite as needed, so it is not available for checking until after we apply it.

Check internal_JMeq_rew_r.

internal_JMeq_rew_r
    : $\forall$ $(A :$ Type$)$ $(x : A)$ $(B :$ Type$)$ $(b : B)$
      $(P : \forall$ *B0* : Type$, B0 \rightarrow$ Type$)$, P B $b \rightarrow x == b \rightarrow P$ A x

The key difference is that whereas the **eq** lemma is parameterized on a predicate of type $A \rightarrow$ Prop, the JMeq lemma is parameterized on a predicate of type more like $\forall\ A$: Type, $A \rightarrow$ Prop. To apply eq_ind_r with a proof of $x = y$, it is only necessary to rearrange the goal into an application of a **fun** abstraction to y. In contrast, to apply internal_JMeq_rew_r, it is necessary to rearrange the goal to an application of a **fun** abstraction to both y and *its type*. In other words, the predicate must be *polymorphic* in y's type; any type must make sense from a type-checking standpoint. There may be cases where the former rearrangement is easy to do in a type-correct way, but the second rearrangement done naïvely leads to a type error.

When `rewrite` cannot figure out how to apply internal_JMeq_rew_r for $x == y$ where x and y have the same type, the tactic can instead use an alternative theorem, which is easy to prove as a composition of eq_ind_r and *JMeq_eq*.

Check JMeq_ind_r.

JMeq_ind_r
  : $\forall\ (A$: Type$)\ (x : A)\ (P : A \rightarrow$ Prop$)$,
    $P\ x \rightarrow \forall\ y : A,\ y == x \rightarrow P\ y$

Ironically, where in the proof of fhapp_assoc' we used `rewrite` app_assoc to make it clear that a use of JMeq was actually homogeneously typed, we created a situation where `rewrite` applied the axiom-based JMeq_ind_r instead of the axiom-free internal_JMeq_rew_r.

For another simple example, consider this theorem, which applies a heterogeneous equality to prove a congruence fact:

Theorem out_of_luck : $\forall\ n\ m$: **nat**,
 $n == m$
 $\rightarrow$ S $n ==$ S m.
intros $n\ m\ H$.

Applying JMeq_ind_r is easy, as the `pattern` tactic transforms the goal into an application of an appropriate **fun** to a term that we want to abstract. (In general, `pattern` abstracts over a term by introducing a new anonymous function taking that term as argument.)

 pattern n.

n : **nat**
m : **nat**
$H : n == m$
============================
 $(\text{fun }n0$: **nat** $\Rightarrow$ S $n0 ==$ S $m)\ n$

apply JMeq_ind_r with $(x := m)$; auto.

However, we run into trouble trying to get the goal into a form compatible with internal_JMeq_rew_r.

Undo 2.

pattern **nat**, n.

```
Error: The abstracted term
"fun (P : Set) (n0 : P) => S n0 == S m"
is not well typed.
Illegal application (Type Error):
The term "S" of type "nat -> nat"
cannot be applied to the term
 "n0" : "P"
This term has type "P" which should be coercible to
"nat".
```

In other words, the successor function S is insufficiently polymorphic. If we try to generalize over the type of n, we find that S is no longer legal to apply to n.

Abort.

Why did we not run into this problem in the proof of fhapp_assoc''? The reason is that the pair constructor is polymorphic in the types of the pair components, whereas functions like S are not polymorphic at all. Use of such nonpolymorphic functions with JMeq tends to push toward use of axioms. The example with **nat** here is a bit unrealistic; more likely cases would involve functions that have *some* polymorphism but not enough to allow abstractions of the sort we attempted with pattern. For instance, we might have an equality between two lists, where the goal only type-checks when the terms involved really are lists, though everything is polymorphic in the types of list data elements. The Heq[6] library builds up a slightly different foundation to help avoid such problems.

10.5 Equivalence of Equality Axioms

Assuming axioms (like axiom K and *JMeq_eq*) is a hazardous business. The due diligence associated with it is necessarily global in scope, since two axioms may be consistent alone but inconsistent together. It turns

---

6. http://www.mpi-sws.org/~gil/Heq/

out that all the major axioms proposed for reasoning about equality in Coq are logically equivalent, so we only need to pick one to assert without proof. This section shows how each of the two previous approaches reduces to the other logically.

To show that JMeq and its axiom let us prove UIP_refl, we start from the lemma UIP_refl'. The rest of the proof is trivial.

Lemma UIP_refl'' : $\forall$ (A : Type) (x : A) (pf : $x = x$), pf = eq_refl x.
  intros; rewrite (UIP_refl' pf); reflexivity.
Qed.

The other direction is perhaps more interesting. Assume that we only have the axiom of the Eqdep module available. We can define JMeq in a way that satisfies the same interface as the combination of the JMeq module's inductive definition and axiom.

Definition JMeq' (A : Type) (x : A) (B : Type) (y : B) : Prop :=
  $\exists$ pf : $B = A$, x = match pf with eq_refl $\Rightarrow$ y end.

Infix "===" := JMeq' (at level 70, no associativity).

By definition, x and y are equal if and only if there exists a proof pf that their types are equal, such that x equals the result of casting y with pf. This statement seems odd from the standpoint of classical math, where proofs are rarely mentioned explicitly with quantifiers in formulas, but it is perfectly legal Coq code.

We can easily prove a theorem with the same type as that of the JMeq_refl constructor of JMeq.

Theorem JMeq_refl' : $\forall$ (A : Type) (x : A), x === x.
  intros; unfold JMeq'; exists eq_refl; reflexivity.
Qed.

The proof of an analogue to *JMeq_eq* is a little more interesting, but most of the action is in appealing to UIP_refl.

Theorem JMeq_eq' : $\forall$ (A : Type) (x y : A),
  x === y $\rightarrow$ $x = y$.
  unfold JMeq'; intros.

  H : $\exists$ pf : $A = A$,
       x = match pf in (_ = T) return T with
         | eq_refl $\Rightarrow$ y
         end
  ============================
  $x = y$

```
destruct H.
```

$x0 : A = A$
$H : x = \text{match } x0 \text{ in } (\_ = T) \text{ return } T \text{ with}$
        | eq_refl $\Rightarrow y$
        end
==
  $x = y$

```
rewrite H.
```

$x0 : A = A$
==
  match $x0$ in $(\_ = T)$ return T with
  | eq_refl $\Rightarrow y$
  end $= y$

```
rewrite (UIP_refl _ _ x0); reflexivity.
Qed.
```

In a very formal sense, we are free to switch back and forth between the two styles of proofs about equality proofs. One style may be more convenient than the other for some proofs, but we can always inter-convert between the results. The style that does not use heterogeneous equality may be preferable in cases where many results do not require the techniques explored in this chapter, since then the use of axioms is avoided altogether for the simple cases, and a wider audience will be able to follow those proofs. On the other hand, heterogeneous equality often makes for shorter and more readable theorem statements.

10.6   Equality of Functions

The following seems like a reasonable theorem to want to hold, and it does hold in set theory.

```
Theorem two_funs : (fun n ⇒ n) = (fun n ⇒ n + 0).
```

Unfortunately, this theorem is not provable in CIC without additional axioms. None of the definitional equality rules force function equality to be *extensional*. That is, the fact that two functions return equal results on equal inputs does not imply that the functions are equal. We can assert function extensionality as an axiom, and indeed the standard library already contains that axiom.

Require Import FunctionalExtensionality.
About functional_extensionality.

functional_extensionality :
$\forall\ (A\ B : \textbf{Type})\ (f\ g : A \to B),\ (\forall\ x : A, f\ x = g\ x) \to f = g$

This axiom has been verified metatheoretically to be consistent with
CIC and the two equality axioms considered previously. With it, the
proof of two_funs is trivial.

Theorem two_funs : (fun $n \Rightarrow n$) = (fun $n \Rightarrow n$ + 0).
  apply functional_extensionality; *crush.*
Qed.

The same axiom can help us prove equality of types, where we need
to reason under quantifiers.

Theorem forall_eq : ($\forall\ x$: **nat**, match x with
                                    | O $\Rightarrow$ **True**
                                    | S _ $\Rightarrow$ **True**
                                  end)
    = ($\forall$ _ : **nat**, **True**).

There are no immediate opportunities to apply functional_extensionality,
but we can use **change** to fix that problem.

    change (($\forall\ x$: **nat**, (fun $x \Rightarrow$ match x with
                                        | 0 $\Rightarrow$ **True**
                                        | S _ $\Rightarrow$ **True**
                                      end) x) = (**nat** $\to$ **True**)).
    rewrite (functional_extensionality (fun $x \Rightarrow$ match x with
                                            | 0 $\Rightarrow$ **True**
                                            | S _ $\Rightarrow$ **True**
                                          end)
                        (fun _ $\Rightarrow$ **True**)).

2 subgoals

  ============================
   (**nat** $\to$ **True**) $=$ (**nat** $\to$ **True**)

subgoal 2 is:
 $\forall\ x$: **nat**, match x with
                  | 0 $\Rightarrow$ **True**
                  | S _ $\Rightarrow$ **True**
                end $=$ **True**

```
reflexivity.
destruct x; constructor.
Qed.
```

Unlike in the case of *eq_rect_eq*, we have no way of deriving this axiom of *functional extensionality* for types with decidable equality. To allow equality reasoning without axioms, it may be worth rewriting a development to replace functions with other representations, such as finite map types for which extensionality is derivable in CIC.

11 Generic Programming

Generic programming makes it possible to write functions that operate over different types of data. Parametric polymorphism in ML and Haskell is one of the simplest examples. ML-style module systems [22] and Haskell type classes [45] are more flexible cases. These language features are often not as powerful as we would like. For instance, while Haskell includes a type class classifying those types whose values can be pretty-printed, per-type pretty-printing is usually either implemented manually or implemented via a *deriving clause* [33], which triggers ad hoc code generation. Some clever encoding techniques have been used to achieve better within Haskell and other languages, but we can do *datatype-generic programming* much more cleanly with dependent types. Thanks to the expressive power of the Calculus of Inductive Constructions (CIC), we need no special language support.

Generic programming can often be very useful in Coq developments. In a proof assistant, there is the new possibility of generic proofs about generic programs.

11.1 Reifying Datatype Definitions

The key to generic programming with dependent types is *universe types*. This concept should not be confused with the idea of *universes* from the metatheory of CIC and related languages (see Chapter 12). Rather, the idea of universe types is to define inductive types that provide *syntactic representations* of Coq types. We cannot directly write CIC programs that do case analysis on types, but we can case-analyze on reified syntactic versions of those types.

Thus, to begin, we define a syntactic representation of some class of datatypes. The running example in this chapter involves basic algebraic datatypes of the kind found in ML and Haskell, but without enhancements like type parameters and mutually recursive definitions.

The first step is to define a representation for constructors of the datatypes. We use the `Record` command as a shorthand for defining an inductive type with a single constructor, plus projection functions for pulling out any of the named arguments to that constructor.

```
Record constructor : Type := Con {
    nonrecursive : Type;
    recursive : nat
}.
```

The idea is that a constructor represented as Con T n has n arguments of the type that we are defining. Additionally, all the other, nonrecursive arguments can be encoded in the type T. When there are no nonrecursive arguments, T can be **unit**. When there are two nonrecursive arguments, of types A and B, T can be $A \times B$. We can generalize to any number of arguments via tupling.

With this definition, it is easy to define a datatype representation in terms of lists of constructors. The intended meaning is that the datatype came from an inductive definition including exactly the constructors in the list.

```
Definition datatype := list constructor.
```

Here are a few example encodings for some common types from the Coq standard library. While the syntax type does not support type parameters directly, we can implement them at the metalevel, via functions from types to **datatypes**.

```
Definition Empty_set_dt : datatype := nil.
Definition unit_dt : datatype := Con unit 0 :: nil.
Definition bool_dt : datatype := Con unit 0 :: Con unit 0 :: nil.
Definition nat_dt : datatype := Con unit 0 :: Con unit 1 :: nil.
Definition list_dt (A : Type) : datatype :=
    Con unit 0 :: Con A 1 :: nil.
```

The type **Empty_set** has no constructors, so its representation is the empty list. The type **unit** has one constructor with no arguments, so its one reified constructor indicates no nonrecursive data and 0 recursive arguments. The representation for **bool** just duplicates this single argumentless constructor. We get from **bool** to **nat** by changing one of the constructors to indicate 1 recursive argument. We get from **nat** to **list** by adding a nonrecursive argument of a parameter type A.

As a further example, we can do the same encoding for a generic binary tree type.

```
Section tree.
```

Variable A : Type.

Inductive **tree** : Type :=
| Leaf : $A \rightarrow$ **tree**
| Node : **tree** $\rightarrow$ **tree** $\rightarrow$ **tree**.
End tree.

Definition tree_dt $(A : \text{Type})$: datatype :=
  Con A 0 :: Con **unit** 2 :: nil.

Each datatype representation stands for a family of inductive types. For a specific real datatype and a reputed representation for it, it is useful to define a type of *evidence* that the datatype is compatible with the encoding.

Section denote.
  Variable T : Type.
  This variable stands for the concrete datatype of interest.

  Definition constructorDenote $(c : \textbf{constructor})$:=
    nonrecursive $c \rightarrow$ **ilist** T (recursive c) $\rightarrow T$.

We write that a constructor is represented as a function returning a T. Such a function takes two arguments, which pack together the nonrecursive and recursive arguments of the constructor. We represent a tuple of all recursive arguments using the length-indexed list type **ilist** (see Chapter 8).

  Definition datatypeDenote := **hlist** constructorDenote.

Finally, the evidence for type T is a heterogeneous list, including a constructor denotation for every constructor encoding in a datatype encoding. Recall that since we are inside a section binding T as a variable, constructorDenote is automatically parameterized by T.

End denote.

Some example pieces of evidence should help clarify the convention. First, we define a helpful notation for constructor denotations. The ASCII ~> from the notation is rendered as $\rightsquigarrow$.

Notation "[v , r ~> x]" :=
  ((fun v r $\Rightarrow$ x) : constructorDenote _ (Con _ _)).

Definition Empty_set_den
  : datatypeDenote **Empty_set** Empty_set_dt := HNil.
Definition unit_den : datatypeDenote **unit** unit_dt :=
  [_, _ $\rightsquigarrow$ tt] ::: HNil.
Definition bool_den : datatypeDenote **bool** bool_dt :=
  [_, _ $\rightsquigarrow$ true] ::: [_, _ $\rightsquigarrow$ false] ::: HNil.
Definition nat_den : datatypeDenote **nat** nat_dt :=

```
  [_, _ ⤳ O] ::: [_, r ⤳ S (hd r)] ::: HNil.
Definition list_den (A : Type) : datatypeDenote (list A) (list_dt A) :=
  [_, _ ⤳ nil] ::: [x, r ⤳ x :: hd r] ::: HNil.
Definition tree_den (A : Type)
  : datatypeDenote (tree A) (tree_dt A) :=
  [v, _ ⤳ Leaf v] ::: [_, r ⤳ Node (hd r) (hd (tl r))] ::: HNil.
```

Recall that the hd and tl calls operate on richly typed lists, where type indices indicate the lengths of lists, guaranteeing the safety of operations like hd. The type annotation attached to each definition provides enough information for Coq to infer list lengths at appropriate points.

11.2   Recursive Definitions

We built these encodings of datatypes to help us write datatype-generic recursive functions. To do so, we want a reified representation of a *recursion scheme* for each type, similar to the T_rect principle generated automatically for an inductive definition of T. A clever reuse of datatypeDenote yields a short definition.

```
Definition fixDenote (T : Type) (dt : datatype) :=
  ∀ (R : Type), datatypeDenote R dt → (T → R).
```

The idea of a recursion scheme is parameterized by a type and a reputed encoding of it. The principle itself is polymorphic in a type R, which is the return type of the recursive function that we mean to write. The next argument is a heterogeneous list of one case of the recursive function definition for each datatype constructor. The datatypeDenote function has just the right definition to express the type we need; a set of function cases is just like an alternative set of constructors where we replace the original type T with the function result type R. Given such a reified definition, a fixDenote invocation returns a function from T to R, which is just what we wanted.

We are ready to write some example functions using one new function from the DepList library (see book source).

```
Check hmake.
```

```
  hmake
    : ∀ (A : Type) (B : A → Type),
      (∀ x : A, B x) → ∀ ls : list A, hlist B ls
```

The function hmake is a kind of map alternative that goes from a regular **list** to an **hlist**. We can use it to define a generic size function that counts the number of constructors used to build a value in a datatype.

Definition size T dt (fx : fixDenote T dt) : $T \to$ **nat** :=
  fx **nat** (hmake ($B :=$ constructorDenote **nat**)
    (fun _ _ $r \Rightarrow$ foldr plus 1 r) dt).

The definition is parameterized over a recursion scheme fx. We instantiate fx by passing it the function result type and a set of function cases, building the latter with hmake. The function argument to hmake takes three arguments: the representation of a constructor, its nonrecursive arguments, and the results of recursive calls on all its recursive arguments. We only need the recursive call results here, so we call them r and bind the other two inputs with wildcards. The actual case body is simple: we add together the recursive call results and increment the result by one (to account for the current constructor). This foldr function is an **ilist**-specific version defined in the DepList module.

It is instructive to build fixDenote values for the example types and see what specialized size functions result from them.

Definition Empty_set_fix : fixDenote **Empty_set** Empty_set_dt :=
  fun R _ $emp \Rightarrow$ match emp with end.
Eval compute in size Empty_set_fix.

     $=$ fun emp : **Empty_set** $\Rightarrow$ match emp return **nat** with
                                 end
     : **Empty_set** $\to$ **nat**

CIC's standard computation rules suffice to normalize the generic size function specialization to exactly what we would have written manually.

Definition unit_fix : fixDenote **unit** unit_dt :=
  fun R $cases$ _ $\Rightarrow$ (hhd $cases$) tt INil.
Eval compute in size unit_fix.

     $=$ fun _ : **unit** $\Rightarrow$ 1
     : **unit** $\to$ **nat**

Again normalization gives us the natural function definition. We see this pattern repeated for the other example types.

Definition bool_fix : fixDenote **bool** bool_dt :=
  fun R $cases$ $b \Rightarrow$ if b
    then (hhd $cases$) tt INil
    else (hhd (htl $cases$)) tt INil.
Eval compute in size bool_fix.

$= \text{fun } b : \textbf{bool} \Rightarrow \text{if } b \text{ then } 1 \text{ else } 1$
$: \textbf{bool} \to \textbf{nat}$

Definition nat_fix : fixDenote **nat** nat_dt :=
  fun R *cases* $\Rightarrow$ fix F (n : **nat**) : R :=
    match n with
      | O $\Rightarrow$ (hhd *cases*) tt INil
      | S n' $\Rightarrow$ (hhd (htl *cases*)) tt (ICons (F n') INil)
    end.

To look at the size function for **nat**, it is useful to avoid full computation, so that the recursive definition of addition is not expanded inline. We can accomplish this with proper flags for the cbv reduction strategy.

Eval cbv beta iota delta -[plus] in size nat_fix.

$= \text{fix } F$ (n : **nat**) : **nat** := match n with
$\qquad\qquad\qquad\qquad\qquad\qquad\qquad$ | $0 \Rightarrow 1$
$\qquad\qquad\qquad\qquad\qquad\qquad\qquad$ | S n' $\Rightarrow$ F n' + 1
$\qquad\qquad\qquad\qquad\qquad\qquad\qquad$ end
$: \textbf{nat} \to \textbf{nat}$

Definition list_fix (A : Type) : fixDenote (**list** A) (list_dt A) :=
  fun R *cases* $\Rightarrow$ fix F (ls : **list** A) : R :=
    match ls with
      | nil $\Rightarrow$ (hhd *cases*) tt INil
      | x :: ls' $\Rightarrow$ (hhd (htl *cases*)) x (ICons (F ls') INil)
    end.
Eval cbv beta iota delta -[plus] in fun $A \Rightarrow$ size (@list_fix A).

$= \text{fun } A : \text{Type} \Rightarrow$
$\quad\text{fix } F$ (ls : **list** A) : **nat** :=
$\qquad$ match ls with
$\qquad$ | nil $\Rightarrow 1$
$\qquad$ | _ :: ls' $\Rightarrow$ F ls' + 1
$\qquad$ end
$\quad: \forall A : \text{Type}, \textbf{list } A \to \textbf{nat}$

Definition tree_fix (A : Type) : fixDenote (**tree** A) (tree_dt A) :=
  fun R *cases* $\Rightarrow$ fix F (t : **tree** A) : R :=
    match t with
      | Leaf x $\Rightarrow$ (hhd *cases*) x INil
      | Node *t1* *t2* $\Rightarrow$

$$(\mathsf{hhd}\ (\mathsf{htl}\ cases))\ \mathsf{tt}\ (\mathsf{ICons}\ (F\ t1)\ (\mathsf{ICons}\ (F\ t2)\ \mathsf{INil}))$$
```
    end.
Eval cbv beta iota delta -[plus] in fun A ⇒ size (@tree_fix A).
```

$$= \mathbf{fun}\ A : \mathsf{Type} \Rightarrow$$
$$\mathbf{fix}\ F\ (t : \mathbf{tree}\ A) : \mathbf{nat} :=$$
$$\mathsf{match}\ t\ \mathsf{with}$$
$$|\ \mathsf{Leaf}\ \_ \Rightarrow 1$$
$$|\ \mathsf{Node}\ t1\ t2 \Rightarrow F\ t1 + (F\ t2 + 1)$$
$$\mathsf{end}$$
$$: \forall\ A : \mathsf{Type},\ \mathbf{tree}\ A \to \mathbf{nat}$$

As the examples show, even recursive datatypes are mapped to normal-looking size functions.

11.2.1 Pretty-Printing

It is useful to do generic pretty-printing of datatype values, rendering them as human-readable strings. To do so, we need a bit of metadata for each constructor, specifically the name to print for the constructor and the function to use to render its nonrecursive arguments. Everything else can be done generically.

```
Record print_constructor (c : constructor) : Type := PI {
  printName : string;
  printNonrec : nonrecursive c → string
}.
```

It is useful to define a shorthand for applying the constructor PI. By applying it explicitly to an unknown application of the constructor Con, we help type inference work.

```
Notation "ˆ" := (PI (Con _ _)).
```

As in earlier examples, we define the type of metadata for a datatype to be a heterogeneous list type collecting metadata for each constructor.

```
Definition print_datatype := hlist print_constructor.
```

For some string manipulation, we import the notations associated with strings.

```
Local Open Scope string_scope.
```

Now it is easy to implement the generic printer, using another function from DepList.

```
Check hmap.

  hmap
```

$: \forall\ (A : \mathsf{Type})\ (B1\ B2 : A \to \mathsf{Type}),$
$\quad (\forall\ x : A,\ B1\ x \to B2\ x) \to$
$\qquad \forall\ ls : \mathsf{list}\ A,\ \mathsf{hlist}\ B1\ ls \to \mathsf{hlist}\ B2\ ls$

Definition print T dt $(pr : \mathsf{print\_datatype}\ dt)$ $(fx : \mathsf{fixDenote}\ T\ dt)$
$\quad : T \to \mathsf{string} :=$
fx **string** (hmap $(B1 := \textbf{print\_constructor})$
$\quad (B2 := \mathsf{constructorDenote}\ \textbf{string})$
$\quad (\mathsf{fun}\ \_\ pc\ x\ r \Rightarrow \mathsf{printName}\ pc\ \text{++}\ "("\ \text{++}\ \mathsf{printNonrec}\ pc\ x$
$\qquad \text{++ foldr (fun}\ s\ acc \Rightarrow ",\ "\ \text{++}\ s\ \text{++}\ acc)\ ")"\ r)\ pr).$

Some simple tests establish that print gets the job done.

Eval compute in print HNil Empty_set_fix.

$\quad = \mathsf{fun}\ emp : \textbf{Empty\_set} \Rightarrow \mathtt{match}\ emp\ \mathtt{return}\ \textbf{string}\ \mathtt{with}$
$\qquad\qquad\qquad\qquad\qquad \mathtt{end}$
$\quad : \textbf{Empty\_set} \to \textbf{string}$

Eval compute in print ($\hat{}$ "tt" (fun _ $\Rightarrow$ "") ::: HNil) unit_fix.

$\quad = \mathsf{fun}\ \_ : \textbf{unit} \Rightarrow "\mathrm{tt}()"$
$\quad : \textbf{unit} \to \textbf{string}$

Eval compute in print ($\hat{}$ "true" (fun _ $\Rightarrow$ "")
$\quad ::: \hat{}$ "false" (fun _ $\Rightarrow$ "")
$\quad :::$ HNil) bool_fix.

$\quad = \mathsf{fun}\ b : \textbf{bool} \Rightarrow \mathtt{if}\ b\ \mathtt{then}\ "\mathrm{true}()"\ \mathtt{else}\ "\mathrm{false}()"$
$\quad : \textbf{bool} \to \textbf{string}$

Definition print_nat := print ($\hat{}$ "O" (fun _ $\Rightarrow$ "")
$\quad ::: \hat{}$ "S" (fun _ $\Rightarrow$ "")
$\quad :::$ HNil) nat_fix.
Eval cbv beta iota delta -[append] in print_nat.

$\quad = \mathtt{fix}\ F\ (n : \textbf{nat}) : \textbf{string} :=$
$\qquad \mathtt{match}\ n\ \mathtt{with}$
$\qquad |\ 0\%\textbf{nat} \Rightarrow "\mathrm{O}"\ \text{++}\ "("\ \text{++}\ ""\ \text{++}\ ")"$
$\qquad |\ \mathsf{S}\ n' \Rightarrow "\mathrm{S}"\ \text{++}\ "("\ \text{++}\ ""\ \text{++}\ ",\ "\ \text{++}\ F\ n'\ \text{++}\ ")"$
$\qquad \mathtt{end}$
$\quad : \textbf{nat} \to \textbf{string}$

Eval simpl in print_nat 0.

$\quad = "\mathrm{O}()"$
$\quad : \textbf{string}$

Eval simpl in print_nat 1.

> = "S(, O())"
> : **string**

Eval simpl in print_nat 2.

> = "S(, S(, O()))"
> : **string**

Eval cbv beta iota delta -[append] in fun A $(pr : A \rightarrow$ **string**$) \Rightarrow$
  print (^ "nil" (fun _ $\Rightarrow$ "")
  : : : ^ "cons" pr
  : : : HNil) (@list_fix A).

> = **fun** $(A :$ **Type**$)$ $(pr : A \rightarrow$ **string**$) \Rightarrow$
>   **fix** F $(ls :$ **list** $A) :$ **string** $:=$
>   match ls with
> | nil $\Rightarrow$ "nil" ++ "(" ++ "" ++ ")"
> | $x :: ls' \Rightarrow$
>   "cons" ++ "(" ++ pr x ++ ", " ++ F ls' ++ ")"
>   end
>   : $\forall$ $A :$ **Type**, $(A \rightarrow$ **string**$) \rightarrow$ **list** $A \rightarrow$ **string**

Eval cbv beta iota delta -[append] in fun A $(pr : A \rightarrow$ **string**$) \Rightarrow$
  print (^ "Leaf" pr
  : : : ^ "Node" (fun _ $\Rightarrow$ "")
  : : : HNil) (@tree_fix A).

> = **fun** $(A :$ **Type**$)$ $(pr : A \rightarrow$ **string**$) \Rightarrow$
>   **fix** F $(t :$ **tree** $A) :$ **string** $:=$
>   match t with
> | Leaf $x \Rightarrow$ "Leaf" ++ "(" ++ pr x ++ ")"
> | Node $t1$ $t2 \Rightarrow$ "Node" ++ "(" ++ "" ++ ", " ++ F $t1$
>   ++ ", " ++ F $t2$ ++ ")"
>   end
>   : $\forall$ $A :$ **Type**, $(A \rightarrow$ **string**$) \rightarrow$ **tree** $A \rightarrow$ **string**

Some of these simplified terms seem overly complex because we have
turned off simplification of calls to append, which is what uses of the
++ operator desugar to. Selective ++ simplification would combine
adjacent string literals, yielding more or less the code we would write
manually to implement this printing scheme.

11.2.2 Mapping

By this point, we have developed enough machinery to define a generic function similar to the list map function.

Definition map T dt (dd : datatypeDenote T dt) (fx : fixDenote T dt)
  (f : $T \rightarrow T$) : $T \rightarrow T$:=
  fx T (hmap ($B1$:= constructorDenote T)
    ($B2$:= constructorDenote T)
    (fun _ c x r $\Rightarrow$ f (c x r)) dd).

Eval compute in map Empty_set_den Empty_set_fix.

  = fun (_ : **Empty_set** $\rightarrow$ **Empty_set**) (emp : **Empty_set**) $\Rightarrow$
    match emp return **Empty_set** with
    end
  : (**Empty_set** $\rightarrow$ **Empty_set**) $\rightarrow$ **Empty_set** $\rightarrow$ **Empty_set**

Eval compute in map unit_den unit_fix.

  = fun (f : **unit** $\rightarrow$ **unit**) (_ : **unit**) $\Rightarrow$ f tt
  : (**unit** $\rightarrow$ **unit**) $\rightarrow$ **unit** $\rightarrow$ **unit**

Eval compute in map bool_den bool_fix.

  = fun (f : **bool** $\rightarrow$ **bool**) (b : **bool**) $\Rightarrow$
    if b then f true else f false
  : (**bool** $\rightarrow$ **bool**) $\rightarrow$ **bool** $\rightarrow$ **bool**

Eval compute in map nat_den nat_fix.

  = fun f : **nat** $\rightarrow$ **nat** $\Rightarrow$
    fix F (n : **nat**) : **nat** :=
      match n with
      | 0%**nat** $\Rightarrow$ f 0%**nat**
      | S n' $\Rightarrow$ f (S (F n'))
      end
  : (**nat** $\rightarrow$ **nat**) $\rightarrow$ **nat** $\rightarrow$ **nat**

Eval compute in fun A $\Rightarrow$ map (list_den A) (@list_fix A).

  = fun (A : Type) (f : **list** A $\rightarrow$ **list** A) $\Rightarrow$
    fix F (ls : **list** A) : **list** A :=
      match ls with
      | nil $\Rightarrow$ f nil
      | x :: ls' $\Rightarrow$ f (x :: F ls')
      end
  : $\forall$ A : Type, (**list** A $\rightarrow$ **list** A) $\rightarrow$ **list** A $\rightarrow$ **list** A

Eval compute in fun A ⇒ map (tree_den A) (@tree_fix A).

$$= \textsf{fun } (A : \textsf{Type}) \; (f : \textbf{tree } A \to \textbf{tree } A) \Rightarrow$$
$$\textsf{fix } F \; (t : \textbf{tree } A) : \textbf{tree } A :=$$
$$\textsf{match } t \textsf{ with}$$
$$| \textsf{ Leaf } x \Rightarrow f \; (\textsf{Leaf } x)$$
$$| \textsf{ Node } t1 \; t2 \Rightarrow f \; (\textsf{Node } (F \; t1) \; (F \; t2))$$
$$\textsf{end}$$
$$: \forall \; A : \textsf{Type}, (\textbf{tree } A \to \textbf{tree } A) \to \textbf{tree } A \to \textbf{tree } A$$

These map functions are just as easy to use as those we write by hand. Readers may want to try figuring out the input-output pattern that map_nat S displays in the following examples.

Definition map_nat := map nat_den nat_fix.
Eval simpl in map_nat S 0.

$$= 1\%\textbf{nat}$$
$$: \textbf{nat}$$

Eval simpl in map_nat S 1.

$$= 3\%\textbf{nat}$$
$$: \textbf{nat}$$

Eval simpl in map_nat S 2.

$$= 5\%\textbf{nat}$$
$$: \textbf{nat}$$

We get map_nat S $n = 2 \times n + 1$, because the mapping process adds an extra S at every level of the inductive tree that defines a natural, including at the last level, the O constructor.

11.3 Proving Theorems about Recursive Definitions

We would like to be able to prove theorems about generic functions. To do so, we need to establish additional well-formedness properties that must hold of pieces of evidence.

Section ok.
  Variable T : Type.
  Variable dt : datatype.

  Variable dd : datatypeDenote T dt.
  Variable fx : fixDenote T dt.

First, we characterize when a piece of evidence about a datatype is acceptable. The basic idea is that the type T should really be an inductive type with the definition given by dd. Semantically, inductive types are characterized by the ability to do induction on them. Therefore, we require that the usual induction principle be true with respect to the constructors given in the encoding dd.

```
Definition datatypeDenoteOk :=
    ∀ P : T → Prop,
      (∀ c (m : member c dt) (x : nonrecursive c)
        (r : ilist T (recursive c)),
        (∀ i : fin (recursive c), P (get r i))
        → P ((hget dd m) x r))
      → ∀ v, P v.
```

This definition can take a while to understand. The quantifier over m : **member** c dt is considering each constructor in turn; as in normal induction principles, each constructor has an associated proof case. The expression hget dd m then names the constructor we have selected. After binding m, we quantify over all possible arguments (encoded with x and r) to the constructor that m selects. Within each specific case, we quantify further over i : **fin** (recursive c) to consider all of the induction hypotheses, one for each recursive argument of the current constructor.

We have completed half the process of defining side conditions. The other half comes in characterizing when a recursion scheme fx is valid. The natural condition is that fx behaves appropriately when applied to any constructor application.

```
Definition fixDenoteOk :=
    ∀ (R : Type) (cases : datatypeDenote R dt)
      c (m : member c dt)
      (x : nonrecursive c) (r : ilist T (recursive c)),
      fx cases ((hget dd m) x r)
      = (hget cases m) x (imap (fx cases) r).
```

As for datatypeDenoteOk, we consider all constructors and all possible arguments to them by quantifying over m, x, and r. The left side of the equality that follows shows a call to the recursive function on the specific constructor application that we selected. The right side shows an application of the function case associated with constructor m, applied to the nonrecursive arguments and to appropriate recursive calls on the recursive arguments.

```
End ok.
```

We are now ready to prove that the size function we defined earlier always returns positive results. First, we establish a simple lemma.

Lemma foldr_plus : $\forall\ n\ (ils : \mathbf{ilist\ nat}\ n)$,
  foldr plus $1\ ils > 0$.
  induction ils; *crush*.
Qed.

Theorem size_positive : $\forall\ T\ dt$
  $(dd : \mathsf{datatypeDenote}\ T\ dt)\ (fx : \mathsf{fixDenote}\ T\ dt)$
  $(dok : \mathsf{datatypeDenoteOk}\ dd)\ (fok : \mathsf{fixDenoteOk}\ dd\ fx)$
  $(v\ :\ T)$,
  size $fx\ v > 0$.
  unfold size; intros.

```
============================
```
  fx **nat**
     (hmake
        (fun $(x : $ constructor$)$ $(_ : $ nonrecursive $x)$
           $(r : $ **ilist nat** $($recursive $x)) \Rightarrow$ foldr plus 1%**nat** $r)\ dt)\ v > 0$

The goal is an inequality over a particular call to size, with its definition expanded. How can we proceed here? We cannot use induction directly because there is no way for Coq to know that T is an inductive type. Instead, we need to use the induction principle encoded in the hypothesis *dok* of type datatypeDenoteOk *dd*. Let us try applying it directly.

  apply *dok*.
Error: Impossible to unify "datatypeDenoteOk dd" with
 "fx nat
    (hmake
       (fun (x : constructor) (_ : nonrecursive x)
          (r : ilist nat (recursive x)) =>
             foldr plus 1%nat r) dt) v > 0".

Matching the type of *dok* with the type of the conclusion requires more than simple first-order unification, so apply is not up to the challenge. We can use the pattern tactic to get the goal into a form that makes it apparent exactly what the induction hypothesis is.

  pattern v.

```
============================
```
  (fun $t\ :\ T \Rightarrow$
     fx **nat**

```
(hmake
    (fun (x : constructor) (_ : nonrecursive x)
        (r : ilist nat (recursive x)) ⇒ foldr plus 1%nat r) dt) t
  > 0) v
```

`apply` *dok*; *crush*.

```
H : ∀ i : fin (recursive c),
    fx nat
        (hmake
            (fun (x : constructor) (_ : nonrecursive x)
                (r : ilist nat (recursive x)) ⇒ foldr plus 1%nat r) dt)
        (get r i) > 0
============================
 hget
    (hmake
        (fun (x0 : constructor) (_ : nonrecursive x0)
            (r0 : ilist nat (recursive x0)) ⇒
            foldr plus 1%nat r0) dt) m x
    (imap
        (fx nat
            (hmake
                (fun (x0 : constructor) (_ : nonrecursive x0)
                    (r0 : ilist nat (recursive x0)) ⇒
                    foldr plus 1%nat r0) dt)) r) > 0
```

An induction hypothesis H is generated, but we do not need it for this example. We can simplify the goal using a library theorem about the composition of hget and hmake.

`rewrite` hget_hmake.

```
============================
 foldr plus 1%nat
    (imap
        (fx nat
            (hmake
                (fun (x0 : constructor) (_ : nonrecursive x0)
                    (r0 : ilist nat (recursive x0)) ⇒
                    foldr plus 1%nat r0) dt)) r) > 0
```

The lemma we proved earlier finishes the proof.

`apply` foldr_plus.

Using hints, we can redo this proof in automated form.

Restart.

Hint Rewrite hget_hmake.
Hint Resolve foldr_plus.

unfold size; intros; pattern v; apply dok; *crush*.
Qed.

In this example, we only needed to use induction degenerately as case analysis. A more involved theorem about map may only be proved using induction hypotheses. I give its proof only in unautomated form and leave effective automation as an exercise for the reader.

In particular, it ought to be the case that generic map applied to an identity function is itself an identity function.

Theorem map_id : $\forall\ T\ dt$
  $(dd : \mathsf{datatypeDenote}\ T\ dt)\ (fx : \mathsf{fixDenote}\ T\ dt)$
  $(dok : \mathsf{datatypeDenoteOk}\ dd)\ (fok : \mathsf{fixDenoteOk}\ dd\ fx)$
  $(v : T),$
  map $dd\ fx$ (fun $x \Rightarrow x$) $v = v$.

Let us begin as we did in the last theorem, after adding another useful library equality as a hint.

Hint Rewrite hget_hmap.

unfold map; intros; pattern v; apply dok; *crush*.

$H : \forall\ i : \mathbf{fin}\ (\mathsf{recursive}\ c),$
    $fx\ T$
      (hmap
        (fun $(x : \mathsf{constructor})\ (c : \mathsf{constructorDenote}\ T\ x)$
            $(x0 : \mathsf{nonrecursive}\ x)\ (r : \mathbf{ilist}\ T\ (\mathsf{recursive}\ x)) \Rightarrow$
          $c\ x0\ r)\ dd)\ (\mathsf{get}\ r\ i) = \mathsf{get}\ r\ i$
==
hget $dd\ m\ x$
  (imap
    ($fx\ T$
      (hmap
        (fun $(x0 : \mathsf{constructor})\ (c0 : \mathsf{constructorDenote}\ T\ x0)$
            $(x1 : \mathsf{nonrecursive}\ x0)\ (r0 : \mathbf{ilist}\ T\ (\mathsf{recursive}\ x0)) \Rightarrow$
          $c0\ x1\ r0)\ dd))\ r) = \mathsf{hget}\ dd\ m\ x\ r$

The goal is an equality whose two sides begin with the same function call and initial arguments. We believe that the remaining arguments are in fact equal as well, and the f_equal tactic applies this reasoning step formally.

f_equal.

```
================================
imap
   (fx T
      (hmap
         (fun (x0 : constructor) (c0 : constructorDenote T x0)
              (x1 : nonrecursive x0) (r0 : ilist T (recursive x0)) ⇒
            c0 x1 r0) dd)) r = r
```

At this point, it is helpful to proceed by an inner induction on the heterogeneous list r of recursive call results. We could arrive at a cleaner proof by breaking this step out into an explicit lemma, but here we do the induction inline to save space.

```
induction r; crush.
```

The base case is discharged automatically. In the following inductive case, H is the outer IH (for induction over T values) and IHr is the inner IH (for induction over the recursive arguments).

```
H : ∀ i : fin (S n),
     fx T
        (hmap
           (fun (x : constructor) (c : constructorDenote T x)
                (x0 : nonrecursive x) (r : ilist T (recursive x)) ⇒
              c x0 r) dd)
        (match i in (fin n') return ((fin (pred n') → T) → T) with
         | First n ⇒ fun _ : fin n → T ⇒ a
         | Next n idx' ⇒ fun get_ls' : fin n → T ⇒ get_ls' idx'
         end (get r)) =
      match i in (fin n') return ((fin (pred n') → T) → T) with
      | First n ⇒ fun _ : fin n → T ⇒ a
      | Next n idx' ⇒ fun get_ls' : fin n → T ⇒ get_ls' idx'
      end (get r)
IHr : (∀ i : fin n,
          fx T
             (hmap
                (fun (x : constructor) (c : constructorDenote T x)
                     (x0 : nonrecursive x) (r : ilist T (recursive x)) ⇒
                  c x0 r) dd) (get r i) = get r i) →
      imap
         (fx T
            (hmap
               (fun (x : constructor) (c : constructorDenote T x)
```

$(x0 : \text{nonrecursive } x)\ (r : \textbf{ilist } T\ (\text{recursive } x)) \Rightarrow$
    $c\ x0\ r)\ dd))\ r = r$
=============================
ICons
   (fx T
      (hmap
         (fun $(x0 : \text{constructor})\ (c0 : \text{constructorDenote } T\ x0)$
            $(x1 : \text{nonrecursive } x0)\ (r0 : \textbf{ilist } T\ (\text{recursive } x0)) \Rightarrow$
         $c0\ x1\ r0)\ dd)\ a)$
      (imap
         (fx T
            (hmap
               (fun $(x0 : \text{constructor})\ (c0 : \text{constructorDenote } T\ x0)$
                  $(x1 : \text{nonrecursive } x0)\ (r0 : \textbf{ilist } T\ (\text{recursive } x0)) \Rightarrow$
               $c0\ x1\ r0)\ dd))\ r) = \text{ICons } a\ r$

We see another opportunity to apply `f_equal`, this time to split the
goal into two different equalities over corresponding arguments. After
that, the form of the first goal matches the outer induction hypothesis H, when we give type inference some help by specifying the right
quantifier instantiation.

```
f_equal.
apply (H First).
```

=============================
imap
   (fx T
      (hmap
         (fun $(x0 : \text{constructor})\ (c0 : \text{constructorDenote } T\ x0)$
            $(x1 : \text{nonrecursive } x0)\ (r0 : \textbf{ilist } T\ (\text{recursive } x0)) \Rightarrow$
         $c0\ x1\ r0)\ dd))\ r = r$

Now the goal matches the inner IH *IHr*.

```
apply IHr; crush.
```

$i : \textbf{fin } n$
=============================
   fx T
      (hmap
         (fun $(x0 : \text{constructor})\ (c0 : \text{constructorDenote } T\ x0)$
            $(x1 : \text{nonrecursive } x0)\ (r0 : \textbf{ilist } T\ (\text{recursive } x0)) \Rightarrow$
         $c0\ x1\ r0)\ dd)\ (\text{get } r\ i) = \text{get } r\ i$

We can finish the proof by applying the outer IH again, specialized to a different **fin** value.

```
apply (H (Next i)).
```
Qed.

The proof involves complex subgoals, but few steps are required and the work may be reused across a variety of datatypes.

12 Universes and Axioms

Many traditional theorems can be proved in Coq without special knowledge of the Calculus of Inductive Constructions (CIC), the logic behind the prover. A development just seems to be using a particular ASCII notation for standard formulas based on set theory. Nonetheless, as noted in Chapter 4, CIC differs from set theory in starting from fewer orthogonal primitives. It is possible to define the usual logical connectives as derived notions. The foundation is a dependently typed functional programming language, based on dependent function types and inductive type families. By using the facilities of this language directly, we can accomplish some things much more easily than in mainstream math.

Gallina, which adds features to the more theoretical CIC [31], is the logic implemented in Coq. It has a relatively simple foundation that can be defined rigorously in a page or two of formal proof rules. Still, there are some important subtleties with practical ramifications. This chapter focuses on those subtleties, avoiding formal metatheory in favor of example code.

12.1 The Type Hierarchy

Every object in Gallina has a type.

Check 0.

> 0
>   : nat

It is natural enough that zero be considered a natural number.

Check nat.

> nat
>   : Set

As in set theory, we consider the natural numbers as a set.

```
Check Set.
```

> ```
> Set
>     : Type
> ```

The type `Set` may be considered to be the set of all sets, a concept that set theory handles in terms of *classes*. In Coq, this more general notion is `Type`.

```
Check Type.
```

> ```
> Type
>     : Type
> ```

Strangely enough, `Type` appears to be its own type. It is known that polymorphic languages with this property are inconsistent, via Girard's paradox [8]. That is, using such a language to encode proofs is unwise, because it is possible to prove any proposition. What is really going on here?

Let us repeat some of our queries after toggling a flag related to Coq's printing behavior.

```
Set Printing Universes.
```

```
Check nat.
```

> ```
> nat
>     : Set
> ```

```
Check Set.
```

> ```
> Set
>     : Type (* (0)+1 *)
> ```

```
Check Type.
```

> ```
> Type (* Top.3 *)
>     : Type (* (Top.3)+1 *)
> ```

Occurrences of `Type` are annotated with some additional information inside comments. These annotations have to do with the fact that `Type` stands for an infinite hierarchy of types. The type of `Set` is $\text{Type}(0)$, the type of $\text{Type}(0)$ is $\text{Type}(1)$, the type of $\text{Type}(1)$ is $\text{Type}(2)$, and so on. This is how we avoid the `Type : Type` paradox. As a convenience, the universe hierarchy drives Coq's one variety of subtyping. Any term whose type is `Type` at level i is automatically also described by `Type` at level j when $j > i$.

In the output of the first `Check` query, we see that the type level of
`Set`'s type is $(0)+1$. Here 0 stands for the level of `Set`, and we increment
it to arrive at the level that *classifies* `Set`.

In the third query's output, we see that the occurrence of `Type` that
we check is assigned a fresh *universe variable* $Top.3$. The output type
increments $Top.3$ to move up a level in the universe hierarchy. As we
write code that uses definitions whose types mention universe variables,
unification may refine the values of those variables. Luckily, the user
rarely has to worry about the details.

Another crucial concept in CIC is *predicativity*. Consider the following
queries.

`Check` $\forall\ T$: **nat**, **fin** T.

> $\forall\ T$: **nat**, **fin** T
> : Set

`Check` $\forall\ T$: Set, T.

> $\forall\ T$: Set, T
> : Type $(*\ max(0, (0)+1)\ *)$

`Check` $\forall\ T$: Type, T.

> $\forall\ T$: Type $(*\ Top.9\ *)$, T
> : Type $(*\ max(Top.9, (Top.9)+1)\ *)$

These outputs demonstrate the rule for determining which universe
a $\forall$ type lives in. In particular, for a type $\forall\ x\ :\ T1,\ T2$, we take the
maximum of the universes of $T1$ and $T2$. In the first example query,
both $T1$ (**nat**) and $T2$ (**fin** T) are in `Set`, so the $\forall$ type is in `Set`, too. In
the second query, $T1$ is `Set`, which is at level $(0)+1$; and $T2$ is T, which
is at level 0. Thus, the $\forall$ exists at the maximum of these two levels.
The third example illustrates the same outcome, where we replace `Set`
with an occurrence of `Type` that is assigned universe variable $Top.9$.
This universe variable appears in the places where 0 appeared in the
previous query.

The behind-the-scenes manipulation of universe variables gives us
predicativity. Consider a simple definition of a polymorphic identity
function, where the first argument T will automatically be marked as
implicit, since it can be inferred from the type of the second argument
x.

`Definition id` $(T : \mathsf{Set})\ (x : T) : T := x$.

`Check id` 0.

id 0
   : **nat**

`Check id Set.`

```
Error: Illegal application (Type Error):
...
The 1st term has type "Type (* (Top.15)+1 *)"
which should be coercible to "Set".
```

The parameter T of id must be instantiated with a `Set`. The type **nat** is a `Set`, but `Set` is not. We can try fixing the problem by generalizing the definition of id.

`Reset id.`
Definition id $(T : \mathsf{Type})\ (x : T) : T := x.$
`Check id 0.`

id 0
   : **nat**

`Check id Set.`

id Set
   : Type (* *Top*.17 *)

`Check id Type.`

id Type (* *Top*.18 *)
   : Type (* *Top*.19 *)

So far, so good. As we apply id to different T values, the inferred index for T's Type occurrence automatically moves higher up the type hierarchy.

`Check id id.`

```
Error: Universe inconsistency
(cannot enforce Top.16 < Top.16).
```

This error message reminds us that the universe variable for T still exists, even though it is usually hidden. To apply id to itself, that variable would need to be less than itself in the type hierarchy. Universe inconsistency error messages announce cases like this, where a term could only type-check by violating an implied constraint over universe variables. Such errors demonstrate that Type is *predicative*; this word has a CIC meaning closely related to its usual mathematical meaning. A predicative system enforces the constraint that when an object is defined using some sort of quantifier, none of the quantifiers may ever be instantiated with the object itself. Impredicativity is associated with popular paradoxes in set theory, involving inconsistent constructions like "the set of all sets that do not contain themselves" (Russell's paradox). Similar paradoxes would result from uncontrolled impredicativity in Coq.

12.1.1 Inductive Definitions

Predicativity restrictions also apply to inductive definitions. As an example, let us consider a type of expression trees that allows injection of any native Coq value. The idea is that an **exp** T stands for an encoded expression of type T.

```
Inductive exp : Set → Set :=
| Const : ∀ T : Set, T → exp T
| Pair : ∀ T1 T2, exp T1 → exp T2 → exp (T1 × T2)
| Eq : ∀ T, exp T → exp T → exp bool.
```

```
Error: Large non-propositional inductive types must be in
Type.
```

This definition is *large* in the sense that at least one of its constructors takes an argument whose type has type **Type**. Coq would be inconsistent if we allowed definitions like this in their full generality. Instead, we must change **exp** to live in **Type** and move **exp**'s index to **Type** as well.

```
Inductive exp : Type → Type :=
| Const : ∀ T, T → exp T
| Pair : ∀ T1 T2, exp T1 → exp T2 → exp (T1 × T2)
| Eq : ∀ T, exp T → exp T → exp bool.
```

Note that we originally had to include an annotation : **Set** for the variable T in Const's type, but we need no annotation now. When the type of a variable is not known, and when that variable is used in a context where only types are allowed, Coq infers that the variable is of type **Type**, the right behavior here, though it was wrong for the **Set** version of **exp**.

The new definition is accepted. We can build some sample expressions.

```
Check Const 0.
```

```
  Const 0
    : exp nat
```

Check Pair (Const 0) (Const tt).

> Pair (Const 0) (Const tt)
>   : **exp** (**nat** × **unit**)

Check Eq (Const Set) (Const Type).

> Eq (Const Set) (Const Type (* *Top.*59 *))
>   : **exp bool**

We can check many expressions, including complex expressions that include types. However, it is not hard to hit a type-checking wall.

Check Const (Const O).

```
Error: Universe inconsistency
(cannot enforce Top.42 < Top.42).
```

We are unable to instantiate the parameter *T* of Const with an **exp** type. To see why, it is helpful to print the annotated version of **exp**'s inductive definition.

Print **exp**.

```
Inductive exp
```
> : Type (* *Top.*8 *) →
>   Type
>   (* *max*(0, (*Top.*11)+1, (*Top.*14)+1, (*Top.*15)+1,
>   (*Top.*19)+1) *) :=
> Const : ∀ *T* : Type (* *Top.*11 *) , *T* → **exp** *T*
> | Pair : ∀ (*T1* : Type (* *Top.*14 *)) (*T2* : Type (* *Top.*15 *)),
>   **exp** *T1* → **exp** *T2* → **exp** (*T1* × *T2*)
> | Eq : ∀ *T* : Type (* *Top.*19 *) , **exp** *T* → **exp** *T* → **exp bool**

We see that the index type of **exp** has been assigned to universe level *Top.*8. In addition, each of the four occurrences of Type in the types of the constructors gets its own universe variable. Each of these variables appears explicitly in the type of **exp**. In particular, any type **exp** *T* lives at a universe level found by incrementing by one the maximum of the four argument variables. Therefore, **exp** *must* live at a higher universe level than any type which may be passed to one of its constructors. This consequence led to the universe inconsistency.

Strangely, the universe variable *Top.*8 only appears in one place. Is there no restriction imposed on which types are valid arguments to **exp**? In fact, there is a restriction, but it only appears in a global set of universe constraints that are maintained but do not appear explicitly in types. We can print the current database.

`Print Universes.`

$Top.19 < Top.9 \leq Top.8$
$Top.15 < Top.9 \leq Top.8 \leq$ Coq.Init.Datatypes.38
$Top.14 < Top.9 \leq Top.8 \leq$ Coq.Init.Datatypes.37
$Top.11 < Top.9 \leq Top.8$

The command outputs many more constraints, but we have collected only those that mention *Top* variables. We see one constraint for each universe variable associated with a constructor argument from **exp**'s definition. Universe variable *Top.*19 is the type argument to Eq. The constraint for *Top.*19 effectively says that *Top.*19 must be less than *Top.*8, the universe of **exp**'s indices; an intermediate variable *Top.*9 appears as an artifact of the way the constraint was generated.

The next constraint, for *Top.*15, is more complicated. This is the universe of the second argument to the Pair constructor. Not only must *Top.*15 be less than *Top.*8 but it is also evident that *Top.*8 must be no greater than Coq.Init.Datatypes.38. What is this new universe variable? It is from the definition of the **prod** inductive family, to which types of the form $A \times B$ are desugared.

`Print` **prod**.

```
Inductive prod (A : Type (* Coq.Init.Datatypes.37 *) )
            (B : Type (* Coq.Init.Datatypes.38 *) )
              : Type (* max(Coq.Init.Datatypes.37,
                          Coq.Init.Datatypes.38) *) :=
      pair : A → B → A × B
```

We see that the constraint is enforcing that indices to **exp** must not live in a higher universe level than B indices to **prod**. The next constraint establishes a symmetric condition for A.

Thus, it is apparent that Coq maintains an elaborate set of universe variable inequalities behind the scenes. It may look like some functions are polymorphic in the universe levels of their arguments, but what is really happening is imperative updating of a system of constraints, such that all uses of a function are consistent with a global set of universe levels. When the constraint system may not be evolved soundly, we get a universe inconsistency error.

The annotated definition of **prod** reveals something interesting. A type **prod** A B lives at a universe that is the maximum of the universes of A and B, though we might expect that **prod**'s universe would in fact need to be *one higher* than the maximum. The critical difference is that in the definition of **prod**, A and B are defined as *parameters*; that is, they appear named to the left of the main colon rather than (possibly unnamed) to the right.

Parameters are not as flexible as normal inductive type arguments. The range types of all constructors of a parameterized type must share the same parameters. Nonetheless, when it is possible to define a polymorphic type in this way, we gain the ability to use the new type family in more ways, without triggering universe inconsistencies. For instance, nested pairs of types are perfectly legal.

Check (**nat**, (Type, Set)).

> (**nat**, (Type (* *Top*.44 *) , Set))
>   : Set × (Type (* *Top*.45 *) × Type (* *Top*.46 *))

The same cannot be done with a counterpart to **prod** that does not use parameters.

Inductive **prod'** : Type → Type → Type :=
| pair' : ∀ A B : Type, A → B → **prod'** A B.

Check (pair' **nat** (pair' Type Set)).

Error: Universe inconsistency
(cannot enforce Top.51 < Top.51).

The key benefit that parameters bring is the ability to avoid quantifying over types in the types of constructors. Such quantification induces less-than constraints, whereas parameters only introduce less-than-or-equal-to constraints.

Coq includes one more (potentially confusing) feature related to parameters. While Gallina does not support real universe polymorphism, there is a convenience facility that mimics universe polymorphism in some cases. We can illustrate what this means with a simple example.

Inductive **foo** (A : Type) : Type :=
| Foo : A → **foo** A.

Check **foo** **nat**.

> **foo** nat
>   : Set

Check **foo** Set.

> **foo** Set
>   : Type

Check **foo** **True**.

foo True
    : Prop

The basic pattern here is that Coq is willing to automatically build a copied-and-pasted version of an inductive definition, where some occurrences of **Type** have been replaced by **Set** or **Prop**. In each context, the type checker tries to find the valid replacements that are lowest in the type hierarchy. Automatic cloning of definitions can be much more convenient than manual cloning. We have already taken advantage of the fact that we may reuse the same families of tuple and list types to form values in **Set** and **Type**.

Imitation polymorphism can be confusing in some contexts. For instance, it is responsible for this odd behavior.

Inductive **bar** : Type := Bar : **bar**.

Check **bar**.

bar
    : Prop

The type that Coq comes up with may be used in strictly more contexts than the type one might have expected.

12.1.2   Deciphering Baffling Messages about Inability to Unify

One of the most confusing sorts of Coq error messages arises from an interplay between universes, syntax notations, and implicit arguments. Consider the following innocuous lemma, which is symmetry of equality for the special case of types.

Theorem symmetry : $\forall$ A B : Type,
    $A = B$
    $\rightarrow B = A$.
    intros ? ? H; rewrite H; reflexivity.
Qed.

Let us attempt an admittedly silly proof of the following theorem.

Theorem illustrative_but_silly_detour : **unit** = **unit**.
    apply symmetry.

Error: Impossible to unify "?35 = ?34" with "unit = unit".

Coq tells us that we cannot apply the lemma **symmetry** here, but the error message seems defective. In particular, one might think that `apply` should unify ?35 and ?34 with **unit** to ensure that the unification goes through. In fact, the issue is in a part of the unification problem that is *not* shown in this error message.

The following command is the secret to getting better error messages in such cases.

```
Set Printing All.

 apply symmetry.
```

```
Error: Impossible to unify "@eq Type ?46 ?45" with
"@eq Set unit unit".
```

Now we can see the problem: it is the first, *implicit* argument to the underlying equality function **eq** that disagrees across the two terms. The universe Set may be both an element and a subtype of Type, but the two are not definitionally equal.

```
Abort.
```

A variety of changes to the theorem statement would lead to use of Type as the implicit argument of **eq**. Here is one such change:

```
Theorem illustrative_but_silly_detour : (unit : Type) = unit.
  apply symmetry; reflexivity.
Qed.
```

Many related issues can come up with error messages, where one or both of notations and implicit arguments hide important details. The `Set Printing All` command turns off all such features and exposes underlying CIC terms.

For completeness, I mention one other class of confusing error messages about inability to unify two terms that look obviously unifiable. Each unification variable has a scope; a unification variable instantiation may not mention variables that were not already defined within that scope, at the point in proof search where the unification variable was introduced. Consider this illustrative example:

```
Unset Printing All.
```

```
Theorem ex_symmetry : (∃ x , x = 0) → (∃ x , 0 = x).
  eexists.
```

$$H : \exists\, x : \mathsf{nat}, x = 0$$
========================
$$0 = ?98$$

```
destruct H.
```

$x : \mathsf{nat}$
$H : x = 0$
================================
$0 = ?99$

symmetry; exact H.

```
Error: In environment
x : nat
H : x = 0
The term "H" has type "x = 0" while it is expected to have
type "?99 = 0".
```

The problem here is that variable x was introduced by destruct *after* we introduced ?99 with eexists, so the instantiation of ?99 may not mention x. A simple reordering of the proof solves the problem.

```
Restart.
  destruct 1 as [x]; apply ex_intro with x; symmetry; assumption.
Qed.
```

This restriction for unification variables may seem counterintuitive, but it follows from the fact that CIC contains no concept of unification variable. Rather, to construct the final proof term, at the point in a proof where the unification variable is introduced, we replace it with the instantiation we eventually find for it. It is simply syntactically illegal to refer there to variables that are not in scope. Without such a restriction, we could trivially prove such nontheorems as $\exists\, n : \mathsf{nat}$, $\forall\, m : \mathsf{nat}$, $n = m$ by econstructor; intro; reflexivity.

12.2 The Prop Universe

Chapter 3 showed parallel versions of useful datatypes for programs and proofs. The convention was that programs live in Set, and proofs live in Prop. Little explanation was given for why it is useful to maintain this distinction. There is certainly documentation value from separating programs from proofs; in practice, different concerns apply to building the two types of objects. It turns out, however, that these concerns motivate formal differences between the two universes in Coq.

Recall the types **sig** and **ex**, which are the program and proof versions of existential quantification. Their definitions differ only in one place, where **sig** uses Type and **ex** uses Prop.

Print **sig**.

```
Inductive sig (A : Type) (P : A → Prop) : Type :=
  exist : ∀ x : A, P x → sig P
```

```
Print ex.
```

```
Inductive ex (A : Type) (P : A → Prop) : Prop :=
  ex_intro : ∀ x : A, P x → ex P
```

It is natural to want a function to extract the first components of data structures like these. Doing so is easy enough for **sig**.

```
Definition projS A (P : A → Prop) (x : sig P) : A :=
  match x with
    | exist v _ ⇒ v
  end.
```

We run into trouble with a version that has been changed to work with **ex**.

```
Definition projE A (P : A → Prop) (x : ex P) : A :=
  match x with
    | ex_intro v _ ⇒ v
  end.
```

```
Error:
Incorrect elimination of "x" in the inductive type "ex":
the return type has sort "Type" while it should be "Prop".
Elimination of an inductive object of sort Prop
is not allowed on a predicate in sort Type
because proofs can be eliminated only to build proofs.
```

In formal Coq parlance, *elimination* means pattern matching. The typing rules of Gallina forbid pattern matching on a discriminee whose type belongs to Prop, whenever the result type of the match has a type besides Prop. This is a sort of information flow policy, where the type system ensures that the details of proofs can never have any effect on parts of a development that are not also marked as proofs.

This restriction matches informal practice. We think of programs and proofs as clearly separated, and outside of constructive logic, the idea of computing with proofs is ill-formed. The distinction also has practical importance in Coq, where it affects the behavior of extraction.

Recall that extraction is Coq's facility for translating Coq developments into programs in general-purpose programming languages like OCaml. Extraction *erases* proofs and leaves programs intact. A simple example with **sig** and **ex** demonstrates the distinction.

```
Definition sym_sig (x : sig (fun n ⇒ n = 0)) : sig (fun n ⇒ 0 = n) :=
```

```
match x with
  | exist n pf ⇒ exist _ n (sym_eq pf)
end.
```

`Extraction sym_sig.`

`(** val sym_sig : nat -> nat **)`

`let sym_sig x = x`

Since extraction erases proofs, the second components of **sig** values are elided, making **sig** a simple identity type family. The sym_sig operation is thus an identity function.

`Definition sym_ex` $(x : \textbf{ex}\ (\texttt{fun}\ n \Rightarrow n = 0)) : \textbf{ex}\ (\texttt{fun}\ n \Rightarrow 0 = n) :=$

```
  match x with
    | ex_intro n pf ⇒ ex_intro _ n (sym_eq pf)
  end.
```

`Extraction sym_ex.`

`(** val sym_ex : __ **)`

`let sym_ex = __`

In this example, the **ex** type itself is in `Prop`, so whole **ex** packages are erased. Coq extracts every proposition as the (Coq-specific) type `__`, whose single constructor is `__`. Not only are proofs replaced by `__` but proof arguments to functions are also removed completely, as we see here.

Extraction is very helpful as an optimization over programs that contain proofs. In languages like Haskell, advanced features make it possible to program with proofs, as a way of convincing the type checker to accept particular definitions. Unfortunately, when proofs are encoded as values in GADTs [50], these proofs exist at run-time and consume resources. In contrast, with Coq, as long as all proofs are kept within `Prop`, extraction is guaranteed to erase them.

Many users of the Curry-Howard correspondence support the idea of *extracting programs from proofs*, but few users of Coq and related tools do this. Instead, extraction is better thought of as an optimization that reduces the run-time costs of expressive typing.

We have seen two differences between proofs and programs: proofs are subject to an elimination restriction and are elided by extraction. The remaining difference is that `Prop` is *impredicative*, as the following example shows.

Check ∀ P Q : Prop, $P \lor Q \to Q \lor P$.

> ∀ P Q : Prop, $P \lor Q \to Q \lor P$
> : Prop

We see that it is possible to define a Prop that quantifies over other Props. This is fortunate, as we want that ability even for such basic purposes as stating propositional tautologies. The next section of this chapter explains why unrestricted impredicativity is undesirable. The impredicativity of Prop interacts crucially with the elimination restriction to avoid those pitfalls.

Impredicativity also allows us to implement a version of our earlier **exp** type that does not suffer from the previous weakness.

```
Inductive expP : Type → Prop :=
| ConstP : ∀ T, T → expP T
| PairP : ∀ T1 T2, expP T1 → expP T2 → expP (T1 × T2)
| EqP : ∀ T, expP T → expP T → expP bool.
```

Check ConstP 0.

> ConstP 0
> : **expP nat**

Check PairP (ConstP 0) (ConstP tt).

> PairP (ConstP 0) (ConstP tt)
> : **expP** (**nat** × **unit**)

Check EqP (ConstP Set) (ConstP Type).

> EqP (ConstP Set) (ConstP Type)
> : **expP bool**

Check ConstP (ConstP O).

> ConstP (ConstP 0)
> : **expP** (**expP nat**)

The new definition is not very helpful in this case. Because we have marked **expP** as a family of proofs, we cannot deconstruct expressions in the usual programmatic ways, which makes them almost useless for the usual purposes. Impredicative quantification is much more useful in defining inductive families that we really think of as judgments. For instance, the following code defines a notion of equality that is strictly more permissive than the base equality $=$.

```
Inductive eqPlus : ∀ T, T → T → Prop :=
| Base : ∀ T (x : T), eqPlus x x
```

```
| Func : ∀ dom ran (f1 f2 : dom → ran),
   (∀ x : dom, eqPlus (f1 x) (f2 x))
   → eqPlus f1 f2.
Check (Base 0).
```

```
   Base 0
      : eqPlus 0 0
```

```
Check (Func (fun n ⇒ n) (fun n ⇒ 0 + n) (fun n ⇒ Base n)).
```

```
   Func (fun n : nat ⇒ n) (fun n : nat ⇒ 0 + n)
   (fun n : nat ⇒ Base n)
      : eqPlus (fun n : nat ⇒ n) (fun n : nat ⇒ 0 + n)
```

```
Check (Base (Base 1)).
```

```
   Base (Base 1)
      : eqPlus (Base 1) (Base 1)
```

For a sense of why a term like the preceding one is useful to write, recall that we have already seen in Chapter 10 the utility of stating equality facts about proofs.

12.3 Axioms

While the specific logic Gallina is hardcoded into Coq's implementation, it is possible to add certain logical rules in a controlled way. In other words, Coq may be used to reason about many different refinements of Gallina where strictly more theorems are provable. We achieve this by asserting *axioms* without proof.

I tour through some standard axioms, as enumerated in Coq's online FAQ, and I add additional commentary as appropriate.

12.3.1 The Basics

One simple example of a useful axiom is the law of the excluded middle.

```
Require Import Classical_Prop.
Print classic.
```

```
   *** [ classic : ∀ P : Prop, P ∨ ¬ P ]
```

In the implementation of module Classical_Prop, this axiom was defined with the command

```
Axiom classic : ∀ P : Prop, P ∨ ¬ P.
```

An `Axiom` may be declared with any type, in any universe. There is a synonym `Parameter` for `Axiom`, and that synonym is often clearer for assertions not of type `Prop`. For instance, we can assert the existence of objects with certain properties.

Parameter *num* : **nat**.
Axiom *positive* : *num* > 0.
Reset *num*.

This kind of axiomatic presentation of a theory is very common outside of higher-order logic. However, in Coq, it is almost always preferable to stick to defining objects, functions, and predicates via inductive definitions and functional programming.

In general, there is a significant burden associated with any use of axioms. It is easy to assert a set of axioms that together is *inconsistent*. That is, a set of axioms may imply **False**, which allows any theorem to be proved, which defeats the purpose of a proof assistant. For example, we could assert the following axiom, which is consistent by itself but inconsistent when combined with *classic*.

Axiom *not_classic* : ¬ ∀ *P* : Prop, *P* ∨ ¬ *P*.

Theorem uhoh : **False**.
  generalize *classic not_classic*; tauto.
Qed.

Theorem uhoh_again : 1 + 1 = 3.
  destruct uhoh.
Qed.

Reset *not_classic*.

On the subject of the law of the excluded middle itself, this axiom is usually quite harmless, and many practical Coq developments assume it. It has been proved metatheoretically to be consistent with CIC. Here, *proved metatheoretically* means that someone proved on paper that excluded middle holds in a *model* of CIC in set theory [48]. All the other axioms surveyed in this section hold in the same model, so they are all consistent together.

Recall that Coq implements *constructive logic* by default, where the law of the excluded middle is not provable. Proofs in constructive logic can be thought of as programs. A ∀ quantifier denotes a dependent function type, and a disjunction denotes a variant type. In such a setting, excluded middle could be interpreted as a decision procedure for arbitrary propositions, which computability theory tells us cannot exist. Thus, constructive logic with excluded middle can no longer be associated with the usual notion of programming.

Given all this, why can one assert excluded middle as an axiom? The intuitive justification is that the elimination restriction for **Prop** prevents us from treating proofs as programs. An excluded middle axiom that quantified over **Set** instead of **Prop** would be problematic. If a development used that axiom, we would not be able to extract the code to OCaml (soundly) without implementing a genuine universal decision procedure. In contrast, values whose types belong to **Prop** are always erased by extraction, so we sidestep the axiom's algorithmic consequences.

Because the proper use of axioms is so precarious, there are helpful commands for determining which axioms a theorem relies on.

Theorem t1 : $\forall P$: Prop, $P \to \neg \neg P$.
  tauto.
Qed.

Print Assumptions t1.

  Closed under the global context

Theorem t2 : $\forall P$: Prop, $\neg \neg P \to P$.
  tauto.

Error: tauto failed.

  intro P; destruct (*classic P*); tauto.
Qed.

Print Assumptions t2.

  Axioms:
  classic : $\forall P$: Prop, $P \vee \neg P$

It is possible to avoid this dependence in some specific cases, where excluded middle is provable, for decidable families of propositions.

Theorem nat_eq_dec : $\forall n\ m$: **nat**, $n = m \vee n \neq m$.
  induction n; destruct m; intuition; generalize (*IHn m*);
    intuition.
Qed.

Theorem t2' : $\forall n\ m$: **nat**, $\neg \neg (n = m) \to n = m$.
  intros $n\ m$; destruct (nat_eq_dec $n\ m$); tauto.
Qed.

Print Assumptions t2'.

Closed under the global context

Mainstream mathematical practice assumes excluded middle, so it can be useful to have it available in Coq developments, though it is also nice to know that a theorem is proved in a simpler formal system than classical logic. The same is true for *proof irrelevance*, which simplifies proof issues that would not even arise in mainstream math.

```
Require Import ProofIrrelevance.
Print proof_irrelevance.
```

*** [*proof_irrelevance* : $\forall$ (P : **Prop**) (p1 p2 : P), p1 = p2]

This axiom asserts that any two proofs of the same proposition are equal. Recall this example function from Chapter 6.

```
Definition pred_strong1 (n : nat) : n > 0 → nat :=
  match n with
    | O ⇒ fun pf : 0 > 0 ⇒ match zgtz pf with end
    | S n' ⇒ fun _ ⇒ n'
  end.
```

We might want to prove that different proofs of $n > 0$ do not lead to different results from the richly typed predecessor function.

```
Theorem pred_strong1_irrel : ∀ n (pf1 pf2 : n > 0),
  pred_strong1 pf1 = pred_strong1 pf2.
  destruct n; crush.
Qed.
```

The proof script is simple, but it involves peeking into the definition of pred_strong1. For more complicated function definitions, one might like to avoid this burden. The **Prop** elimination restriction makes it impossible to write any function that discriminates on details of proof arguments, but this is only true metatheoretically, unless we assert an axiom like *proof_irrelevance*. With that axiom, we can prove the theorem without consulting the definition of pred_strong1.

```
Theorem pred_strong1_irrel' : ∀ n (pf1 pf2 : n > 0),
  pred_strong1 pf1 = pred_strong1 pf2.
  intros; f_equal; apply proof_irrelevance.
Qed.
```

Chapter 10 discussed some axioms related to proof irrelevance. In particular, Coq's standard library includes this axiom:

```
Require Import Eqdep.
Import Eq_rect_eq.
Print eq_rect_eq.
```

*** [eq_rect_eq :
$\forall$ (U : Type) (p : U) (Q : U $\rightarrow$ Type) (x : Q p) (h : $p = p$),
x = eq_rect p Q x p h]

This axiom says that it is permissible to simplify pattern matches over proofs of equalities like $e = e$. The axiom is logically equivalent to some simpler corollaries. In the theorem names, UIP stands for "unicity of identity proofs," where *identity* is a synonym for *equality*.

Corollary UIP_refl : $\forall$ A (x : A) (pf : $x = x$), pf = eq_refl x.
  intros; replace pf with (eq_rect x (**eq** x) (eq_refl x) x pf); [
    symmetry; apply eq_rect_eq
    | exact (match pf as pf' return match pf' in _ = y
                           return $x = y$ with
                           | eq_refl $\Rightarrow$ eq_refl x
                   end = pf' with
        | eq_refl $\Rightarrow$ eq_refl _
      end)].
Qed.

Corollary UIP : $\forall$ A (x y : A) ($pf1$ $pf2$: $x = y$), $pf1$ = $pf2$.
  intros; generalize $pf1$ $pf2$; subst; intros;
    match goal with
      | [$\vdash$?$pf1$ = ?$pf2$] $\Rightarrow$ rewrite (UIP_refl $pf1$);
        rewrite (UIP_refl $pf2$); reflexivity
    end.
Qed.

These corollaries are special cases of proof irrelevance. In developments that only need proof irrelevance for equality, there is no need to assert full irrelevance.

Another facet of proof irrelevance is that, like excluded middle, it is often provable for specific propositions. For instance, UIP is provable whenever the type A has a decidable equality operation. The module Eqdep_dec of the standard library contains a proof. A similar phenomenon applies to other notable cases, including less-than proofs. Thus, it is often possible to use proof irrelevance without asserting axioms.

There are two more basic axioms that are often assumed, to avoid complications that do not arise in set theory.

Require Import FunctionalExtensionality.
Print functional_extensionality_dep.

*** | *functional_extensionality_dep* :
$\forall (A : \mathtt{Type}) (B : A \to \mathtt{Type}) (f \ g : \forall \ x : A, \ B \ x),$
$(\forall \ x : A, f \ x = g \ x) \to f = g$]

This axiom says that two functions are equal if they map equal inputs to equal outputs. Such facts are not provable in general in CIC, but it is consistent to assume that they are.

A simple corollary shows that the same property applies to predicates.

Corollary predicate_extensionality : $\forall (A : \mathtt{Type}) (B : A \to \mathtt{Prop})$
$(f \ g : \forall \ x : A, \ B \ x),$
$(\forall \ x : A, f \ x = g \ x) \to f = g.$
intros; apply *functional_extensionality_dep*; assumption.
Qed.

In some cases, one might prefer to assert this corollary as the axiom, to restrict the consequences to proofs and not programs.

12.3.2   Axioms of Choice

Some Coq axioms are also points of contention in mainstream math. The most prominent example is the axiom of choice. In fact, there are multiple versions, and considered in isolation, none of these versions means quite what it means in classical set theory.

First, it is possible to implement a choice operator *without* axioms in some cases.

Require Import ConstructiveEpsilon.
Check constructive_definite_description.

constructive_definite_description
       : $\forall (A : \mathtt{Set}) (f : A \to \mathtt{nat}) (g : \mathtt{nat} \to A),$
       $(\forall \ x : A, g \ (f \ x) = x) \to$
       $\forall P : A \to \mathtt{Prop},$
       $(\forall \ x : A, \{P \ x\} + \{ \neg P \ x\}) \to$
       $(\exists! \ x : A, P \ x) \to \{x : A \mid P \ x\}$

Print Assumptions constructive_definite_description.

Closed under the global context

This function transforms a decidable predicate P into a function that produces an element satisfying P from a proof that such an element exists. The functions f and g, in conjunction with an associated injectivity property, are used to express the idea that the set A is countable. Under these conditions, a simple brute force algorithm gets the job done: we just enumerate all elements of A, stopping when we find one satisfying P. The existence proof, specified in terms of *unique* existence $\exists!$, guarantees termination. The definition of this operator in Coq uses some interesting techniques, as seen in the implementation of the ConstructiveEpsilon module.

Countable choice is provable in set theory without appealing to the general axiom of choice. To support the more general principle in Coq, we must also add an axiom. Here is a functional version of the axiom of unique choice:

```
Require Import ClassicalUniqueChoice.
Check dependent_unique_choice.
```

> dependent_unique_choice
>   : $\forall$ $(A : \mathtt{Type})$ $(B : A \to \mathtt{Type})$ $(R : \forall\, x : A,\ B\ x \to \mathtt{Prop})$,
> $(\forall\, x : A,\ \exists!\ y : B\ x,\ R\ x\ y) \to$
> $\exists\, f : \forall\, x : A,\ B\ x$,
> $\forall\, x : A,\ R\ x\ (f\ x)$

This axiom lets us convert a relational specification R into a function implementing that specification. We need only prove that R is truly a function. A stronger formulation applies to cases where R maps each input to one or more outputs. We also simplify the statement of the theorem by considering only nondependent function types.

```
Require Import ClassicalChoice.
Check choice.
```

> choice
>   : $\forall$ $(A\ B : \mathtt{Type})$ $(R : A \to B \to \mathtt{Prop})$,
> $(\forall\, x : A,\ \exists\, y : B,\ R\ x\ y) \to$
> $\exists\, f : A \to B,\ \forall\, x : A,\ R\ x\ (f\ x)$

This principle is proved as a theorem, based on the unique choice axiom and an additional axiom of relational choice from the RelationalChoice module.

In set theory, the axiom of choice is a fundamental philosophical commitment one makes about the universe of sets. In Coq, the choice axioms say something weaker. For instance, consider the simple restatement of the choice axiom where we replace existential quantification by its Curry-Howard analogue, subset types.

```
Definition choice_Set (A B : Type) (R : A → B → Prop)
```

$(H : \forall\ x : A,\ \{y\ :\ B\ |\ R\ x\ y\})$
$:\{f\ :\ A \rightarrow B\ |\ \forall\ x : A,\ R\ x\ (f\ x)\} :=$
exist $(\mathtt{fun}\ f \Rightarrow \forall\ x : A,\ R\ x\ (f\ x))$
$(\mathtt{fun}\ x \Rightarrow \mathtt{proj1\_sig}\ (H\ x))\ (\mathtt{fun}\ x \Rightarrow \mathtt{proj2\_sig}\ (H\ x)).$

Via the Curry-Howard correspondence, this axiom can be taken to have the same meaning as the original. It is implemented trivially as a transformation not much deeper than uncurrying. Thus, the utility of the axioms mentioned earlier comes in their usage to build programs from proofs. Normal set theory has no explicit proofs, so the meaning of the usual axiom of choice is subtly different. In Gallina, the axioms implement a controlled relaxation of the restrictions on information flow from proofs to programs.

However, when we combine an axiom of choice with the law of the excluded middle, the idea of choice becomes more interesting. Excluded middle gives us a highly noncomputational way of constructing proofs, but it does not change the computational nature of programs. Thus, the axiom of choice can still be used to translate between two different sorts of programs, but the input programs (which are proofs) may be written in a rich language that goes beyond normal computability. This combination truly is more than repackaging a function with a different type.

An even stronger and more direct bridge between the two worlds comes from Hilbert's epsilon operator:

Require Import ClassicalEpsilon.
Check *constructive_indefinite_description*.

constructive_indefinite_description
    $: \forall\ (A : \mathtt{Type})\ (P : A \rightarrow \mathtt{Prop}),$
    $(\exists\ x : A,\ P\ x) \rightarrow \{x : A\ |\ P\ x\}$

This operator lets us translate directly from the Prop version of existential quantification into the Set version. With such an axiom plus others like excluded middle, computation in all of Coq's universes goes beyond the usual bounds of computability, so one should appeal to the axiom with care. Program extraction will not be feasible for functions that use this operator, but it may be useful in formalizing standard mathematical constructs programmatically, for instance, to materialize the limit of an infinite series that can be proved to converge.

The Coq tools support a command line flag -impredicative-set, which modifies Gallina in a more fundamental way by making Set impredicative. A term like $\forall\ T : \mathtt{Set},\ T$ has type Set, and inductive definitions in Set may have constructors that quantify over arguments of any types. To maintain consistency, an elimination restriction must be imposed, similarly to the restriction for Prop. The restriction only applies to large inductive types, where some constructor quantifies over a type of type Type. In such cases, a value in this inductive type may only be pattern-matched over to yield a result type whose type is Set or Prop. This rule contrasts with the rule for Prop, where the restriction applies even to nonlarge inductive types, and where the result type may only have type Prop.

In old versions of Coq, Set was impredicative by default. Later versions make Set predicative to avoid inconsistency with some classical axioms. In particular, one should watch out when using impredicative Set with axioms of choice. In combination with excluded middle or predicate extensionality, inconsistency can result. Impredicative Set can be useful for modeling inherently impredicative mathematical concepts, but almost all Coq developments do fine without it.

12.3.3   Axioms and Computation

One additional axiom-related concern arises from an aspect of Gallina that is very different from set theory: a notion of *computational equivalence* is central to the definition of the formal system. Axioms tend not to play well with computation. Consider this example. We start by implementing a function that uses a type equality proof to perform a safe type cast.

```
Definition cast (x y : Set) (pf : x = y) (v : x) : y :=
  match pf with
    | eq_refl ⇒ v
  end.
```

Computation over programs that use cast can proceed smoothly.

```
Eval compute in (cast (eq_refl (nat → nat)) (fun n ⇒ S n)) 12.
```

```
    = 13
    : nat
```

Things do not go as smoothly when we use cast with proofs that rely on axioms.

```
Theorem t3 : (∀ n : nat, fin (S n)) = (∀ n : nat, fin (n + 1)).
  change ((∀ n : nat, (fun n ⇒ fin (S n)) n)
    = (∀ n : nat, (fun n ⇒ fin (n + 1)) n));
    rewrite (functional_extensionality (fun n ⇒ fin (n + 1))
      (fun n ⇒ fin (S n))); crush.
```

Qed.

Eval compute in (cast t3 (fun _ ⇒ First)) 12.

> = match t3 in (_ = P) return P with
> | eq_refl ⇒ fun n : **nat** ⇒ First
>   end 12
> : **fin** $(12 + 1)$

Computation gets stuck in a pattern match on the proof t3. The structure of t3 is not known, so the match cannot proceed. It turns out a more basic problem leads to this particular situation. We ended the proof of t3 with Qed, so the definition of t3 is not available to computation. That mistake is easily fixed.

Reset t3.

Theorem t3 : $(\forall\ n$: **nat**, **fin** $(S\ n)) = (\forall\ n$: **nat**, **fin** $(n + 1))$.
   change $((\forall\ n$: **nat**, $(\text{fun}\ n \Rightarrow$ **fin** $(S\ n))\ n)$
    $= (\forall\ n$: **nat**, $(\text{fun}\ n \Rightarrow$ **fin** $(n + 1))\ n))$;
    rewrite (functional_extensionality (fun $n \Rightarrow$ **fin** $(n + 1)$)
     (fun $n \Rightarrow$ **fin** $(S\ n)))$; *crush*.
Defined.

Eval compute in (cast t3 (fun _ ⇒ First)) 12.

> = match
>   match
>   match
>   functional_extensionality
>
>   ....

Most of the details are elided. A very unwieldy tree of nested matches on equality proofs appears. This time evaluation really *is* stuck on a use of an axiom.

If we are careful in using tactics to prove an equality, we can still compute with casts over the proof.

Lemma plus1 : $\forall\ n$, S $n = n + 1$.
   induction n; simpl; intuition.
Defined.

Theorem t4 : $\forall\ n$, **fin** $(S\ n) =$ **fin** $(n + 1)$.
   intro; f_equal; apply plus1.
Defined.

Eval compute in cast (t4 13) First.

> = First

: **fin** $(13 + 1)$

This simple computational reduction hides the use of a recursive function to produce a suitable eq_refl proof term. The recursion originates in the use of induction in t4's proof.

12.3.4   Methods for Avoiding Axioms

The previous section demonstrated one reason to avoid axioms: they interfere with computational behavior of terms. A further reason is to reduce the philosophical commitment of a theorem. The more axioms one assumes, the harder it becomes to convince oneself that the formal system corresponds appropriately to one's intuitions. A refinement of this last point, in applications like proof-carrying code [27] in computer security, has to do with minimizing the size of a *trusted code base*. To convince ourselves that a theorem is true, we must convince ourselves of the correctness of the program that checks the theorem. Axioms effectively become new source code for the checking program, increasing the effort required to perform a correctness audit.

Section 12.3 gave one example of avoiding an axiom. We proved that pred_strong1 is agnostic to details of the proofs passed to it as arguments, by unfolding the definition of the function. A different proof keeps the function definition opaque and instead applies a proof irrelevance axiom. By accepting a more complex proof, we reduce the philosophical commitment and trusted base. (By the way, the less-than relation that the proofs here prove admits proof irrelevance as a theorem provable within normal Gallina.)

We used the *dep_destruct* tactic several times in a way that silently generates proof terms referring to an axiom. Consider this simple case analysis principle for **fin** values:

Theorem fin_cases : $\forall n$ $(f$: **fin** $(S\ n))$, f = First $\lor \exists f'$, f = Next f'.
  intros; *dep_destruct* f; eauto.
Qed.

Print Assumptions fin_cases.

Axioms:
JMeq_eq : $\forall$ $(A$: Type$)$ $(x\ y$: $A)$, JMeq $x\ y \rightarrow x = y$

The proof depends on the *JMeq_eq* axiom (see Chapter 10). However, a smarter tactic could have avoided an axiom dependence. Here is a different proof via a slightly strange-looking lemma:

Lemma fin_cases_again' : $\forall n$ $(f$: **fin** $n)$,
  match n return **fin** $n \rightarrow$ Prop with

```
    | O ⇒ fun _ ⇒ False
    | S n' ⇒ fun f ⇒ f = First ∨ ∃ f', f = Next f'
  end f.
  destruct f; eauto.
Qed.
```

We apply a variant of the convoy pattern, which we are used to seeing in function implementations. Here, the pattern helps us state a lemma in a form where the argument to **fin** is a variable. Recall that, thanks to basic typing rules for pattern matching, `destruct` will only work effectively on types whose nonparameter arguments are variables. The `exact` tactic, which takes as argument a literal proof term, now gives us an easy way of proving the original theorem.

```
Theorem fin_cases_again : ∀ n (f : fin (S n)),
  f = First ∨ ∃ f', f = Next f'.
  intros; exact (fin_cases_again' f).
Qed.
```

```
Print Assumptions fin_cases_again.
Closed under the global context
```

As the Curry-Howard correspondence might lead us to expect, the same pattern may be applied in programming as in proving. Axioms are relevant in programming, too, because, while Coq includes useful extensions like `Program` that make dependently typed programming more straightforward, in general these extensions generate code that relies on axioms about equality. We can use clever pattern matching to write code axiom-free.

As an example, consider a `Set` version of `fin_cases`. We use `Set` types instead of `Prop` types, so that return values have computational content and may be used to guide the behavior of algorithms. Besides that, we are essentially writing the same "proof" in a more explicit way.

```
Definition finOut n (f : fin n)
  : match n return fin n → Type with
      | O ⇒ fun _ ⇒ Empty_set
      | _ ⇒ fun f ⇒ {f' : _ | f = Next f'} + {f = First}
    end f :=
  match f with
    | First _ ⇒ inright _ eq_refl
    | Next _ f' ⇒ inleft _ (exist _ f' eq_refl)
  end.
```

As another example, consider the following type of formulas in first-order logic. The intent of the type definition is not important in what follows, but we give a quick intuition. The formulas may include ∀ quantification over arbitrary Types, and we index formulas by environments telling which variables are in scope and what their types are; such an environment is a **list** Type. A constructor Inject lets us include any Coq Prop as a formula, and VarEq and Lift can be used for variable references, in what is essentially the de Bruijn index convention.

```
Inductive formula : list Type → Type :=
| Inject : ∀ Ts, Prop → formula Ts
| VarEq : ∀ T Ts, T → formula (T :: Ts)
| Lift : ∀ T Ts, formula Ts → formula (T :: Ts)
| Forall : ∀ T Ts, formula (T :: Ts) → formula Ts
| And : ∀ Ts, formula Ts → formula Ts → formula Ts.
```

This example is based on my own experiences implementing variants of a program logic called XCAP [28], which also includes an inductive predicate for characterizing which formulas are provable. Here I include a pared-down version of such a predicate, with only two constructors, which is sufficient to illustrate certain issues.

```
Inductive proof : formula nil → Prop :=
| PInject : ∀ (P : Prop), P → proof (Inject nil P)
| PAnd : ∀ p q, proof p → proof q → proof (And p q).
```

Let us prove a lemma showing that a "$P \land Q \to P$" rule is derivable within the rules of **proof**.

```
Theorem proj1 : ∀ p q, proof (And p q) → proof p.
  destruct 1.
```

```
p : formula nil
q : formula nil
P : Prop
H : P
============================
  proof p
```

We are reminded that `induction` and `destruct` do not work effectively on types with nonvariable arguments. The first subgoal is clearly unprovable. (Consider the case where $p = $ Inject nil **False**.)

An application of the `dependent destruction` tactic (the basis for *dep_destruct*) solves the problem handily. We use a shorthand with the `intros` tactic that lets us use question marks for variable names that do not matter.

```
Restart.
Require Import Program.
 intros ? ? H; dependent destruction H; auto.
Qed.
```

```
Print Assumptions proj1.
```

Axioms:
$eq\_rect\_eq : \forall\ (U : \mathsf{Type})\ (p : U)\ (Q : U \to \mathsf{Type})\ (x : Q\ p)$
$\qquad\qquad (h : p = p),\ x = \mathsf{eq\_rect}\ p\ Q\ x\ p\ h$

Unfortunately, that built-in tactic appeals to an axiom. It is still possible to avoid axioms by giving the proof via another lemma. Here is a first attempt that fails at remaining axiom-free, using a common equality-based trick for supporting induction on nonvariable arguments to type families. The trick works fine without axioms for datatypes more traditional than **formula**, but we run into trouble with the current type.

Lemma proj1_again' : $\forall\ r$, **proof** r
    $\to \forall\ p\ q,\ r =$ And $p\ q \to$ **proof** p.
 destruct 1; *crush*.

$H0$: Inject $[]\ P =$ And $p\ q$
=================================
  proof p

The first goal looks reasonable. Hypothesis $H0$ is clearly contradictory, as `discriminate` can show.

 discriminate.

H : **proof** p
$H1$: And $p\ q =$ And $p0\ q0$
=================================
  proof $p0$

It looks like we are almost done. Hypothesis $H1$ gives $p = p0$ by injectivity of constructors, and then H finishes the case.

 injection $H1$; intros.

Unfortunately, the equality that we expected between p and $p0$ comes in a strange form.

$H3$: existT (fun Ts : **list** Type $\Rightarrow$ **formula** Ts) $[]$%**list** $p =$
    existT (fun Ts : **list** Type $\Rightarrow$ **formula** Ts) $[]$%**list** $p0$
=================================
  proof $p0$

Reviewing the discussion in Chapter 3 of writing injection principles manually, we see that an existT type is the most direct way to express the output of injection on a dependently typed constructor. The constructor And is dependently typed, since it takes a parameter Ts upon which the types of p and q depend. Let us not dwell further here on why this goal appears; readers may like to attempt the (impossible) exercise of building a better injection lemma for And without using axioms.

How exactly does an axiom come into the picture here? Let us ask *crush* to finish the proof.

   crush.
Qed.

Print Assumptions proj1_again'.

Axioms:
eq_rect_eq : ∀ (U : Type) (p : U) (Q : U → Type) (x : Q p)
             (h : $p = p$), x = eq_rect p Q x p h

It turns out that this familiar axiom about equality (or some other axiom) is required to deduce $p = p0$ from the hypothesis *H3* above. The soundness of that proof step is neither provable nor disprovable in Gallina.

We can produce an even stranger-looking lemma, which gives us the theorem without axioms. As always when we want to do case analysis on a term with a tricky dependent type, the key is to refactor the theorem statement so that every term we match on has *variables* as its type indices; so instead of talking about proofs of And p q, we talk about proofs of an arbitrary r, but we only conclude anything interesting when r is an And.

Lemma proj1_again'' : ∀ r, **proof** r
   → match r with
       | And Ps p _ ⇒ match Ps return **formula** Ps → Prop with
                           | nil ⇒ fun p ⇒ **proof** p
                           | _ ⇒ fun _ ⇒ **True**
                          end p
       | _ ⇒ **True**
     end.
   destruct 1; auto.
Qed.

Theorem proj1_again : ∀ p q, **proof** (And p q) → **proof** p.
   intros ? ? H; exact (proj1_again'' H).
Qed.

Print Assumptions proj1_again.

```
Closed under the global context
```

This example illustrates again how some of the design patterns for dependently typed programming can be used fruitfully in theorem statements.

Consider one final way to avoid dependence on axioms. Often this task is equivalent to writing definitions such that they *compute*. That is, we want Coq's normal reduction to be able to run certain programs to completion. Here is a simple example where such computation can get stuck. In proving properties of such functions, we would need to apply axioms like K manually to make progress.

Imagine we are working with deeply embedded syntax of some programming language, where each term is considered to be in the scope of a number of free variables that hold normal Coq values. To enforce proper typing, we need to model a Coq typing environment somehow. One natural choice is as a list of types, where variable number i is treated as a reference to the ith element of the list.

```
Section withTypes.
   Variable types : list Set.
```

To give the semantics of terms, we need to represent value environments, which assign each variable a term of the proper type.

```
   Variable values : hlist (fun x : Set ⇒ x) types.
```

Now imagine that we are writing some procedure that operates on a distinguished variable of type **nat**. A hypothesis formalizes this assumption, using the standard library function nth_error for looking up list elements by position.

```
   Variable natIndex : nat.
   Variable natIndex_ok : nth_error types natIndex = Some nat.
```

It is not hard to use this hypothesis to write a function for extracting the **nat** value in position *natIndex* of *values*, starting with two helpful lemmas, each of which we finish with Defined to mark the lemma as transparent, so that its definition may be expanded during evaluation.

```
   Lemma nth_error_nil : ∀ A n x,
      nth_error (@nil A) n = Some x
      → False.
      destruct n; simpl; unfold error; congruence.
   Defined.

   Implicit Arguments nth_error_nil [A n x].
   Lemma Some_inj : ∀ A (x y : A),
```

```
    Some x = Some y
    → x = y.
    congruence.
  Defined.
  Fixpoint getNat (types' : list Set)
    (values' : hlist (fun x : Set ⇒ x) types')
    (natIndex : nat)
    : (nth_error types' natIndex = Some nat) → nat :=
    match values' with
      | HNil ⇒ fun pf ⇒ match nth_error_nil pf with end
      | HCons t ts x values'' ⇒
        match natIndex return nth_error (t :: ts) natIndex
          = Some nat → nat with
          | O ⇒ fun pf ⇒
            match Some_inj pf in _ = T return T with
              | eq_refl ⇒ x
            end
          | S natIndex' ⇒ getNat values'' natIndex'
        end
    end.
End withTypes.
```

The problem becomes apparent when we experiment with running getNat on a concrete *types* list.

```
Definition myTypes := unit :: nat :: bool :: nil.
Definition myValues : hlist (fun x : Set ⇒ x) myTypes :=
  tt ::: 3 ::: false ::: HNil.
```

```
Definition myNatIndex := 1.
```

```
Theorem myNatIndex_ok : nth_error myTypes myNatIndex = Some nat.
  reflexivity.
Defined.
```

```
Eval compute in getNat myValues myNatIndex myNatIndex_ok.
```

```
    = 3
```

We have not hit the problem yet, since we proceeded with a concrete equality proof for **myNatIndex_ok**. However, consider a case where we want to reason about the behavior of **getNat** *independently* of a specific proof.

```
Theorem getNat_is_reasonable : ∀ pf,
  getNat myValues myNatIndex pf = 3.
  intro; compute.
```

```
1 subgoal
```
  pf : nth_error myTypes myNatIndex $=$ Some **nat**
  ============================
```
  match
    match
      pf in (_ = y)
      return (nat = match y with
                    | Some H ⇒ H
                    | None ⇒ nat
                    end)
    with
    | eq_refl ⇒ eq_refl
    end in (_ = T) return T
  with
  | eq_refl ⇒ 3
  end = 3
```

Since the details of the equality proof pf are not known, computation can proceed no further. A rewrite with axiom K would allow us to make progress, but we can rethink the definitions a bit to avoid depending on axioms.

```
Abort.
```

Here is a definition of a function that turns out to be useful. A call **update** ls n x overwrites the nth position of the list ls with the value x, padding the end of the list with extra x values as needed to ensure sufficient length.

```
Fixpoint copies A (x : A) (n : nat) : list A :=
  match n with
    | O ⇒ nil
    | S n' ⇒ x :: copies x n'
  end.
```
```
Fixpoint update A (ls : list A) (n : nat) (x : A) : list A :=
  match ls with
    | nil ⇒ copies x n ++ x :: nil
    | y :: ls' ⇒ match n with
                   | O ⇒ x :: ls'
                   | S n' ⇒ y :: update ls' n' x
                 end
  end.
```

Now let us revisit the definition of getNat.

```
Section withTypes'.
```

Variable *types* : **list** Set.
Variable *natIndex* : **nat**.

Instead of asserting properties about the list *types*, we build a new list that is *guaranteed by construction* to have those properties.

Definition types' := update *types* *natIndex* **nat**.

Variable *values* : **hlist** (**fun** x : Set $\Rightarrow$ x) types'.

Now a bit of dependent pattern matching helps us rewrite getNat in a way that avoids any use of equality proofs.

Fixpoint skipCopies (n : **nat**)
 : **hlist** (**fun** x : Set $\Rightarrow$ x) (copies **nat** n ++ **nat** :: nil) $\rightarrow$ **nat** :=
 match n with
  | O $\Rightarrow$ **fun** vs $\Rightarrow$ hhd vs
  | S n' $\Rightarrow$ **fun** vs $\Rightarrow$ skipCopies n' (htl vs)
 end.

Fixpoint getNat' (*types''* : **list** Set) (*natIndex* : **nat**)
 : **hlist** (**fun** x : Set $\Rightarrow$ x) (update *types''* *natIndex* **nat**) $\rightarrow$ **nat** :=
 match *types''* with
  | nil $\Rightarrow$ skipCopies *natIndex*
  | t :: *types0* $\Rightarrow$
    match *natIndex* **return** **hlist** (**fun** x : Set $\Rightarrow$ x)
      (update (t :: *types0*) *natIndex* **nat**) $\rightarrow$ **nat** with
     | O $\Rightarrow$ **fun** vs $\Rightarrow$ hhd vs
     | S *natIndex'* $\Rightarrow$ **fun** vs $\Rightarrow$ getNat' *types0* *natIndex'* (htl vs)
    end
 end.
End withTypes'.

The surprise comes in how easy it is to use getNat'. While typing works by modification of a types list, we can choose parameters so that the modification has no effect.

Theorem getNat_is_reasonable
 : getNat' myTypes myNatIndex myValues = 3.
 reflexivity.
Qed.

The same parameters as before work without alteration, and we avoid use of axioms.

PART III

Proof Engineering

13   Proof Search by Logic Programming

The Curry-Howard correspondence tells us that proving is just programming, but the pragmatics of the two activities are very different. Generally we care about properties of a program besides its type, but the same is not true for proofs. Any proof of a theorem will do just as well. As a result, automated proof search is conceptually simpler than automated programming.

The paradigm of logic programming [21], as embodied in languages like Prolog [42], is a good match for proof search in higher-order logic. This chapter introduces the details, attempting to avoid any dependence on past logic programming experience.

13.1   Introducing Logic Programming

Recall the definition of addition from the standard library.

```
Print plus.
```

plus =
fix plus $(n\ m : \mathbf{nat}) : \mathbf{nat} := \mathrm{match}\ n\ \mathrm{with}$
$\qquad\qquad | \ 0 \Rightarrow m$
$\qquad\qquad | \ \mathsf{S}\ p \Rightarrow \mathsf{S}\ (\mathsf{plus}\ p\ m)$
$\qquad\qquad \mathrm{end}$

This is a recursive definition, in the style of functional programming. We might also follow the style of logic programming, which corresponds to the inductive relations defined in previous chapters.

```
Inductive plusR : nat → nat → nat → Prop :=
```
$| \ \mathsf{PlusO} : \forall\ m,\ \mathbf{plusR}\ \mathsf{O}\ m\ m$
$| \ \mathsf{PlusS} : \forall\ n\ m\ r,\ \mathbf{plusR}\ n\ m\ r$
$\quad \rightarrow \mathbf{plusR}\ (\mathsf{S}\ n)\ m\ (\mathsf{S}\ r).$

Intuitively, a fact **plusR** $n\ m\ r$ only holds when **plus** $n\ m = r$. It is not hard to prove this correspondence formally.

Hint Constructors **plusR**.

Theorem plus_plusR : ∀ n m,
  plusR n m $(n + m)$.
  induction n; *crush*.
Qed.

Theorem plusR_plus : ∀ n m r,
  plusR n m r
  → $r = n + m$.
  induction 1; *crush*.
Qed.

With the functional definition of **plus**, simple equalities about arithmetic follow by computation.

Example four_plus_three : $4 + 3 = 7$.
  reflexivity.
Qed.

Print four_plus_three.

four_plus_three $=$ eq_refl

With the relational definition, the same equalities take more steps to prove, but the process is completely mechanical. For example, consider this manual proof search strategy. The steps with error messages shown afterward will be omitted from the final script.

Example four_plus_three' : **plusR** 4 3 7.
  apply PlusO.

Error: Impossible to unify "plusR 0 ?24 ?24"
with "plusR 4 3 7".

  apply PlusS.
  apply PlusO.

Error: Impossible to unify "plusR 0 ?25 ?25"
with "plusR 3 3 6".

  apply PlusS.
  apply PlusO.

Error: Impossible to unify "plusR 0 ?26 ?26"
with "plusR 2 3 5".

  apply PlusS.
  apply PlusO.

```
Error: Impossible to unify "plusR 0 ?27 ?27"
with "plusR 1 3 4".
```

```
  apply PlusS.
  apply PlusO.
```

At this point the proof is completed. It is no doubt clear that a simple procedure could find all proofs of this kind. We are just exploring all possible proof trees, built from the two candidate steps `apply PlusO` and `apply PlusS`. The built-in tactic `auto` follows exactly this strategy, since we used `Hint Constructors` to register the two candidate proof steps as hints.

```
Restart.
  auto.
Qed.
```

```
Print four_plus_three'.
```

```
four_plus_three' = PlusS (PlusS (PlusS (PlusS (PlusO 3))))
```

Let us try the same approach on a slightly more complex goal.

```
Example five_plus_three : plusR 5 3 8.
  auto.
```

This time, `auto` is not enough to make any progress. Since even a single candidate step may lead to an infinite space of possible proof trees, `auto` is parameterized on the maximum depth of trees to consider. The default depth is 5, and it turns out that we need depth 6 to prove the goal.

```
  auto 6.
```

Sometimes it is useful to see a description of the proof tree that `auto` finds, with the `info` tactical. (This tactical is not available in Coq 8.4, but I hope it reappears soon. The special case `info_auto` tactic is provided as a replacement for `auto`.)

```
Restart.
  info auto 6.
```

```
== apply PlusS; apply PlusS; apply PlusS; apply PlusS;
   apply PlusS; apply PlusO.
```

```
Qed.
```

The two key components of logic programming are *backtracking* and *unification*. To see these techniques in action, consider this frivolous example. Here the candidate proof steps are reflexivity and quantifier instantiation.

Example seven_minus_three : $\exists\,x$, $x + 3 = 7$.

For explanatory purposes, let us proceed in the manner of a user with minimal understanding of arithmetic. We start by choosing an instantiation for the quantifier. Recall that ex_intro is the constructor for existentially quantified formulas.

```
apply ex_intro with 0.
reflexivity.
```

Error: Impossible to unify "7" with "0 + 3".

This seems to be a dead end. Let us backtrack to the point where we ran apply and make a better choice.

```
Restart.
apply ex_intro with 4.
reflexivity.
Qed.
```

This is a fairly tame example of backtracking. In general, any node in an under-construction proof tree may be the destination of backtracking an arbitrarily large number of times, as different candidate proof steps are found not to lead to full proof trees, within the depth bound passed to auto.

Next I demonstrate unification, which is easier when we switch to the relational formulation of addition.

Example seven_minus_three' : $\exists\,x$, **plusR** x 3 7.

We could attempt to guess the quantifier instantiation manually as before, but there is no need. Instead of apply, we use eapply, which proceeds with placeholder *unification variables* standing in for those parameters we wish to postpone guessing.

```
eapply ex_intro.
```

1 subgoal

```
============================
```

  plusR ?70 3 7

Now we can finish the proof with the right applications of **plusR**'s constructors. Note that new unification variables are being generated to stand for new unknowns.

```
apply PlusS.
```

```
============================
```

plusR ?71 3 6

```
apply PlusS. apply PlusS. apply PlusS.
```

=============================

plusR ?74 3 3

```
apply PlusO.
```

The `auto` tactic will not perform these sorts of steps that introduce unification variables, but the `eauto` tactic will. It is helpful to work with two separate tactics, because proof search in the `eauto` style can uncover many more potential proof trees and hence take much longer to run.

```
Restart.
  info eauto 6.
```

```
 == eapply ex_intro; apply PlusS; apply PlusS;
    apply PlusS; apply PlusS; apply PlusO.
```

```
Qed.
```

This proof is the first example showing that logic programming simplifies proof search compared to functional programming. In general, functional programs are only meant to be run in a single direction; a function has disjoint sets of inputs and outputs. The last example effectively ran a logic program backwards, deducing an input that gives rise to a certain output. The same works for deducing an unknown value of the other input.

```
Example seven_minus_four' : ∃ x, plusR 4 x 7.
  eauto 6.
Qed.
```

By proving the right auxiliary facts, we can reason about specific functional programs in the same way as for a logic program. Let us prove that the constructors of **plusR** have natural interpretations as lemmas about **plus**. We can find the first such lemma already proved in the standard library, using the `SearchRewrite` command to find a library theorem proving an equality whose left or right side matches a pattern with wildcards.

```
SearchRewrite (O + _).
```

```
plus_O_n: ∀ n : nat, 0 + n = n
```

The command `Hint Immediate` asks `auto` and `eauto` to consider this lemma as a candidate step for any leaf of a proof tree.

```
Hint Immediate plus_O_n.
```

The counterpart to PlusS is proved here.

```
Lemma plusS : ∀ n m r,
  n + m = r
  → S n + m = S r.
  crush.
Qed.
```

The command `Hint Resolve` adds a new candidate proof step, to be attempted at any level of a proof tree, not just at leaves.

```
Hint Resolve plusS.
```

Now that we have registered the proper hints, we can replicate the previous examples with the normal, functional addition plus.

```
Example seven_minus_three" : ∃ x, x + 3 = 7.
  eauto 6.
Qed.

Example seven_minus_four : ∃ x, 4 + x = 7.
  eauto 6.
Qed.
```

This new hint database is far from a complete decision procedure, as we see in a further example that `eauto` does not finish.

```
Example seven_minus_four_zero : ∃ x, 4 + x + 0 = 7.
  eauto 6.
Abort.
```

A further lemma will be helpful.

```
Lemma plusO : ∀ n m,
  n = m
  → n + 0 = m.
  crush.
Qed.

Hint Resolve plusO.
```

Note that if we consider the inputs to plus as the inputs of a corresponding logic program, the new rule plusO introduces an ambiguity. For instance, a sum $0 + 0$ would match both of plus_O_n and plusO, depending on which operand we focus on. This ambiguity may increase the number of potential search trees, slowing proof search, but semantically it presents no problems, and in fact it leads to an automated proof of the present example.

Example seven_minus_four_zero : $\exists\, x$, $4 + x + 0 = 7$.
    eauto 7.
Qed.

Just how much damage can be done by adding hints that increase the space of possible proof trees? A classic example comes from unrestricted use of transitivity, as embodied in this library theorem about equality:

Check eq_trans.

eq_trans
        : $\forall\, (A : \mathsf{Type})\ (x\ y\ z : A),\ x = y \rightarrow y = z \rightarrow x = z$

Hints are scoped over sections, so let us enter a section to contain the effects of an unfortunate hint choice.

Section slow.
    Hint Resolve eq_trans.

The following fact is false, but that does not stop eauto from taking a very long time to search for proofs of it. We use the handy Time command to measure how long a proof step takes to run. None of the following steps makes any progress.

    Example zero_minus_one : $\exists\, x$, $1 + x = 0$.
        Time eauto 1.
Finished transaction in 0. secs (0.u,0.s)

    Time eauto 2.
Finished transaction in 0. secs (0.u,0.s)

    Time eauto 3.
Finished transaction in 0. secs (0.008u,0.s)

    Time eauto 4.
Finished transaction in 0. secs (0.068005u,0.004s)

    Time eauto 5.
Finished transaction in 2. secs (1.92012u,0.044003s)

We see worrying exponential growth in running time, and the debug tactical helps us see where eauto is wasting its time, outputting a trace of every proof step that is attempted. The rule eq_trans applies at every node of a proof tree, and eauto tries all such positions.

    debug eauto 3.

1 *depth*=3
1.1 *depth*=2 eapply ex_intro
1.1.1 *depth*=1 apply plusO
1.1.1.1 *depth*=0 eapply eq_trans
1.1.2 *depth*=1 eapply eq_trans
1.1.2.1 *depth*=1 apply plus_n_O
1.1.2.1.1 *depth*=0 apply plusO
1.1.2.1.2 *depth*=0 eapply eq_trans
1.1.2.2 *depth*=1 apply @eq_refl
1.1.2.2.1 *depth*=0 apply plusO
1.1.2.2.2 *depth*=0 eapply eq_trans
1.1.2.3 *depth*=1 apply eq_add_S ; trivial
1.1.2.3.1 *depth*=0 apply plusO
1.1.2.3.2 *depth*=0 eapply eq_trans
1.1.2.4 *depth*=1 apply eq_sym ; trivial
1.1.2.4.1 *depth*=0 eapply eq_trans
1.1.2.5 *depth*=0 apply plusO
1.1.2.6 *depth*=0 apply plusS
1.1.2.7 *depth*=0 apply f_equal (*A*:=**nat**)
1.1.2.8 *depth*=0 apply f_equal2 (*A1*:=**nat**) (*A2*:=**nat**)
1.1.2.9 *depth*=0 eapply eq_trans

```
  Abort.
End slow.
```

Sometimes, though, transitivity is just what is needed to get a proof to go through automatically with `eauto`. For those cases, we can use named *hint databases* to segregate hints into different groups that may be called on as needed. Here we put `eq_trans` into the database slow.

`Hint Resolve eq_trans` : *slow*.

`Example three_minus_four_zero` : $\exists\, x,\ 1 + x = 0$.
  `Time eauto`.

`Finished transaction in 0. secs (0.004u,0.s)`

This `eauto` fails to prove the goal, but at least it takes substantially less than the 2 seconds required previously.

`Abort`.

One simple example from before runs in the same amount of time, avoiding pollution by transitivity.

`Example seven_minus_three_again` : $\exists\, x,\ x + 3 = 7$.

```
Time eauto 6.
```

```
Finished transaction in 0. secs (0.004001u,0.s)
Qed.
```

When we *do* need transitivity, we ask for it explicitly.

Example needs_trans : $\forall \; x \; y, \; 1 + x = y$
  $\rightarrow y = 2$
  $\rightarrow \exists \; z, \; z + x = 3.$
  info eauto with *slow*.

  == intro x; intro y; intro H; intro $H0$; simple eapply ex_intro;
     apply plusS; simple eapply eq_trans.
     exact H.

     exact $H0$.

Alternatively, we can invoke **eauto** with a **using** clause, to specify extra hints without adding them to a database ahead of time.

```
Restart.
```

```
eauto using eq_trans.
Qed.
```

The **info** trace shows that **eq_trans** was used in just the position where it is needed to complete the proof. We also see that **auto** and **eauto** always perform **intro** steps without counting them toward the bound on proof tree depth.

13.2 Searching for Underconstrained Values

Recall the definition of the list length function.

Print length.

length =
fun A : Type $\Rightarrow$
fix length (l : **list** A) : **nat** :=
  match l with
  | nil $\Rightarrow$ 0
  | _ :: l' $\Rightarrow$ S (length l')
  end

This function is easy to reason about in the forward direction, computing output from input.

Example length_1_2 : length (1 :: 2 :: nil) = 2.

```
   auto.
Qed.
```

```
Print length_1_2.
```

```
length_1_2 = eq_refl
```

As in Section 13.1, we will prove some lemmas to recast length in logic programming style, to help us compute inputs from outputs.

```
Theorem length_O : ∀ A, length (nil (A := A)) = O.
   crush.
Qed.
```

```
Theorem length_S : ∀ A (h : A) t n,
   length t = n
   → length (h :: t) = S n.
   crush.
Qed.
```

```
Hint Resolve length_O length_S.
```

Let us apply these hints to prove that a **list nat** of length 2 exists. (Here we register length_O with `Hint Resolve` instead of `Hint Immediate` merely as a convenience to use the same command as for length_S; `Resolve` and `Immediate` have the same meaning for a premise-free hint.)

```
Example length_is_2 : ∃ ls : list nat, length ls = 2.
   eauto.
```

```
No more subgoals but non-instantiated existential variables:
Existential 1 = ?20249 : [ |- nat]
Existential 2 = ?20252 : [ |- nat]
```

Coq complains that we finished the proof without determining the values of some unification variables created during proof search. The error message may seem a bit silly, since *any* value of type **nat** (for instance, 0) can be plugged in for either variable. However, for more complex types, finding their inhabitants may be as complex as theorem proving in general.

The `Show Proof` command shows exactly which proof term `eauto` has found, with the undetermined unification variables appearing explicitly where they are used.

```
   Show Proof.
```

```
Proof: ex_intro (fun ls : list nat => length ls = 2)
          (?20249 :: ?20252 :: nil)
```

```
      (length_S ?20249 (?20252 :: nil)
         (length_S ?20252 nil (length_O nat)))
Abort.
```

We see that the two unification variables stand for the two elements of
the list. Indeed, list length is independent of data values. Paradoxically,
we can make the proof search process easier by constraining the list
further, so that proof search naturally locates appropriate data elements
by unification. The library predicate **Forall** will be helpful.

Print **Forall**.

Inductive **Forall** $(A : \text{Type})$ $(P : A \to \text{Prop})$: **list** $A \to \text{Prop}$:=
    Forall_nil : **Forall** P nil
  | Forall_cons : $\forall$ $(x : A)$ $(l : \textbf{list } A)$,
               P $x \to$ **Forall** P $l \to$ **Forall** P $(x :: l)$

Example length_is_2 : $\exists$ ls : **list nat,** length ls = 2
  $\wedge$ **Forall** (fun $n \Rightarrow n \geq 1$) ls.
  eauto 9.
Qed.

We can see which list `eauto` found by printing the proof term.

Print length_is_2.

length_is_2 =
ex_intro
  (fun ls : **list nat** $\Rightarrow$ length ls = 2 $\wedge$ **Forall** (fun n : **nat** $\Rightarrow n \geq 1$) ls)
  (1 :: 1 :: nil)
  (conj (length_S 1 (1 :: nil) (length_S 1 nil (length_O **nat**)))
    (Forall_cons 1 (le_n 1)
      (Forall_cons 1 (le_n 1) (Forall_nil (fun n : **nat** $\Rightarrow n \geq 1$)))))

Let us try one more example. First, we use a standard higher-order
function to define a function for summing all data elements of a list.

Definition sum := fold_right plus O.

Another basic lemma is helpful to guide proof search.

Lemma plusO' : $\forall$ n m,
  $n = m$
  $\to 0 + n = m$.
  crush.
Qed.

Hint Resolve plusO'.

Finally, we meet `Hint Extern`, the command to register a custom hint. That is, we provide a pattern to match against goals during proof search. Whenever the pattern matches, a tactic (given to the right of an arrow $\Rightarrow$) is attempted. In the following, the number 1 gives a priority for this step. Lower priorities are tried before higher priorities, which can have a significant effect on proof search time.

`Hint Extern 1 (sum _ = _) ` $\Rightarrow$ ` simpl.`

Now we can find a length 2 list whose sum is 0.

`Example length_and_sum : ` $\exists$ `ls : ` **list nat**`, length ` *ls* ` = 2`
  $\wedge$ `sum ` *ls* ` = O.`
  `eauto 7.`
`Qed.`

Printing the proof term shows the unsurprising list that is found. Here is an example where it is less obvious which list will be used. Can you guess which list `eauto` will choose?

`Example length_and_sum' : ` $\exists$ `ls : ` **list nat**`, length ` *ls* ` = 5`
  $\wedge$ `sum ` *ls* ` = 42.`
  `eauto 15.`
`Qed.`

I give away part of the answer and say that this list is less interesting than one would like, because it contains too many zeroes. A further constraint forces a different solution for a smaller instance of the problem.

`Example length_and_sum'' : ` $\exists$ `ls : ` **list nat**`, length ` *ls* ` = 2`
  $\wedge$ `sum ` *ls* ` = 3`
  $\wedge$ **Forall** `(fun ` n ` ` $\Rightarrow$ ` ` $n \neq 0$`) ` *ls*`.`
  `eauto 11.`
`Qed.`

We could continue through exercises of this kind, but even more interesting than finding lists automatically is finding *programs* automatically.

13.3   Synthesizing Programs

Here is a simple syntax type for arithmetic expressions, similar to those used earlier. In this case, we allow expressions to mention exactly one distinguished variable.

`Inductive ` **exp** ` : Set :=`

```
| Const : nat → exp
| Var : exp
| Plus : exp → exp → exp.
```

An inductive relation specifies the semantics of an expression, relating a variable value and an expression to the expression value.

```
Inductive eval (var : nat) : exp → nat → Prop :=
| EvalConst : ∀ n, eval var (Const n) n
| EvalVar : eval var Var var
| EvalPlus : ∀ e1 e2 n1 n2, eval var e1 n1
    → eval var e2 n2
    → eval var (Plus e1 e2) (n1 + n2).
```

```
Hint Constructors eval.
```

We can use `auto` to execute the semantics for specific expressions.

```
Example eval1 : ∀ var,
  eval var (Plus Var (Plus (Const 8) Var)) (var + (8 + var)).
  auto.
Qed.
```

Unfortunately, just the constructors of `eval` are not enough to prove theorems like the following, which depends on an arithmetic identity.

```
Example eval1' : ∀ var,
  eval var (Plus Var (Plus (Const 8) Var)) (2 × var + 8).
  eauto.
Abort.
```

To help prove eval1', we prove an alternative version of EvalPlus that inserts an extra equality premise. This sort of staging is helpful to get around limitations of `eauto`'s unification: EvalPlus as a direct hint will only match goals whose results are already expressed as additions rather than as constants. In the following version, to prove the first two premises, `eauto` is given free reign in deciding the values of $n1$ and $n2$; the third premise can then be proved by `reflexivity`, no matter how each of its sides is decomposed as a tree of additions.

```
Theorem EvalPlus' : ∀ var e1 e2 n1 n2 n, eval var e1 n1
    → eval var e2 n2
    → n1 + n2 = n
    → eval var (Plus e1 e2) n.
  crush.
Qed.
```

```
Hint Resolve EvalPlus'.
```

Further, we instruct `eauto` to apply `omega`, a standard tactic that provides a complete decision procedure for quantifier-free linear arithmetic. Via `Hint Extern`, we ask for use of `omega` on any equality goal. The `abstract` tactical generates a new lemma for every such successful proof, so that in the final proof term, the lemma may be referenced in place of dropping in the full proof of the arithmetic equality.

Hint Extern 1 (_ = _) ⇒ abstract omega.

Now we can return to eval1' and prove it automatically.

Example eval1' : ∀ *var*,
    eval *var* (Plus Var (Plus (Const 8) Var)) ($2 \times var + 8$).
    eauto.
Qed.

Print eval1'.

eval1' =
fun *var* : **nat** ⇒
EvalPlus' (EvalVar *var*) (EvalPlus (EvalConst *var* 8) (EvalVar *var*))
    (eval1'_subproof *var*)
        : ∀ *var* : **nat**,
            eval *var* (Plus Var (Plus (Const 8) Var)) ($2 \times var + 8$)

The lemma eval1'_subproof was generated by `abstract omega`.

Now we are ready to take advantage of logic programming's flexibility by searching for a program (arithmetic expression) that always evaluates to a particular symbolic value.

Example synthesize1 : ∃ *e* , ∀ *var*, **eval** *var* *e* (*var* + 7).
    eauto.
Qed.

Print synthesize1.

synthesize1 =
ex_intro (fun *e* : **exp** ⇒ ∀ *var* : **nat**, eval *var* *e* (*var* + 7))
    (Plus Var (Const 7))
    (fun *var* : **nat** ⇒ EvalPlus (EvalVar *var*) (EvalConst *var* 7))

Here are two more examples demonstrating program synthesis:

Example synthesize2 : ∃ *e* , ∀ *var*, **eval** *var* *e* ($2 \times var + 8$).
    eauto.
Qed.

Example synthesize3 : ∃ *e* , ∀ *var*, **eval** *var* *e* ($3 \times var + 42$).
    eauto.

Qed.

These examples show linear expressions over the variable *var*. Any such expression is equivalent to $k \times var + n$ for some k and n. We can prove that any expression's semantics is equivalent to some such linear expression, but it is tedious to prove such a fact manually. We use `eauto` to complete the proof, finding k and n values automatically.

We prove a series of lemmas and add them as hints. We have alternative `eval` constructor lemmas and some facts about arithmetic.

Theorem EvalConst' : $\forall$ *var n m*, $n = m$
  $\rightarrow$ **eval** *var* (Const n) m.
  crush.
Qed.

Hint Resolve EvalConst'.

Theorem zero_times : $\forall$ *n m r*,
  $r = m$
  $\rightarrow r = 0 \times n + m$.
  crush.
Qed.

Hint Resolve zero_times.

Theorem EvalVar' : $\forall$ *var n*,
  var = n
  $\rightarrow$ **eval** *var* Var n.
  crush.
Qed.

Hint Resolve EvalVar'.

Theorem plus_0 : $\forall$ *n r*,
  $r = n$
  $\rightarrow r = n + 0$.
  crush.
Qed.

Theorem times_1 : $\forall$ *n*, $n = 1 \times n$.
  crush.
Qed.

Hint Resolve plus_0 times_1.

We finish with one more arithmetic lemma that is particularly specialized to this theorem. This fact follows by the axioms of the *ring* algebraic structure; since the naturals form a semiring, we can use the built-in tactic `ring`.

```
Require Import Arith Ring.
```
Theorem combine : ∀ x k1 k2 n1 n2,
  (k1 × x + n1) + (k2 × x + n2) = (k1 + k2) × x + (n1 + n2).
  `intros; ring.`
`Qed.`

```
Hint Resolve combine.
```

This choice of hints is cheating, to an extent, by telegraphing the procedure for choosing values of k and n. Nonetheless, with these lemmas in place, we achieve an automated proof without explicitly orchestrating the lemmas' composition.

Theorem linear : ∀ e, ∃ k , ∃ n ,
  ∀ var, **eval** var e (k × var + n).
  `induction` e; *crush*; `eauto.`
`Qed.`

By printing the proof term, it is possible to see the procedure that is used to choose the constants for each input term.

13.4   More on `auto` Hints

Let us take stock of the possibilities for `auto` and `eauto` hints. Hints are contained within *hint databases*, which we have seen extended in many examples so far. When no hint database is specified, a default database is used. Hints in the default database are always used by `auto` or `eauto`. The chance to extend hint databases imperatively is important, because, in Ltac programming, we cannot create global variables whose values can be extended seamlessly by different modules in different source files. We have seen the advantages of hints so far, where *crush* can be defined once and for all, while still automatically applying the hints added throughout developments. In fact, *crush* is defined in terms of `auto`, which explains how we achieve this extensibility. Other user-defined tactics can take similar advantage of `auto` and `eauto`.

The basic hints for `auto` and `eauto` are `Hint Immediate` *lemma*, asking to try solving a goal immediately by applying a lemma and discharging any hypotheses with a single proof step each; `Resolve` *lemma*, which does the same but may add new premises that are themselves to be subjects of nested proof search; `Constructors` *typename*, which acts like `Resolve` applied to every constructor of an inductive type; and `Unfold` *ident*, which tries unfolding *ident* when it appears at the head of a proof goal. Each of these `Hint` commands may be used with a suffix, as in `Hint Resolve` *lemma* : *my_db*, to add the hint only to the

specified database, so that it would only be used by, for instance, auto
with *my_db*. An additional argument to auto specifies the maximum
depth of proof trees to search in depth-first order, as in auto 8 or auto
8 with *my_db*. The default depth is 5.

All these Hint commands can be expressed with a more primitive
hint kind, Extern. A few more examples of Hint Extern illustrate the
possibilities.

Theorem bool_neq : true $\neq$ false.
    auto.

A call to *crush* would have discharged this goal, but the default hint
database for auto contains no hint that applies.

Abort.

It is hard to come up with a **bool**-specific hint that is not just a
restatement of the theorem we mean to prove. Luckily, a simpler form
suffices, by appealing to the built-in tactic congruence, a complete procedure for the theory of equality, uninterpreted functions, and datatype
constructors.

Hint Extern 1 (_ $\neq$ _) $\Rightarrow$ congruence.

Theorem bool_neq : true $\neq$ false.
    auto.
Qed.

A Hint Extern may be implemented with the full Ltac language. This
example shows a case where a hint uses a match.

Section forall_and.
    Variable A : Set.
    Variables P Q : $A \rightarrow$ Prop.

    Hypothesis *both* : $\forall$ x, P x $\wedge$ Q x.

    Theorem forall_and : $\forall$ z, P z.
        crush.

The *crush* invocation makes no progress beyond what intros would
have accomplished. An auto invocation will not apply the hypothesis
both to prove the goal, because the conclusion of *both* does not unify
with the conclusion of the goal. However, we can teach auto to handle
this kind of goal.

    Hint Extern 1 (P ?X) $\Rightarrow$
        match goal with
            | [H : $\forall$ x, P x $\wedge$ _ $\vdash$ _] $\Rightarrow$ apply (proj1 (H X))

```
        end.

    auto.
  Qed.
```

We see that an `Extern` pattern may bind unification variables used in the associated tactic. The function `proj1` is from the standard library, for extracting a proof of U from a proof of $U \wedge V$.

End forall_and.

We might get more ambitious and seek to generalize the hint to all possible predicates P.

```
Hint Extern 1 (?P ?X) ⇒
  match goal with
    | [ H : ∀ x, P x ∧ _ ⊢ _ ] ⇒ apply (proj1 (H X))
  end.
```

```
User error: Bound head variable
```

Coq's `auto` hint databases work as tables mapping *head symbols* to lists of tactics to try. Because of this, the constant head of an `Extern` pattern must be determinable statically. In the first `Extern` hint, the head symbol was `not`, since $x \neq y$ desugars to `not` (**eq** x y); and in the second example, the head symbol was P.

Fortunately, a more basic form of `Hint Extern` also applies. We may simply leave out the pattern to the left of the ⇒, incorporating the corresponding logic into the Ltac script.

```
Hint Extern 1 ⇒
  match goal with
    | [ H : ∀ x, ?P x ∧ _ ⊢ ?P ?X ] ⇒ apply (proj1 (H X))
  end.
```

Be forewarned that a `Hint Extern` of this kind will be applied at *every* node of a proof tree, so an extensive Ltac script may slow proof search significantly.

13.5 Rewrite Hints

Another dimension of extensibility with hints is rewriting with quantified equalities. We have used the associated command `Hint Rewrite` in many examples so far. The *crush* tactic uses these hints by calling the built-in tactic `autorewrite`. The rewrite hints have taken the form `Hint Rewrite` *lemma*, which by default adds them to the default hint database *core*; but other hint databases may also be specified, just as with `Hint Resolve`, for instance.

The next example shows a direct use of `autorewrite`. Note that whereas `Hint Rewrite` uses a default database, `autorewrite` requires that a database be named.

```
Section autorewrite.
  Variable A : Set.
  Variable f : A → A.

  Hypothesis f_f : ∀ x, f (f x) = f x.

  Hint Rewrite f_f.

  Lemma f_f_f : ∀ x, f (f (f x)) = f x.
    intros; autorewrite with core; reflexivity.
  Qed.
```

There are a few ways in which `autorewrite` can lead to trouble when insufficient care is taken in choosing hints. First, the set of hints may define a nonterminating rewrite system, in which case invocations to `autorewrite` may not terminate. Second, we may add hints that lead `autorewrite` down the wrong path. For instance,

```
Section garden_path.
  Variable g : A → A.
  Hypothesis f_g : ∀ x, f x = g x.
  Hint Rewrite f_g.

  Lemma f_f_f' : ∀ x, f (f (f x)) = f x.
    intros; autorewrite with core.
```

```
============================
```

$$g \ (g \ (g \ x)) = g \ x$$

```
  Abort.
```

The new hint was used to rewrite the goal into a form where the old hint could no longer be applied. This nonmonotonicity of rewrite hints contrasts with the situation for `auto`, where new hints may slow down proof search but can never break old proofs. The key difference is that `auto` either solves a goal or makes no changes to it, whereas `autorewrite` may change goals without solving them. The situation for `eauto` is slightly more complicated, as changes to hint databases may change the proof found for a particular goal, and that proof may influence the settings of unification variables that appear elsewhere in the proof state.

```
Reset garden_path.
```

The `autorewrite` tactic also works with quantified equalities that include additional premises, but we must be careful to avoid similar incorrect rewritings.

```
Section garden_path.
  Variable P : A → Prop.
  Variable g : A → A.
  Hypothesis f_g : ∀ x, P x → f x = g x.
  Hint Rewrite f_g.

  Lemma f_f_f' : ∀ x, f (f (f x)) = f x.
    intros; autorewrite with core.
```

$$============================$$
$$g\ (g\ (g\ x)) = g\ x$$

```
subgoal 2 is:
 P x
subgoal 3 is:
 P (f x)
subgoal 4 is:
 P (f x)
```

```
  Abort.
```

The inappropriate rule fired the same three times as before, even though we know we will not be able to prove the premises.

```
Reset garden_path.
```

The final, successful, attempt uses an extra argument to `Hint Rewrite` that specifies a tactic to apply to generated premises. Such a hint is only used when the tactic succeeds for all premises, possibly leaving further subgoals for some premises.

```
Section garden_path.
  Variable P : A → Prop.
  Variable g : A → A.
  Hypothesis f_g : ∀ x, P x → f x = g x.
  Hint Rewrite f_g using assumption.

  Lemma f_f_f' : ∀ x, f (f (f x)) = f x.
    intros; autorewrite with core; reflexivity.
  Qed.
```

We may still use `autorewrite` to apply *f_g* when the generated premise is among the assumptions.

> Lemma f_f_f_g : $\forall\ x,\ P\ x \rightarrow f\ (f\ x) = g\ x$.
>   intros; autorewrite with *core*; reflexivity.
> Qed.

End garden_path.

It can also be useful to apply the `autorewrite with` *db* `in` * form, which does rewriting in hypotheses as well as in the conclusion.

> Lemma in_star : $\forall\ x\ y,\ f\ (f\ (f\ (f\ x))) = f\ (f\ y)$
> $\rightarrow f\ x = f\ (f\ (f\ y))$.
>   intros; autorewrite with *core* in *; assumption.
> Qed.

End autorewrite.

Many proofs can be automated in modular ways with deft combinations of `auto` and `autorewrite`.

14 Proof Search in Ltac

We have seen many examples of proof automation so far, some with code snippets from Ltac, Coq's domain-specific language for proof search procedures. This chapter gives a bottom-up presentation of the features of Ltac, focusing in particular on the Ltac `match` construct, which supports a novel approach to backtracking search. First, the chapter runs through some useful automation tactics that are built into Coq. They are described in detail in the Coq manual, so I only outline what is possible.

14.1 Some Built-in Automation Tactics

A number of tactics are called repeatedly by *crush*. The `intuition` tactic simplifies propositional structure of goals. The `congruence` tactic applies the rules of equality and congruence closure, plus properties of constructors of inductive types. The `omega` tactic provides a complete decision procedure for a theory called quantifier-free linear arithmetic or Presburger arithmetic by different communities. That is, `omega` proves any goal that follows from looking only at parts of that goal that can be interpreted as propositional formulas whose atomic formulas are basic comparison operations on natural numbers or integers, with operands built from constants, variables, addition, and subtraction (with multiplication by a constant available as a shorthand for addition or subtraction).

The `ring` tactic solves goals by appealing to the axioms of rings or semirings (as in algebra), depending on the type involved. Coq developments may declare new types to be parts of rings and semirings by proving the associated axioms. There is a similar tactic, `field`, for simplifying values in fields by conversion to fractions over rings. Both `ring` and `field` can only solve goals that are equalities. The `fourier` tactic uses Fourier's method to prove inequalities over real numbers, which are axiomatized in the Coq standard library.

The *setoid* facility makes it possible to register new equivalence relations to be understood by tactics like `rewrite`. For instance, `Prop` is registered as a setoid with the equivalence relation "if and only if." The ability to register new setoids can be very useful in proofs of a kind common in math, where all reasoning is done after modding out by a relation.

There are several other built-in automation tactics described in the Coq manual. The real promise of Coq, though, is in the coding of problem-specific tactics with Ltac.

14.2 Ltac Programming Basics

We have already seen many examples of Ltac programs. This chapter gives a thorough introduction to the important features and design patterns.

One common use for `match` tactics is identification of subjects for case analysis, as we see in this tactic definition:

```
Ltac find_if :=
  match goal with
    | [ ⊢ if ?X then _ else _ ] ⇒ destruct X
  end.
```

The tactic checks if the conclusion is an `if`, `destruct`ing the test expression if so. Certain classes of theorem are trivial to prove automatically with such a tactic.

```
Theorem hmm : ∀ (a b c : bool),
  if a
    then if b
      then True
      else True
    else if c
      then True
      else True.
  intros; repeat find_if; constructor.
Qed.
```

The `repeat` used here is called a *tactical*, or tactic combinator. The behavior of `repeat t` is to loop through running t, running t on all generated subgoals, running t on *their* generated subgoals, and so on. When t fails at any point in this search tree, that particular subgoal is left to be handled by later tactics. Thus, it is important never to use `repeat` with a tactic that always succeeds.

Another very useful Ltac building block is *context patterns*.

Ltac *find_if_inside* :=
  `match goal with`
    `| [ ⊢ context[if ?X then _ else _] ] ⇒ destruct` X
  `end.`

The behavior of this tactic is to find any subterm of the conclusion that is an `if` and then `destruct` the test expression. This version subsumes *find_if*:

Theorem hmm' : ∀ (a b c : **bool**),
  `if` a
    `then if` b
      `then` **True**
      `else` **True**
    `else if` c
      `then` **True**
      `else` **True**.
  `intros; repeat` *find_if_inside*; `constructor`.
Qed.

We can also use *find_if_inside* to prove goals that *find_if* does not simplify sufficiently.

Theorem hmm2 : ∀ (a b : **bool**),
  (`if` a `then` 42 `else` 42) = (`if` b `then` 42 `else` 42).
  `intros; repeat` *find_if_inside*; `reflexivity`.
Qed.

Many decision procedures can be coded in Ltac via `repeat match` loops. For instance, we can implement a subset of the functionality of `tauto`.

Ltac *my_tauto* :=
  `repeat match goal with`
            `| [` H `:` $?P$ ⊢ $?P$ `] ⇒ exact` H

            `| [ ⊢` **True** `] ⇒ constructor`
            `| [ ⊢ _ ∧ _ ] ⇒ constructor`
            `| [ ⊢ _ → _ ] ⇒ intro`

            `| [` H `:` **False** ⊢ _ `] ⇒ destruct` H
            `| [` H `:` _ ∧ _ ⊢ _ `] ⇒ destruct` H
            `| [` H `:` _ ∨ _ ⊢ _ `] ⇒ destruct` H

$$| \ [\ H1 : ?P \to ?Q, \ H2 : ?P \vdash \_ \ ] \Rightarrow \texttt{specialize} \ (H1 \ H2)$$
end.

Since `match` patterns can share unification variables between hypothesis and conclusion patterns, it is easy to figure out when the conclusion matches a hypothesis. The `exact` tactic solves a goal completely when given a proof term of the proper type.

It is also trivial to implement the introduction rules (in the sense of natural deduction [37]) for a few of the connectives. Implementing elimination rules is only a little more work, since we must give a name for a hypothesis to `destruct`.

The last rule implements modus ponens, using a tactic `specialize`, which will replace a hypothesis with a version that is specialized to a provided set of arguments (for quantified variables or local hypotheses from implications). By convention, when the argument to `specialize` is an application of a hypothesis H to a set of arguments, the result of the specialization replaces H. For other terms, the outcome is the same as with `generalize`.

```
Section propositional.
  Variables P Q R : Prop.

  Theorem propositional : (P ∨ Q ∨ False) ∧ (P → Q) → True ∧ Q.
    my_tauto.
  Qed.
End propositional.
```

It was relatively easy to implement modus ponens because we do not lose information by clearing every implication that we use. If we want to implement a similarly complete procedure for quantifier instantiation, we need a way to ensure that a particular proposition is not already included among the hypotheses. To do that effectively, we first need to know a bit more about the semantics of `match`.

It is tempting to assume that `match` works as it does in ML. In fact, there are a few critical differences in its behavior. One is that we may include arbitrary expressions in patterns instead of being restricted to variables and constructors. Another is that the same variable may appear multiple times, inducing an implicit equality constraint.

A related pair of two other differences is much more important than the others. The `match` construct has a *backtracking semantics for failure*. In ML, pattern matching works by finding the first pattern to match and then executing its body. If the body raises an exception, then the overall match raises the same exception. In Coq, failures in case bodies instead trigger continued search through the list of cases.

For instance, this proof script works:

```
Theorem m1 : True.
  match goal with
    | [ ⊢ _ ] ⇒ intro
    | [ ⊢ True ] ⇒ constructor
  end.
Qed.
```

The first case matches trivially, but its body tactic fails, since the conclusion does not begin with a quantifier or implication. In a similar ML match, the whole pattern match would fail. In Coq, we backtrack and try the next pattern, which also matches. Its body tactic succeeds, so the overall tactic succeeds as well.

The example shows how failure can move to a different pattern within a match. Failure can also trigger an attempt to find *a different way of matching a single pattern*. Consider another example.

```
Theorem m2 : ∀ P Q R : Prop, P → Q → R → Q.
  intros; match goal with
            | [ H : _ ⊢ _ ] ⇒ idtac H
          end.
```

Coq prints "*H1*". By applying `idtac` with an argument, a convenient debugging tool for leaking information out of `match`es, we see that this `match` first tries binding H to *H1*, which cannot be used to prove Q. Nonetheless, the following variation on the tactic succeeds at proving the goal.

```
match goal with
  | [ H : _ ⊢ _ ] ⇒ exact H
end.
Qed.
```

The tactic first unifies H with *H1*, as before, but `exact` H fails in that case, so the tactic engine searches for more possible values of H. Eventually, it arrives at the correct value, so that `exact` H and the overall tactic succeed.

Now we are equipped to implement a tactic for checking that a proposition is not among the hypotheses.

```
Ltac notHyp P :=
  match goal with
    | [ _ : P ⊢ _ ] ⇒ fail 1
    | _ ⇒
```

```
    match P with
      | ?P1 ∧ ?P2 ⇒ first [ notHyp P1 | notHyp P2 | fail 2 ]
      | _ ⇒ idtac
    end
end.
```

We use the equality checking that is built into pattern matching to
see if there is a hypothesis that matches the proposition exactly. If so,
we use the `fail` tactic. Without arguments, `fail` signals normal tactic
failure, as one might expect. When `fail` is passed an argument n, n
is used to count outwards through the enclosing cases of backtracking
search. In this case, `fail 1` says "fail not just in this pattern-matching
branch but for the whole `match`." The second case will never be tried
when the `fail 1` is reached.

This second case, used when P matches no hypothesis, checks if P is
a conjunction. Other simplifications may have split conjunctions into
their component formulas, so we need to check that at least one of those
components is also not represented. To achieve this, we apply the `first`
tactical, which takes a list of tactics and continues down the list until
one of them does not fail. The `fail 2` at the end says to `fail` both the
`first` and the `match` wrapped around it.

The body of the $?P1$ ∧ $?P2$ case guarantees that if it is reached,
we either succeed completely or fail completely. Thus, if we reach the
wildcard case, P is not a conjunction. We use `idtac`, a tactic that would
not be applied on its own, since its effect is to succeed at doing nothing.
Nonetheless, `idtac` is a useful placeholder for cases like this.

With the nonpresence check implemented, it is easy to build a tactic that takes as input a proof term and adds its conclusion as a
new hypothesis, only if that conclusion is not already present, failing
otherwise.

```
Ltac extend pf :=
  let t := type of pf in
    notHyp t; generalize pf; intro.
```

We see the useful `type of` operator of Ltac. This operator could not
be implemented in Gallina, but it is easy to support in Ltac. We end up
with t bound to the type of *pf*. We check that t is not already present. If
so, we use a `generalize`/`intro` combo to add a new hypothesis proved
by *pf*. The tactic `generalize` takes as input a term t (for instance, a
proof of some proposition) and then changes the conclusion from G to
$T \rightarrow G$, where T is the type of t (for instance, the proposition proved
by the proof t).

With these tactics defined, we can write a tactic *completer* for, among other things, adding to the context all consequences of a set of simple first-order formulas.

Ltac *completer* :=
  repeat match goal with
                | [⊢ _ ∧ _] ⇒ constructor
                | [H : _ ∧ _ ⊢ _] ⇒ destruct H
                | [H : ?P → ?Q, H' : ?P ⊢ _] ⇒ specialize (H H')
                | [⊢ ∀ x, _] ⇒ intro

                | [H : ∀ x, ?P x → _, H' : ?P ?X ⊢ _] ⇒
                   extend (H X H')
          end.

We use the same kind of conjunction and implication handling as previously. Note that since → is the special nondependent case of ∀, the fourth rule handles intro for implications, too.

In the fifth rule, when we find a ∀ fact H with a premise matching one of the hypotheses, we add the appropriate instantiation of H's conclusion, if we have not already added it.

We can check that *completer* is working properly, with a theorem that introduces a spurious variable.

Section firstorder.
  Variable A : Set.
  Variables $P\ Q\ R\ S : A →$ Prop.

  Hypothesis $H1$: ∀ x, $P\ x → Q\ x ∧ R\ x$.
  Hypothesis $H2$: ∀ x, $R\ x → S\ x$.

  Theorem fo : ∀ $(y\ x : A)$, $P\ x → S\ x$.
    completer.

$y : A$
$x : A$
$H : P\ x$
$H0 : Q\ x$
$H3 : R\ x$
$H4 : S\ x$
============================
  $S\ x$

    assumption.
  Qed.

End firstorder.

We narrowly avoided a subtle pitfall in the definition of *completer*. Let us try another definition that even seems preferable to the original, to the untrained eye. (We change the second `match` case a bit to make the tactic smart enough to handle some subtleties of Ltac behavior that had not been exercised previously.)

```
Ltac completer' :=
    repeat match goal with
            | [ ⊢ _ ∧ _ ] ⇒ constructor
            | [ H : ?P ∧ ?Q ⊢ _ ] ⇒ destruct H;
              repeat match goal with
                      | [ H' : P ∧ Q ⊢ _ ] ⇒ clear H'
                    end
            | [ H : ?P → _, H' : ?P ⊢ _ ] ⇒ specialize (H H')
            | [ ⊢ ∀ x, _ ] ⇒ intro

            | [ H : ∀ x, ?P x → _, H' : ?P ?X ⊢ _ ] ⇒
              extend (H X H')
          end.
```

The only other difference is in the modus ponens rule, where we have replaced an unused unification variable $?Q$ with a wildcard. Let us try our example again with this version:

```
Section firstorder'.
    Variable A : Set.
    Variables P Q R S : A → Prop.

    Hypothesis H1 : ∀ x, P x → Q x ∧ R x.
    Hypothesis H2 : ∀ x, R x → S x.

    Theorem fo' : ∀ (y x : A), P x → S x.
        completer'.
```

```
y : A
H1 : P y → Q y ∧ R y
H2 : R y → S y
x : A
H : P x
============================
    S x
```

The quantified theorems have been instantiated with y instead of x, reducing a provable goal to one that is unprovable. The code in the last match case for *completer'* is careful only to instantiate quantifiers along with suitable hypotheses, so why were incorrect choices made?

```
  Abort.
End firstorder'.
```

A few examples should illustrate the issue. This match-based proof works fine:

```
Theorem t1 : ∀ x : nat, x = x.
  match goal with
    | [ ⊢ ∀ x, _ ] ⇒ trivial
  end.
Qed.
```

This one fails:

```
Theorem t1' : ∀ x : nat, x = x.
  match goal with
    | [ ⊢ ∀ x, ?P ] ⇒ trivial
  end.
```

```
User error: No matching clauses for match goal
```

```
Abort.
```

The problem is that unification variables may not contain locally bound variables. In this case, ?P would need to be bound to $x = x$, which contains the local quantified variable x. By using a wildcard in the earlier version, we avoided this restriction. To understand why this restriction affects the behavior of the *completer* tactic, recall that, in Coq, implication is shorthand for degenerate universal quantification where the quantified variable is not used. Nonetheless, in an Ltac pattern, Coq matches a wildcard implication against a universal quantification.

The Coq 8.2 release includes a special pattern form for a unification variable with an explicit set of free variables. That unification variable is then bound to a function from the free variables to the real value. In Coq 8.1 and earlier, there is no such work-around. Section 15.5 shows an example of this binding form.

No matter which Coq version is used, it is important to be aware of this restriction. As mentioned, the restriction is the culprit behind the surprising behavior of *completer'*. We unintentionally match quantified facts with the modus ponens rule, circumventing the check that a suitably matching hypothesis is available and leading to different behavior, where wrong quantifier instantiations are chosen. The earlier *completer* tactic uses a modus ponens rule that matches the implication conclusion with a variable, which blocks matching against nontrivial universal quantifiers.

Actually, the behavior demonstrated here applies to Coq version 8.4, but not 8.4pl1. The latter version will allow regular Ltac pattern variables to match terms that contain locally bound variables, but a tactic failure occurs if the variable is later used as a Gallina term.

14.3   Functional Programming in Ltac

Ltac supports quite convenient functional programming, with a Lisp-with-syntax kind of flavor. However, there are a few syntactic conventions involved in getting programs to be accepted. The Ltac syntax is optimized for tactic writing, so one has to deal with some inconveniences in writing more standard functional programs.

To illustrate, let us try to write a simple list length function. We start out writing it just as in Gallina, simply replacing `Fixpoint` (and its annotations) with `Ltac`.

```
Ltac length ls :=
  match ls with
  | nil ⇒ O
  | _ :: ls' ⇒ S (length ls')
  end.
```

```
Error: The reference ls' was not found in the current environment
```

At this point, recall that pattern variable names must be prefixed by question marks in Ltac.

```
Ltac length ls :=
  match ls with
  | nil ⇒ O
  | _ :: ?ls' ⇒ S (length ls')
  end.
```

```
Error: The reference S was not found in the current environment
```

The problem is that Ltac treats the expression S (length ls') as an invocation of a tactic S with argument length ls'. We need to use a special annotation to escape into the Gallina parsing nonterminal.

```
Ltac length ls :=
  match ls with
```

```
  | nil ⇒ O
  | _ :: ?ls' ⇒ constr:(S (length ls'))
end.
```

This definition is accepted. It can be a little awkward to test Ltac definitions like this one. Here is one method:

```
Goal False.
  let n := length (1 :: 2 :: 3 :: nil) in
    pose n.
```

```
n := S (length (2 :: 3 :: nil)) : nat
============================
  False
```

We use the `pose` tactic, which extends the proof context with a new variable that is set equal to a particular term. We could also have used `idtac n` in place of `pose n`, which would have printed the result without changing the context.

The value of n only has the length calculation unrolled one step. What has happened here is that by escaping into the `constr` nonterminal, we referred to the length function of Gallina rather than to the length Ltac function that we are defining.

```
Abort.
```

```
Reset length.
```

Gallina terms built by tactics must be bound explicitly via `let` or a similar technique rather than inserting Ltac calls directly in other Gallina terms.

```
Ltac length ls :=
  match ls with
    | nil ⇒ O
    | _ :: ?ls' ⇒
      let ls'' := length ls' in
        constr:(S ls'')
  end.
```

```
Goal False.
  let n := length (1 :: 2 :: 3 :: nil) in
    pose n.
```

```
n := 3 : nat
============================
  False
```

```
Abort.
```

We can also use anonymous function expressions and local function definitions in Ltac, as this example of a standard list **map** function shows:

Ltac *map* T f :=
  let rec *map'* ls :=
    match ls with
      | nil $\Rightarrow$ constr:(@nil T)
      | ?x :: ?ls' $\Rightarrow$
        let x' := f x in
          let ls'' := *map'* ls' in
            constr:(x' :: ls'')
    end in
   map'.

Ltac functions can have no implicit arguments. It may seem surprising that we need to pass T, the carried type of the output list, explicitly. We cannot just use **type of** f, because f is an Ltac term, not a Gallina term, and Ltac programs are dynamically typed. The function f could use very syntactic methods to decide to return differently typed terms for different inputs. We also could not replace constr:(@nil T) with constr:nil, because we have no strongly typed context to use to infer the parameter to nil. Luckily, we do have sufficient context within constr:(x' :: ls'').

Sometimes we need to employ the opposite direction of nonterminal escape, when we want to pass a complicated tactic expression as an argument to another tactic, as we might want to do in invoking *map*.

Goal **False**.
  let ls := *map* (**nat** $\times$ **nat**)%type ltac:(fun x $\Rightarrow$ constr:(x, x))
    (1 :: 2 :: 3 :: nil) in
   pose ls.

l := (1, 1) :: (2, 2) :: (3, 3) :: nil : **list** (**nat** $\times$ **nat**)
============================
  False

```
Abort.
```

Each position within an Ltac script has a default applicable nonterminal, where constr and ltac are the main options, standing respectively for terms of Gallina and Ltac. The explicit colon notation can always be used to override the default nonterminal choice, though code being parsed as Gallina can no longer use such overrides. Within the `ltac` nonterminal, top-level function applications are treated as applications in Ltac, not Gallina; but the *arguments* to such functions are parsed with `constr` by default. This choice may seem strange, until we realize that we have been relying on it all along in proof scripts. For instance, the `apply` tactic is an Ltac function, and it is natural to interpret its argument as a term of Gallina, not Ltac. We use an `ltac` prefix to parse Ltac function arguments as Ltac terms themselves, as in the call to *map* in the previous example. For some simple cases, Ltac terms may be passed without an extra prefix. For instance, an identifier that has an Ltac meaning but no Gallina meaning will be interpreted in Ltac automatically.

One other problem shows up when we want to debug Ltac functional programs. We might expect the following code to work, to yield a version of *length* that prints a debug trace of the arguments it is called with.

`Reset length.`

```
Ltac length ls :=
   idtac ls;
   match ls with
     | nil ⇒ O
     | _ :: ?ls' ⇒
       let ls'' := length ls' in
         constr:(S ls'')
   end.
```

Coq accepts the tactic definition, but the code is fatally flawed and will always lead to dynamic type errors.

`Goal False.`

```
   let n := length (1 :: 2 :: 3 :: nil) in
      pose n.
```

`Error: variable n should be bound to a term.`

`Abort.`

What is going wrong here? The problem has to do with the dual status of Ltac as both a purely functional and an imperative programming language. The basic programming language is purely functional, but tactic scripts are one "datatype" that can be returned by such programs, and Coq will run such a script using an imperative semantics that mutates proof states. Readers familiar with monadic programming in Haskell [44, 34] may recognize a similarity. Haskell programs with side effects can be thought of as pure programs that return *the code of programs in an imperative language*, where some out-of-band mechanism takes responsibility for running these derived programs. In this way, Haskell remains pure while supporting usual input-output side effects and more. Ltac uses the same basic mechanism, but in a dynamically typed setting. Here the embedded imperative language includes all the tactics we have applied so far.

Even basic `idtac` is an embedded imperative program, so we may not automatically mix it with purely functional code. In fact, a semicolon operator alone marks a span of Ltac code as an embedded tactic script. This makes some sense, since pure functional languages have no need for sequencing. Because they lack side effects, there is no reason to run an expression and then just throw away its value and move on to another expression.

Another explanation that avoids an analogy to Haskell monads is that an Ltac tactic program returns a function that, when run later, will perform the desired proof modification. These functions are distinct from other types of data, like numbers or Gallina terms. The prior, correctly working version of length computed solely with Gallina terms, but the new one implicitly returns a tactic function, as indicated by the use of `idtac` and semicolon. However, the new version's recursive call to length is structured to expect a Gallina term, not a tactic function, as output. As a result, we have a basic dynamic type error, perhaps obscured by the involvement of first-class tactic scripts.

The solution is like the one in Haskell: we must monadify the pure program to give it access to side effects. The trouble is that the embedded tactic language has no **return** construct. Proof scripts are about proving theorems, not calculating results. We can apply a somewhat awkward work-around that requires translating the program into *continuation-passing style* [39], a program-structuring idea popular in functional programming.

Reset length.

```
Ltac length ls k :=
  idtac ls;
  match ls with
    | nil ⇒ k O
    | _ :: ?ls' ⇒ length ls' ltac:(fun n ⇒ k (S n))
  end.
```

The new length takes a new input: a *continuation* k, which is a function to be called to continue whatever proving process we were in the middle of when we called *length*. The argument passed to k may be thought of as the return value of *length*.

Goal **False**.
   length $(1 :: 2 :: 3 :: \mathsf{nil})$ ltac:(fun n $\Rightarrow$ pose n).

$(1 :: 2 :: 3 :: \mathsf{nil})$
$(2 :: 3 :: \mathsf{nil})$
$(3 :: \mathsf{nil})$
nil

Abort.

We see exactly the trace of function arguments that we expected initially, and an examination of the proof state afterward would show that variable n has been added with value 3.

Considering the comparison with Haskell's IO monad, there is an important subtlety that deserves to be mentioned. A Haskell IO computation represents (theoretically, at least) a transformer from one state of the real world to another, plus a pure value to return. Some of the state can be very specific to the program, as in the case of heap-allocated mutable references, but some can be along the lines of the example "launch missile," where the program has a side effect on the real world that is not possible to undo.

In contrast, Ltac scripts can be thought of as controlling just two simple kinds of mutable state. First, there is the current sequence of proof subgoals. Second, there is a partial assignment of discovered values to unification variables introduced by proof search (for instance, by eauto, as shown in Chapter 13). Crucially, *every mutation of this state can be undone* during backtracking introduced by match, auto, and other built-in Ltac constructs. Ltac proof scripts have state, but it is purely local, and all changes to it are reversible, which is a very useful semantics for proof search.

14.4   Recursive Proof Search

Deciding how to instantiate quantifiers is one of the hardest parts of automated first-order theorem proving. For a given problem, we can consider all possible bounded-length sequences of quantifier instantiations, applying only propositional reasoning at the end. This is probably a bad idea for almost all goals, but it makes for a nice example of recursive proof search procedures in Ltac.

We can consider the maximum dependency chain length for a first-order proof. We define the chain length for a hypothesis to be 0, and the chain length for an instantiation of a quantified fact to be one greater than the length for that fact. The tactic *inster n* is meant to try all possible proofs with chain length at most *n*.

```
Ltac inster n :=
  intuition;
    match n with
      | S ?n' ⇒
        match goal with
          | [ H : ∀ x : ?T, _, y : ?T ⊢ _ ] ⇒
            generalize (H y); inster n'
        end
    end.
```

The tactic begins by applying propositional simplification. Next, it checks if any chain length remains, failing if not. Otherwise, it tries all possible ways of instantiating quantified hypotheses with properly typed local variables. It is critical to realize that if the recursive call *inster n'* fails, then the `match goal` just seeks out another way of unifying its pattern against proof state. Thus, this small amount of code provides an elegant demonstration of how backtracking `match` enables exhaustive search.

We can verify the efficacy of *inster* with two short examples. The built-in `firstorder` tactic (with no extra arguments) is able to prove the first but not the second.

```
Section test_inster.
  Variable A : Set.
  Variables P Q : A → Prop.
  Variable f : A → A.
  Variable g : A → A → A.

  Hypothesis H1 : ∀ x y, P (g x y) → Q (f x).

  Theorem test_inster : ∀ x, P (g x x) → Q (f x).
    inster 2.
  Qed.

  Hypothesis H3 : ∀ u v, P u ∧ P v ∧ u ≠ v → P (g u v).
  Hypothesis H4 : ∀ u, Q (f u) → P u ∧ P (f u).

  Theorem test_inster2 : ∀ x y, x ≠ y → P x → Q (f y) → Q (f x).
    inster 3.
  Qed.
End test_inster.
```

The style employed in the definition of *inster* can seem counterintuitive to functional programmers. Usually, functional programs accumulate state changes in explicit arguments to recursive functions. In Ltac, the state of the current subgoal is always implicit. Nonetheless, in accord with the discussion at the end of Section 14.3, in contrast to general imperative programming, it is easy to undo any changes to this state, and indeed such undoing happens automatically at failures within `matches`. In this way, Ltac programming is similar to programming in Haskell with a stateful failure monad that supports a composition operator along the lines of the `first` tactical.

Functional programming purists may reject programming in this way. Nonetheless, as with other kinds of monadic programming, many problems are much simpler to solve with Ltac than they would be with explicit, pure proof manipulation in ML or Haskell. To demonstrate, we write a basic simplification procedure for logical implications.

This procedure is inspired by one for separation logic [40], where conjuncts in formulas are thought of as resources, such that we lose no completeness by crossing out equal conjuncts on the two sides of an implication. This process is complicated by the fact that, for reasons of modularity, the formulas can have arbitrary nested tree structure (branching at conjunctions) and may include existential quantifiers. It is helpful for the matching process to "go under" quantifiers and in fact decide how to instantiate existential quantifiers in the conclusion.

To distinguish the implications that the tactic handles from the implications that show up as plumbing in various lemmas, we define a wrapper definition, a notation, and a tactic.

Definition imp (*P1 P2* : Prop) := *P1* → *P2*.
Infix "->" := imp (no associativity, at level 95).
Ltac *imp* := unfold imp; firstorder.

The following lemmas about imp will be useful in writing the tactic.

Theorem and_True_prem : ∀ *P Q*,
  (*P* ∧ **True** -> *Q*)
  → (*P* -> *Q*).
  imp.
Qed.

Theorem and_True_conc : ∀ *P Q*,
  (*P* -> *Q* ∧ **True**)
  → (*P* -> *Q*).
  imp.
Qed.

Theorem pick_prem1 : $\forall \, P \; Q \; R \; S,$
   $(P \wedge (Q \wedge R) \; \text{->} \; S)$
   $\rightarrow ((P \wedge Q) \wedge R \; \text{->} \; S).$
   imp.
Qed.

Theorem pick_prem2 : $\forall \, P \; Q \; R \; S,$
   $(Q \wedge (P \wedge R) \; \text{->} \; S)$
   $\rightarrow ((P \wedge Q) \wedge R \; \text{->} \; S).$
   imp.
Qed.

Theorem comm_prem : $\forall \, P \; Q \; R,$
   $(P \wedge Q \; \text{->} \; R)$
   $\rightarrow (Q \wedge P \; \text{->} \; R).$
   imp.
Qed.

Theorem pick_conc1 : $\forall \, P \; Q \; R \; S,$
   $(S \; \text{->} \; P \wedge (Q \wedge R))$
   $\rightarrow (S \; \text{->} \; (P \wedge Q) \wedge R).$
   imp.
Qed.

Theorem pick_conc2 : $\forall \, P \; Q \; R \; S,$
   $(S \; \text{->} \; Q \wedge (P \wedge R))$
   $\rightarrow (S \; \text{->} \; (P \wedge Q) \wedge R).$
   imp.
Qed.

Theorem comm_conc : $\forall \, P \; Q \; R,$
   $(R \; \text{->} \; P \wedge Q)$
   $\rightarrow (R \; \text{->} \; Q \wedge P).$
   imp.
Qed.

The first order of business in crafting the *matcher* tactic is to include
auxiliary support for searching through formula trees. The *search_prem*
tactic implements running its tactic argument *tac* on every subformula
of an imp premise. As it traverses a tree, *search_prem* applies some of the
preceding lemmas to rewrite the goal to bring different subformulas to
the head of the goal. That is, for every subformula P of the implication
premise, we want P to have a turn, where the premise is rearranged
into the form $P \wedge Q$ for some Q. The tactic *tac* should expect to see
a goal in this form and focus its attention on the first conjunct of the
premise.

```
Ltac search_prem tac :=
  let rec search P :=
    tac
    || (apply and_True_prem; tac)
    || match P with
         | ?P1 ∧ ?P2 ⇒
             (apply pick_prem1; search P1)
             || (apply pick_prem2; search P2)
       end
  in match goal with
       | [ ⊢ ?P ∧ _ -> _ ] ⇒ search P
       | [ ⊢ _ ∧ ?P -> _ ] ⇒ apply comm_prem; search P
       | [ ⊢ _ -> _ ] ⇒ progress (tac || (apply and_True_prem; tac))
     end.
```

To understand how *search_prem* works, we turn first to the final
match. If the premise begins with a conjunction, we call the *search*
procedure on each of the conjuncts, or only the first conjunct if that
already yields a case where *tac* does not fail. The call *search P* expects
and maintains the invariant that the premise is of the form $P \wedge Q$ for
some Q. We pass P explicitly as a kind of decreasing induction measure,
to avoid looping forever when *tac* always fails. The second match case
calls a commutativity lemma to realize this invariant, before passing
control to *search*. The final match case tries applying *tac* directly and
then, if that fails, changes the form of the goal by adding an extraneous
True conjunct and calls *tac* again. The progress tactical fails when its
argument tactic succeeds without changing the current subgoal.

The *search* function itself tries the same routine as in the last case
of the final match, using the || operator as a shorthand for trying one
tactic and then, if the first fails, trying another. Additionally, if neither
works, it checks if P is a conjunction. If so, it calls itself recursively
on each conjunct, first applying associativity/commutativity lemmas
to maintain the goal-form invariant.

We also want a dual function *search_conc*, which does tree search
through an imp conclusion.

```
Ltac search_conc tac :=
  let rec search P :=
    tac
    || (apply and_True_conc; tac)
    || match P with
         | ?P1 ∧ ?P2 ⇒
             (apply pick_conc1; search P1)
```

```
            || (apply pick_conc2; search P2)
        end
    in match goal with
          | [ ⊢ _ -> ?P ∧ _ ] ⇒ search P
          | [ ⊢ _ -> _ ∧ ?P ] ⇒ apply comm_conc; search P
          | [ ⊢ _ -> _ ] ⇒ progress (tac || (apply and_True_conc; tac))
    end.
```

Now we can prove a number of lemmas that are suitable for application by the search tactics. A lemma that is meant to handle a premise should have the form $P \land Q \to R$ for some interesting P, and a lemma that is meant to handle a conclusion should have the form $P \to Q \land R$ for some interesting Q.

```
Theorem False_prem : ∀ P Q,
    False ∧ P -> Q.
    imp.
Qed.
```

```
Theorem True_conc : ∀ P Q : Prop,
    (P -> Q)
    → (P -> True ∧ Q).
    imp.
Qed.
```

```
Theorem Match : ∀ P Q R : Prop,
    (Q -> R)
    → (P ∧ Q -> P ∧ R).
    imp.
Qed.
```

```
Theorem ex_prem : ∀ (T : Type) (P : T → Prop) (Q R : Prop),
    (∀ x, P x ∧ Q -> R)
    → (ex P ∧ Q -> R).
    imp.
Qed.
```

```
Theorem ex_conc : ∀ (T : Type) (P : T → Prop) (Q R : Prop) x,
    (Q -> P x ∧ R)
    → (Q -> ex P ∧ R).
    imp.
Qed.
```

We also want a base case lemma for finishing proofs where cancellation has removed every constituent of the conclusion.

```
Theorem imp_True : ∀ P,
```

P -> **True**.
imp.
Qed.

The final *matcher* tactic is now straightforward. First, we intros all variables into scope. Then we attempt simple premise simplifications, finishing the proof upon finding **False** and eliminating any existential quantifiers that we find. After that, we search through the conclusion. We remove **True** conjuncts, remove existential quantifiers by introducing unification variables for their bound variables, and search for matching premises to cancel. Finally, when no more progress is made, we see if the goal has become trivial and can be solved by imp_True. In each case, we use the tactic simple apply in place of apply to use a simpler, less expensive unification algorithm.

```
Ltac matcher :=
  intros;
    repeat search_prem ltac:(simple apply False_prem
      || (simple apply ex_prem; intro));
    repeat search_conc ltac:(simple apply True_conc
      || simple eapply ex_conc
      || search_prem ltac:(simple apply Match));
    try simple apply imp_True.
```

The tactic succeeds at proving a simple example.

Theorem t2 : $\forall P \; Q$: Prop,
  $Q \wedge (P \wedge$ **False**$) \wedge P$ -> $P \wedge Q$.
  matcher.
Qed.

In the generated proof, we find a trace of the workings of the search tactics.

Print t2.

t2 =
fun $P \; Q$: Prop $\Rightarrow$
comm_prem (pick_prem1 (pick_prem2
  (False_prem $(P:=P \wedge P \wedge Q) \; (P \wedge Q)$))))
    : $\forall P \; Q$: Prop, $Q \wedge (P \wedge$ **False**$) \wedge P$ -> $P \wedge Q$

We can also see that *matcher* is well-suited for cases where some human intervention is needed after the automation finishes.

Theorem t3 : $\forall P \; Q \; R$: Prop,
  $P \wedge Q$ -> $Q \wedge R \wedge P$.

matcher.

```
============================
```
True $-> R$

The tactic canceled those conjuncts that it was able to cancel, leaving a simplified subgoal, much as `intuition` does.

`Abort.`

The *matcher* tactic even succeeds at guessing quantifier instantiations. It is the unification that occurs in uses of the **Match** lemma that does the real work here.

`Theorem t4` $: \forall\ (P : \textbf{nat} \to \text{Prop})\ Q,\ (\exists\ x,\ P\ x \land Q)$
   $-> Q \land (\exists\ x,\ P\ x).$
   matcher.
`Qed.`

`Print t4.`

`t4 =`
`fun` $(P : \textbf{nat} \to \text{Prop})\ (Q : \text{Prop}) \Rightarrow$
`and_True_prem`
   $(\textsf{ex\_prem}\ (P:=\textbf{fun}\ x : \textbf{nat} \Rightarrow P\ x \land Q)$
      $(\textbf{fun}\ x : \textbf{nat} \Rightarrow$
        `pick_prem2`
           $(\textsf{Match}\ (P:=Q)$
              $(\textsf{and\_True\_conc}$
                 $(\textsf{ex\_conc}\ (\textbf{fun}\ x0 : \textbf{nat} \Rightarrow P\ x0)\ x$
                    $(\textsf{Match}\ (P:=P\ x)\ (\textsf{imp\_True}\ (P:=\textbf{True})))))))))$
      $: \forall\ (P : \textbf{nat} \to \text{Prop})\ (Q : \text{Prop}),$
         $(\exists\ x : \textbf{nat},\ P\ x \land Q)\ -> Q \land (\exists\ x : \textbf{nat},\ P\ x)$

We can be glad that we did not have to build this proof term manually.

14.5   Creating Unification Variables

A final useful ingredient in tactic crafting is the ability to allocate new unification variables explicitly. Tactics like `eauto` introduce unification variables internally to support flexible proof search. While `eauto` and its relatives do *backward* reasoning, we often want to do similar *forward* reasoning, where unification variables can be useful for similar reasons.

For example, we can write a tactic that instantiates the quantifiers of a universally quantified hypothesis. The tactic should not need to know what the appropriate instantiations are; rather, we want these choices filled with placeholders. We hope that when we apply the specialized hypothesis later, syntactic unification will determine concrete values.

Before we are ready to write a tactic, we can try out its ingredients one at a time.

```
Theorem t5 : (∀ x : nat, S x > x) → 2 > 1.
  intros.
```

$H : \forall x : \textbf{nat}, S\ x > x$
============================
$2 > 1$

To instantiate H generically, we first need to name the value to be used for x.

```
  evar (y : nat).
```

$H : \forall x : \textbf{nat}, S\ x > x$
$y := ?279 : \textbf{nat}$
============================
$2 > 1$

The proof context is extended with a new variable y, which has been assigned to be equal to a fresh unification variable ?279. We want to instantiate H with ?279. To get hold of the new unification variable rather than just its alias y, we perform a trivial unfolding in the expression y, using the **eval** Ltac construct, which works with the same reduction strategies seen in tactics (e.g., `simpl`, `compute`, etc.).

```
  let y' := eval unfold y in y in
    clear y; specialize (H y').
```

$H : S\ ?279 > ?279$
============================
$2 > 1$

The instantiation was successful. We can finish the proof by using `apply`'s unification to figure out the proper value of ?279.

```
  apply H.
```

Qed.

Now we can write a tactic that encapsulates the pattern we just employed, instantiating all quantifiers of a particular hypothesis.

Ltac *insterU H* :=
  repeat match type of *H* with
        | $\forall x : ?T, \_ \Rightarrow$
           let *x* := fresh "x" in
             evar $(x : T)$;
             let *x'* := eval unfold *x* in *x* in
               clear *x*; specialize $(H\ x')$
       end.

Theorem t5' : $(\forall x : \mathbf{nat}, S\ x > x) \to 2 > 1$.
  intro *H*; *insterU H*; apply *H*.
Qed.

This particular example is somewhat trivial, since **apply** by itself would have solved the goal originally. Separate forward reasoning is more useful on hypotheses that end in existential quantifications. Before we go through an example, it is useful to define a variant of *insterU* that does not clear the base hypothesis we pass to it. We use the Ltac construct **fresh** to generate a hypothesis name that is not already used, based on a string suggesting a good name.

Ltac *insterKeep H* :=
  let *H'* := fresh "H'" in
    generalize *H*; intro *H'*; *insterU H'*.

Section t6.
  Variables $A\ B$: Type.
  Variable $P : A \to B \to$ Prop.
  Variable $f : A \to A \to A$.
  Variable $g : B \to B \to B$.

  Hypothesis *H1* : $\forall v, \exists u,\ P\ v\ u$.
  Hypothesis *H2* : $\forall v1\ u1\ v2\ u2,$
    $P\ v1\ u1$
    $\to P\ v2\ u2$
    $\to P\ (f\ v1\ v2)\ (g\ u1\ u2)$.

  Theorem t6 : $\forall v1\ v2, \exists u1, \exists u2,\ P\ (f\ v1\ v2)\ (g\ u1\ u2)$.
    intros.

Neither **eauto** nor **firstorder** is clever enough to prove this goal. We can help out by doing some of the work with quantifiers, abbreviating the proof with the do tactical for repetition of a tactic a set number of times.

>   do 2 *insterKeep H1.*

The proof state is extended with two generic instances of *H1.*

>   *H' : ∃ u : B, P ?4289 u*
>   *H'0 : ∃ u : B, P ?4288 u*
>   ================================
>   *∃ u1 : B, ∃ u2 : B, P (f v1 v2) (g u1 u2)*

Normal eauto still cannot prove the goal, so we eliminate the two new existential quantifiers. (Recall that ex is the underlying type family to which uses of the ∃ syntax are compiled.)

>   repeat match goal with
> | [*H* : ex _ ⊢ _] ⇒ destruct *H*
>   end.

Now the goal is simple enough to solve by logic programming.

>   eauto.
>   Qed.
> End t6.

The *insterU* tactic does not fare so well with quantified hypotheses that also contain implications. We can see the problem in a slight modification of the last example. We introduce a new unary predicate *Q* and use it to state an additional requirement of the hypothesis *H1.*

Section t7.
  Variables *A B* : Type.
  Variable *Q* : *A* → Prop.
  Variable *P* : *A* → *B* → Prop.
  Variable *f* : *A* → *A* → *A.*
  Variable *g* : *B* → *B* → *B.*

  Hypothesis *H1* : ∀ *v*, *Q v* → ∃ *u*, *P v u.*
  Hypothesis *H2* : ∀ *v1 u1 v2 u2*,
    P v1 u1
    → *P v2 u2*
    → *P (f v1 v2) (g u1 u2).*

  Theorem t7 : ∀ *v1 v2*, *Q v1* → *Q v2* → ∃ *u1* , ∃ *u2* ,
    P (f v1 v2) (g u1 u2).
    intros; do 2 *insterKeep H1*;

```
repeat match goal with
       | [ H : ex _ ⊢ _ ] ⇒ destruct H
     end; eauto.
```

This proof script does not hit any errors until the very end, when an error message like this one is displayed:

```
No more subgoals but non-instantiated existential variables :
Existential 1 =
```
$?4384 : [A : \mathtt{Type}$
$\qquad B : \mathtt{Type}$
$\qquad Q : A \to \mathtt{Prop}$
$\qquad P : A \to B \to \mathtt{Prop}$
$\qquad f : A \to A \to A$
$\qquad g : B \to B \to B$
$\qquad H1 : \forall\, v : A,\; Q\; v \to \exists\, u : B,\; P\; v\; u$
$\qquad H2 : \forall\, (v1 : A)\; (u1 : B)\; (v2 : A)\; (u2 : B),$
$\qquad\qquad P\; v1\; u1 \to P\; v2\; u2 \to P\; (f\; v1\; v2)\; (g\; u1\; u2)$
$\qquad v1 : A$
$\qquad v2 : A$
$\qquad H : Q\; v1$
$\qquad H0 : Q\; v2$
$\qquad H' : Q\; v2 \to \exists\, u : B,\; P\; v2\; u \vdash Q\; v2]$

There is another similar line about a different existential variable. Here, *existential variable* means what we have also called unification variable. In the course of the proof, some unification variable ?4384 was introduced but never unified. Unification variables are just a device to structure proof search; the language of Gallina proof terms does not include them. Thus, we cannot produce a proof term without instantiating the variable.

The error message shows that ?4384 is meant to be a proof of $Q\; v2$ in a particular proof state, whose variables and hypotheses are displayed. It turns out that ?4384 was created by *insterU*, as the value of a proof to pass to *H1*. Recall that, in Gallina, implication is just a degenerate case of $\forall$ quantification, so the *insterU* code to match against $\forall$ also matched the implication. Since any proof of $Q\; v2$ is as good as any other in this context, there was never any opportunity to use unification to determine exactly which proof is appropriate. We expect similar problems with any implications in arguments to *insterU*.

```
  Abort.
End t7.
```

```
Reset insterU.
```

We can redefine *insterU* to treat implications differently. In particular, we pattern-match on the type of the type T in $\forall\ x : ?T, \ldots$. If T has type Prop, then x's instantiation should be thought of as a proof. Thus, instead of picking a new unification variable for it, we apply a user-supplied tactic *tac*. It is important that we end this special Prop case with $\|$ fail 1, so that, if *tac* fails to prove T, we abort the instantiation rather than continuing on to the default quantifier handling. Also recall that the tactic form solve [t] fails if t does not completely solve the goal.

Ltac *insterU tac H* :=
  repeat match type of H with
        | $\forall\ x : ?T,$ _ $\Rightarrow$
          match type of T with
           | Prop $\Rightarrow$
             (let H' := fresh "H'" in
               assert $(H' : T)$ by solve [*tac*];
                 specialize $(H\ H')$; clear H')
             $\|$ fail 1
           | _ $\Rightarrow$
             let x := fresh "x" in
               evar $(x : T)$;
               let x' := eval unfold x in x in
                 clear x; specialize $(H\ x')$
         end
      end.

Ltac *insterKeep tac H* :=
  let H' := fresh "H'" in
    generalize H; intro H'; *insterU tac H'*.

Section t7.
  Variables $A\ B$: Type.
  Variable $Q : A \rightarrow$ Prop.
  Variable $P : A \rightarrow B \rightarrow$ Prop.
  Variable $f : A \rightarrow A \rightarrow A$.
  Variable $g : B \rightarrow B \rightarrow B$.

  Hypothesis $H1 : \forall\ v,\ Q\ v \rightarrow \exists\ u,\ P\ v\ u.$
  Hypothesis $H2 : \forall\ v1\ u1\ v2\ u2,$
    $P\ v1\ u1$
    $\rightarrow P\ v2\ u2$
    $\rightarrow P\ (f\ v1\ v2)\ (g\ u1\ u2).$

  Theorem t7 : $\forall\ v1\ v2,\ Q\ v1 \rightarrow Q\ v2 \rightarrow \exists\ u1,\ \exists\ u2,$

$$P\ (f\ v1\ v2)\ (g\ u1\ u2).$$

We can prove the goal by calling *insterKeep* with a tactic that tries to find and apply a Q hypothesis over a variable about which we do not yet know any P facts. We need to begin this tactic code with `idtac`; to get around a strange limitation in Coq's proof engine, where a first-class tactic argument may not begin with a `match`.

```
intros; do 2 insterKeep
  ltac:(idtac; match goal with
                 | [ H : Q ?v ⊢ _ ] ⇒
                   match goal with
                     | [ _ : context[P v _] ⊢ _ ] ⇒ fail 1
                     | _ ⇒ apply H
                   end
               end) H1;
  repeat match goal with
           | [ H : ex _ ⊢ _ ] ⇒ destruct H
         end; eauto.
Qed.
End t7.
```

It is often useful to instantiate existential variables explicitly. A built-in tactic provides one way of doing so.

```
Theorem t8 : ∃ p : nat × nat, fst p = 3.
  econstructor; instantiate (1 := (3, 2)); reflexivity.
Qed.
```

The 1 identifies an existential variable appearing in the current goal, with the last existential assigned number 1, the second-last assigned number 2, and so on. The named existential is replaced everywhere by the term to the right of the :=.

The `instantiate` tactic can be convenient for exploratory proving, but it leads to very brittle proof scripts that are unlikely to adapt to changing theorem statements. It is often more helpful to have a tactic that can be used to assign a value to a term that is known to be an existential. By employing a roundabout implementation technique, we can build a tactic that generalizes this functionality. In particular, the tactic *equate* will assert that two terms are equal. If one of the terms happens to be an existential, then it will be replaced everywhere with the other term.

```
Ltac equate x y :=
  let dummy := constr:(eq_refl : x = y) in idtac.
```

This tactic fails if it is not possible to prove $x = y$ by eq_refl. We check the proof only for its unification side effects, ignoring the associated variable *dummy*. With *equate*, we can build a less brittle version of the prior example.

Theorem t9 : $\exists\, p$: **nat** $\times$ **nat**, fst p = 3.
  econstructor; match goal with
                 | [$\vdash$ fst $?x$ = 3] $\Rightarrow$ *equate* x (3, 2)
          end; reflexivity.
Qed.

This technique is even more useful within recursive and iterative tactics that are meant to solve broad classes of goals.

15   Proof by Reflection

The last chapter highlighted a heuristic approach to proving. In this chapter, we study an alternative technique, *proof by reflection* [2]. We write, in Gallina, decision procedures with proofs of correctness and appeal to these procedures in writing very short proofs. Such a proof is checked by running the decision procedure. The term *reflection* applies because we need to translate Gallina propositions into values of inductive types representing syntax, so that Gallina programs may analyze them, and translating such a term back to the original form is called *reflecting* it.

15.1   Proving Evenness

Proving that particular natural number constants are even is certainly something we would rather have happen automatically. The Ltac programming techniques explained in Chapter 14 make it easy to implement such a procedure.

```
Inductive isEven : nat → Prop :=
| Even_O : isEven O
| Even_SS : ∀ n, isEven n → isEven (S (S n)).
```

```
Ltac prove_even := repeat constructor.
```

```
Theorem even_256 : isEven 256.
  prove_even.
Qed.
```

```
Print even_256.
```

```
even_256 =
Even_SS
  (Even_SS
    (Even_SS
      (Even_SS
```

and so on. This procedure always works (at least on machines with infinite resources), but it has a serious drawback, which we see when we print the proof it generates that 256 is even. The final proof term has length superlinear in the input value. Coq's implicit arguments mechanism is hiding the values given for parameter n of Even_SS, which is why the proof term only appears linear here. Also, proof terms are represented internally as syntax trees, with the opportunity for sharing node representations, but in this chapter we measure proof term size as simple textual length or as the number of nodes in the term's syntax tree, two measures that are approximately equivalent. Sometimes apparently large proof terms have enough internal sharing that they take up less memory than we expect, but one avoids having to reason about such sharing by ensuring that the size of a sharing-free version of a term is low enough.

Superlinear evenness proof terms seem excessively large, since we could write a trivial and trustworthy program to verify evenness of constants. The proof checker could simply call the program where needed. There are also no static typing guarantees that the tactic always behaves appropriately. Other invocations of similar tactics might fail with dynamic type errors, and we would not know about the bugs behind these errors until we attempted to prove complex goals.

The techniques of proof by reflection address both complaints. We can write proofs like the preceding example with constant size overhead beyond the size of the input, and do it with verified decision procedures written in Gallina.

We begin by using a type from the MoreSpecif module (see the book source) to write a certified evenness checker.

```
Print partial.
```

```
Inductive partial (P : Prop) : Set := Proved : P → [P]
  | Uncertain : [P]
```

A **partial** P value is an optional proof of P. The notation $[P]$ stands for **partial** P.

```
Local Open Scope partial_scope.
```

We bring into scope some notations for the **partial** type. These overlap with some of the notations seen previously for specification types, so they were placed in a separate scope that needs separate opening.

```
Definition check_even : ∀ n : nat, [isEven n].
  Hint Constructors isEven.

  refine (fix F (n : nat) : [isEven n] :=
```

```
    match n with
      | 0 ⇒ Yes
      | 1 ⇒ No
      | S (S n') ⇒ Reduce (F n')
    end); auto.
Defined.
```

The function check_even may be viewed as a *verified decision procedure*, because its type guarantees that it never returns Yes for inputs that are not even.

Now we can use dependent pattern matching to write a function that performs a surprising feat. When given a **partial** P, this function partialOut returns a proof of P if the **partial** value contains a proof, and it returns a (useless) proof of **True** otherwise. From the standpoint of ML and Haskell programming, it seems impossible to write such a type, but it is trivial with a **return** annotation.

Definition partialOut $(P : \text{Prop})$ $(x : [P]) :=$
  match x return (match x with
                   | Proved _ ⇒ P
                   | Uncertain ⇒ **True**
                 end) with
    | Proved pf ⇒ pf
    | Uncertain ⇒ I
  end.

A function like this is useful in writing a reflective version of the earlier *prove_even* tactic.

Ltac *prove_even_reflective* :=
  match goal with
    | [⊢ **isEven** ?N] ⇒ exact (partialOut (check_even N))
  end.

We identify which natural number we are considering and prove its evenness by pulling the proof out of the appropriate check_even call. Recall that the exact tactic proves a proposition P when given a proof term of precisely type P.

Theorem even_256' : **isEven** 256.
  prove_even_reflective.
Qed.

Print even_256'.

even_256' = partialOut (check_even 256)
     : **isEven** 256

We can see a constant wrapper around the object of the proof. For any even number, this form of proof will suffice. The size of the proof term is now linear in the number being checked, containing two repetitions of the unary form of that number, one of which is hidden within the implicit argument to partialOut.

What happens if we try the tactic with an odd number?

Theorem even_255 : isEven 255.
  prove_even_reflective.

```
User error: No matching clauses for match goal
```

The tactic fails. To see more precisely what goes wrong, we can run manually the body of the `match`.

  exact (partialOut (check_even 255)).

```
Error: The term "partialOut (check_even 255)" has type
"match check_even 255 with
 | Yes => isEven 255
 | No => True
 end" while it is expected to have type "isEven 255"
```

As usual, the type checker performs no reductions to simplify error messages. If we reduced the first term, we would see that check_even 255 reduces to a No, so that the first term is equivalent to **True**, which certainly does not unify with isEven 255.

```
Abort.
```

The tactic *prove_even_reflective* is reflective because it performs a proof search process (a trivial one, in this case) wholly within Gallina, where the only use of Ltac is to translate a goal into an appropriate use of check_even.

15.2   Reifying the Syntax of a Trivial Tautology Language

We might also like to have reflective proofs of trivial tautologies like this one:

Theorem true_galore : (**True** ∧ **True**)
    → (**True** ∨ (**True** ∧ (**True** → **True**))).
  tauto.
Qed.

Print true_galore.

```
true_galore =
fun H : True ∧ True ⇒
and_ind (fun _ _ : True ⇒ or_introl (True ∧ (True → True)) I) H
     : True ∧ True → True ∨ True ∧ (True → True)
```

As we might expect, the proof that `tauto` builds contains explicit applications of natural deduction rules. For large formulas, this can add a superlinear amount of proof size overhead, beyond the size of the input.

To write a reflective procedure for this class of goals, we need to get into the actual "reflection" part of "proof by reflection." It is impossible to case-analyze a `Prop` in any way in Gallina. We must *reify* `Prop` into some type that we can analyze. This inductive type is a good candidate:

```
Inductive taut : Set :=
| TautTrue : taut
| TautAnd : taut → taut → taut
| TautOr : taut → taut → taut
| TautImp : taut → taut → taut.
```

We write a recursive function to *reflect* this syntax back to `Prop`. Such functions are also called *interpretation functions*; they were used in previous examples to give semantics to small programming languages.

```
Fixpoint tautDenote (t : taut) : Prop :=
  match t with
    | TautTrue ⇒ True
    | TautAnd t1 t2 ⇒ tautDenote t1 ∧ tautDenote t2
    | TautOr t1 t2 ⇒ tautDenote t1 ∨ tautDenote t2
    | TautImp t1 t2 ⇒ tautDenote t1 → tautDenote t2
  end.
```

It is easy to prove that every formula in the range of `tautDenote` is true.

```
Theorem tautTrue : ∀ t, tautDenote t.
  induction t; crush.
Qed.
```

To use `tautTrue` to prove particular formulas, we need to implement the syntax reification process. A recursive Ltac function does the job.

```
Ltac tautReify P :=
  match P with
    | True ⇒ TautTrue
    | ?P1 ∧ ?P2 ⇒
```

```
    let t1 := tautReify P1 in
    let t2 := tautReify P2 in
      constr:(TautAnd t1 t2)
  | ?P1 ∨ ?P2 ⇒
    let t1 := tautReify P1 in
    let t2 := tautReify P2 in
      constr:(TautOr t1 t2)
  | ?P1 → ?P2 ⇒
    let t1 := tautReify P1 in
    let t2 := tautReify P2 in
      constr:(TautImp t1 t2)
end.
```

With *tautReify* available, it is easy to finish the reflective tactic. We look at the goal formula, reify it, and apply tautTrue to the reified formula.

```
Ltac obvious :=
  match goal with
    | [ ⊢ ?P ] ⇒
      let t := tautReify P in
        exact (tautTrue t)
  end.
```

We can verify that *obvious* solves the original example, with a proof term that does not mention details of the proof.

```
Theorem true_galore' : (True ∧ True)
  → (True ∨ (True ∧ (True → True))).
  obvious.
Qed.
```

```
Print true_galore'.
```

```
true_galore' =
tautTrue
  (TautImp (TautAnd TautTrue TautTrue)
    (TautOr TautTrue (TautAnd TautTrue
    (TautImp TautTrue TautTrue))))
    : True ∧ True → True ∨ True ∧ (True → True)
```

It is worth considering how the reflective tactic improves on a pure Ltac implementation. The formula reification process is just as ad hoc as before, so we gain little there. In general, proofs are more complicated than formula translation, and the generic proof rule applied here is on much better formal footing than a recursive Ltac function. The dependent type of the proof guarantees that it works on any input formula. This benefit is in addition to the proof size improvement that we have already seen.

It may also be worth pointing out that the previous example of evenness testing used a function partialOut for sound handling of input goals that the verified decision procedure fails to prove. Here, we prove that the procedure tautTrue (recall that an inductive proof may be viewed as a recursive procedure) is able to prove any goal representable in **taut**, so no extra step is necessary.

15.3 A Monoid Expression Simplifier

Proof by reflection does not require encoding of all the syntax in a goal. We can insert variables into syntax types to allow injection of arbitrary pieces, even if we cannot apply specialized reasoning to them. In this section, we explore that possibility by writing a tactic for normalizing monoid equations.

```
Section monoid.
  Variable A : Set.
  Variable e : A.
  Variable f : A → A → A.

  Infix "+" := f.

  Hypothesis assoc : ∀ a b c, (a + b) + c = a + (b + c).
  Hypothesis identl : ∀ a, e + a = a.
  Hypothesis identr : ∀ a, a + e = a.
```

We add variables and hypotheses characterizing an arbitrary instance of the algebraic structure of monoids. We have an associative binary operator and an identity element for it.

It is easy to define an expression tree type for monoid expressions. A Var constructor is a catch-all case for subexpressions that we cannot model. These subexpressions could be actual Gallina variables, or they could just use functions that the tactic is unable to understand.

```
  Inductive mexp : Set :=
  | Ident : mexp
  | Var : A → mexp
  | Op : mexp → mexp → mexp.
```

Next, we write an interpretation function.

```
  Fixpoint mdenote (me : mexp) : A :=
    match me with
```

```
        | Ident ⇒ e
        | Var v ⇒ v
        | Op me1 me2 ⇒ mdenote me1 + mdenote me2
    end.
```

We normalize expressions by flattening them into lists, via associativity, so it is helpful to have a denotation function for lists of monoid values.

```
Fixpoint mldenote (ls : list A) : A :=
    match ls with
        | nil ⇒ e
        | x :: ls' ⇒ x + mldenote ls'
    end.
```

The flattening function itself is easy to implement.

```
Fixpoint flatten (me : mexp) : list A :=
    match me with
        | Ident ⇒ nil
        | Var x ⇒ x :: nil
        | Op me1 me2 ⇒ flatten me1 ++ flatten me2
    end.
```

This function has a straightforward correctness proof in terms of the *denote* functions.

```
Lemma flatten_correct' : ∀ ml2 ml1,
    mldenote ml1 + mldenote ml2 = mldenote (ml1 ++ ml2).
    induction ml1; crush.
Qed.

Theorem flatten_correct : ∀ me, mdenote me = mldenote (flatten me).
    Hint Resolve flatten_correct'.

    induction me; crush.
Qed.
```

Now it is easy to prove a theorem that will be the main tool behind the simplification tactic.

```
Theorem monoid_reflect : ∀ me1 me2,
    mldenote (flatten me1) = mldenote (flatten me2)
    → mdenote me1 = mdenote me2.
    intros; repeat rewrite flatten_correct; assumption.
Qed.
```

We implement reification into the **mexp** type.

```
Ltac reify me :=
```

```
match me with
  | e ⇒ Ident
  | ?me1 + ?me2 ⇒
    let r1 := reify me1 in
    let r2 := reify me2 in
      constr:(Op r1 r2)
  | _ ⇒ constr:(Var me)
end.
```

The final monoid tactic works on goals that equate two monoid terms. We reify each and change the goal to refer to the reified versions, finishing off by applying monoid_reflect and simplifying uses of mldenote. Recall that the change tactic replaces a conclusion formula with another that is definitionally equal to it.

```
Ltac monoid :=
  match goal with
    | [ ⊢ ?me1 = ?me2 ] ⇒
      let r1 := reify me1 in
      let r2 := reify me2 in
        change (mdenote r1 = mdenote r2);
          apply monoid_reflect; simpl
  end.
```

We can make short work of theorems like this one:

Theorem t1 : ∀ a b c d, a + b + c + d = a + (b + c) + d.
  intros; *monoid*.

$$============================$$
$$a + (b + (c + (d + e))) = a + (b + (c + (d + e)))$$

The tactic has canonicalized both sides of the equality, such that we can finish the proof by reflexivity.

  reflexivity.
Qed.

It is interesting to look at the form of the proof.

  Print t1.

```
t1 =
fun a b c d : A ⇒
monoid_reflect (Op (Op (Op (Var a) (Var b)) (Var c)) (Var d))
  (Op (Op (Var a) (Op (Var b) (Var c))) (Var d)) eq_refl
```

$$: \forall \ a \ b \ c \ d : A, \ a + b + c + d = a + (b + c) + d$$

The proof term contains only restatements of the equality operands in reified form, followed by a use of reflexivity on the shared canonical form.

End monoid.

Extensions of this basic approach are used in the implementations of the `ring` and `field` tactics that come packaged with Coq.

15.4   A Smarter Tautology Solver

Now we are ready to revisit the tautology solver example. We want to broaden the scope of the tactic to include formulas whose truth is not syntactically apparent. We want to allow injection of arbitrary formulas, just as arbitrary monoid expressions were allowed in the last example. Since we are working in a richer theory, it is important to be able to use equalities between different injected formulas. For instance, we cannot prove $P \to P$ by translating the formula into a value like Imp (Var P) (Var P), because a Gallina function has no way of comparing the two Ps for equality.

To arrive at an implementation satisfying these criteria, we introduce the `quote` tactic and its associated library.

Require Import Quote.

```
Inductive formula : Set :=
| Atomic : index → formula
| Truth : formula
| Falsehood : formula
| And : formula → formula → formula
| Or : formula → formula → formula
| Imp : formula → formula → formula.
```

The type **index** comes from the Quote library and represents a countable variable type. The rest of **formula**'s definition should be familiar by now.

The `quote` tactic implements injection from Prop into **formula**, but it is not quite as smart as we might like. In particular, it wants to treat function types specially, so it gets confused if function types are part of the structure we want to encode syntactically. To trick `quote` into not noticing our uses of function types to express logical implication, we need to declare a wrapper definition for implication (see related code in Section 14.4).

Definition imp $(P1\ P2 : \text{Prop}) := P1 \rightarrow P2$.
Infix "–>" := imp (no associativity, at level 95).

Now we can define the denotation function.

Definition asgn := **varmap** Prop.

Fixpoint formulaDenote $(atomics : \text{asgn})\ (f : \textbf{formula}) : \text{Prop} :=$
  match f with
    | Atomic $v \Rightarrow$ varmap_find **False** v *atomics*
    | Truth $\Rightarrow$ **True**
    | Falsehood $\Rightarrow$ **False**
    | And $f1\ f2 \Rightarrow$
      formulaDenote *atomics f1* $\wedge$ formulaDenote *atomics f2*
    | Or $f1\ f2 \Rightarrow$
      formulaDenote *atomics f1* $\vee$ formulaDenote *atomics f2*
    | Imp $f1\ f2 \Rightarrow$
      formulaDenote *atomics f1* –> formulaDenote *atomics f2*
  end.

The **varmap** type family implements maps from **index** values. In this case, we define an assignment as a map from variables to Props. The interpretation function formulaDenote works with an assignment, and we use the **varmap_find** function to consult the assignment in the Atomic case. The first argument to **varmap_find** is a default value, in case the variable is not found.

Section my_tauto.
  Variable *atomics* : asgn.

  Definition holds $(v : \textbf{index}) :=$ varmap_find **False** v *atomics*.

We define some shorthand for a particular variable's being true, and now we are ready to define some helpful functions based on the ListSet module of the standard library, which presents a view of lists as sets.

  Require Import ListSet.

  Definition index_eq : $\forall\ x\ y : \textbf{index},\ \{x = y\} + \{x \neq y\}$.
    decide equality.
  Defined.

  Definition add $(s : \text{set}\ \textbf{index})\ (v : \textbf{index}) :=$ set_add index_eq $v\ s$.

  Definition In_dec : $\forall\ v\ (s : \text{set}\ \textbf{index}),\ \{\text{In}\ v\ s\} + \{\neg\ \text{In}\ v\ s\}$.
    Local Open Scope *specif_scope*.

    intro; refine (fix $F\ (s : \text{set}\ \textbf{index}) : \{\text{In}\ v\ s\} + \{\neg\ \text{In}\ v\ s\} :=$
      match s with
        | nil $\Rightarrow$ No

```
        | v' :: s' ⇒ index_eq v' v || F s'
    end); crush.
Defined.
```

We define what it means for all members of an index set to represent true propositions, and we prove some lemmas about this notion.

```
Fixpoint allTrue (s : set index) : Prop :=
  match s with
    | nil ⇒ True
    | v :: s' ⇒ holds v ∧ allTrue s'
  end.

Theorem allTrue_add : ∀ v s,
  allTrue s
  → holds v
  → allTrue (add s v).
  induction s; crush;
    match goal with
      | [ ⊢ context[if ?E then _ else _] ] ⇒ destruct E
    end; crush.
Qed.

Theorem allTrue_In : ∀ v s,
  allTrue s
  → set_In v s
  → varmap_find False v atomics.
  induction s; crush.
Qed.

Hint Resolve allTrue_add allTrue_In.

Local Open Scope partial_scope.
```

Now we can write a function forward that implements deconstruction of hypotheses, expanding a compound formula into a set of sets of atomic formulas covering all possible cases introduced with use of Or. To handle consideration of multiple cases, the function takes in a continuation argument, which will be called once for each case.

The forward function has a dependent type, in the style of Chapter 6, guaranteeing correctness. The arguments to forward are a goal formula *f*, a set *known* of atomic formulas that we may assume are true, a hypothesis formula *hyp*, and a success continuation *cont* that we call when we have extended *known* to hold new truths implied by *hyp*.

```
Definition forward : ∀ (f : formula) (known : set index)
  (hyp : formula)
```

```
      (cont : ∀ known', [allTrue known' → formulaDenote atomics f]),
      [allTrue known → formulaDenote atomics hyp
         → formulaDenote atomics f].
    refine (fix F (f : formula) (known : set index) (hyp : formula)
      (cont : ∀ known', [allTrue known' → formulaDenote atomics f])
      : [allTrue known → formulaDenote atomics hyp
         → formulaDenote atomics f] :=
    match hyp with
       | Atomic v ⇒ Reduce (cont (add known v))
       | Truth ⇒ Reduce (cont known)
       | Falsehood ⇒ Yes
       | And h1 h2 ⇒
          Reduce (F (Imp h2 f) known h1 (fun known' ⇒
             Reduce (F f known' h2 cont)))
       | Or h1 h2 ⇒ F f known h1 cont && F f known h2 cont
       | Imp _ _ ⇒ Reduce (cont known)
    end); crush.
Defined.
```

A backward function implements analysis of the final goal. It calls forward to handle implications.

```
Definition backward : ∀ (known : set index) (f : formula),
   [allTrue known → formulaDenote atomics f].
   refine (fix F (known : set index) (f : formula)
     : [allTrue known → formulaDenote atomics f] :=
     match f with
        | Atomic v ⇒ Reduce (In_dec v known)
        | Truth ⇒ Yes
        | Falsehood ⇒ No
        | And f1 f2 ⇒ F known f1 && F known f2
        | Or f1 f2 ⇒ F known f1 || F known f2
        | Imp f1 f2 ⇒
           forward f2 known f1 (fun known' ⇒ F known' f2)
     end); crush; eauto.
Defined.
```

A simple wrapper around backward gives us the usual type of a partial decision procedure.

```
Definition my_tauto : ∀ f : formula, [formulaDenote atomics f].
   intro; refine (Reduce (backward nil f)); crush.
Defined.
End my_tauto.
```

The final tactic implementation is now fairly straightforward. First, we intro all quantifiers that do not bind Props. Then we call the quote tactic, which implements the reification. Finally, we are able to construct an exact proof via partialOut and the my_tauto Gallina function.

Ltac *my_tauto* :=
  repeat match goal with
         | [⊢ ∀ x : ?P, _] ⇒
           match type of P with
             | Prop ⇒ fail 1
             | _ ⇒ intro
           end
        end;
  quote *formulaDenote*;
  match goal with
    | [⊢ formulaDenote ?m ?f] ⇒ exact (partialOut (my_tauto *m f*))
  end.

A few examples demonstrate how the tactic works.

Theorem mt1 : **True**.
  my_tauto.
Qed.

Print mt1.

mt1 = partialOut (my_tauto (Empty_vm Prop) Truth)
    : **True**

We see my_tauto applied with an empty **varmap**, since every subformula is handled by formulaDenote.

Theorem mt2 : ∀ x y : **nat**, $x = y$ -> $x = y$.
  my_tauto.
Qed.

Print mt2.

mt2 =
fun x y : **nat** ⇒
partialOut
  (my_tauto (Node_vm ($x = y$) (Empty_vm Prop) (Empty_vm Prop))
    (Imp (Atomic End_idx) (Atomic End_idx)))
      : ∀ x y : **nat**, $x = y$ -> $x = y$

Crucially, both instances of $x = y$ are represented with the same index, End_idx. The value of this index only needs to appear once in the **varmap**, whose form reveals that **varmap**s are represented as binary trees, where **index** values denote paths from tree roots to leaves.

Theorem mt3 : ∀ x y z,
  $(x < y \land y > z) \lor (y > z \land x < $ S $y)$
  -> $y > z \land (x < y \lor x < $ S $y)$.
  my_tauto.
Qed.

Print mt3.

fun x y z : **nat** ⇒
partialOut
  (my_tauto
    (Node_vm $(x < $ S $y)$ (Node_vm $(x < y)$ (Empty_vm Prop)
      (Empty_vm Prop))
      (Node_vm $(y > z)$ (Empty_vm Prop) (Empty_vm Prop)))
    (Imp
      (Or (And (Atomic (Left_idx End_idx))
        (Atomic (Right_idx End_idx)))
        (And (Atomic (Right_idx End_idx)) (Atomic End_idx)))
      (And (Atomic (Right_idx End_idx))
        (Or (Atomic (Left_idx End_idx)) (Atomic End_idx)))))
    : ∀ x y z : **nat**,
      $x < y \land y > z \lor y > z \land x < $ S y
      -> $y > z \land (x < y \lor x < $ S $y)$

The goal contained three distinct atomic formulas, and we see that a three-element **varmap** is generated.

It can be interesting to observe differences between the level of repetition in proof terms generated by `my_tauto` and `tauto` for especially trivial theorems.

Theorem mt4 :
  True ∧ **True** ∧ **True** ∧ **True** ∧ **True** ∧ **True** ∧ **False** -> **False**.
  my_tauto.
Qed.

Print mt4.

mt4 =
partialOut
  (my_tauto (Empty_vm Prop)
    (Imp
      (And Truth
        (And Truth

```
        (And Truth (And Truth (And Truth
            (And Truth Falsehood))))))
      Falsehood))
   : True ∧ True ∧ True ∧ True ∧ True ∧ True ∧ False -> False
```

```
Theorem mt4' :
  True ∧ True ∧ True ∧ True ∧ True ∧ True ∧ False → False.
  tauto.
Qed.
```

```
Print mt4'.
```

```
mt4' =
fun H : True ∧ True ∧ True ∧ True ∧ True ∧ True ∧ False ⇒
and_ind
  (fun (_ : True)
    (H1 : True ∧ True ∧ True ∧ True ∧ True ∧ False) ⇒
    and_ind
      (fun (_ : True) (H3 : True ∧ True ∧ True ∧ True ∧ False) ⇒
      and_ind
        (fun (_ : True) (H5 : True ∧ True ∧ True ∧ False) ⇒
        and_ind
          (fun (_ : True) (H7 : True ∧ True ∧ False) ⇒
          and_ind
            (fun (_ : True) (H9 : True ∧ False) ⇒
            and_ind (fun (_ : True) (H11 : False) ⇒
            False_ind False H11)
            H9) H7) H5) H3) H1) H
   : True ∧ True ∧ True ∧ True ∧ True ∧ True ∧ False → False
```

The traditional `tauto` tactic introduces a quadratic blow-up in the size of the proof term, whereas proofs produced by `my_tauto` always have linear size.

15.4.1   Manual Reification of Terms with Variables

The action of the `quote` tactic may seem like magic. Somehow it performs equality comparison between subterms of arbitrary types, so that these subterms may be represented with the same reified variable. While `quote` is implemented in OCaml, we can code the reification process completely in Ltac as well. To make the job simpler, we represent variables as **nat**s, indexing into a simple list of variable values that may be referenced.

Step one of the process is to crawl over a term, building a duplicate-free list of all values that appear in positions encoded as variables. A useful helper function adds an element to a list, preventing duplicates. Note how we use Ltac pattern matching to implement an equality test on Gallina terms; this is simple syntactic equality, not even the richer definitional equality. We also represent lists as nested tuples, to allow different list elements to have different Gallina types.

```
Ltac inList x xs :=
  match xs with
    | tt ⇒ false
    | (x, _) ⇒ true
    | (_, ?xs') ⇒ inList x xs'
  end.
```

```
Ltac addToList x xs :=
  let b := inList x xs in
    match b with
      | true ⇒ xs
      | false ⇒ constr:(x, xs)
    end.
```

Now we can write the recursive function to calculate the list of variable values we want to use to represent a term.

```
Ltac allVars xs e :=
  match e with
    | True ⇒ xs
    | False ⇒ xs
    | ?e1 ∧ ?e2 ⇒
      let xs := allVars xs e1 in
        allVars xs e2
    | ?e1 ∨ ?e2 ⇒
      let xs := allVars xs e1 in
        allVars xs e2
    | ?e1 → ?e2 ⇒
      let xs := allVars xs e1 in
        allVars xs e2
    | _ ⇒ addToList e xs
  end.
```

We will also need a way to map a value to its position in a list.

```
Ltac lookup x xs :=
  match xs with
    | (x, _) ⇒ O
```

```
      | (_, ?xs') ⇒
          let n := lookup x xs' in
              constr:(S n)
  end.
```

The next building block is a procedure for reifying a term, given a list of all allowed variable values. We are free to make this procedure partial, where tactic failure may be triggered upon attempting to reify a term containing subterms not included in the list of variables. The type of the output term is a copy of **formula** where **index** is replaced by **nat**, in the type of the constructor for atomic formulas.

```
Inductive formula' : Set :=
| Atomic' : nat → formula'
| Truth' : formula'
| Falsehood' : formula'
| And' : formula' → formula' → formula'
| Or' : formula' → formula' → formula'
| Imp' : formula' → formula' → formula'.
```

Note that when we write the Ltac procedure, we can work directly with the normal → operator rather than needing to introduce a wrapper for it.

```
Ltac reifyTerm xs e :=
  match e with
    | True ⇒ constr:Truth'
    | False ⇒ constr:Falsehood'
    | ?e1 ∧ ?e2 ⇒
      let p1 := reifyTerm xs e1 in
      let p2 := reifyTerm xs e2 in
        constr:(And' p1 p2)
    | ?e1 ∨ ?e2 ⇒
      let p1 := reifyTerm xs e1 in
      let p2 := reifyTerm xs e2 in
        constr:(Or' p1 p2)
    | ?e1 → ?e2 ⇒
      let p1 := reifyTerm xs e1 in
      let p2 := reifyTerm xs e2 in
        constr:(Imp' p1 p2)
    | _ ⇒
      let n := lookup e xs in
        constr:(Atomic' n)
  end.
```

Finally, we bring all the pieces together.

```
Ltac reify :=
  match goal with
    | [ ⊢ ?G ] ⇒ let xs := allVars tt G in
      let p := reifyTerm xs G in
        pose p
  end.
```

A quick test verifies that we are doing reification correctly.

```
Theorem mt3' : ∀ x y z,
  (x < y ∧ y > z) ∨ (y > z ∧ x < S y)
  → y > z ∧ (x < y ∨ x < S y).
do 3 intro; reify.
```

A simple tactic adds the translated term as a new variable.

f := Imp'
       (Or' (And' (Atomic' 2) (Atomic' 1))
        (And' (Atomic' 1) (Atomic' 0)))
       (And' (Atomic' 1) (Or' (Atomic' 2) (Atomic' 0))) : **formula'**

```
Abort.
```

More work would be needed to complete the reflective tactic, as we must connect the new syntax type with the real meanings of formulas, but the details are the same as in the prior implementation with `quote`.

15.5 Building a Reification Tactic That Recurses under Binders

All examples so far have stayed away from reifying the syntax of terms that use such features as quantifiers and `fun` function abstractions. Such cases are complicated by the fact that different subterms may be allowed to reference different sets of free variables. Some cleverness is needed to clear this hurdle, but a few simple patterns will suffice. Consider this example of a simple dependently typed term language, where a function abstraction body is represented conveniently with a Coq function:

```
Inductive type : Type :=
| Nat : type
| NatFunc : type → type.

Inductive term : type → Type :=
| Const : nat → term Nat
| Plus : term Nat → term Nat → term Nat
```

| Abs : ∀ t, (**nat** → **term** t) → **term** (NatFunc t).

Fixpoint typeDenote (t : **type**) : Type :=
  match t with
    | Nat ⇒ **nat**
    | NatFunc t ⇒ **nat** → typeDenote t
  end.

Fixpoint termDenote t (e : **term** t) : typeDenote t :=
  match e with
    | Const n ⇒ n
    | Plus $e1$ $e2$ ⇒ termDenote $e1$ + termDenote $e2$
    | Abs _ $e1$ ⇒ fun x ⇒ termDenote ($e1$ x)
  end.

Here is a naïve first attempt at a reification tactic:

Ltac *refl'* e :=
  match e with
    | ?$E1$ + ?$E2$ ⇒
      let $r1$:= *refl'* $E1$ in
      let $r2$:= *refl'* $E2$ in
        constr:(Plus $r1$ $r2$)

    | fun x : **nat** ⇒ ?$E1$ ⇒
      let $r1$:= *refl'* $E1$ in
        constr:(Abs (fun x ⇒ $r1$ x))

    | _ ⇒ constr:(Const e)
  end.

Recall that a regular Ltac pattern variable ?X only matches terms that *do not mention new variables introduced within the pattern.* In the naïve implementation, the case for matching function abstractions matches the function body in a way that prevents it from mentioning the function argument. The code structures the function body in a way that leads to independent problems, but we could change it so that it handles function abstractions that ignore their arguments.

To handle functions in general, we use the pattern variable form @?X, which allows X to mention newly introduced variables that are declared explicitly. A use of @?X must be followed by a list of the local variables that may be mentioned. The variable X then comes to stand for a Gallina function over the values of those variables. For instance,

Reset *refl'*.
Ltac *refl'* e :=

```
match e with
  | ?E1 + ?E2 ⇒
    let r1 := refl' E1 in
    let r2 := refl' E2 in
      constr:(Plus r1 r2)

  | fun x : nat ⇒ @?E1 x ⇒
    let r1 := refl' E1 in
      constr:(Abs r1)

  | _ ⇒ constr:(Const e)
end.
```

Now, in the abstraction case, we bind *E1* as a function from an *x* value to the value of the abstraction body. Unfortunately, the recursive call there is not destined for success. It will match the same abstraction pattern and trigger another recursive call, and so on, through infinite recursion. One last refactoring yields a working procedure. The key idea is to consider every input to *refl'* as *a function over the values of variables introduced during recursion*.

```
Reset refl'.
Ltac refl' e :=
  match eval simpl in e with
    | fun x : ?T ⇒ @?E1 x + @?E2 x ⇒
      let r1 := refl' E1 in
      let r2 := refl' E2 in
        constr:(fun x ⇒ Plus (r1 x) (r2 x))

    | fun (x : ?T) (y : nat) ⇒ @?E1 x y ⇒
      let r1 := refl' (fun p : T × nat ⇒ E1 (fst p) (snd p)) in
        constr:(fun x ⇒ Abs (fun y ⇒ r1 (x, y)))

    | _ ⇒ constr:(fun x ⇒ Const (e x))
end.
```

Note how even the addition case now works in terms of functions, with @?*X* patterns. The abstraction case introduces a new variable by extending the type used to represent the free variables. In particular, the argument to *refl'* uses type *T* to represent all free variables. We extend the type to *T* × **nat** for the type representing free variable values within the abstraction body. A bit of bookkeeping with pairs and their projections produces an appropriate version of the abstraction body to pass in a recursive call. To ensure that this repackaging of terms does

not interfere with pattern matching, we add an extra `simpl` reduction
on the function argument, in the first line of the body of *refl'*.

Now one more tactic provides an example of how to apply reification.
Let us consider goals that are equalities between terms that can be reified. We want to change such goals into equalities between appropriate
calls to termDenote.

Ltac *refl* :=
  match goal with
    | [⊢ ?*E1* = ?*E2*] ⇒
      let *E1'* := *refl'* (fun _ : **unit** ⇒ *E1*) in
      let *E2'* := *refl'* (fun _ : **unit** ⇒ *E2*) in
        change (termDenote (*E1'* tt) = termDenote (*E2'* tt));
          cbv beta iota delta [fst snd]
  end.

Goal (fun (x y : **nat**) ⇒ x + y + 13) = (fun (_ z : **nat**) ⇒ z).
  refl.

  =================================

  termDenote
    (Abs
      (fun y : **nat** ⇒
      Abs (fun $y0$: **nat** ⇒ Plus (Plus (Const y) (Const $y0$))
      (Const 13)))) =
  termDenote (Abs (fun _ : **nat** ⇒ Abs (fun $y0$: **nat** ⇒ Const $y0$)))

Abort.

The encoding here uses Coq functions to represent binding within
the terms we reify, which makes it difficult to implement certain functions over reified terms. An alternative would be to represent variables
with numbers. This can be done by writing a slightly smarter reification function that identifies variable references by detecting when term
arguments are just compositions of **fst** and **snd**; from the order of the
compositions we may read off the variable number. The details are left
as an exercise (though not a trivial one) for the reader.

PART IV

The Big Picture

16   Proving in the Large

It is somewhat unfortunate that the term *theorem proving* looks so much like the word *theory*. Most researchers and practitioners in software assume that mechanized theorem proving is profoundly impractical. Indeed, until recently, most advances in theorem proving for higher-order logics have been largely theoretical. However, starting at the beginning of the twenty-first century, there was a surge in the use of proof assistants in serious verification efforts. That line of work is still quite new, but I believe it is not too soon to distill some lessons on how to work effectively with large formal proofs.

Thus, this chapter discusses structuring and maintaining large Coq developments.

16.1 Ltac Antipatterns

In this book, I follow an unusual style in which proofs are not considered finished until they are fully automated, in a certain sense. Each such theorem is proved by a single tactic. Since Ltac is a Turing-complete programming language, it is not hard to squeeze arbitrary heuristics into single tactics, using operators like the semicolon to combine steps. In contrast, most Ltac proofs "in the wild" consist of many steps, performed by individual tactics followed by periods. Is it really worth drawing a distinction between proof steps terminated by semicolons and steps terminated by periods?

I argue that this is, in fact, a very important distinction, with serious consequences for a majority of important verification domains. The more uninteresting drudge work a proof domain involves, the more important it is to prove theorems with single tactics. From an automation standpoint, single-tactic proofs can be extremely effective, and automation becomes more and more critical as proofs are populated by more uninteresting detail. In this section, I give some examples of the consequences of more common proof styles.

As a running example, consider a basic language of arithmetic expressions, an interpreter for it, and a transformation that scales up every constant in an expression.

```
Inductive exp : Set :=
| Const : nat → exp
| Plus : exp → exp → exp.
```

```
Fixpoint eval (e : exp) : nat :=
  match e with
    | Const n ⇒ n
    | Plus e1 e2 ⇒ eval e1 + eval e2
  end.
```

```
Fixpoint times (k : nat) (e : exp) : exp :=
  match e with
    | Const n ⇒ Const (k × n)
    | Plus e1 e2 ⇒ Plus (times k e1) (times k e2)
  end.
```

We can write a manual proof that **times** really implements multiplication.

```
Theorem eval_times : ∀ k e,
  eval (times k e) = k × eval e.
  induction e.

  trivial.

  simpl.
  rewrite IHe1.
  rewrite IHe2.
  rewrite mult_plus_distr_l.
  trivial.
Qed.
```

We use spaces to separate the two inductive cases, but note that these spaces have no real semantic content; Coq does not enforce that spacing matches the real case structure of a proof. The second case mentions automatically generated hypothesis names explicitly. As a result, innocuous changes to the theorem statement can invalidate the proof.

```
Reset eval_times.
```

```
Theorem eval_times : ∀ k x,
  eval (times k x) = k × eval x.
```

```
  induction x.
  trivial.
  simpl.
  rewrite IHe1.
```

Error: The reference IHe1 was not found in the current
environment.

The inductive hypotheses are named *IHx1* and *IHx2* now, not *IHe1*
and *IHe2*.

Abort.

We might decide to use a more explicit invocation of induction to
give explicit binders for all the names that will be referenced later in
the proof.

```
Theorem eval_times : ∀ k  e,
    eval (times k  e) = k × eval e.
    induction e as [ | ? IHe1 ? IHe2 ].

  trivial.

  simpl.
  rewrite IHe1.
  rewrite IHe2.
  rewrite mult_plus_distr_l.
  trivial.
Qed.
```

We pass induction an *intro pattern*, using a | character to sepa-
rate instructions for the different inductive cases. Within a case, we
write ? to ask Coq to generate a name automatically, and we write an
explicit name to assign that name to the corresponding new variable. It
is apparent that in order to use intro patterns to avoid proof brittleness,
we need to keep track of the seemingly unimportant facts of the orders
in which variables are introduced. Thus, the script keeps working if we
replace *e* by *x*, but it has become more cluttered. Arguably, neither
proof is easy to follow.

That category of complaint has to do with understanding proofs as
static artifacts. As with programming in general, with serious projects
it is more important to be able to support evolution of proofs as specifications change. Unstructured proofs like the preceding examples can be
very hard to update in concert with theorem statements. For instance,
consider how the last proof script plays out when we modify times to
introduce a bug.

```
Reset times.
Fixpoint times (k : nat) (e : exp) : exp :=
  match e with
    | Const n ⇒ Const (1 + k × n)
    | Plus e1 e2 ⇒ Plus (times k e1) (times k e2)
  end.
```

```
Theorem eval_times : ∀ k e,
  eval (times k e) = k × eval e.
  induction e as [ | ? IHe1 ? IHe2 ].

  trivial.

  simpl.

  rewrite IHe1.
```

```
Error: The reference IHe1 was not found in the current
environment.
```

```
Abort.
```

What went wrong? The problem is that `trivial` never fails. Originally, `trivial` had been succeeding in proving an equality that follows by reflexivity. The change to `times` leads to a case where that equality is no longer true. The invocation `trivial` leaves the false equality in place, and we continue on to the span of tactics intended for the second inductive case. Unfortunately, those tactics end up being applied to the *first* case instead.

The problem with `trivial` could be solved by writing `solve [ trivial ]` instead, for instance, so that an error is signaled early on if something unexpected happens. However, the root problem is that the syntax of a tactic invocation does not imply how many subgoals it produces. Even more confusing instances of this problem are possible. For example, if a lemma L is modified to take an extra hypothesis, then uses of `apply L` will generate more subgoals than before. Old unstructured proof scripts will become hopelessly jumbled, with tactics applied to inappropriate subgoals. Because of the lack of structure, there is usually relatively little to be gleaned from knowledge of the precise point in a proof script where an error is raised.

```
Reset times.
Fixpoint times (k : nat) (e : exp) : exp :=
  match e with
    | Const n ⇒ Const (k × n)
    | Plus e1 e2 ⇒ Plus (times k e1) (times k e2)
```

end.

Many real developments try to make essentially unstructured proofs look structured by applying careful indentation conventions, idempotent case marker tactics included solely to serve as documentation, and so on. All these strategies suffer from the same kind of failure of abstraction that was just demonstrated. I like to say that if one finds oneself caring about indentation in a proof script, it is a sign that the script is structured poorly.

We can rewrite the current proof with a single tactic.

```
Theorem eval_times : ∀ k e,
  eval (times k e) = k × eval e.
  induction e as [ | ? IHe1 ? IHe2 ]; [
    trivial
    | simpl; rewrite IHe1; rewrite IHe2; rewrite mult_plus_distr_l;
      trivial ].
Qed.
```

We use the form of the semicolon operator that allows a different tactic to be specified for each generated subgoal. This change improves the robustness of the script: we no longer need to worry about tactics from one case being applied to a different case. Still, the proof script is not especially readable. Probably most readers would not find it helpful in explaining why the theorem is true. The same could be said for scripts using the *bullets* or curly braces provided by Coq 8.4, which allow code like this to be stepped through interactively, with periods in place of the semicolons, while representing proof structure in a way that is enforced by Coq. Interactive replay of scripts becomes easier, but readability is not really helped.

The situation gets worse in considering extensions to the theorem we want to prove. Let us add multiplication nodes to the **exp** type and see how the proof fares.

```
Reset exp.
```

```
Inductive exp : Set :=
| Const : nat → exp
| Plus : exp → exp → exp
| Mult : exp → exp → exp.
```

```
Fixpoint eval (e : exp) : nat :=
  match e with
    | Const n ⇒ n
    | Plus e1 e2 ⇒ eval e1 + eval e2
    | Mult e1 e2 ⇒ eval e1 × eval e2
```

```
   end.
Fixpoint times (k : nat) (e : exp) : exp :=
   match e with
     | Const n ⇒ Const (k × n)
     | Plus e1 e2 ⇒ Plus (times k e1) (times k e2)
     | Mult e1 e2 ⇒ Mult (times k e1) e2
   end.
Theorem eval_times : ∀ k e,
   eval (times k e) = k × eval e.
   induction e as [ | ? IHe1 ? IHe2 ]; [
     trivial
     | simpl; rewrite IHe1; rewrite IHe2; rewrite mult_plus_distr_l;
       trivial ].
```

```
Error: Expects a disjunctive pattern with 3 branches.
```

```
Abort.
```

Unsurprisingly, the old proof fails, because it explicitly says that there are two inductive cases. To update the script, we must, at a minimum, remember the order in which the inductive cases are generated, so that we can insert the new case in the appropriate place. Even then, it will be painful to add the case, because we cannot walk through proof steps interactively when they occur inside an explicit set of cases.

```
Theorem eval_times : ∀ k e,
   eval (times k e) = k × eval e.
   induction e as [ | ? IHe1 ? IHe2 | ? IHe1 ? IHe2 ]; [
     trivial
     | simpl; rewrite IHe1; rewrite IHe2; rewrite mult_plus_distr_l;
       trivial
     | simpl; rewrite IHe1; rewrite mult_assoc; trivial ].
Qed.
```

Now we are in a position to see that the style of proof followed in most of this book is preferable.

```
Reset eval_times.
```

```
Hint Rewrite mult_plus_distr_l.
```

```
Theorem eval_times : ∀ k e,
   eval (times k e) = k × eval e.
   induction e; crush.
Qed.
```

This style is motivated by a hard truth: one person's manual proof script is almost always inscrutable to everyone else. I claim that step-by-step formal proofs are a poor way of conveying information. Thus, we might as well cut out the steps and automate as much as possible.

What about the illustrative value of proofs? Most informal proofs are read to convey the big ideas of proofs. How can reading `induction` e; *crush* convey any big ideas? My position is that any ideas that standard automation can find are not very big, and big ideas should be expressed through lemmas that are added as hints.

An example should help illustrate what I mean. Consider this function, which rewrites an expression using associativity of addition and multiplication:

```
Fixpoint reassoc (e : exp) : exp :=
  match e with
    | Const _ ⇒ e
    | Plus e1 e2 ⇒
      let e1' := reassoc e1 in
      let e2' := reassoc e2 in
        match e2' with
          | Plus e21 e22 ⇒ Plus (Plus e1' e21) e22
          | _ ⇒ Plus e1' e2'
        end
    | Mult e1 e2 ⇒
      let e1' := reassoc e1 in
      let e2' := reassoc e2 in
        match e2' with
          | Mult e21 e22 ⇒ Mult (Mult e1' e21) e22
          | _ ⇒ Mult e1' e2'
        end
  end.

Theorem reassoc_correct : ∀ e, eval (reassoc e) = eval e.
  induction e; crush;
    match goal with
      | [ ⊢ context[match ?E with Const _ ⇒ _ | _ ⇒ _ end] ] ⇒
        destruct E; crush
    end.
```

One subgoal remains.

```
IHe2 : eval e3 × eval e4 = eval e2
============================
  eval e1 × eval e3 × eval e4 = eval e1 × eval e2
```

The *crush* tactic does not know how to finish this goal. We could finish the proof manually.

    rewrite ← *IHe2*; *crush.*

However, the proof would be easier to understand and maintain if we separated this insight into a separate lemma.

    Abort.

    Lemma rewr : ∀ a b c d, $b \times c = d \rightarrow a \times b \times c = a \times d$.
      crush.
    Qed.

    Hint Resolve rewr.

    Theorem reassoc_correct : ∀ e, eval (reassoc e) = eval e.
      induction e; *crush*;
        match goal with
          | [⊢ context[match ?E with Const _ ⇒ _ | _ ⇒ _ end]] ⇒
            destruct E; *crush*
        end.
    Qed.

In the limit, a complicated inductive proof might rely on one hint for each inductive case. The lemma for each hint could restate the associated case. Compared to manual proof scripts, we arrive at more readable results. Scripts no longer need to depend on the order in which cases are generated. The lemmas are easier to digest separately than are fragments of tactic code, since lemma statements include complete proof contexts. Such contexts can only be extracted from monolithic manual proofs by stepping through scripts interactively.

The more common situation is that a large induction has several easy cases that automation makes short work of. In the remaining cases, automation performs some standard simplification. Among these cases, some may require quite involved proofs; such a case may deserve a hint lemma of its own, where the lemma statement may copy the simplified version of the case. Alternatively, the proof script for the main theorem may be extended with some automation code targeted at the specific case. Even such targeted scripting is more desirable than manual proving, because it may be read and understood without knowledge of a proof's hierarchical structure, case ordering, or name-binding structure.

A competing alternative to the common style of Coq tactics is the *declarative style*, most frequently associated today with the Isar [47] language. A declarative proof script is very explicit about subgoal structure and introduction of local names, aiming for human readability. The coding of proof automation is taken to be outside the scope of the proof language, an assumption related to the idea that it is not worth building new automation for each serious theorem. I have shown many examples of theorem-specific automation, which I believe is crucial for scaling to significant results. Declarative proof scripts make it easier to read scripts to modify them for theorem statement changes, but the alternative *adaptive style* in this book allows use of the *same* scripts for many versions of a theorem.

Perhaps I am a pessimist for thinking that fully formal proofs will inevitably consist of details that are uninteresting to people, but it is my preference to focus on conveying proof-specific details through choice of lemmas. Additionally, adaptive Ltac scripts contain bits of automation that can be understood in isolation. For instance, in a big `repeat match` loop, each case can generally be digested separately, which is a big contrast from trying to understand the hierarchical structure of a script in a more common style. Adaptive scripts rely on variable binding, but generally only over very small scopes, whereas understanding a traditional script requires tracking the identities of local variables potentially across pages of code.

One might also wonder why it makes sense to prove all theorems automatically (in the sense of adaptive proof scripts) but not construct all programs automatically. My view is that *program synthesis* is a very useful idea that deserves broader application. In practice, there are difficult obstacles in the way of finding a program automatically from its specification. A typical specification is not exhaustive in its description of program properties. For instance, details of performance on particular machine architectures are often omitted. As a result, a synthesized program may be correct in some sense while suffering from deficiencies in other senses. Program synthesis research will continue to come up with ways of dealing with this problem, but the situation for theorem proving is fundamentally different. Following mathematical practice, the only property of a formal proof that we care about is which theorem it proves, and it is trivial to check this property automatically. In other words, with a simple criterion for what makes a proof acceptable, automatic search is straightforward. Of course, in practice we also care about understandability of proofs to facilitate long-term maintenance, which is what motivates the techniques I have just outlined. The next section gives some related advice.

16.2   Debugging and Maintaining Automation

Fully automated proofs are desirable because they open up possibilities for automatic adaptation to changes of specification. A well-engineered script within a narrow domain can survive many changes to the formulation of the problem it solves. Still, when one works with higher-order logic, most theorems fall within no obvious decidable theories. It is inevitable that most long-lived automated proofs will need updating.

Before we are ready to update proofs, we need to write them. While fully automated scripts are most robust to changes of specification, it is hard to write every new proof directly in that form. Instead, it is useful to begin a theorem with exploratory proving and then gradually refine it into a suitable automated form.

Consider this theorem from Chapter 8, which we begin by proving in a mostly manual way, invoking *crush* after each step to discharge any simple cases first. The manual effort involves choosing which expressions to case-analyze on.

Theorem cfold_correct : $\forall$ t (e : **exp** t),
  expDenote e = expDenote (cfold e).
  induction e; *crush*.

  dep_destruct (cfold *e1*); *crush.*
  dep_destruct (cfold *e2*); *crush.*

  dep_destruct (cfold *e1*); *crush.*
  dep_destruct (cfold *e2*); *crush.*

  dep_destruct (cfold *e1*); *crush.*
  dep_destruct (cfold *e2*); *crush.*

  dep_destruct (cfold *e1*); *crush.*
  dep_destruct (expDenote *e1*); *crush.*

  dep_destruct (cfold *e*); *crush.*

  dep_destruct (cfold *e*); *crush.*
Qed.

In this complete proof, it is hard to avoid noticing a pattern. We rework the proof, abstracting over the patterns we find.

Reset cfold_correct.

Theorem cfold_correct : $\forall$ t (e : **exp** t),
  expDenote e = expDenote (cfold e).
  induction e; *crush*.

The expression we want to destruct here turns out to be the discriminee of a `match`, and we can easily write a tactic that destructs all such expressions.

Ltac t :=
  repeat (match goal with
            | [⊢ context[match ?E with NConst _ ⇒ _
                           | _ ⇒ _ end]] ⇒
        dep_destruct E
     end; *crush*).

  t.

This tactic invocation discharges the whole case. It does the same on the next two cases, but it gets stuck on the fourth case.

  t.

  t.

  t.

The subgoal's conclusion is

  ============================

  (if expDenote $e1$ then expDenote (cfold $e2$)
     else expDenote (cfold $e3$)) =
  expDenote (if expDenote $e1$ then cfold $e2$ else cfold $e3$)

We need to expand the t tactic to handle this case.

Ltac t' :=
  repeat (match goal with
            | [⊢ context[match ?E with NConst _ ⇒ _
                           | _ ⇒ _ end]] ⇒
        dep_destruct E
        | [⊢ (if ?E then _ else _) = _] ⇒ destruct E
     end; *crush*).

  t'.

Now the goal is discharged, but t' has no effect on the next subgoal.

  t'.

A final revision of t finishes the proof.

Ltac t'' :=
  repeat (match goal with
            | [⊢ context[match ?E with NConst _ ⇒ _
                           | _ ⇒ _ end]] ⇒
        dep_destruct E

$$| [\vdash (\text{if } ?E \text{ then } \_ \text{ else } \_) = \_] \Rightarrow \text{destruct } E$$
$$| [\vdash \text{context}[\text{match pairOut } ?E \text{ with Some } \_ \Rightarrow \_$$
$$| \text{ None} \Rightarrow \_ \text{ end}]] \Rightarrow$$
$$dep\_destruct\ E$$
end; *crush*).

t''.

t''.

Qed.

We can take the final tactic and move it into the initial part of the proof script, arriving at a nicely automated proof.

Reset t.

Theorem cfold_correct : $\forall\ t\ (e : \mathbf{exp}\ t)$,
   expDenote e = expDenote (cfold e).
   induction e; *crush*;
      repeat (match goal with
                  $| [\vdash \text{context}[\text{match } ?E \text{ with NConst } \_ \Rightarrow \_$
                              $| \_ \Rightarrow \_ \text{ end}]] \Rightarrow$
                  $dep\_destruct\ E$
                  $| [\vdash (\text{if } ?E \text{ then } \_ \text{ else } \_) = \_] \Rightarrow \text{destruct } E$
                  $| [\vdash \text{context}[\text{match pairOut } ?E \text{ with Some } \_ \Rightarrow \_$
                              $| \text{ None} \Rightarrow \_ \text{ end}]] \Rightarrow$
                  $dep\_destruct\ E$
               end; *crush*).

Qed.

Even after we put together automated proofs, we must deal with specification changes that can invalidate them. It is not generally possible to step through single-tactic proofs interactively. There is a command Debug On that lets us step through points in tactic execution, but the debugger tends to make counterintuitive choices of which points we would like to stop at, and per-point output is quite verbose, so most Coq users do not find this debugging mode very helpful. How are we to understand what has broken in a script that used to work?

An example helps demonstrate a useful approach. Consider what would have happened in the proof of reassoc_correct if we had first added a misleading rewrite hint.

Reset reassoc_correct.

Theorem confounder : $\forall\ e1\ e2\ e3$,
   eval $e1$ × eval $e2$ × eval $e3$ = eval $e1$ × (eval $e2$ + 1 - 1) × eval $e3$.
   crush.

Qed.

Hint Rewrite confounder.

Theorem reassoc_correct : ∀ *e*, eval (reassoc *e*) = eval *e*.
  induction *e*; *crush*;
    match goal with
      | [⊢ context[match ?*E* with Const _ ⇒ _ | _ ⇒ _ end]] ⇒
        destruct *E*; *crush*
    end.

One subgoal remains.

===============================
  eval *e1* × (eval *e3* + 1 - 1) × eval *e4* = eval *e1* × eval *e2*

The poorly chosen rewrite rule fired, changing the goal to a form where another hint no longer applies. Imagine that we are in the middle of a large development with many hints. How would we diagnose the problem? We might not be sure which case of the inductive proof has gone wrong. It is useful to separate out the automation procedure and apply it manually.

Restart.

Ltac *t* := *crush*; match goal with
          | [⊢ context[match ?*E* with Const _ ⇒ _
                | _ ⇒ _ end]] ⇒
        destruct *E*; *crush*
      end.

  induction *e*.

Since we see the subgoals before any simplification occurs, it is clear that we are looking at the case for constants. Then we can make short work of it.

  t.

The next subgoal, for addition, is also discharged without trouble.

  t.

The final subgoal is for multiplication, and it is here that the proof got stuck.

  t.

What is *t* doing? The **info** command can help us find out. (In the most recent Coq release, **info** no longer functions, but I hope it returns.)

```
Undo.
info t.
```

```
== simpl in *; intuition; subst; autorewrite with core in *;
     simpl in *; intuition; subst; autorewrite with core in *;
     simpl in *; intuition; subst; destruct (reassoc e2).
   simpl in *; intuition.
```

```
   simpl in *; intuition.
```

```
   simpl in *; intuition; subst; autorewrite with core in *;
       refine (eq_ind_r
                 (fun n : nat ⇒
                    n × (eval e3 + 1 - 1) × eval e4
                    = eval e1 × eval e2) _ IHe1);
       autorewrite with core in *; simpl in *; intuition;
     subst; autorewrite with core in *; simpl in *;
   intuition; subst.
```

A detailed trace of t's execution appears. Since we are using the very general *crush* tactic, many of these steps have no effect and only occur as instances of a more general strategy. We can copy-and-paste the details to see where things go wrong.

```
Undo.
```

We arbitrarily split the script into chunks. The first few seem not to do any harm.

```
simpl in *; intuition; subst; autorewrite with core in *.
simpl in *; intuition; subst; autorewrite with core in *.
simpl in *; intuition; subst; destruct (reassoc e2).
simpl in *; intuition.
simpl in *; intuition.
```

The next step is revealed as the culprit, bringing us to the final unproved subgoal.

```
simpl in *; intuition; subst; autorewrite with core in *.
```

We can split the steps further to determine the problem.

```
Undo.
```

```
simpl in *.
intuition.
subst.
```

```
autorewrite with core in *.
```

It is the final of these four tactics that made the rewrite. We can find out exactly what happened. The `info` command presents hierarchical views of proof steps, and we can zoom down to a lower level of detail by applying `info` to one of the steps in the original trace.

```
Undo.
```

```
info autorewrite with core in *.
```

$$== \mathsf{refine}\ (\mathsf{eq\_ind\_r}\ (\mathsf{fun}\ n : \mathbf{nat} \Rightarrow n = \mathsf{eval}\ e1 \times \mathsf{eval}\ e2)\ \_$$
$$(\mathsf{confounder}\ (\mathsf{reassoc}\ e1)\ e3\ e4)).$$

We can see that theorem **confounder** is the final culprit. At this point, we could remove that hint, prove an alternative version of the key lemma **rewr**, or find some other remedy. Fixing this kind of problem tends to be relatively easy once the problem is revealed.

```
Abort.
```

Sometimes a change to a development has undesirable performance consequences, even if it does not prevent any proof scripts from completing. If the performance consequences are severe enough, the proof scripts can be considered broken for practical purposes.

Here is one example of a performance surprise:

```
Section slow.
  Hint Resolve eq_trans.
```

The central element of the problem is the addition of transitivity as a hint. With transitivity available, it is easy for proof search to wind up exploring exponential search spaces. We also add a few other arbitrary variables and hypotheses that will lead to trouble later.

```
Variable A : Set.
Variables P Q R S : A → A → Prop.
Variable f : A → A.
```
$$\mathsf{Hypothesis}\ H1 : \forall\ x\ y,\ P\ x\ y \to Q\ x\ y \to R\ x\ y \to f\ x = f\ y.$$
$$\mathsf{Hypothesis}\ H2 : \forall\ x\ y,\ S\ x\ y \to R\ x\ y.$$

We prove a simple lemma very quickly, using the `Time` command to measure exactly how quickly.

$$\mathsf{Lemma\ slow} : \forall\ x\ y,\ P\ x\ y \to Q\ x\ y \to S\ x\ y \to f\ x = f\ y.$$
```
    Time eauto 6.
```

```
Finished transaction in 0. secs (0.068004u,0.s)
```

```
Qed.
```

Now we add a different hypothesis, which is innocent enough; in fact, it is even provable as a theorem.

```
Hypothesis H3 : ∀ x y, x = y → f x = f y.
```

```
Lemma slow' : ∀ x y, P x y → Q x y → S x y → f x = f y.
   Time eauto 6.
```

```
Finished transaction in 2. secs (1.264079u,0.s)
```

Why has the search time gone up so much? The `info` command is not much help, since it only shows the result of search, not all the paths that turned out to be worthless.

```
Restart.
info eauto 6.
```

```
== intro x; intro y; intro H; intro H0; intro H4;
      simple eapply eq_trans.
   simple apply eq_refl.

   simple eapply eq_trans.
   simple apply eq_refl.

   simple eapply eq_trans.
   simple apply eq_refl.

   simple apply H1.
   eexact H.

   eexact H0.

   simple apply H2; eexact H4.
```

This output does not reveal why proof search takes so long, but it does provide a clue that is useful if we have forgotten that we added transitivity as a hint. The `eauto` tactic is applying depth-first search, and the relevant proof script is buried inside a chain of pointless invocations of transitivity, where each invocation uses reflexivity to discharge one subgoal. Each increment to the depth argument to `eauto` adds another unnecessary call to transitivity. This wasted proof effort only adds linear time overhead, as long as proof search never makes false steps. No false steps were made before we added the new hypothesis, but somehow the

addition made possible a new faulty path. To understand which paths
we enabled, we can use the **debug** command.

```
Restart.
debug eauto 6.
```

The output is a large proof tree. The beginning of the tree is enough
to reveal what is happening:

1 *depth*=6
1.1 *depth*=6 intro
1.1.1 *depth*=6 intro
1.1.1.1 *depth*=6 intro
1.1.1.1.1 *depth*=6 intro
1.1.1.1.1.1 *depth*=6 intro
1.1.1.1.1.1.1 *depth*=5 apply *H3*
1.1.1.1.1.1.1.1 *depth*=4 eapply eq_trans
1.1.1.1.1.1.1.1.1 *depth*=4 apply eq_refl
1.1.1.1.1.1.1.1.1.1.1 *depth*=3 eapply eq_trans
1.1.1.1.1.1.1.1.1.1.1.1 *depth*=3 apply eq_refl
1.1.1.1.1.1.1.1.1.1.1.1.1.1 *depth*=2 eapply eq_trans
1.1.1.1.1.1.1.1.1.1.1.1.1.1 *depth*=2 apply eq_refl
1.1.1.1.1.1.1.1.1.1.1.1.1.1.1.1 *depth*=1 eapply eq_trans
1.1.1.1.1.1.1.1.1.1.1.1.1.1.1.1 *depth*=1 apply eq_refl
1.1.1.1.1.1.1.1.1.1.1.1.1.1.1.1.1 *depth*=0 eapply eq_trans
1.1.1.1.1.1.1.1.1.1.1.1.1.1.1.2 *depth*=1 apply sym_eq ; trivial
1.1.1.1.1.1.1.1.1.1.1.1.1.1.2.1 *depth*=0 eapply eq_trans
1.1.1.1.1.1.1.1.1.1.1.1.1.1.3 *depth*=0 eapply eq_trans
1.1.1.1.1.1.1.1.1.1.1.1.1.2 *depth*=2 apply sym_eq ; trivial
1.1.1.1.1.1.1.1.1.1.1.1.1.2.1 *depth*=1 eapply eq_trans
1.1.1.1.1.1.1.1.1.1.1.1.1.2.1.1 *depth*=1 apply eq_refl
1.1.1.1.1.1.1.1.1.1.1.1.1.2.1.1.1 *depth*=0 eapply eq_trans
1.1.1.1.1.1.1.1.1.1.1.1.1.2.1.2 *depth*=1 apply sym_eq ; trivial
1.1.1.1.1.1.1.1.1.1.1.1.1.2.1.2.1 *depth*=0 eapply eq_trans
1.1.1.1.1.1.1.1.1.1.1.1.1.2.1.3 *depth*=0 eapply eq_trans

The first choice **eauto** makes is to apply *H3*, since *H3* has the fewest
hypotheses of all the hypotheses and hints that match. However, it
turns out that the single hypothesis generated is unprovable. That does
not stop **eauto** from trying to prove it with an exponentially sized tree
of applications of transitivity, reflexivity, and symmetry of equality. It is
the children of the initial **apply** *H3* that account for all the additional
time in proof execution. In a more realistic development, we might

conclude from this output of `debug` that adding transitivity as a hint was a bad idea.

```
  Qed.
End slow.
```

Even greater problems can result from importing library modules with commands like `Require Import`. Such a command imports not just the Gallina terms from a module but also all the hints for `auto`, `eauto`, and `autorewrite`. Some very recent versions of Coq include mechanisms for removing hints from databases, but the proper solution is to be very conservative in exporting hints from modules. Consider putting hints in named databases, so that they may be used only when called upon explicitly, as demonstrated in Chapter 13.

It is also easy to end up with a proof script that uses too much memory. As tactics run, they avoid generating proof terms, since serious proof search will consider many possible avenues, and we do not want to build proof terms for subproofs that end up unused. Instead, tactic execution maintains *thunks* (suspended computations, represented with closures), such that a tactic's proof-producing thunk is only executed when we run `Qed`. These thunks can use up large amounts of space, such that a proof script exhausts available memory, even when we know that we could have used much less memory by forcing some thunks earlier.

The `abstract` tactical helps us force thunks by proving some subgoals as their own lemmas. For instance, a proof `induction` x; *crush* can in many cases be made to use significantly less peak memory by changing it to `induction` x; `abstract` *crush*. The main limitation of `abstract` is that it can only be applied to subgoals that are proved completely, with no undetermined unification variables in their initial states. Still, many large automated proofs can realize vast memory savings via `abstract`.

16.3 Modules

The examples in Chapter 15 of proof by reflection demonstrate opportunities for implementing abstract proof strategies with stronger formal guarantees than can be had with Ltac scripting. Coq's *module system* provides another tool for more rigorous development of generic theorems. This feature is inspired by the module systems found in Standard ML [22] and OCaml, and the discussion that follows assumes familiarity with the basics of one of those systems.

ML modules facilitate the grouping of abstract types with operations over those types. Moreover, there is support for *functors*, which are functions from modules to modules. A canonical example of a functor is one that builds a data structure implementation from a module that describes a domain of keys and its associated comparison operations.

When we add modules to a base language with dependent types, it becomes possible to use modules and functors to formalize kinds of reasoning that are common in algebra. For instance, the following module signature captures the essence of the algebraic structure known as a group. A group consists of a carrier set G, an associative binary operation f, a left identity element id for f, and an operation i that is a left inverse for f.

Module Type GROUP.
  Parameter G : Set.
  Parameter $f : G \rightarrow G \rightarrow G$.
  Parameter $id : G$.
  Parameter $i : G \rightarrow G$.

  Axiom *assoc* : $\forall\ a\ b\ c,\ f\ (f\ a\ b)\ c = f\ a\ (f\ b\ c)$.
  Axiom *ident* : $\forall\ a,\ f\ id\ a = a$.
  Axiom *inverse* : $\forall\ a,\ f\ (i\ a)\ a = id$.
End GROUP.

Many useful theorems hold of arbitrary groups. We capture some such theorem statements in another module signature.

Module Type GROUP_THEOREMS.
  Declare Module M : GROUP.

  Axiom *ident'* : $\forall\ a,\ M.f\ a\ M.id = a$.

  Axiom *inverse'* : $\forall\ a,\ M.f\ a\ (M.i\ a) = M.id$.

  Axiom *unique_ident* : $\forall\ id',\ (\forall\ a,\ M.f\ id'\ a = a) \rightarrow id' = M.id$.
End GROUP_THEOREMS.

We implement generic proofs of these theorems with a functor, whose input is an arbitrary group M.

Module GROUPPROOFS (M : GROUP) : GROUP_THEOREMS
  with Module M := M.

As in ML, Coq provides multiple options for ascribing signatures to modules. Here we use just the colon operator, which implements *opaque ascription*, hiding all details of the module not exposed by the signature. Another option is *transparent ascription* via the $<:$ operator, which checks for signature compatibility without hiding implementation details. Here we stick with opaque ascription but employ the `with` operation to add more detail to a signature, exposing just those implementation details that we need to. For instance, here we expose the underlying group representation set and operator definitions. Without such a refinement, we would get an output module proving theorems about some unknown group, which is not very useful. Also note that opaque ascription can in Coq have some undesirable consequences without analogues in ML, since not just the types but also the *definitions* of identifiers have significance in type checking and theorem proving.

```
Module M := M.
```
To ensure that the module we are building meets its signature, we add an extra local name for *M*, the functor argument.

```
Import M.
```
It would be inconvenient to repeat the prefix *M.* everywhere in theorem statements and proofs, so we bring all the identifiers of *M* into the local scope unqualified.

Now we are ready to prove the three theorems. The proofs are completely manual, which may seem ironic given the content of the previous sections. Nonetheless, short proof scripts that change infrequently may be worth leaving unautomated. It would take some effort to build suitable generic automation for these theorems about groups, so I stick with manual proof scripts to avoid distracting from the main message here. We take the proofs from the Wikipedia page on elementary group theory.

```
Theorem inverse' : ∀ a, f a (i a) = id.
  intro.
  rewrite ← (ident (f a (i a))).
  rewrite ← (inverse (f a (i a))) at 1.
  rewrite assoc.
  rewrite assoc.
  rewrite ← (assoc (i a) a (i a)).
  rewrite inverse.
  rewrite ident.
  apply inverse.
Qed.

Theorem ident' : ∀ a, f a id = a.
  intro.
  rewrite ← (inverse a).
  rewrite ← assoc.
  rewrite inverse'.
  apply ident.
Qed.

Theorem unique_ident : ∀ id', (∀ a, f id' a = a) → id' = id.
  intros.
```

```
      rewrite ← (H id).
      symmetry.
      apply ident'.
   Qed.
End GROUPPROOFS.
```

We can show that the integers with + form a group.

```
Require Import ZArith.
Open Scope Z_scope.

Module INT.
   Definition G := Z.
   Definition f x y := x + y.
   Definition id := 0.
   Definition i x := -x.

   Theorem assoc : ∀ a b c, f (f a b) c = f a (f b c).
      unfold f; crush.
   Qed.
   Theorem ident : ∀ a, f id a = a.
      unfold f, id; crush.
   Qed.
   Theorem inverse : ∀ a, f (i a) a = id.
      unfold f, i, id; crush.
   Qed.
End INT.
```

Next, we can produce integer-specific versions of the generic group theorems.

```
Module INTPROOFS := GROUPPROOFS(INT).

Check IntProofs.unique_ident.
```

> *IntProofs.unique_ident*
>   : ∀ e' : Int.G, (∀ a : Int.G, Int.f e' a = a) → e' = Int.e

Projections like *Int.G* are known to be definitionally equal to the concrete values we have assigned to them, so this theorem yields as a trivial corollary the following more natural restatement.

```
Theorem unique_ident : ∀ id', (∀ a, id' + a = a) → id' = 0.
   exact IntProofs.unique_ident.
Qed.
```

As in ML, the module system provides an effective way to structure large developments. Unlike in ML, Coq modules add no expressiveness; we can implement any module as an inhabitant of a dependent record

type. It is the second-class nature of modules that makes them easier
to use than dependent records in many cases. Because modules may
only be used in quite restricted ways, it is easier to support convenient
module coding through special commands and editing modes, as the
preceding example demonstrates. An isomorphic implementation with
records would have suffered from lack of such conveniences as module
subtyping and importation of the fields of a module. On the other hand,
all module values must be determined statically, so modules may not
be computed, for instance, within the definitions of normal functions,
based on particular function parameters.

16.4   Build Processes

As in software development, large Coq projects are much more manage-
able when split across multiple files and when decomposed into libraries.
Coq and Proof General provide very good support for these activities.

Consider a library that I name LIB, housed in directory LIB and split
between files A.v, B.v, and C.v. A simple Makefile will compile the
library, relying on the standard Coq tool `coq_makefile` to do the hard
work.

```
MODULES := A B C
VS      := $(MODULES:%=%.v)

.PHONY: coq clean

coq: Makefile.coq
        $(MAKE) -f Makefile.coq

Makefile.coq: Makefile $(VS)
        coq_makefile -R . Lib $(VS) -o Makefile.coq

clean:: Makefile.coq
        $(MAKE) -f Makefile.coq clean
        rm -f Makefile.coq
```

The Makefile begins by defining a variable VS holding the list of
filenames to be included in the project. The primary target is `coq`,
which depends on the construction of an auxiliary Makefile called
`Makefile.coq`. Another rule explains how to build that file. We call
`coq_makefile`, using the -R flag to specify that files in the current directory should be considered to belong to the library LIB. This Makefile

will build a compiled version of each module, such that `X.v` is compiled into `X.vo`.

Now code in `B.v` may refer to definitions in `A.v` after running

`Require Import` Lib.A.

Library Lib is presented as a module, containing a submodule A, which contains the definitions from `A.v`. These are genuine modules in the sense of Coq's module system, and they may be passed to functors, and so on.

The command `Require Import` is a convenient combination of two more primitive commands. The `Require` command finds the `.vo` file containing the named module, ensuring that the module is loaded into memory. The `Import` command loads all top-level definitions of the named module into the current namespace, and it may be used with local modules that do not have corresponding `.vo` files. Another command, `Load`, is for inserting the contents of a named file verbatim. It is generally better to use the module-based commands, since they avoid rerunning proof scripts, and they facilitate reorganization of directory structure without the need to change code.

Now we would like to use the library from a different development, called Client and found in directory `CLIENT`, which has its own Makefile.

```
MODULES := D E
VS      := $(MODULES:%=%.v)

.PHONY: coq clean

coq: Makefile.coq
	$(MAKE) -f Makefile.coq

Makefile.coq: Makefile $(VS)
	coq_makefile -R LIB Lib -R . Client $(VS) \
		-o Makefile.coq

clean:: Makefile.coq
	$(MAKE) -f Makefile.coq clean
	rm -f Makefile.coq
```

We change the `coq_makefile` call to indicate where the library Lib is found. Now `D.v` and `E.v` can refer to definitions from Lib module A after running

Require Import Lib.A.

and E.v can refer to definitions from D.v by running

Require Import Client.D.

It can be useful to split a library into several files, but it is also inconvenient for client code to import library modules individually. We can get the best of both worlds by, for example, adding an extra source file Lib.v to Lib's directory and Makefile, where that file contains just this line:

Require Export Lib.A Lib.B Lib.C.

Now client code can import all definitions from all of Lib's modules simply by running

Require Import Lib.

The two Makefiles above share a lot of code, so, in practice, it is useful to define a common Makefile that is included by multiple library-specific Makefiles.

The remaining ingredient is the proper way of editing library code files in Proof General. Recall this snippet of .emacs code from Chapter 1, which tells Proof General where to find the library associated with this book:

```
(custom-set-variables
  ...
  '(coq-prog-args '("-I" "/path/to/cpdt/src"))
  ...
)
```

To do interactive editing of the current example, we just need to change the flags to point to the right places.

```
(custom-set-variables
  ...
; '(coq-prog-args '("-I" "/path/to/cpdt/src"))
  '(coq-prog-args '("-R" "LIB" "Lib" "-R" "CLIENT" "Client"))
  ...
)
```

When working on multiple projects, it is useful to leave multiple versions of this setting in the .emacs file, commenting out all but one of them at any moment. To switch between projects, change the commenting structure and restart Emacs.

Alternatively, we can revisit the directory-local settings approach and write the following into a file `.dir-locals.el` in `CLIENT`.

```
((coq-mode . ((coq-prog-args .
  ("-emacs-U" "-R" "LIB" "Lib" "-R" "CLIENT" "Client")))))
```

A downside of this approach is that users of the code may not want to trust the arbitrary Emacs Lisp programs that are allowed to be placed in such files and prefer to add mappings manually.

17   Reasoning about Programming Language Syntax

Reasoning about the syntax and semantics of programming languages is a popular application of proof assistants. Before proving the first theorem of this kind, it is necessary to choose a formal encoding of the informal notions of syntax, dealing with such issues as variable-binding conventions. I believe the pragmatic questions in this domain are far from settled and remain important open research problems. However, in this chapter, I demonstrate two underused encoding approaches. Note that I am not recommending either approach as a complete solution for all contexts. For a broader introduction to programming language formalization, using more elementary techniques, see *Software Foundations* by Pierce et al.[7]

This chapter is meant to serve as a case study, bringing together concepts from previous chapters. There is a concrete example of the importance of representation choices. Translating mathematics to Coq is not a deterministic process, and different creative choices can have big impacts. We will also see dependent types and scripted proof automation in action, applied to solve a particular problem as well as possible rather than to demonstrate new Coq concepts.

I make a few remarks intended to relate the material with common ideas in semantics, but readers not familiar with the theory of programming language semantics can safely disregard them.

We study a small programming language and reason about its semantics, expressed as an interpreter into Coq terms, much as in examples throughout the book. It is helpful to build a slight extension of *crush* that tries to apply the functional extensionality axiom, which says that two functions are equal if they map equal inputs to equal outputs (see Section 10.6).

```
Ltac ext := let x := fresh "x" in extensionality x.
```

---

7. http://www.cis.upenn.edu/~bcpierce/sf/

Ltac *pl* := *crush*; repeat (*ext* || f_equal; *crush*).

At this point in the book source, some auxiliary proofs also appear.

Here is a definition of the type system used throughout this chapter. It is for simply typed lambda calculus with natural numbers as the base type.

Inductive **type** : Type :=
| Nat : **type**
| Func : **type** → **type** → **type**.

Fixpoint typeDenote (t : **type**) : Type :=
  match t with
    | Nat ⇒ **nat**
    | Func $t1$ $t2$ ⇒ typeDenote $t1$ → typeDenote $t2$
  end.

Now we can choose how to represent the syntax of programs. The two sections of the chapter explore two such choices, demonstrating the effect the choice has on proof complexity.

17.1   Dependent de Bruijn Indices

The first encoding is the *dependent de Bruijn index encoding* (see Chapter 9). We represent program syntax terms in a type family parameterized by a list of types, representing the *typing context*, or information on which free variables are in scope and what their types are. Variables are represented in a way isomorphic to the natural numbers, where number 0 represents the first element in the context, number 1 the second element, and so on. Actually, instead of numbers, we use the **member** dependent type family from Chapter 9.

Module FIRSTORDER.

Here is the definition of the **term** type, including variables, constants, addition, function abstraction and application, and let binding of local variables:

Inductive **term** : **list type** → **type** → Type :=
| Var : ∀ G t, **member** t G → **term** G t

| Const : ∀ G, **nat** → **term** G Nat
| Plus : ∀ G, **term** G Nat → **term** G Nat → **term** G Nat

| Abs : ∀ G *dom ran*,

term (*dom* :: *G*) *ran* → **term** *G* (Func *dom ran*)
| App : ∀ *G dom ran*,
   term *G* (Func *dom ran*) → **term** *G dom* → **term** *G ran*

| Let : ∀ *G t1 t2*, **term** *G t1* → **term** (*t1* :: *G*) *t2* → **term** *G t2*.

Implicit Arguments Const [*G*].

Here are two example term encodings, the first of addition packaged as a two-argument curried function, and the second of a sample application of addition to constants:

Example add : **term** nil (Func Nat (Func Nat Nat)) :=
   Abs (Abs (Plus (Var (HNext HFirst)) (Var HFirst))).

Example three_the_hard_way : **term** nil Nat :=
   App (App add (Const 1)) (Const 2).

Since dependent typing ensures that any term is well-formed in its context and has a particular type, it is easy to translate syntactic terms into Coq values.

Fixpoint termDenote *G t* (*e* : **term** *G t*)
   : **hlist** typeDenote *G* → typeDenote *t* :=
   match *e* with
      | Var _ _ *x* ⇒ fun *s* ⇒ hget *s x*

      | Const _ *n* ⇒ fun _ ⇒ *n*
      | Plus _ *e1 e2* ⇒ fun *s* ⇒ termDenote *e1 s* + termDenote *e2 s*

      | Abs _ _ _ *e1* ⇒ fun *s* ⇒ fun *x* ⇒ termDenote *e1* (*x* ::: *s*)
      | App _ _ _ *e1 e2* ⇒ fun *s* ⇒
         (termDenote *e1 s*) (termDenote *e2 s*)

      | Let _ _ _ *e1 e2* ⇒ fun *s* ⇒
         termDenote *e2* (termDenote *e1 s* ::: *s*)
   end.

With this term representation, some program transformations are easy to implement and prove correct. Certainly we would worry if this were not the case for the *identity* transformation, which takes a term apart and reassembles it.

Fixpoint ident *G t* (*e* : **term** *G t*) : **term** *G t* :=
   match *e* with
      | Var _ _ *x* ⇒ Var *x*

```
    | Const _ n ⇒ Const n
    | Plus _ e1 e2 ⇒ Plus (ident e1) (ident e2)

    | Abs _ _ _ e1 ⇒ Abs (ident e1)
    | App _ _ _ e1 e2 ⇒ App (ident e1) (ident e2)

    | Let _ _ _ e1 e2 ⇒ Let (ident e1) (ident e2)
  end.

Theorem identSound : ∀ G t (e : term G t) s,
  termDenote (ident e) s = termDenote e s.
  induction e; pl.
Qed.
```

A slightly more ambitious transformation belongs to the family of *constant folding* optimizations used as examples in other chapters.

```
Fixpoint cfold G t (e : term G t) : term G t :=
  match e with
    | Plus _ e1 e2 ⇒
      let e1' := cfold e1 in
      let e2' := cfold e2 in
      let maybeOpt := match e1' return _ with
                        | Const _ n1 ⇒
                          match e2' return _ with
                            | Const _ n2 ⇒
                              Some (Const (n1 + n2))
                            | _ ⇒ None
                          end
                        | _ ⇒ None
                      end in
      match maybeOpt with
        | None ⇒ Plus e1' e2'
        | Some e' ⇒ e'
      end

    | Abs _ _ _ e1 ⇒ Abs (cfold e1)
    | App _ _ _ e1 e2 ⇒ App (cfold e1) (cfold e2)

    | Let _ _ _ e1 e2 ⇒ Let (cfold e1) (cfold e2)

    | e ⇒ e
  end.
```

The correctness proof is more complex, but only slightly so.

```
Theorem cfoldSound : ∀ G t (e : term G t) s,
   termDenote (cfold e) s = termDenote e s.
   induction e; pl;
     repeat (match goal with
               | [ ⊢ context[match ?E with Var _ _ _ ⇒ _
                                     | _ ⇒ _ end] ] ⇒
                  dep_destruct E
             end; pl).
Qed.
```

The transformations so far have been straightforward because they do not have interesting effects on the variable-binding structure of terms. The dependent de Bruijn representation is called *first-order* because it encodes variable identity explicitly; all such representations incur bookkeeping overheads in transformations that rearrange binding structure.

As an example of a more complex transformation, consider one that removes all uses of "let $x = e1$ in $e2$" by substituting $e1$ for x in $e2$. We implement the translation by pairing the compile-time typing environment with a run-time value environment or *substitution*, mapping each variable to a value to be substituted for it. Such a substitute term may be placed within a program in a position with a larger typing environment than applied at the point where the substitute term was chosen. To support such context transplantation, we need *lifting*, a standard de Bruijn indices operation. With dependent typing, lifting corresponds to weakening for typing judgments.

The fundamental goal of lifting is to add a new variable to a typing context, maintaining the validity of a term in the expanded context. To express the operation of adding a type to a context, we use a helper function insertAt.

```
Fixpoint insertAt (t : type) (G : list type) (n : nat) {struct n}
   : list type :=
   match n with
     | O ⇒ t :: G
     | S n' ⇒ match G with
                | nil ⇒ t :: G
                | t' :: G' ⇒ t' :: insertAt t G' n'
              end
   end.
```

Another function lifts bound variable instances, which we represent with **member** values.

```
Fixpoint liftVar t G (x : member t G) t' n
  : member t (insertAt t' G n) :=
  match x with
    | HFirst G' ⇒ match n return member t
                    (insertAt t' (t :: G') n) with
                    | O ⇒ HNext HFirst
                    | _ ⇒ HFirst
                  end
    | HNext t'' G' x' ⇒ match n return member t
                    (insertAt t' (t'' :: G') n) with
                    | O ⇒ HNext (HNext x')
                    | S n' ⇒ HNext (liftVar x' t' n')
                  end
end.
```

The final helper function for lifting allows us to insert a new variable anywhere in a typing context.

```
Fixpoint lift' G t' n t (e : term G t) : term (insertAt t' G n) t :=
  match e with
    | Var _ _ x ⇒ Var (liftVar x t' n)

    | Const _ n ⇒ Const n
    | Plus _ e1 e2 ⇒ Plus (lift' t' n e1) (lift' t' n e2)

    | Abs _ _ _ e1 ⇒ Abs (lift' t' (S n) e1)
    | App _ _ _ e1 e2 ⇒ App (lift' t' n e1) (lift' t' n e2)

    | Let _ _ _ e1 e2 ⇒ Let (lift' t' n e1) (lift' t' (S n) e2)
end.
```

In the Let removal transformation, we only need to apply lifting to add a new variable at the *beginning* of a typing context, so we package lifting into this final, simplified form.

```
Definition lift G t' t (e : term G t) : term (t' :: G) t :=
  lift' t' O e.
```

Finally, we can implement Let removal. The argument of type **hlist** (**term** G') G represents a substitution mapping each variable from context G into a term that is valid in context G'. Note how the Abs case (1) extends via lifting the substitution s to hold in the broader context of the abstraction body $e1$, and (2) maps the new first variable to itself.

It is only the Let case that maps a variable to any substitute besides itself.

Fixpoint unlet G t (e : **term** G t) G'
  : **hlist** (**term** G') G → **term** G' t :=
  match e with
    | Var _ _ x ⇒ fun s ⇒ hget s x

    | Const _ n ⇒ fun _ ⇒ Const n
    | Plus _ $e1$ $e2$ ⇒ fun s ⇒ Plus (unlet $e1$ s) (unlet $e2$ s)

    | Abs _ _ _ $e1$ ⇒ fun s ⇒
      Abs (unlet $e1$ (Var HFirst ::: hmap (lift _) s))
    | App _ _ _ $e1$ $e2$ ⇒ fun s ⇒ App (unlet $e1$ s) (unlet $e2$ s)

    | Let _ _ _ $e1$ $e2$ ⇒ fun s ⇒ unlet $e2$ (unlet $e1$ s ::: s)
  end.

We have finished defining the transformation, but the parade of helper functions is not done. To prove correctness, we use one more helper function and a few lemmas. First, we need an operation to insert a new value into a substitution at a particular position.

Fixpoint insertAtS (t : **type**) (x : typeDenote t) (G : **list type**)
  (n : **nat**) {struct n}
  : **hlist** typeDenote G → **hlist** typeDenote (insertAt t G n) :=
  match n with
    | O ⇒ fun s ⇒ x ::: s
    | S n' ⇒ match G return **hlist** typeDenote G
                        → **hlist** typeDenote
                        (insertAt t G (S n')) with
         | nil ⇒ fun s ⇒ x ::: s
         | t' :: G' ⇒ fun s ⇒
           hhd s ::: insertAtS t x n' (htl s)
       end
  end.

Implicit Arguments insertAtS [t G].

Next we prove that liftVar is correct. That is, a lifted variable retains its value with respect to a substitution when we perform an analogue to lifting by inserting a new mapping into the substitution.

Lemma liftVarSound : ∀ t' (x : typeDenote t') t G (m : **member** t G)
  s n,
  hget s m = hget (insertAtS x n s) (liftVar m t' n).

```
        induction m; destruct n; dep_destruct s; pl.
Qed.

Hint Resolve liftVarSound.
```

An analogous lemma establishes correctness of lift'.

```
Lemma lift'Sound : ∀ G t' (x : typeDenote t') t (e : term G t) n s,
    termDenote e s = termDenote (lift' t' n e) (insertAtS x n s).
    induction e; pl;
      repeat match goal with
                  | [ IH : ∀ n s, _ = termDenote (lift' _ n ?E) _
                        ⊢ context[lift' _ (S ?N) ?E] ] ⇒
                      specialize (IH (S N))
                end; pl.
Qed.
```

Correctness of lift itself is an easy corollary.

```
Lemma liftSound : ∀ G t' (x : typeDenote t') t (e : term G t) s,
    termDenote (lift t' e) (x ::: s) = termDenote e s.
    unfold lift; intros; rewrite (lift'Sound _ x e O); trivial.
Qed.

Hint Rewrite hget_hmap hmap_hmap liftSound.
```

Finally, we prove correctness of unlet for terms in arbitrary typing environments.

```
Lemma unletSound' : ∀ G t (e : term G t) G' (s : hlist (term G') G)
    s1,
    termDenote (unlet e s) s1
    = termDenote e (hmap (fun t' (e' : term G' t') ⇒
      termDenote e' s1) s).
    induction e; pl.
Qed.
```

The lemma statement is complex, with all its details of typing contexts and substitutions. It is usually prudent to state a final theorem in as simple a way as possible, to make clear that the statement properly formalizes its informal counterpart. We do that here for the simple case of terms with empty typing contexts.

```
Theorem unletSound : ∀ t (e : term nil t),
    termDenote (unlet e HNil) HNil = termDenote e HNil.
    intros; apply unletSound'.
Qed.

End FIRSTORDER.
```

The Let removal optimization is a good case study of a simple transformation that may turn out to be much more work than expected, based on representation choices. In the next section, we consider a better choice.

17.2 Parametric Higher-Order Abstract Syntax

In contrast to first-order encodings, *higher-order encodings* avoid explicit modeling of variable identity. Instead, the binding constructs of an object language (the language being formalized) can be represented using the binding constructs of the metalanguage (the language in which the formalization is done). The best known higher-order encoding is called *higher-order abstract syntax* (HOAS) [35]. We start by attempting to apply it directly in Coq.

Module HIGHERORDER.

With HOAS, each object language binding construct is represented with a *function* of the metalanguage. Here is the result of applying that idea within an inductive definition of term syntax:

```
Inductive term : type → Type :=
| Const : nat → term Nat
| Plus : term Nat → term Nat → term Nat

| Abs : ∀ dom ran, (term dom → term ran) → term (Func dom ran)
| App : ∀ dom ran, term (Func dom ran) → term dom → term ran

| Let : ∀ t1 t2, term t1 → (term t1 → term t2) → term t2.
```

However, Coq rejects this definition for failing to meet the strict positivity restriction. For instance, the constructor Abs takes an argument that is a function over the same type family term that we are defining. Inductive definitions of this kind can be used to write nonterminating Gallina programs, which breaks the consistency of Coq's logic.

An alternative higher-order encoding is *parametric HOAS* (PHOAS), as introduced by Washburn and Weirich [46] for Haskell and tweaked by me [5] for use in Coq. Here the idea is to parameterize the syntax type by a type family standing for a *representation of variables*.

```
Section var.
  Variable var : type → Type.

  Inductive term : type → Type :=
  | Var : ∀ t, var t → term t
```

```
| Const : nat → term Nat
| Plus : term Nat → term Nat → term Nat

| Abs : ∀ dom ran, (var dom → term ran) → term (Func dom ran)
| App : ∀ dom ran, term (Func dom ran) → term dom → term ran

| Let : ∀ t1 t2, term t1 → (var t1 → term t2) → term t2.
End var.
```

```
Implicit Arguments Var [var t].
Implicit Arguments Const [var].
Implicit Arguments Abs [var dom ran].
```

Coq accepts this definition because the embedded functions now merely take *variables* as arguments instead of arbitrary terms. One might wonder whether there is an easy loophole to exploit here, instantiating the parameter *var* as **term** itself. However, to do that, we would need to choose a variable representation for this nested mention of **term**, and so on, through an infinite descent into **term** arguments.

We write the final type of a closed term using polymorphic quantification over all possible choices of *var* type family.

```
Definition Term t := ∀ var, term var t.
```

Here are the new representations of the example terms from the last section. Note how each is written as a function over a *var* choice, such that the specific choice has no impact on the structure of the term.

```
Example add : Term (Func Nat (Func Nat Nat)) := fun var ⇒
    Abs (fun x ⇒ Abs (fun y ⇒ Plus (Var x) (Var y))).
```

```
Example three_the_hard_way : Term Nat := fun var ⇒
    App (App (add var) (Const 1)) (Const 2).
```

The argument *var* does not even appear in the function body for **add**. How can that be? By giving the terms expressive types, we allow Coq to infer many arguments for us. In fact, we do not even need to name the *var* argument.

```
Example add' : Term (Func Nat (Func Nat Nat)) := fun _ ⇒
    Abs (fun x ⇒ Abs (fun y ⇒ Plus (Var x) (Var y))).
```

```
Example three_the_hard_way' : Term Nat := fun _ ⇒
    App (App (add' _) (Const 1)) (Const 2).
```

Even though the *var* formal parameters appear as underscores, they *are* mentioned in the function bodies that type inference calculates.

17.2.1   Functional Programming with PHOAS

It may not be obvious that the PHOAS representation admits the crucial computable operations. The key to effective deconstruction of PHOAS terms is one principle: treat the *var* parameter as an unconstrained choice of *which data should be annotated on each variable*. We begin with a simple example, that of counting how many variable nodes appear in a PHOAS term. This operation requires no data annotated on variables, so we simply annotate variables with **unit** values. Note that when we go under binders in the cases for Abs and Let, we must provide the data value to annotate on the new variable we pass beneath. For the current choice of **unit** data, we always pass tt.

```
Fixpoint countVars t (e : term (fun _ ⇒ unit) t) : nat :=
  match e with
    | Var _ _ ⇒ 1

    | Const _ ⇒ 0
    | Plus e1 e2 ⇒ countVars e1 + countVars e2

    | Abs _ _ e1 ⇒ countVars (e1 tt)
    | App _ _ e1 e2 ⇒ countVars e1 + countVars e2

    | Let _ _ e1 e2 ⇒ countVars e1 + countVars (e2 tt)
  end.
```

This definition may seem a bit peculiar. Why may we represent variables as **unit** values? Recall that the final representation of closed terms is as polymorphic functions. We merely specialize a closed term to exactly the right variable representation for the transformation we wish to perform.

```
Definition CountVars t (E : Term t) :=
  countVars (E (fun _ ⇒ unit)).
```

It is easy to test that CountVars operates properly.

```
Eval compute in CountVars three_the_hard_way.
```

$$= 2$$

In fact, PHOAS can be used anywhere that first-order representations can. I do not go into detail here, but the intuition is that it is possible to interconvert between PHOAS and any reasonable first-order representation. Here is a suggestive example, translating PHOAS terms into strings giving a first-order rendering. To implement this translation, the key insight is to tag variables with strings, giving their names.

The function takes as an additional input a string giving the name to be assigned to the next variable introduced. We evolve this name by adding a prime to its end. To avoid getting bogged down in orthogonal details, we render all constants as the string $"N"$.

```
Require Import String.
Open Scope string_scope.

Fixpoint pretty t (e : term (fun _ ⇒ string) t) (x : string)
  : string :=
  match e with
    | Var _ s ⇒ s

    | Const _ ⇒ "N"
    | Plus e1 e2 ⇒ "(" ++ pretty e1 x ++ " + " ++ pretty e2 x ++ ")"

    | Abs _ _ e1 ⇒
      "(fun " ++ x ++ " => " ++ pretty (e1 x) (x ++ "'") ++ ")"
    | App _ _ e1 e2 ⇒
      "(" ++ pretty e1 x ++ " " ++ pretty e2 x ++ ")"

    | Let _ _ e1 e2 ⇒ "(let " ++ x ++ " = " ++ pretty e1 x ++ " in "
      ++ pretty (e2 x) (x ++ "'") ++ ")"
  end.

Definition Pretty t (E : Term t) := pretty (E (fun _ ⇒ string)) "x".

Eval compute in Pretty three_the_hard_way.
```

$$= \text{"(((fun x => (fun x' => (x + x'))) N) N)"}$$

However, it is not necessary to convert to first-order form to support many common operations on terms. For instance, we can implement substitution of terms for variables. The key insight here is to *tag variables with terms*, so that on encountering a variable, we can simply replace it by the term in its tag. We call this function initially on a term with exactly one free variable, tagged with the appropriate substitute. During recursion, new variables are added, but they are only tagged with their own term equivalents. Note that this function squash is parameterized over a specific *var* choice.

```
Fixpoint squash var t (e : term (term var) t) : term var t :=
  match e with
    | Var _ e1 ⇒ e1

    | Const n ⇒ Const n
```

| Plus $e1$ $e2$ $\Rightarrow$ Plus (squash $e1$) (squash $e2$)

| Abs _ _ $e1$ $\Rightarrow$ Abs (fun x $\Rightarrow$ squash ($e1$ (Var x)))
| App _ _ $e1$ $e2$ $\Rightarrow$ App (squash $e1$) (squash $e2$)

| Let _ _ $e1$ $e2$ $\Rightarrow$ Let (squash $e1$) (fun x $\Rightarrow$ squash ($e2$ (Var x)))
  end.

To define the final substitution function over terms with single free variables, we define Term1, an analogue to Term that was defined before for closed terms.

Definition Term1 ($t1$ $t2$: **type**) := $\forall$ var, var $t1$ $\rightarrow$ **term** var $t2$.

Substitution is defined by (1) instantiating a Term1 to tag variables with terms, and (2) applying the result to a specific term to be substituted. Note how the parameter *var* of squash is instantiated: the body of Subst is itself a polymorphic quantification over *var*, standing for a variable tag choice in the output term; and we use that input to compute a tag choice for the input term.

Definition Subst ($t1$ $t2$: **type**) (E : Term1 $t1$ $t2$) (E' : Term $t1$)
  : Term $t2$:= fun *var* $\Rightarrow$ squash (E (**term** var) (E' var)).

Eval compute in Subst (fun _ x $\Rightarrow$ Plus (Var x) (Const 3))
  three_the_hard_way.

  = fun *var* : type $\rightarrow$ Type $\Rightarrow$
    Plus
      (App
        (App
          (Abs
            (fun x : *var* Nat $\Rightarrow$
             Abs (fun y : *var* Nat $\Rightarrow$ Plus (Var x) (Var y))))
        (Const 1)) (Const 2)) (Const 3)

One further development is that we can also implement a usual term denotation function, when we *tag variables with their denotations*.

Fixpoint termDenote t (e : **term** typeDenote t) : typeDenote t :=
  match e with
    | Var _ v $\Rightarrow$ v

    | Const n $\Rightarrow$ n
    | Plus $e1$ $e2$ $\Rightarrow$ termDenote $e1$ + termDenote $e2$

    | Abs _ _ $e1$ $\Rightarrow$ fun x $\Rightarrow$ termDenote ($e1$ x)

```
    | App _ _ e1 e2 ⇒ (termDenote e1) (termDenote e2)

    | Let _ _ e1 e2 ⇒ termDenote (e2 (termDenote e1))
  end.
Definition TermDenote t (E : Term t) : typeDenote t :=
  termDenote (E typeDenote).
```

Eval compute in TermDenote three_the_hard_way.

$= 3$

To summarize, the PHOAS representation has all the expressive power of more standard first-order encodings, and a variety of translations are actually much more pleasant to implement than usual, thanks to the novel ability to tag variables with data.

17.2.2 Verifying Program Transformations

Let us now revisit the three example program transformations from Section 17.1. Each is easy to implement with PHOAS, and the last is substantially easier than with first-order representations.

First, we have the recursive identity function, following the same pattern as earlier, with a helper function, polymorphic in a tag choice; and a final function that instantiates the choice appropriately.

```
Fixpoint ident var t (e : term var t) : term var t :=
  match e with
    | Var _ x ⇒ Var x

    | Const n ⇒ Const n
    | Plus e1 e2 ⇒ Plus (ident e1) (ident e2)

    | Abs _ _ e1 ⇒ Abs (fun x ⇒ ident (e1 x))
    | App _ _ e1 e2 ⇒ App (ident e1) (ident e2)

    | Let _ _ e1 e2 ⇒ Let (ident e1) (fun x ⇒ ident (e2 x))
  end.
Definition Ident t (E : Term t) : Term t := fun var ⇒
  ident (E var).
```

Proving correctness is both easier and harder than before, easier because we do not need to manipulate substitutions, and harder because we do the induction in an extra lemma about ident, to establish the correctness theorem for Ident.

Lemma identSound : $\forall$ t (e : **term** typeDenote t),
   termDenote (ident e) = termDenote e.
   induction e; pl.
Qed.

Theorem IdentSound : $\forall$ t (E : Term t),
   TermDenote (Ident E) = TermDenote E.
   intros; apply identSound.
Qed.

The translation of the constant-folding function and its proof work more or less the same way.

Fixpoint cfold var t (e : **term** var t) : **term** var t :=
  match e with
    | Plus $e1$ $e2$ $\Rightarrow$
      let $e1'$:= cfold $e1$ in
      let $e2'$:= cfold $e2$ in
        match $e1'$, $e2'$ with
          | Const $n1$, Const $n2$ $\Rightarrow$ Const ($n1$ + $n2$)
          | _, _ $\Rightarrow$ Plus $e1'$ $e2'$
        end

    | Abs _ _ $e1$ $\Rightarrow$ Abs (fun x $\Rightarrow$ cfold ($e1$ x))
    | App _ _ $e1$ $e2$ $\Rightarrow$ App (cfold $e1$) (cfold $e2$)

    | Let _ _ $e1$ $e2$ $\Rightarrow$ Let (cfold $e1$) (fun x $\Rightarrow$ cfold ($e2$ x))

    | e $\Rightarrow$ e
  end.

Definition Cfold t (E : Term t) : Term t := fun var $\Rightarrow$
  cfold (E var).

Lemma cfoldSound : $\forall$ t (e : **term** typeDenote t),
  termDenote (cfold e) = termDenote e.
  induction e; pl;
    repeat (match goal with
          | [$\vdash$ context[match ?E with Var _ _ $\Rightarrow$ _
                  | _ $\Rightarrow$ _ end]] $\Rightarrow$
        $dep\_destruct$ E
       end; pl).
Qed.

Theorem CfoldSound : $\forall$ t (E : Term t),
  TermDenote (Cfold E) = TermDenote E.

```
    intros; apply cfoldSound.
  Qed.
```

Things get more interesting in the Let removal optimization. The recursive helper function adapts the key idea from earlier definitions of squash and Subst: tag variables with terms. We have a straightforward generalization of squash, where only the Let case has changed, to tag the new variable with the term it is bound to rather than just tagging the variable with itself as a term.

```
  Fixpoint unlet var t (e : term (term var) t) : term var t :=
    match e with
      | Var _ e1 ⇒ e1

      | Const n ⇒ Const n
      | Plus e1 e2 ⇒ Plus (unlet e1) (unlet e2)

      | Abs _ _ e1 ⇒ Abs (fun x ⇒ unlet (e1 (Var x)))
      | App _ _ e1 e2 ⇒ App (unlet e1) (unlet e2)

      | Let _ _ e1 e2 ⇒ unlet (e2 (unlet e1))
    end.
```

```
  Definition Unlet t (E : Term t) : Term t := fun var ⇒
    unlet (E (term var)).
```

We can test Unlet first on an uninteresting example, three_the_hard_way, which does not use Let.

```
  Eval compute in Unlet three_the_hard_way.
```

```
    = fun var : type → Type ⇒
      App
        (App
          (Abs
            (fun x : var Nat ⇒
              Abs (fun x0 : var Nat ⇒ Plus (Var x) (Var x0))))
          (Const 1)) (Const 2)
```

Next, we try a more interesting example, with some extra Lets introduced in three_the_hard_way.

```
  Definition three_a_harder_way : Term Nat := fun _ ⇒
    Let (Const 1) (fun x ⇒ Let (Const 2) (fun y ⇒
      App (App (add _) (Var x)) (Var y))).
```

```
  Eval compute in Unlet three_a_harder_way.
```

```
= fun var : type → Type ⇒
  App
    (App
      (Abs
        (fun x : var Nat ⇒
          Abs (fun x0 : var Nat ⇒ Plus (Var x) (Var x0))))
      (Const 1)) (Const 2)
```

The output is the same as in the previous test, confirming that Unlet operates properly here.

Now we need to state a correctness theorem for Unlet, based on an inductively proved lemma about unlet. It is not obvious how to arrive at a proper induction principle for the lemma. The problem is that we want to relate two instantiations of the same Term, in a way where we know they share the same structure. Note that whereas Unlet is defined to consider all possible *var* choices in the output term, the correctness proof conveniently only depends on the case of *var* := typeDenote. Thus, one parallel instantiation will set *var* := typeDenote to take the denotation of the original term. The other parallel instantiation will set *var* := **term** typeDenote to perform the unlet transformation in the original term.

Here is a relation formalizing the idea that two terms are structurally the same, differing only by replacing the variable data of one with another isomorphic set of variable data in some possibly different type family:

```
Section wf.
  Variables var1 var2 : type → Type.
```

To formalize the tag isomorphism, we use lists of values with the following record type. Each entry has an object language type and an appropriate tag for that type, in each of the two tag families *var1* and *var2*.

```
Record varEntry := {
  Ty : type;
  First : var1 Ty;
  Second : var2 Ty
}.
```

Here is the inductive relation definition. An instance wf *G e1 e2* asserts that terms *e1* and *e2* are equivalent up to the variable tag isomorphism *G*. Note how the Var rule looks up an entry in *G*, and the Abs and Let rules include recursive wf invocations inside the scopes of quantifiers to introduce parallel tag values to be considered as isomorphic.

```
Inductive wf : list varEntry → ∀ t, term var1 t → term var2 t
    → Prop :=
| WfVar : ∀ G t x x', In {| Ty := t; First := x; Second := x' |} G
    → wf G (Var x) (Var x')

| WfConst : ∀ G n, wf G (Const n) (Const n)

| WfPlus : ∀ G e1 e2 e1' e2', wf G e1 e1'
    → wf G e2 e2'
    → wf G (Plus e1 e2) (Plus e1' e2')

| WfAbs : ∀ G dom ran (e1 : _ dom → term _ ran) e1',
    (∀ x1 x2,
        wf ({| First := x1; Second := x2 |} :: G) (e1 x1) (e1' x2))
    → wf G (Abs e1) (Abs e1')

| WfApp : ∀ G dom ran (e1 : term _ (Func dom ran))
    (e2 : term _ dom) e1' e2',
    wf G e1 e1'
    → wf G e2 e2'
    → wf G (App e1 e2) (App e1' e2')

| WfLet : ∀ G t1 t2 e1 e1' (e2 : _ t1 → term _ t2) e2',
    wf G e1 e1'
    → (∀ x1 x2,
        wf ({| First := x1; Second := x2 |} :: G) (e2 x1) (e2' x2))
    → wf G (Let e1 e2) (Let e1' e2').
End wf.
```

We can state a well-formedness condition for closed terms: for any two choices of tag type families, the parallel instantiations belong to the `wf` relation, starting from an empty variable isomorphism.

```
Definition Wf t (E : Term t) := ∀ var1 var2,
    wf nil (E var1) (E var2).
```

After digesting the syntactic details of Wf, it is probably not hard to see that reasonable term encodings will satisfy it. For example,

```
Theorem three_the_hard_way_Wf : Wf three_the_hard_way.
    red; intros; repeat match goal with
                            | [ ⊢ wf _ _ _ ] ⇒ constructor; intros
```

```
                        end; intuition.
  Qed.
```

Now we are ready to give a simple proof of correctness for unlet. First, we add one hint to apply a small variant of a standard library theorem connecting Forall, a higher-order predicate asserting that every element of a list satisfies some property, and In, the list membership predicate.

```
Hint Extern 1 ⇒ match goal with
                | [ H1 : Forall _ _, H2 : In _ _ ⊢ _ ] ⇒
                    apply (Forall_In H1 _ H2)
              end.
```

The rest of the proof is about as automated as we could hope for.

```
Lemma unletSound : ∀ G t (e1 : term _ t) e2,
   wf G e1 e2
   → Forall (fun ve ⇒ termDenote (First ve) = Second ve) G
   → termDenote (unlet e1) = termDenote e2.
   induction 1; pl.
Qed.

Theorem UnletSound : ∀ t (E : Term t), Wf E
   → TermDenote (Unlet E) = TermDenote E.
   intros; eapply unletSound; eauto.
Qed.
```

With this example, it is not obvious that the PHOAS encoding is more tractable than dependent de Bruijn. Where the de Bruijn version had lift and its helper functions, here we have Wf and its auxiliary definitions. In practice, Wf is defined once per object language, whereas such operations as lift often need to operate differently for different examples, forcing new implementations for new transformations.

Readers may also have identified another objection: via Curry-Howard, wf proofs may be thought of as first-order encodings of term syntax. For instance, the In hypothesis of rule WfVar is equivalent to a **member** value. There is some merit to this objection. However, as the preceding proofs show, we are able to reason about transformations using first-order representation only for their inputs, not their outputs. Furthermore, explicit numbering of variables remains absent from the proofs.

Have we really avoided first-order reasoning about the output terms of translations? The answer depends on some subtle issues.

17.2.3   Establishing Term Well-Formedness

Can there be values of type Term t that are not well-formed according to Wf? We expect that Gallina satisfies key *parametricity* [38] properties, which indicate how polymorphic types may only be inhabited by specific values. We omit details of parametricity theorems here, but $\forall\ t\ (E :$ Term $t)$, Wf E follows the flavor of such theorems. One option would be to assert that fact as an axiom, "proving" that any output of any of the translations is well-formed. We could even prove the soundness of the theorem on paper metatheoretically, say, by considering some particular model of the Calculus of Inductive Constructions.

To be more cautious, we could prove Wf for every term that interests us, threading such proofs through all transformations. Here is an example exercise of that kind, for Unlet.

First, we prove that `wf` is monotone, in that a given instance continues to hold as we add new variable pairs to the variable isomorphism.

```
Hint Constructors wf.
Hint Extern 1 (In _ _) ⇒ simpl; tauto.
Hint Extern 1 (Forall _ _) ⇒
  eapply Forall_weaken; [ eassumption | simpl ].

Lemma wf_monotone : ∀ var1 var2 G t (e1 : term var1 t)
  (e2 : term var2 t),
  wf G e1 e2
  → ∀ G', Forall (fun x ⇒ In x G') G
    → wf G' e1 e2.
  induction 1; pl; auto 6.
Qed.

Hint Resolve wf_monotone Forall_In'.
```

Now we are ready to prove that unlet preserves any `wf` instance. The key invariant has to do with the parallel execution of unlet on two different *var* instantiations of a particular term. Since unlet uses **term** as the type of variable data, the variable isomorphism context G contains pairs of terms, which allows us to state the invariant that any pair of terms in the context is also related by `wf`.

```
Hint Extern 1 (wf _ _ _) ⇒ progress simpl.

Lemma unletWf : ∀ var1 var2 G t (e1 : term (term var1) t)
  (e2 : term (term var2) t),
  wf G e1 e2
  → ∀ G', Forall (fun ve ⇒ wf G' (First ve) (Second ve)) G
    → wf G' (unlet e1) (unlet e2).
```

```
   induction 1; pl; eauto 9.
Qed.
```

Repackaging unletWf into a theorem about Wf and Unlet is straight-forward.

```
Theorem UnletWf : ∀ t (E : Term t), Wf E
   → Wf (Unlet E).
   red; intros; apply unletWf with nil; auto.
Qed.
```

This example demonstrates how we may need to use reasoning rem-iniscent of that associated with first-order representations, though the bookkeeping details are generally easier to manage, and bookkeeping theorems may generally be proved separately from the independently interesting theorems about program transformations.

17.2.4   A Few Additional Remarks

Higher-order encodings derive their strength from reuse of the metalan-guage's binding constructs. As a result, we can write encoded terms so that they look very similar to their informal counterparts, without vari-able numbering schemes like those for de Bruijn indices. The example encodings demonstrated this fact, but modulo the clunkiness of explicit use of the constructors of **term**. After defining a few new Coq syntax notations, we can work with terms in an even more standard form.

```
Infix "->" := Func (right associativity, at level 52).

Notation "^" := Var.
Notation "#" := Const.
Infix "@" := App (left associativity, at level 50).
Infix "@+" := Plus (left associativity, at level 50).
Notation "\ x : t , e" := (Abs (dom := t) (fun x ⇒ e))
   (no associativity, at level 51, x at level 0).
Notation "[ e ]" := (fun _ ⇒ e).

Example Add : Term (Nat -> Nat -> Nat) :=
   [\x : Nat, \y : Nat, ^x @+ ^y].

Example Three_the_hard_way : Term Nat :=
   [Add _ @ #1 @ #2].

Eval compute in TermDenote Three_the_hard_way.

   = 3
```

End HigherOrder.

The PHOAS approach shines here because we are working with an object language that has an easy embedding into Coq. That is, there is a straightforward recursive function translating object terms into terms of Gallina. All Gallina programs terminate, so clearly we cannot hope to find such embeddings for Turing-complete languages; and non-Turing-complete languages may still require much more involved translations. I have some work [6] on modeling semantics of Turing-complete languages with PHOAS, but my impression is that many more advances are still to be made in this field, possibly with completely new term representations that have not yet been devised.

Conclusion

This book presented the key ideas needed to get started with productive use of Coq. Many people have learned to use Coq through a variety of resources, yet there is a distinct lack of agreement on structuring principles and techniques for easing the evolution of Coq developments over time. Here I have emphasized two unusual techniques: programming with dependent types and proving with scripted proof automation. I have also presented other material relevant to keeping Coq code beautiful and scalable.

Part of the attraction of Coq and similar tools is that their logical foundations are small. A few pages of LaTeX code suffice to define CIC, Coq's logic, yet there do not seem to be any practical limits on which mathematical concepts may be encoded on top of this modest base. At the same time, the *pragmatic* foundation of Coq is vast, encompassing tactics, libraries, and design patterns for programs, theorem statements, and proof scripts. I hope the preceding chapters have given a sense of just how much there is to learn before it is possible to use Coq with the same ease with which many readers write informal proofs. The payoff of this learning process is that proofs, especially those with many details to check, become much easier to write than they are on paper. Further, the truth of such theorems may be established with much greater confidence, even without reading proof details.

I have not attempted to describe all the many parts of Coq. My advice to readers is to read through the Coq manual, front to back, at some level of detail. Get a sense for which bits of functionality are available. Dig more into those categories that sound relevant to the developments you want to build, and keep the rest in mind in case they come in handy later.

In a domain as rich as this one, the learning process never ends. The Coq Club mailing list (linked from the Coq home page) is a great place to get involved in discussions of the latest improvements, or to ask questions about stumbling blocks that you encounter. I believe the best way to learn is to get started using Coq to build some development that interests you.

References

[1] Yves Bertot and Pierre Castéran. *Interactive Theorem Proving and Program Development: Coq'Art: The Calculus of Inductive Constructions*. Texts in Theoretical Computer Science. Springer, 2004.

[2] Samuel Boutin. Using reflection to build efficient and certified decision procedures. In *Proceedings of the Third International Symposium on Theoretical Aspects of Computer Software*, pages 515–529, 1997.

[3] Robert S. Boyer, Matt Kaufmann, and J Strother Moore. The Boyer-Moore theorem prover and its interactive enhancement. *Computers and Mathematics with Applications*, 29(2):27–62, 1995.

[4] Venanzio Capretta. General recursion via coinductive types. *Logical Methods in Computer Science*, 1(2):1–18, 2005.

[5] Adam Chlipala. Parametric higher-order abstract syntax for mechanized semantics. In *Proceedings of the 13th ACM SIGPLAN International Conference on Functional Programming*, pages 143–156, 2008.

[6] Adam Chlipala. A verified compiler for an impure functional language. In *Proceedings of the 37th ACM SIGPLAN-SIGACT Symposium on Principles of Programming Languages*, pages 93–106, 2010.

[7] Coq Development Team. The Coq proof assistant reference manual, version 8.4. 2012.

[8] Thierry Coquand. An analysis of Girard's paradox. In *Proceedings of the Symposium on Logic in Computer Science*, pages 227–236, 1986.

[9] Thierry Coquand and Gérard Huet. The Calculus of Constructions. *Information and Computation*, 76(2-3), 1988.

[10] H. B. Curry. Functionality in combinatory logic. *Proceedings of the National Academy of Sciences of the United States of America*, 20(11):584–590, 1934.

[11] Nicolas G. de Bruijn. Lambda-calculus notation with nameless dummies: A tool for automatic formal manipulation with application to the Church-Rosser theorem. *Indagationes Mathematicae*, 34(5):381–392, 1972.

[12] Eduardo Giménez. A tutorial on recursive types in Coq. Technical Report 0221, INRIA, May 1998.

[13] Georges Gonthier. Formal proof—the four-color theorem. *Notices of the American Mathematical Society*, 55(11):1382–1393, 2008.

[14] William A. Howard. The formulae-as-types notion of construction. In Jonathan P. Seldin and J. Roger Hindley, editors, *To H.B. Curry: Essays on Combinatory Logic, Lambda Calculus and Formalism*, pages 479–490. Academic Press, 1980. Original paper manuscript from 1969.

[15] Gérard Huet. The undecidability of unification in third order logic. *Information and Control*, pages 257–267, 1973.

[16] John Hughes. Why functional programming matters. *Computer Journal*, 32:98–107, 1984.

[17] Matt Kaufmann, Panagiotis Manolios, and J Strother Moore. *Computer-Aided Reasoning: An Approach*. Kluwer Academic Publishers, 2000.

[18] Gerwin Klein, Kevin Elphinstone, Gernot Heiser, June Andronick, David Cock, Philip Derrin, Dhammika Elkaduwe, Kai Engelhardt, Rafal Kolanski, Michael Norrish, Thomas Sewell, Harvey Tuch, and Simon Winwood. seL4: Formal verification of an OS kernel. In *Proceedings of the 22nd ACM Symposium on Operating Systems Principles*, pages 207–220, 2009.

[19] Xavier Leroy. A formally verified compiler back-end. *Journal of Automated Reasoning*, 43(4):363–446, 2009.

[20] Xavier Leroy and Hervé Grall. Coinductive big-step operational semantics. In *Proceedings of the 15th European Symposium on Programming*, pages 54–68, 2006.

[21] John W. Lloyd. *Foundations of Logic Programming*. Springer, 2nd edition, 1987.

[22] David MacQueen. Modules for Standard ML. In *Proceedings of the 1984 ACM Symposium on LISP and Functional Programming*, pages 198–207, 1984.

[23] Conor McBride. Elimination with a motive. In *Proceedings of the International Workshop on Types for Proofs and Programs*, pages 197–216, 2000.

[24] Adam Megacz. A coinductive monad for Prop-bounded recursion. In *Proceedings of the ACM Workshop Programming Languages Meets Program Verification*, pages 11–20, 2007.

[25] J Strother Moore. *Piton: A Mechanically Verified Assembly-Level Language*. Automated Reasoning Series. Kluwer Academic Publishers, 1996.

[26] J Strother Moore, Tom Lynch, and Matt Kaufmann. A mechanically checked proof of the correctness of the kernel of the AMD5k86 floating-point division algorithm. *IEEE Transactions on Computers*, 47(9):913–926, 1998.

[27] George C. Necula. Proof-carrying code. In *Proceedings of the 24th ACM SIGPLAN-SIGACT Symposium on Principles of Programming Languages*, pages 106–119, 1997.

[28] Zhaozhong Ni and Zhong Shao. Certified assembly programming with embedded code pointers. In *Proceedings of the 33rd ACM SIGPLAN-SIGACT Symposium on Principles of Programming Languages*, pages 320–333, 2006.

[29] Tobias Nipkow, Lawrence C. Paulson, and Markus Wenzel. *Isabelle/HOL—A Proof Assistant for Higher-Order Logic*, volume 2283 of *Lecture Notes in Computer Science*. Springer, 2002.

[30] Chris Okasaki. Red-black trees in a functional setting. *Journal of Functional Programming*, 9:471–477, 1999.

[31] Christine Paulin-Mohring. Inductive definitions in the system Coq—rules and properties. In *Proceedings of the International Conference on Typed Lambda Calculi and Applications*, pages 328–345, 1993.

[32] Lawrence C. Paulson. *Isabelle: A Generic Theorem Prover*, volume 828 of *Lecture Notes in Computer Science*. Springer, 1994.

[33] Simon Peyton Jones, Lennart Augustsson, Dave Barton, Brian Boutel, Warren Burton, Joseph Fasel, Kevin Hammond, Ralf Hinze, Paul Hudak, John Hughes, Thomas Johnsson, Mark Jones, John Launchbury, Erik Meijer, John Peterson, Alastair Reid, Colin Runciman, and Philip Wadler. *Haskell 98 Language and Libraries: The Revised Report*. 1998. Section 4.3.3.

[34] Simon L. Peyton Jones and Philip Wadler. Imperative functional programming. In *Proceedings of the 20th ACM SIGPLAN-SIGACT Symposium on Principles of Programming Languages*, pages 71–84, 1993.

[35] Frank Pfenning and Conal Elliott. Higher-order abstract syntax. In *Proceedings of the ACM SIGPLAN 1988 Conference on Programming Language Design and Implementation*, pages 199–208, 1988.

[36] Benjamin C. Pierce. *Types and Programming Languages*. MIT Press, 2002.

[37] Benjamin C. Pierce. *Types and Programming Languages*. MIT Press, 2002. Section 9.4.

[38] John C. Reynolds. Types, abstraction, and parametric polymorphism. *Information Processing*, pages 513–523, 1983.

[39] John C. Reynolds. The discoveries of continuations. *Lisp and Symbolic Computation*, 6(3-4):233–248, November 1993.

[40] John C. Reynolds. Separation logic: A logic for shared mutable data structures. In *Proceedings of the IEEE Symposium on Logic in Computer Science*, pages 55–74, 2002.

[41] John Alan Robinson. A machine-oriented logic based on the resolution principle. *Journal of the ACM*, 12(1):23–41, January 1965.

[42] Leon Sterling and Ehud Shapiro. *The Art of Prolog*. MIT Press, 2nd edition, 1994.

[43] Thomas Streicher. *Semantical Investigations into Intensional Type Theory*. Habilitationsschrift, LMU München, 1993.

[44] Philip Wadler. The essence of functional programming. In *Proceedings of the 19th ACM SIGPLAN-SIGACT Symposium on Principles of Programming Languages*, pages 1–14, 1992.

[45] Philip Wadler and Stephen Blott. How to make ad-hoc polymorphism less ad hoc. In *Proceedings of the 16th ACM SIGPLAN-SIGACT Symposium on Principles of Programming Languages*, pages 60–76, 1989.

[46] Geoffrey Washburn and Stephanie Weirich. Boxes go bananas: Encoding higher-order abstract syntax with parametric polymorphism. *Journal of Functional Programming*, 18(1):87–140, 2008.

[47] Markus Wenzel. Isar—A generic interpretative approach to readable formal proof documents. In *Proceedings of the 12th International Conference on Theorem Proving in Higher Order Logics*, pages 167–184, 1999.

[48] Benjamin Werner. Sets in types, types in sets. In *Proceedings of the Third International Symposium on Theoretical Aspects of Computer Software*, pages 530–546, 1997.

[49] Glynn Winskel. *The Formal Semantics of Programming Languages*. MIT Press, 1993. Chapter 8.

[50] Hongwei Xi, Chiyan Chen, and Gang Chen. Guarded recursive datatype constructors. In *Proceedings of the 30th ACM SIGPLAN-SIGACT Symposium on Principles of Programming Languages*, pages 224–235, 2003.

Index